Praise for

DATA AND GOLIATH

An Amazon 2015 Best Book of the Year

"Schneier has encyclopedic knowledge of not just the uses and abuses of data collection around the globe but the dizzying array of laws, regulations, international accords and not-so-secret orders governing these practices. A half-dozen members of Congress invited Mr. Schneier to brief *them* about the unpublished Snowden documents."
—*New York Times*

"*Data and Goliath* is deeply informed and accessibly written analysis of mass surveillance by firms and the government." —*Lawfare*

"Makes a convincing case that America's intelligence community has unprecedented powers that, if unchecked, undermine a free society. . . . Offers a deep but accessible look at surveillance in the post-Snowden, big-data era." —*Economist*

"It's easy to feel daunted by the substantial threats to privacy and civil liberties that we are facing as a society. That's exactly why *Data and Goliath* is so essential. Knowledge is power."
—*Electronic Frontier Foundation*

"Schneier's lucid and compelling *Data and Goliath* is free of the hysteria that often accompanies discussions about surveillance."
—*Washington Post*

"A thought-provoking, absorbing, and comprehensive guide to our new big data world. Most important, it's a call for a serious discussion and urgent action to stop the harms caused by the mass collection and mining of data by governments and corporations."

—*Forbes*

"A lucid, sophisticated overview of how corporate and governmental surveillance works, how it doesn't, and what we can do about it."

—*Los Angeles Times*

"No one explains security, privacy, crypto and safety better. . . . Schneier offers hope."   —Cory Doctorow, *BoingBoing*

"Superior work—*Data and Goliath* will go far in furthering the much-needed debate about the fight to maintain our fundamental rights of privacy and free speech."   —J. Kirk Wiebe, former NSA senior intelligence analyst and NSA whistleblower

"A thoroughly convincing and brilliant book about big data, mass surveillance and the ensuing privacy dangers facing everyone. . . . This is a book that must be read, for your freedom."   —*Slashdot*

"[Schneier's] understanding of encryption, cyberattacks and vulnerabilities, and his ability to explain them in a relatively accessible way, is impressive and admirable. . . . [*Data and Goliath*] is a book full of rage, but ultimately also full of hope—and realism."

—*Times Higher Education*

"A handbook for the information age. . . . Security expert Bruce Schneier examines how governments, corporations, individuals and society as a whole can deliver a better balance between security and privacy."   —*ZDNet*

"Schneier's book gives us a road map to more intelligent policies that better balance security and privacy. I already consider it my bible when discussing privacy issues." —Roger A. Grimes, *InfoWorld*

"You should probably stop reading this review and just buy the book! ... The notes alone are worth the sticker price." —*Virus Bulletin*

"Schneier exposes the many and surprising ways governments and corporations monitor all of us, providing a must-read User's Guide to Life in the Data Age. His recommendations for change should be part of a much-needed public debate." —Richard A. Clarke, former chief counterterrorism adviser on the National Security Council under Presidents Bill Clinton and George W. Bush, and author of *Cyber War*

"Schneier did not need the Snowden revelations, as important as they are, to understand the growing threat to personal privacy worldwide from government and corporate surveillance—he's been raising the alarm for nearly two decades. But this important book does more than detail the threat; it tells the average low-tech citizen what steps he or she can take to limit surveillance, and thus fight those who are seeking to strip privacy from all of us." —Seymour M. Hersh, Pulitzer Prize–winning journalist

"Bruce Schneier is the most consistently sober, authoritative, and knowledgeable voice on security and privacy issues in our time. This book brings his experience and sharp analytical skills to important and fast-evolving technology and human rights issues. Much has been said about the way our government, financial institutions, and online entities gather data, but less is said about how that seemingly infinite ocean of data is used, or might be used. In the face of a vast spectrum of possibility, clouded in secrecy, Bruce's book is a voice of steady reason." —Xeni Jardin, co-editor of *BoingBoing*

"A pithy, pointed, and highly readable explanation of what we know in the wake of the Snowden revelations, with practical steps that ordinary people can take if they want to do something about the threats to privacy and liberty posed not only by the government but by the Big Data industry."

—Neal Stephenson, author of *Reamde*

"A judicious and incisive analysis of one of the most pressing new issues of our time, written by a true expert." —Steven Pinker, Johnstone Professor of Psychology, Harvard University, and author of *The Better Angels of Our Nature*

"As it becomes increasingly clear that surveillance has surpassed anything that Orwell imagined, we need a guide to how and why we're being snooped and what we can do about it. Bruce Schneier is that guide—step by step he outlines the various ways we are being monitored, and after scaring the pants off us, he tells us how to fight back."

—Steven Levy, editor-in-chief of *Backchannel* and author of *Crypto* and *Hackers*

"The internet is a surveillance state, and like any technology, surveillance has both good and bad uses. Bruce Schneier draws on his vast range of technical and historical skills to sort them out. He analyzes both the challenge of big brother and many little brothers. Anyone interested in security, liberty, privacy, and justice in this cyber age must read this book." —Joseph S. Nye Jr., Harvard University Distinguished Service Professor and author of *The Future of Power*

"*Data and Goliath* is the indispensable guide to understanding the most important current threat to freedom in democratic market societies. Whether you worry about government surveillance in the post-Snowden era, or about Facebook and Google manipulating you based on their vast data collections, Schneier, the leading, truly independent expert writing about these threats today, offers a rich overview of the technologies and practices leading us toward surveillance society and the diverse solutions we must pursue to save us from that fate." —Yochai Benkler, Berkman Professor of Entrepreneurial Legal Studies at Harvard Law School and author of *The Wealth of Networks*

"Data, algorithms, and thinking machines give our corporations and political institutions immense and far-reaching powers. Bruce Schneier has done a remarkable job of breaking down their impact on our privacy, our lives, and our society. *Data and Goliath* should be on everyone's must-read list." —Om Malik, founder of Gigaom

DATA AND GOLIATH

SELECTED BOOKS BY BRUCE SCHNEIER

Carry On: Sound Advice from Schneier on Security (2013)

Liars and Outliers: Enabling the Trust That Society Needs to Thrive (2012)

Schneier on Security (2008)

Beyond Fear: Thinking Sensibly about Security in an Uncertain World (2003)

Secrets and Lies: Digital Security in a Networked World (2000)

Applied Cryptography: Protocols, Algorithms, and Source Code in C (1994 and 1996)

DATA
AND
GOLIATH

The Hidden Battles to Collect
Your Data and Control Your World

BRUCE SCHNEIER

W. W. NORTON & COMPANY
INDEPENDENT PUBLISHERS SINCE 1923
NEW YORK · LONDON

For information about permission to reproduce selections from this book, write to Permissions, W. W. Norton & Company, Inc., 500 Fifth Avenue, New York, NY 10110

For information about special discounts for bulk purchases, please contact W. W. Norton Special Sales at specialsales@wwnorton.com or 800-233-4830

Manufacturing by RR Donnelley Harrisonburg
Book design by Daniel Lagin
Production manager: Julia Druskin

Schneier, Bruce, 1963–
  Data and Goliath : the hidden battles to collect your data and control your world / Bruce Schneier. — First edition.
     pages cm
  Includes bibliographical references and index.
  ISBN 978-0-393-24481-6 (hardcover)
  1. Electronic surveillance—Social aspects. 2. Information technology—Social aspects. 3. Computer security. 4. Privacy, Right of. 5. Social control. I. Title.
  HM846.S362 2015
  005.8—dc23
                          2014048365

ISBN: 978-0-393-35217-7 pbk.

W. W. Norton & Company, Inc.
500 Fifth Avenue, New York, N.Y. 10110
www.wwnorton.com

W. W. Norton & Company Ltd.
Castle House, 75/76 Wells Street, London W1T 3QT

1 2 3 4 5 6 7 8 9 0

To Karen: DMASC

Contents

DATA AND GOLIATH

Introduction

I f you need to be convinced that you're living in a science-fiction world, look at your cell phone. This cute, sleek, incredibly powerful tool has become so central to our lives that we take it for granted. It seems perfectly normal to pull this device out of your pocket, no matter where you are on the planet, and use it to talk to someone else, no matter where the person is on the planet.

Yet every morning when you put your cell phone in your pocket, you're making an implicit bargain with the carrier: "I want to make and receive mobile calls; in exchange, I allow this company to know where I am at all times." The bargain isn't specified in any contract, but it's inherent in how the service works. You probably hadn't thought about it, but now that I've pointed it out, you might well think it's a pretty good bargain. Cell phones really are great, and they can't work unless the cell phone companies know where you are, which means they keep you under their surveillance.

This is a very intimate form of surveillance. Your cell phone tracks where you live and where you work. It tracks where you like to spend your weekends and evenings. It tracks how often you go to church (and which church), how much time you spend in a bar, and whether you speed when you drive. It tracks—since it knows about all the other phones in your area—whom you spend your days with, whom you meet for lunch, and whom you sleep with. The accumulated data can probably paint a better picture of how you spend your time than you can, because it doesn't have to rely on human memory. In 2012, researchers were able to use this data to predict where people would be *24 hours later*, to within 20 meters.

Before cell phones, if someone wanted to know all of this, he would have had to hire a private investigator to follow you around taking notes. Now that job is obsolete; the cell phone in your pocket does all of this automatically. It might be that no one retrieves that information, but it is there for the taking.

Your location information is valuable, and everyone wants access to it. The police want it. Cell phone location analysis is useful in criminal investigations in several different ways. The police can "ping" a particular phone to determine where it is, use historical data to determine where it has been, and collect all the cell phone location data from a specific area to figure out who was there and when. More and more, police are using this data for exactly these purposes.

Governments also use this same data for intimidation and social control. In 2014, the government of Ukraine sent this positively Orwellian text message to people in Kiev whose phones were at a certain place during a certain time period: "Dear subscriber, you have been registered as a participant in a mass disturbance." Don't think this behavior is limited to totalitarian countries; in 2010, Michigan police sought information about every cell phone in service near an expected labor protest. They didn't bother getting a warrant first.

There's a whole industry devoted to tracking you in real time. Companies use your phone to track you in stores to learn how you shop, track you on the road to determine how close you might be to a particular store, and deliver advertising to your phone based on where you are right now.

Your location data is so valuable that cell phone companies are now selling it to data brokers, who in turn resell it to anyone willing to pay for it. Companies like Sense Networks specialize in using this data to build personal profiles of each of us.

Phone companies are not the only source of cell phone data. The US company Verint sells cell phone tracking systems to both corporations and governments worldwide. The company's website says that it's "a global leader in Actionable Intelligence solutions for customer engagement optimization, security intelligence, and fraud, risk and compliance," with clients in "more than 10,000 organizations in over 180 countries." The UK company Cobham sells a system that allows someone to send a "blind" call to a phone—one that doesn't ring, and isn't detectable. The blind call forces the phone to transmit on a certain frequency, allowing the sender to track that phone to within one meter. The company boasts government customers in Algeria, Brunei, Ghana, Pakistan, Saudi Arabia, Singapore, and the United States. Defentek, a company mysteriously registered in Panama, sells a system that can "locate and track any phone number in the world . . . undetected and unknown by the network, carrier, or the target." It's not an idle boast; telecommunications researcher Tobias Engel demonstrated the same thing at a hacker conference in 2008. Criminals do the same today.

All this location tracking is based on the cellular system. There's another entirely different and more accurate location system built into your smartphone: GPS. This is what provides location data to the various apps running on your phone. Some apps use location data to deliver service: Google Maps, Uber, Yelp. Others, like Angry Birds, just want to be able to collect and sell it.

You can do this, too. HelloSpy is an app that you can surreptitiously install on someone else's smartphone to track her. Perfect for an anxious mom wanting to spy on her teenager—or an abusive man wanting to spy on his wife or girlfriend. Employers have used apps like this to spy on their employees.

The US National Security Agency (NSA) and its UK counterpart, Government Communications Headquarters (GCHQ), use location data to track people. The NSA collects cell phone location data from a variety of sources: the cell towers that phones connect to, the location of Wi-Fi networks that phones log on to, and GPS location data from Internet apps. Two of the NSA's internal databases, code-named HAPPYFOOT and FASCIA, contain comprehensive location information of devices worldwide. The NSA uses the databases to track people's movements, identify people who associate with people of interest, and target drone strikes.

The NSA can allegedly track cell phones even when they are turned off.

I've just been talking about location information from one source—your cell phone—but the issue is far larger than this. The computers you interact with are constantly producing intimate personal data about you. It includes what you read, watch, and listen to. It includes whom you talk to and what you say. Ultimately, it covers what you're thinking about, at least to the extent that your thoughts lead you to the Internet and search engines. We are living in the golden age of surveillance.

Sun Microsystems' CEO Scott McNealy said it plainly way back in 1999: "You have zero privacy anyway. Get over it." He's wrong about how we should react to surveillance, of course, but he's right that it's becoming harder and harder to avoid surveillance and maintain privacy.

Surveillance is a politically and emotionally loaded term, but I use it deliberately. The US military defines surveillance as "systematic observation." As I'll explain, modern-day electronic surveillance is exactly that. We're all open books to both governments and corporations; their ability to peer into our collective personal lives is greater than it has ever been before.

The bargain you make, again and again, with various companies is surveillance in exchange for free service. Google's chairman Eric Schmidt and its director of ideas Jared Cohen laid it out in their 2013 book, *The New Digital Age*. Here I'm paraphrasing their message: if you let us have all your data, we will show you advertisements you want to see and we'll throw in free web search, e-mail, and all sorts of other services. It's convenience, basically. We are social animals, and there's nothing more powerful or rewarding than communicating with other people. Digital means have become the easiest and quickest way to communicate. And why do we allow governments access? Because we fear the terrorists, fear the strangers abducting our children, fear the drug dealers, fear whatever bad guy is in vogue at the moment. That's the NSA's justification for its mass-surveillance programs; if you let us have all of your data, we'll relieve your fear.

The problem is that these aren't good or fair bargains, at least as they're structured today. We've been accepting them too easily, and without really understanding the terms.

Here is what's true. Today's technology gives governments and corporations robust capabilities for mass surveillance. Mass surveillance is dangerous. It enables discrimination based on almost any criteria: race, religion, class, political beliefs. It is being used to control what we see, what we can do, and, ultimately, what we say. It is being done without offering citizens recourse or any real ability to opt out, and without any meaningful checks and balances. It makes us less safe. It makes us less free. The rules we had established to protect us from these dangers under earlier technological regimes are now woefully insufficient; they are not working. We need to fix that, and we need to do it very soon.

In this book, I make that case in three parts.

Part One describes the surveillance society we're living in. Chapter 1 looks at the varieties of personal data we generate as we go about our lives. It's not just the cell phone location data I've described. It's also data about our phone calls, e-mails, and text messages, plus all the webpages we read, our financial transaction data, and much more. Most of us don't realize the degree to which computers are integrated into everything we do, or that computer storage has become cheap enough to make it feasible to indefinitely save all the data we churn out. Most of us also underestimate just how easy it has become to identify us using data that we consider anonymous.

Chapter 2 shows how all this data is used for surveillance. It happens everywhere. It happens automatically, without human intervention. And it's largely hidden from view. This is ubiquitous mass surveillance.

It's easy to focus on how data is collected by corporations and governments, but that gives a distorted picture. The real story is how the different streams of data are processed, correlated, and analyzed. And it's not just one person's data; it's everyone's data. Ubiquitous mass surveillance is fundamentally different from just a lot of individual surveillance, and it's happening on a scale we've never seen before. I talk about this in Chapter 3.

Surveillance data is largely collected by the corporations that we interact with, either as customers or as users. Chapter 4 talks about business models of surveillance, primarily personalized advertising. An entire data broker industry has sprung up around profiting from our data, and our personal information is being bought and sold without our knowledge and consent. This is being driven by a new model of computing, where our data is stored in the cloud and accessed by devices like the iPhone that are under strict manufacturer control. The result is unprecedented corporate access to and control over our most intimate information.

Chapter 5 turns to government surveillance. Governments around the world are surveilling their citizens, and breaking into computers both domestically and internationally. They want to spy on everyone to find terrorists and criminals, and—depending on the government—political activists, dissidents, environmental activists, consumer advocates, and freethinkers. I focus mainly on the NSA, because this is the secret government agency we know best, because of the documents Edward Snowden released.

Corporations and governments alike have an insatiable appetite for our data, and I discuss how the two work together in Chapter 6. I call it a "public-private surveillance partnership," and it's an alliance that runs deep. It's the primary reason that surveillance is so pervasive, and it will impede attempts to reform the system.

All of this matters, even if you trust the corporations you interact with and the government you're living under. With that in mind, Part Two turns to the many interrelated harms that arise from ubiquitous mass surveillance.

In Chapter 7, I discuss the harms caused by government surveillance. History has repeatedly demonstrated the dangers of allowing governments to conduct unchecked mass surveillance on their citizens. Potential harms include discrimination and control, chilling effects on free speech and free thought, inevitable abuse, and loss of democracy and liberty. The Internet has the potential to be an enormous driver of freedom and liberty around the world; we're squandering that potential by allowing governments to conduct worldwide surveillance.

Chapter 8 turns to the harms caused by unfettered corporate surveillance. Private companies now control the "places" on the Internet where we gather, and they're mining the information we leave there for their own benefit. By allowing companies to know everything about us, we're permitting them to categorize and manipulate us. This manipulation is largely hidden and unregulated, and will become more effective as technology improves.

Ubiquitous surveillance leads to other harms as well. Chapter 9 discusses the economic harms, primarily to US businesses, that arise when the citizens of different countries try to defend themselves against surveillance by the NSA and its allies. The Internet is a global platform, and attempts by countries like Germany and Brazil to build national walls around their data will cost companies that permit government surveillance—particularly American companies—considerably.

In Chapter 10, I discuss the harms caused by a loss of privacy. Defenders of surveillance—from the Stasi of the German Democratic Republic to the Chilean dictator Augusto Pinochet to Google's Eric Schmidt—have always relied on the old saw "If you have nothing to hide, then you have nothing to fear." This is a dangerously narrow conception of the value of privacy. Privacy is an essential human need, and central to our ability to control how we relate to the world. Being stripped of privacy is fundamentally dehumanizing, and it makes no difference whether the surveillance is conducted by an undercover policeman following us around or by a computer algorithm tracking our every move.

In Chapter 11, I turn to the harms to security caused by surveillance. Government mass surveillance is often portrayed as a security benefit, something that protects us from terrorism. Yet there's no actual proof of any real successes against terrorism as a result of mass surveillance, and significant evidence of harm. Enabling ubiquitous mass surveillance requires maintaining an insecure Internet, which makes us all less safe from rival governments, criminals, and hackers.

Finally, Part Three outlines what we need to do to protect ourselves from government and corporate surveillance. The remedies are as complicated as the issues, and often require fine attention to detail. Before I delve into specific technical and policy recommendations, though, Chapter 12 offers eight general principles that should guide our thinking.

The following two chapters lay out specific policy recommendations: for governments in Chapter 13, and for corporations in Chapter 14. Some of these recommendations are more detailed than others, and some are aspirational rather than immediately implementable. All are important, though, and any omissions could subvert the other solutions.

Chapter 15 turns to what each of us can do individually. I offer some practical technical advice, as well as suggestions for political action. We're living in a world where technology can trump politics, and also where politics can trump technology. We need both to work together.

I end, in Chapter 16, by looking at what we must do collectively as a society. Most of the recommendations in Chapters 13 and 14 require a shift in how we perceive surveillance and value privacy, because we're not going to get any serious legal reforms until society starts demanding them. There is enormous value in aggregating our data for medical research, improving education, and other tasks that benefit society. We need to figure out how to collectively get that value while minimizing the harms. This is the fundamental issue that underlies everything in this book.

This book encompasses a lot, and necessarily covers ground quickly. The endnotes include extensive references for those interested in delving deeper. Those are on the book's website as well: www.schneier.com/dg.html. There you'll also find any updates to the book, based on events that occurred after I finished the manuscript.

I write with a strong US bias. Most of the examples are from the

US, and most of the recommendations best apply to the US. For one thing, it's what I know. But I also believe that the US serves as a singular example of how things went wrong, and is in a singular position to change things for the better.

My background is security and technology. For years, I have been writing about how security technologies affect people, and vice versa. I have watched the rise of surveillance in the information age, and have seen the many threats and insecurities in this new world. I'm used to thinking about security problems, and about broader social issues through the lens of security problems. This perspective gives me a singular understanding of both the problems and the solutions.

I am not, and this book is not, anti-technology. The Internet, and the information age in general, has brought enormous benefits to society. I believe they will continue to do so. I'm not even anti-surveillance. The benefits of computers knowing what we're doing have been life-transforming. Surveillance has revolutionized traditional products and services, and spawned entirely new categories of commerce. It has become an invaluable tool for law enforcement. It helps people all around the world in all sorts of ways, and will continue to do so far into the future.

Nevertheless, the threats of surveillance are real, and we're not talking about them enough. Our response to all this creeping surveillance has largely been passive. We don't think about the bargains we're making, because they haven't been laid out in front of us. Technological changes occur, and we accept them for the most part. It's hard to blame us; the changes have been happening so fast that we haven't really evaluated their effects or weighed their consequences. This is how we ended up in a surveillance society. The surveillance society snuck up on us.

It doesn't have to be like this, but we have to take charge. We can start by renegotiating the bargains we're making with our data. We need to be proactive about how we deal with new technologies. We need to think about what we want our technological infrastructure to be, and what values we want it to embody. We need to balance the value of our data to society with its personal nature. We need to examine our fears, and decide how much of our privacy we are really willing to sacrifice for convenience. We need to understand the many harms of overreaching surveillance.

And we need to fight back.

—Minneapolis, Minnesota, and
Cambridge, Massachusetts, October 2014

PART ONE
THE WORLD
WE'RE CREATING

1

Data as a By-product of Computing

Computers constantly produce data. It's their input and output, but it's also a by-product of everything they do. In the normal course of their operations, computers continuously document what they're doing. They sense and record more than you're aware of.

For instance, your word processor keeps a record of what you've written, including your drafts and changes. When you hit "save," your word processor records the new version, but your computer doesn't erase the old versions until it needs the disk space for something else. Your word processor automatically saves your document every so often; Microsoft Word saves mine every 20 minutes. Word also keeps a record of who created the document, and often of who else worked on it.

Connect to the Internet, and the data you produce multiplies: records of websites you visit, ads you click on, words you type. Your computer, the sites you visit, and the computers in the network each produce data. Your browser sends data to websites about what software you have, when it was installed, what features you've

enabled, and so on. In many cases, this data is enough to uniquely identify your computer.

Increasingly we communicate with our family, friends, co-workers, and casual acquaintances via computers, using e-mail, text messaging, Facebook, Twitter, Instagram, SnapChat, WhatsApp, and whatever else is hot right now. Data is a by-product of this high-tech socialization. These systems don't just transfer data; they also create data records of your interactions with others.

Walking around outside, you might not think that you're producing data, but you are. Your cell phone is constantly calculating its location based on which cell towers it's near. It's not that your cell phone company particularly cares where you are, but it needs to know where your cell phone is to route telephone calls to you.

Of course, if you actually use that phone, you produce more data: numbers dialed and calls received, text messages sent and received, call duration, and so on. If it's a smartphone, it's also a computer, and all your apps produce data when you use them—and sometimes even when you're not using them. Your phone probably has a GPS receiver, which produces even more accurate location information than the cell tower location alone. The GPS receiver in your smartphone pinpoints you to within 16 to 27 feet; cell towers, to about 2,000 feet.

Purchase something in a store, and you produce more data. The cash register is a computer, and it creates a record of what you purchased and the time and date you purchased it. That data flows into the merchant's computer system. Unless you paid cash, your credit card or debit card information is tied to that purchase. That data is also sent to the credit card company, and some of it comes back to you in your monthly bill.

There may be a video camera in the store, installed to record evidence in case of theft or fraud. There's another camera recording you when you use an ATM. There are more cameras outside, monitoring buildings, sidewalks, roadways, and other public spaces.

Get into a car, and you generate yet more data. Modern cars are loaded with computers, producing data on your speed, how hard you're pressing on the pedals, what position the steering wheel is in, and more. Much of that is automatically recorded in a black box recorder, useful for figuring out what happened in an accident. There's even a computer in each tire, gathering pressure data. Take your car into the shop, and the first thing the mechanic will do is access all that data to diagnose any problems. A self-driving car could produce a gigabyte of data per second.

Snap a photo, and you're at it again. Embedded in digital photos is information such as the date, time, and location—yes, many cameras have GPS—of the photo's capture; generic information about the camera, lens, and settings; and an ID number of the camera itself. If you upload the photo to the web, that information often remains attached to the file.

It wasn't always like this. In the era of newspapers, radio, and television, we received information, but no record of the event was created. Now we get our news and entertainment over the Internet. We used to speak to people face-to-face and then by telephone; we now have conversations over text or e-mail. We used to buy things with cash at a store; now we use credit cards over the Internet. We used to pay with coins at a tollbooth, subway turnstile, or parking meter. Now we use automatic payment systems, such as EZPass, that are connected to our license plate number and credit card. Taxis used to be cash-only. Then we started paying by credit card. Now we're using our smartphones to access networked taxi systems like Uber and Lyft, which produce data records of the transaction, plus our pickup and drop-off locations. With a few specific exceptions, computers are now everywhere we engage in commerce and most places we engage with our friends.

Last year, when my refrigerator broke, the serviceman replaced the computer that controls it. I realized that I had been thinking about the refrigerator backwards: it's not a refrigerator with a computer, it's a computer that keeps food cold. Just like that, everything is turning into a computer. Your phone is a computer that makes calls. Your car is a computer with wheels and an engine. Your oven is a computer that bakes lasagnas. Your camera is a computer that takes pictures. Even our pets and livestock are now regularly chipped; my cat is practically a computer that sleeps in the sun all day.

Computers are getting embedded into more and more kinds of products that connect to the Internet. A company called Nest, which Google purchased in 2014 for more than $3 billion, makes an Internet-enabled thermostat. The smart thermostat adapts to your behavior patterns and responds to what's happening on the power grid. But to do all that, it records more than your energy usage: it also tracks and records your home's temperature, humidity, ambient light, and any nearby movement. You can buy a smart refrigerator that tracks the expiration dates of food, and a smart air conditioner that can learn your preferences and maximize energy efficiency. There's more coming: Nest is now selling a smart smoke and carbon monoxide detector and is planning a whole line of additional home sensors. Lots of other companies are working on a wide range of smart appliances. This will all be necessary if we want to build the smart power grid, which will reduce energy use and greenhouse gas emissions.

We're starting to collect and analyze data about our bodies as a means of improving our health and well-being. If you wear a fitness tracking device like Fitbit or Jawbone, it collects information about your movements awake and asleep, and uses that to analyze both your exercise and sleep habits. It can determine when you're having sex. Give the device more information about yourself—how much you weigh, what you eat—and you can learn even more. All of this data you share is available online, of course.

Many medical devices are starting to be Internet-enabled, collecting and reporting a variety of biometric data. There are already—or will be soon—devices that continually measure our vital signs, our moods, and our brain activity. It's not just specialized devices; current smartphones have some pretty sensitive motion sensors. As the price of DNA sequencing continues to drop, more of us are signing up to generate and analyze our own genetic data. Companies like 23andMe hope to use genomic data from their customers to find genes associated with disease, leading to new and highly profitable cures. They're also talking about personalized marketing, and insurance companies may someday buy their data to make business decisions.

Perhaps the extreme in the data-generating-self trend is lifelogging: continuously capturing personal data. Already you can install lifelogging apps that record your activities on your smartphone, such as when you talk to friends, play games, watch movies, and so on. But this is just a shadow of what lifelogging will become. In the future, it will include a video record. Google Glass is the first wearable device that has this potential, but others are not far behind.

These are examples of the Internet of Things. Environmental sensors will detect pollution levels. Smart inventory and control systems will reduce waste and save money. Internet-connected computers will be in everything—smart cities, smart toothbrushes, smart lightbulbs, smart sidewalk squares, smart pill bottles, smart clothing—because why not? Estimates put the current number of Internet-connected devices at 10 billion. That's already more than the number of people on the planet, and I've seen predictions that it will reach 30 billion by 2020. The hype level is pretty high, and we don't yet know which applications will work and which will be duds. What we do know is that they're all going to produce data, lots of data. The things around us will become the eyes and ears of the Internet.

The privacy implications of all this connectivity are profound. All those smart appliances will reduce greenhouse gas emissions— and they'll also stream data about how people move around within their houses and how they spend their time. Smart streetlights will gather data on people's movements outside. Cameras will only get better, smaller, and more mobile. Raytheon is planning to fly a blimp over Washington, DC, and Baltimore in 2015 to test its ability to track "targets"—presumably vehicles—on the ground, in the water, and in the air.

The upshot is that we interact with hundreds of computers every day, and soon it will be thousands. Every one of those computers produces data. Very little of it is the obviously juicy kind: what we ordered at a restaurant, our heart rate during our evening jog, or the last love letter we wrote. Rather, much of it is a type of data called *metadata*. This is data about data—information a computer system uses to operate or data that's a by-product of that operation. In a text message system, the messages themselves are data, but the accounts that sent and received the message, and the date and time of the message, are all metadata. An e-mail system is similar: the text of the e-mail is data, but the sender, receiver, routing data, and message size are all metadata—and we can argue about how to classify the subject line. In a photograph, the image is data; the date and time, camera settings, camera serial number, and GPS coordinates of the photo are metadata. Metadata may sound uninteresting, but, as I'll explain, it's anything but.

Still, this smog of data we produce is not necessarily a result of deviousness on anyone's part. Most of it is simply a natural by-product of computing. This is just the way technology works right now. Data is the exhaust of the information age.

HOW MUCH DATA?

Some quick math. Your laptop probably has a 500-gigabyte hard drive. That big backup drive you might have purchased with it can probably store two or three terabytes. Your corporate network might have one thousand times that: a petabyte. There are names for bigger numbers. A thousand petabytes is an exabyte (a billion billion bytes), a thousand exabytes is a zettabyte, and a thousand zettabytes is a yottabyte. To put it in human terms, an exabyte of data is 500 billion pages of text.

All of our data exhaust adds up. By 2010, we as a species were creating more data per day than we did from the beginning of time until 2003. By 2015, 76 exabytes of data will travel across the Internet every year.

As we start thinking of all this data, it's easy to dismiss concerns about its retention and use based on the assumption that there's simply too much of it to save, and in any case it would be too hard to sift through for nuggets of meaningful information. This used to be true. In the early days of computing, most of this data—and certainly most of the metadata—was thrown away soon after it was created. Saving it took too much memory. But the cost of all aspects of computing has continuously fallen over the years, and amounts of data that were impractical to store and process a decade ago are easy to deal with today. In 2015, a petabyte of cloud storage will cost $100,000 per year, down 90% from $1 million in 2011. The result is that more and more data is being stored.

You could probably store every tweet ever sent on your home computer's disk drive. Storing the voice conversation from every phone call made in the US requires less than 300 petabytes, or $30 million, per year. A continuous video lifelogger would require 700 gigabytes per year per person. Multiply that by the US population and you get 2 exabytes per year, at a current cost of $200 million.

That's expensive but plausible, and the price will only go down. In 2013, the NSA completed its massive Utah Data Center in Bluffdale. It's currently the third largest in the world, and the first of several that the NSA is building. The details are classified, but experts believe it can store about 12 exabytes of data. It has cost $1.4 billion so far. Worldwide, Google has the capacity to store 15 exabytes.

What's true for organizations is also true for individuals, and I'm a case study. My e-mail record stretches back to 1993. I consider that e-mail archive to be part of my brain. It's my memories. There isn't a week that goes by that I don't search that archive for something: a restaurant I visited some years ago, an article someone once told me about, the name of someone I met. I send myself reminder e-mails all the time; not just reminders of things to do when I get home, but reminders of things that I might want to recall years in the future. Access to that data trove is access to me.

I used to carefully sort all that e-mail. I had to decide what to save and what to delete, and I would put saved e-mails into hundreds of different folders based on people, companies, projects, and so on. In 2006, I stopped doing that. Now, I save everything in one large folder. In 2006, for me, saving and searching became easier than sorting and deleting.

To understand what all this data hoarding means for individual privacy, consider Austrian law student Max Schrems. In 2011, Schrems demanded that Facebook give him all the data the company had about him. This is a requirement of European Union (EU) law. Two years later, after a court battle, Facebook sent him a CD with a 1,200-page PDF: not just the friends he could see and the items on his newsfeed, but all of the photos and pages he'd ever clicked on and all of the advertising he'd ever viewed. Facebook doesn't use all of this data, but instead of figuring out what to save, the company finds it easier to just save everything.

2

Data as Surveillance

Governments and corporations gather, store, and analyze the tremendous amount of data we chuff out as we move through our digitized lives. Often this is without our knowledge, and typically without our consent. Based on this data, they draw conclusions about us that we might disagree with or object to, and that can impact our lives in profound ways. We may not like to admit it, but we are under mass surveillance.

Much of what we know about the NSA's surveillance comes from Edward Snowden, although people both before and after him also leaked agency secrets. As an NSA contractor, Snowden collected tens of thousands of documents describing many of the NSA's surveillance activities. In 2013, he fled to Hong Kong and gave them to select reporters. For a while I worked with Glenn Greenwald and the *Guardian* newspaper, helping analyze some of the more technical documents.

The first news story to break that was based on the Snowden documents described how the NSA collects the cell phone call records of every American. One government defense, and a sound bite repeated ever since, is that the data collected is "only metadata." The intended point was that the NSA wasn't collecting the words we spoke during our phone conversations, only the phone numbers of the two parties, and the date, time, and duration of the call. This seemed to mollify many people, but it shouldn't have. Collecting metadata on people means putting them under surveillance.

An easy thought experiment demonstrates this. Imagine that you hired a private detective to eavesdrop on someone. The detective would plant bugs in that person's home, office, and car. He would eavesdrop on that person's phone and computer. And you would get a report detailing that person's conversations.

Now imagine that you asked the detective to put that person under surveillance. You would get a different but nevertheless comprehensive report: where he went, what he did, who he spoke with and for how long, who he wrote to, what he read, and what he purchased. That's metadata.

Eavesdropping gets you the conversations; surveillance gets you everything else.

Telephone metadata alone reveals a lot about us. The timing, length, and frequency of our conversations reveal our relationships with others: our intimate friends, business associates, and everyone in-between. Phone metadata reveals what and who we're interested in and what's important to us, no matter how private. It provides a window into our personalities. It yields a detailed summary of what's happening to us at any point in time.

A Stanford University experiment examined the phone metadata of about 500 volunteers over several months. The personal nature of what the researchers could deduce from the metadata surprised even them, and the report is worth quoting:

- Participant A communicated with multiple local neurology groups, a specialty pharmacy, a rare-condition management service, and a hotline for a pharmaceutical used solely to treat relapsing multiple sclerosis.

- Participant B spoke at length with cardiologists at a major medical center, talked briefly with a medical laboratory, received calls from a pharmacy, and placed short calls to a home reporting hotline for a medical device used to monitor cardiac arrhythmias.
- Participant C made a number of calls to a firearms store that specializes in the AR semiautomatic rifle platform, and also spoke at length with customer service for a firearm manufacturer that produces an AR line.
- In a span of three weeks, Participant D contacted a home improvement store, locksmiths, a hydroponics dealer, and a head shop.
- Participant E had a long early morning call with her sister. Two days later, she placed a series of calls to the local Planned Parenthood location. She placed brief additional calls two weeks later, and made a final call a month after.

That's a multiple sclerosis sufferer, a heart attack victim, a semi-automatic weapons owner, a home marijuana grower, and someone who had an abortion, all from a single stream of metadata.

Web search data is another source of intimate information that can be used for surveillance. (You can argue whether this is data or metadata. The NSA claims it's metadata because your search terms are embedded in the URLs.) We don't lie to our search engine. We're more intimate with it than with our friends, lovers, or family members. We always tell it exactly what we're thinking about, in words as clear as possible. Google knows what kind of porn each of us searches for, which old lovers we still think about, our shames, our concerns, and our secrets. If Google decided to, it could figure out which of us is worried about our mental health, thinking about tax evasion, or planning to protest a particular government policy. I used to say that Google knows more about what I'm thinking of than my wife does. But that doesn't go far enough. Google knows more about what I'm thinking of *than I do*, because Google remembers all of it perfectly and forever.

I did a quick experiment with Google's autocomplete feature. This is the feature that offers to finish typing your search queries in real time, based on what other people have typed. When I typed "should I tell my w," Google suggested "should i tell my wife i had an affair" and "should i tell my work about dui" as the most popular completions. Google knows who clicked on those completions, and everything else they ever searched on.

Google's CEO Eric Schmidt admitted as much in 2010: "We know where you are. We know where you've been. We can more or less know what you're thinking about."

If you have a Gmail account, you can check for yourself. You can look at your search history for any time you were logged in. It goes back for as long as you've had the account, probably for years. Do it; you'll be surprised. It's more intimate than if you'd sent Google your diary. And even though Google lets you modify your ad preferences, you have no rights to delete anything you don't want there.

There are other sources of intimate data and metadata. Records of your purchasing habits reveal a lot about who you are. Your tweets tell the world what time you wake up in the morning, and what time you go to bed each night. Your buddy lists and address books reveal your political affiliation and sexual orientation. Your e-mail headers reveal who is central to your professional, social, and romantic life.

One way to think about it is that data is content, and metadata is context. Metadata can be much more revealing than data, especially when collected in the aggregate. When you have one person under surveillance, the contents of conversations, text messages, and e-mails can be more important than the metadata. But when you have an entire population under surveillance, the metadata is far more meaningful, important, and useful.

As former NSA general counsel Stewart Baker said, "Metadata absolutely tells you everything about somebody's life. If you have enough metadata you don't really need content." In 2014, former NSA and CIA director Michael Hayden remarked, "We kill people based on metadata."

The truth is, though, that the difference is largely illusory. It's all data about us.

CHEAPER SURVEILLANCE

Historically, surveillance was difficult and expensive. We did it only when it was important: when the police needed to tail a suspect, or a business required a detailed purchasing history for billing purposes. There were exceptions, and they were extreme and expensive. The exceptionally paranoid East German government had 102,000 Stasi surveilling a population of 17 million: that's one spy for every 166 citizens, or one for every 66 if you include civilian informants.

Corporate surveillance has grown from collecting as little data as necessary to collecting as much as possible. Corporations always collected information on their customers, but in the past they didn't collect very much of it and held it only as long as necessary. Credit card companies collected only the information about their customers' transactions that they needed for billing. Stores hardly ever collected information about their customers, and mail-order companies only collected names and addresses, and maybe some purchasing history so they knew when to remove someone from their mailing list. Even Google, back in the beginning, collected far less information about its users than it does today. When surveillance information was expensive to collect and store, corporations made do with as little as possible.

The cost of computing technology has declined rapidly in recent decades. This has been a profoundly good thing. It has become cheaper and easier for people to communicate, to publish their thoughts, to access information, and so on. But that same decline in price has also brought down the price of surveillance. As computer technologies improved, corporations were able to collect more information on everyone they did business with. As the cost of data storage became cheaper, they were able to save more data and for a longer time. As big data analysis tools became more powerful, it became profitable to save more information. This led to the surveillance-based business models I'll talk about in Chapter 4.

Government surveillance has gone from collecting data on as few people as necessary to collecting it on as many as possible. When surveillance was manual and expensive, it could only be justified in extreme cases. The warrant process limited police surveillance, and resource constraints and the risk of discovery limited national intelligence surveillance. Specific individuals were targeted for surveillance, and maximal information was collected on them alone. There were also strict minimization rules about not collecting information on other people. If the FBI was listening in on a mobster's phone, for example, the listener was supposed to hang up and stop recording if the mobster's wife or children got on the line.

As technology improved and prices dropped, governments broadened their surveillance. The NSA could surveil large groups— the Soviet government, the Chinese diplomatic corps, leftist political organizations and activists—not just individuals. Roving wiretaps meant that the FBI could eavesdrop on people regardless of the device they used to communicate with. Eventually, US agencies could spy on entire populations and save the data for years. This dovetailed with a changing threat, and they continued espionage against specific governments, while expanding mass surveillance of broad populations to look for potentially dangerous individuals. I'll talk about this in Chapter 5.

The result is that corporate and government surveillance interests have converged. Both now want to know everything about everyone. The motivations are different, but the methodologies are the same. That is the primary reason for the strong public-private security partnership that I'll talk about in Chapter 6.

To see what I mean about the cost of surveillance technology, just look how cheaply ordinary consumers can obtain sophisticated spy gadgets. On a recent flight, I was flipping through an issue of *SkyMall*, a catalog that airlines stick in the pocket of every domestic airplane seat. It offered an $80 pen with a hidden camera and microphone, so I could secretly record any meeting I might want evidence about later. I can buy a camera hidden in a clock radio for $100, or one disguised to look like a motion sensor alarm unit on a wall. I can set either one to record continuously or only when it detects motion. Another device allows me to see all the data on someone else's smartphone—either iPhone or Android—assuming I can get my hands on it. "Read text messages even after they've been deleted. See photos, contacts, call histories, calendar appointments and websites visited. Even tap into the phone's GPS data to find out where it's been." Only $120.

From other retailers I can buy a keyboard logger, or keylogger, to learn what someone else types on her computer—assuming I have physical access to it—for under $50. I can buy call intercept software to listen in on someone else's cell phone calls for $100. Or I can buy a remote-controlled drone helicopter with an onboard camera and use it to spy on my neighbors for under $1,000.

These are the consumer items, and some of them are illegal in some jurisdictions. Professional surveillance devices are also getting cheaper and better. For the police, the declining costs change everything. Following someone covertly, either on foot or by car, costs around $175,000 per month—primarily for the salary of the agents doing the following. But if the police can place a tracker in the suspect's car, or use a fake cell tower device to fool the suspect's cell phone into giving up its location information, the cost drops to about $70,000 per month, because it only requires one agent. And if the police can hide a GPS receiver in the suspect's car, suddenly the price drops to about $150 per month—mostly for the surreptitious installation of the device. Getting location information from the suspect's cell provider is even cheaper: Sprint charges law enforcement only $30 per month.

The difference is between fixed and marginal costs. If a police department performs surveillance on foot, following two people costs twice as much as following one person. But with GPS or cell phone surveillance, the cost is primarily for setting up the system. Once it is in place, the additional marginal cost of following one, ten, or a thousand more people is minimal. Or, once someone spends the money designing and building a telephone eavesdropping system that collects and analyzes all the voice calls in Afghanistan, as the NSA did to help defend US soldiers from improvised explosive devices, it's cheap and easy to deploy that same technology against the telephone networks of other countries.

MASS SURVEILLANCE

The result of this declining cost of surveillance technology is not just a difference in price; it's a difference in kind. Organizations end up doing more surveillance—a lot more. For example, in 2012, after a Supreme Court ruling, the FBI was required to either obtain warrants for or turn off 3,000 GPS surveillance devices installed in cars. It would simply be impossible for the FBI to follow 3,000 cars without automation; the agency just doesn't have the manpower. And now the prevalence of cell phones means that everyone can be followed, all of the time.

Another example is license plate scanners, which are becoming more common. Several companies maintain databases of vehicle license plates whose owners have defaulted on their auto loans. Spotter cars and tow trucks mount cameras on their roofs that continually scan license plates and send the data back to the companies, looking for a hit. There's big money to be made in the repossession business, so lots of individuals participate—all of them feeding data into the companies' centralized databases. One scanning company, Vigilant Solutions of Livermore, California, claims to have 2.5 billion records and collects 70 million scans in the US per month, along with date, time, and GPS location information.

In addition to repossession businesses, scanning companies also sell their data to divorce lawyers, private investigators, and others. They sometimes relay it, in real time, to police departments, which combine it with scans they get from interstate highway on-ramps, toll plazas, border crossings, and airport parking lots. They're looking for stolen vehicles and drivers with outstanding warrants and unpaid tickets. Already, the states' driver's license databases are being used by the FBI to identify people, and the US Department of Homeland Security wants all this data in a single national database. In the UK, a similar government-run system based on fixed cameras is deployed throughout the country. It enforces London's automobile congestion charge system, and searches for vehicles that are behind on their mandatory inspections.

Expect the same thing to happen with automatic face recognition. Initially, the data from private cameras will most likely be used by bounty hunters tracking down bail jumpers. Eventually, though, it will be sold for other uses and given to the government. Already the FBI has a database of 52 million faces, and facial recognition software that's pretty good. The Dubai police are integrating custom facial recognition software with Google Glass to automatically identify suspects. With enough cameras in a city, police officers will be able to follow cars and people around without ever leaving their desks.

This is mass surveillance, impossible without computers, networks, and automation. It's not "follow that car"; it's "follow every car." Police could always tail a suspect, but with an urban mesh of cameras, license plate scanners, and facial recognition software, they can tail everyone—suspect or not.

Similarly, putting a device called a pen register on a suspect's land line to record the phone numbers he calls used to be both time-consuming and expensive. But now that the FBI can demand that data from the phone companies' databases, it can acquire that information about everybody in the US. And it has.

In 2008, the company Waze (acquired by Google in 2013) introduced a new navigation system for smartphones. The idea was that by tracking the movements of cars that used Waze, the company could infer real-time traffic data and route people to the fastest roads. We'd all like to avoid traffic jams. In fact, all of society, not just Waze's customers, benefits when people are steered away from traffic jams so they don't add to them. But are we aware of how much data we're giving away?

For the first time in history, governments and corporations have the ability to conduct mass surveillance on entire populations. They can do it with our Internet use, our communications, our financial transactions, our movements . . . everything. Even the East Germans couldn't follow everybody all of the time. Now it's easy.

HIDDEN SURVEILLANCE

If you're reading this book on a Kindle, Amazon knows. Amazon knows when you started reading and how fast you read. The company knows if you're reading straight through, or if you read just a few pages every day. It knows if you skip ahead to the end, go back and reread a section, or linger on a page—or if you give up and don't finish the book. If you highlight any passages, Amazon knows about that, too. There's no light that flashes, no box that pops up, to warn you that your Kindle is sending Amazon data about your reading habits. It just happens, quietly and constantly.

We tolerate a level of electronic surveillance online that we would never allow in the physical world, because it's not obvious or advertised. It's one thing for a clerk to ask to see an ID card, or a tollbooth camera to photograph a license plate, or an ATM to ask for a card and a PIN. All of these actions generate surveillance records—the first case may require the clerk to copy or otherwise capture the data on the ID card—but at least they're overt. We know they're happening.

Most electronic surveillance doesn't happen that way. It's covert. We read newspapers online, not realizing that the articles we read are recorded. We browse online stores, not realizing that both the things we buy and the things we look at and decide not to buy are being monitored. We use electronic payment systems, not thinking about how they're keeping a record of our purchases. We carry our cell phones with us, not understanding that they're constantly tracking our location.

Buzzfeed is an entertainment website that collects an enormous amount of information about its users. Much of the data comes from traditional Internet tracking, but Buzzfeed also has a lot of fun quizzes, some of which ask very personal questions. One of them—"How Privileged Are You?"—asks about financial details, job stability, recreational activities, and mental health. Over two million people have taken that quiz, not realizing that Buzzfeed saves data from its quizzes. Similarly, medical information sites like WebMD collect data on what pages users search for and read.

Lest you think it's only your web browsing, e-mails, phone calls, chats, and other electronic communications that are monitored, old-fashioned paper mail is tracked as well. Through a program called Isolation Control and Tracking, the US Postal Service photographs the exterior, front and back, of *every piece of mail sent in the US*. That's about 160 billion pieces annually. This data is available to law enforcement, and certainly other government agencies as well.

Off the Internet, many surveillance technologies are getting smaller and less obtrusive. In some cities, video cameras capture our images hundreds of times a day. Some are obvious, but we don't see a CCTV camera embedded in a ceiling light or ATM, or a gigapixel camera a block away. Drones are getting smaller and harder to see; they're now the size of insects and soon the size of dust.

Add identification software to any of these image collection systems, and you have an automatic omnipresent surveillance system. Face recognition is the easiest way to identify people on camera, and the technology is getting better every year. In 2014, face recognition algorithms started outperforming people. There are other image identification technologies in development: iris scanners that work at a distance, gait recognition systems, and so on.

There's more hidden surveillance going on in the streets. Those contactless RFID chip cards in your wallet can be used to track people. Many retail stores are surreptitiously tracking people by the MAC addresses and Bluetooth IDs—which are basically identification numbers—broadcast by their smartphones. The goal is to record which aisles they walk down, which products they stop to look at, and so on. People can be tracked at public events by means of both these approaches.

In 2014, a senior executive from the Ford Motor Company told an audience at the Consumer Electronics Show, "We know everyone who breaks the law, we know when you're doing it. We have GPS in your car, so we know what you're doing." This came as a shock and surprise, since no one knew Ford had its car owners under constant surveillance. The company quickly retracted the remarks, but the comments left a lot of wiggle room for Ford to collect data on its car owners. We know from a Government Accountability Office report that both automobile companies and navigational aid companies collect a lot of location data from their users.

Radar in the terahertz range can detect concealed weapons on people, and objects through eight inches of concrete wall. Cameras can "listen" to phone conversations by focusing on nearby objects like potato chip bags and measuring their vibrations. The NSA, and presumably others, can turn your cell phone's microphone on remotely, and listen to what's going on around it.

There are body odor recognition systems under development, too. On the Internet, one company is working on identifying people by their typing style. There's research into identifying people by their writing style. Both corporations and governments are harvesting tens of millions of voiceprints—yet another way to identify you in real time.

This is the future. Store clerks will know your name, address, and income level as soon as you walk through the door. Billboards will know who you are, and record how you respond to them. Grocery store shelves will know what you usually buy, and exactly how to entice you to buy more of it. Your car will know who is in it, who is driving, and what traffic laws that driver is following or ignoring. Even now, it feels a lot like science fiction.

As surveillance fades into the background, it becomes easier to ignore. And the more intrusive a surveillance system is, the more likely it is to be hidden. Many of us would refuse a drug test before being hired for an office job, but many companies perform invasive background checks on all potential employees. Likewise, being tracked by hundreds of companies on the Internet—companies you've never interacted with or even heard of—feels much less intrusive than a hundred market researchers following us around taking notes.

In a sense, we're living in a unique time in history; many of our surveillance systems are still visible to us. Identity checks are common, but they still require us to show our ID. Cameras are everywhere, but we can still see them. In the near future, because these systems will be hidden, we may unknowingly acquiesce to even more surveillance.

AUTOMATIC SURVEILLANCE

A surprising amount of surveillance happens to us automatically, even if we do our best to opt out. It happens because we interact with others, and *they're* being monitored.

Even though I never post or friend anyone on Facebook—I have a professional page, but not a personal account—Facebook tracks me. It maintains a profile of non-Facebook users in its database. It tracks me whenever I visit a page with a Facebook "Like" button. It can probably make good guesses about who my friends are based on tagged photos, and it may well have the profile linked to other information it has purchased from various data brokers. My friends, and those sites with the Like buttons, allow Facebook to surveil me through them.

I try not to use Google search. But Google still collects a lot of information about the websites I visit, because so many of them use Google Analytics to track their visitors. Again, those sites let

Google track me through them. I use various blockers in my browser so Google can't track me very well, but it's working on technologies that will circumvent my privacy practices.

I also don't use Gmail. Instead, I use a local ISP and store all of my e-mail on my computer. Even so, Google has about a third of my messages, because many of the people I correspond with use Gmail. It's not just Gmail.com addresses; Google hosts a lot of organizations' e-mail, even though those organizations keep their domain name addresses. There are other examples. Apple has a worldwide database of Wi-Fi passwords, including my home network's, from people backing up their iPhones. Many companies have my contact information because my friends and colleagues back up their address books in the cloud. If my sister publishes her genetic information, then half of mine becomes public as well.

Sometimes data we only intend to share with a few becomes surveillance data for the world. Someone might take a picture of a friend at a party and post it on Facebook so her other friends can see it. Unless she specifies otherwise, that picture is public. It's still hard to find, of course—until it's tagged by an automatic face recognition system and indexed by a search engine. Now that photo can be easily found with an image search.

I am constantly appearing on other people's surveillance cameras. In cities like London, Chicago, Mexico City, and Beijing, the police forces have installed surveillance cameras all over the place. In other cities, like New York, the cameras are mostly privately owned. We saw the difference in two recent terrorism cases. The London subway bombers were identified by government cameras, and the Boston Marathon bombers by private cameras attached to businesses.

That data is almost certainly digital. Often it's just stored on the camera, on an endless loop that erases old data as it records new data. But increasingly, that surveillance video is available on the Internet and being saved indefinitely—and a lot of it is publicly searchable.

Unless we take steps to prevent it, being captured on camera will get even less avoidable as life recorders become more prevalent. Once enough people regularly record video of what they are seeing, you'll be in enough of their video footage that it'll no longer matter whether or not you're wearing one. It's kind of like herd immunity, but in reverse.

UBIQUITOUS SURVEILLANCE

Philosopher Jeremy Bentham conceived of his "panopticon" in the late 1700s as a way to build cheaper prisons. His idea was a prison where every inmate could be surveilled at any time, unawares. The inmate would have no choice but to assume that he was always being watched, and would therefore conform. This idea has been used as a metaphor for mass personal data collection, both on the Internet and off.

On the Internet, surveillance is ubiquitous. All of us are being watched, all the time, and that data is being stored forever. This is what an information-age surveillance state looks like, and it's efficient beyond Bentham's wildest dreams.

3

Analyzing Our Data

In 2012, the *New York Times* published a story on how corporations analyze our data for advertising advantages. The article revealed that Target Corporation could determine from a woman's buying patterns that she was pregnant, and would use that information to send the woman ads and coupons for baby-related items. The story included an anecdote about a Minneapolis man who'd complained to a Target store that had sent baby-related coupons to his teenage daughter, only to find out later that Target was right.

The general practice of amassing and saving all kinds of data is called "big data," and the science and engineering of extracting useful information from it is called "data mining." Companies like Target mine data to focus their advertising. Barack Obama mined data extensively in his 2008 and 2012 presidential campaigns for the same purpose. Auto companies mine the data from your car to design better cars; municipalities mine data from roadside sensors to understand driving conditions. Our genetic data is mined for all sorts of medical research. Companies like Facebook and Twitter mine our data for advertising purposes, and have allowed academics to mine their data for social research.

Most of these are secondary uses of the data. That is, they are not the reason the data was collected in the first place. In fact, that's the basic promise of big data: save everything you can, and someday you'll be able to figure out some use for it all.

Big data sets derive value, in part, from the inferences that can be made from them. Some of these are obvious. If you have someone's detailed location data over the course of a year, you can infer what his favorite restaurants are. If you have the list of people he calls and e-mails, you can infer who his friends are. If you have the list of Internet sites he visits—or maybe a list of books he's purchased—you can infer his interests.

Some inferences are more subtle. A list of someone's grocery purchases might imply her ethnicity. Or her age and gender, and possibly religion. Or her medical history and drinking habits. Marketers are constantly looking for patterns that indicate someone is about to do something expensive, like get married, go on vacation, buy a home, have a child, and so on. Police in various countries use these patterns as evidence, either in a court or in secret. Facebook can predict race, personality, sexual orientation, political ideology, relationship status, and drug use on the basis of Like clicks alone. The company knows you're engaged before you announce it, and gay before you come out—and its postings may reveal that to other people without your knowledge or permission. Depending on the country you live in, that could merely be a major personal embarrassment—or it could get you killed.

There are a lot of errors in these inferences, as all of us who've seen Internet ads that are only vaguely interesting can attest. But when the ads are on track, they can be eerily creepy—and we often don't like it. It's one thing to see ads for hemorrhoid suppositories or services to help you find a girlfriend on television, where we know they're being seen by everyone. But when we know they're targeted at us specifically, based on what we've posted or liked on the Internet, it can feel much more invasive. This makes for an interesting tension: data we're willing to share can imply conclusions that we don't want to share. Many of us are happy to tell Target our buying patterns for discounts and notifications of new products we might like to buy, but most of us don't want Target to figure out that we're pregnant. We also don't want the large data thefts and fraud that inevitably accompany these large databases.

When we think of computers using all of our data to make inferences, we have a very human way of thinking about it. We imagine how we would make sense of the data, and project that process onto computers. But that's not right. Computers and people have different strengths, weaknesses, and limits. Computers can't abstractly reason nearly as well as people, but they can process enormous amounts of data ever more quickly. (If you think about it, this means that computers are better at working with metadata than they are at handling conversational data.) And they're constantly improving; computing power is still doubling every eighteen months, while our species' brain size has remained constant. Computers are already far better than people at processing quantitative data, and they will continue to improve.

Right now, data mining is a hot technology, and there's a lot of hype and opportunism around it. It's not yet entirely clear what kinds of research will be possible, or what the true potential of the field is. But what is clear is that data-mining technology is becoming increasingly powerful and is enabling observers to draw ever more startling conclusions from big data sets.

SURVEILLING BACKWARDS IN TIME

One new thing you can do by applying data-mining technology to mass-surveillance data is go backwards in time. Traditional surveillance can only learn about the present and future: "Follow him and find out where he's going next." But if you have a database of historical surveillance information on everyone, you can do something new: "Look up that person's location information, and find out where he's been." Or: "Listen to his phone calls from last week."

Some of this has always been possible. Historically, governments have collected all sorts of data about the past. In the McCarthy era, for example, the government used political party registrations, subscriptions to magazines, and testimonies from friends, neighbors, family, and colleagues to gather data on people. The difference now is that the capability is more like a Wayback Machine: the data is more complete and far cheaper to get, and the technology has evolved to enable sophisticated historical analysis.

For example, in recent years Credit Suisse, Standard Chartered Bank, and BNP Paribas all admitted to violating laws prohibiting money transfer to sanctioned groups. They deliberately altered transactions to evade algorithmic surveillance and detection by "OFAC filters"—that's the Office of Foreign Assets Control within the Department of the Treasury. Untangling this sort of wrongdoing involved a massive historical analysis of banking transactions and employee communications.

Similarly, someone could go through old data with new analytical tools. Think about genetic data. There's not yet a lot we can learn from someone's genetic data, but ten years from now—who knows? We saw something similar happen during the Tour de France doping scandals; blood taken from riders years earlier was tested with new technologies, and widespread doping was detected.

The NSA stores a lot of historical data, which I'll talk about more in Chapter 5. We know that in 2008 a database called XKEYSCORE routinely held voice and e-mail content for just three days, but it held metadata for a month. One called MARINA holds a year's worth of people's browsing history. Another NSA database, MYS-

TIC, was able to store recordings of *all* the phone conversations for Bermuda. The NSA stores telephone metadata for five years.

These storage limits pertain to the raw trove of all data gathered. If an NSA analyst touches something in the database, the agency saves it for much longer. If your data is the result of a query into these databases, your data is saved indefinitely. If you use encryption, your data is saved indefinitely. If you use certain keywords, your data is saved indefinitely.

How long the NSA stores data is more a matter of storage capacity than a respect for privacy. We know the NSA needed to increase its storage capacity to hold all the cell phone location data it was collecting. As data storage gets cheaper, assume that more of this data will be stored longer. This is the point of the NSA's Utah Data Center.

The FBI stores our data, too. During the course of a legitimate investigation in 2013, the FBI obtained a copy of all the data on a site called Freedom Hosting, including stored e-mails. Almost all the data was unrelated to the investigation, but the FBI kept a copy of the entire site and has been accessing it for unrelated investigations ever since. The state of New York retains license plate scanning data for at least five years and possibly indefinitely.

Any data—Facebook history, tweets, license plate scanner data— can basically be retained forever, or until the company or government agency decides to delete it. In 2010, different cell phone companies held text messages for durations ranging from 90 days to 18 months. AT&T beat them all, hanging on to the data for seven years.

MAPPING RELATIONSHIPS

Mass-surveillance data permits mapping of interpersonal relationships. In 2013, when we first learned that the NSA was collecting telephone calling metadata on every American, there was much ado about so-called hop searches and what they mean. They're a new type of search, theoretically possible before computers but only really practical in a world of mass surveillance. Imagine that the NSA is interested in Alice. It will collect data on her, and then data on everyone she communicates with, and then data on everyone they communicate with, and then data on everyone *they* communicate with. That's three hops away from Alice, which is the maximum the NSA worked with.

The intent of hop searches is to map relationships and find conspiracies. Making sense of the data requires being able to cull out the overwhelming majority of innocent people who are caught in this dragnet, and the phone numbers common to unrelated people: voice mail services, pizza restaurants, taxi companies, and so on.

NSA documents note that the agency had 117,675 "active surveillance targets" on one day in 2013. Even using conservative estimates of how many conversants each person has and how much they overlap, the total number of people being surveilled by this system easily exceeded 20 million. It's the classic "six degrees of separation" problem; most of us are only a few hops away from everyone else. In 2014, President Obama directed the NSA to conduct two-hop analysis only on telephone metadata collected under one particular program, but he didn't place any restrictions on NSA hops for all the other data it collects.

Metadata from various sources is great for mapping relationships. Most of us use the Internet for social interaction, and our relationships show up in that. This is what both the NSA and Facebook do, and it's why the latter is so unnervingly accurate when it suggests people you might know whom you're not already Facebook friends with. One of Facebook's most successful advertising programs involves showing ads not just to people who Like a particular page or product, but to their friends and to friends of their friends.

FINDING US BY WHAT WE DO

Once you have collected data on everyone, you can search for individuals based on their behavior. Maybe you want to find everyone who frequents a certain gay bar, or reads about a particular topic, or has a particular political belief. Corporations do this regularly, using mass-surveillance data to find potential customers with particular characteristics, or looking for people to hire by searching for people who have published on a particular topic.

One can search for things other than names and other personal identifiers like identification numbers, phone numbers, and so on. Google, for example, searches all of your Gmail and uses keywords it finds to more intimately understand you, for advertising purposes. The NSA does something similar: what it calls "about" searches. Basically, it searches the contents of everyone's communications for a particular name or word—or maybe a phrase. So in addition to examining Alice's data and the data of everyone within two or three hops of her, it can search everyone else—the entire database of communications—for mentions of her name. Or if it doesn't know a name, but knows the name of a particular location or project, or a code name that someone has used, it can search on that. For example, the NSA targets people who search for information on popular Internet privacy and anonymity tools.

We don't know the details, but the NSA chains together hops based on any connection, not just phone connections. This could include being in the same location as a target, having the same calling pattern, and so on. These types of searches are made possible by having access to everyone's data.

You can use mass surveillance to find individuals. If you know that a particular person was at a specific restaurant one evening, a train station three days later in the afternoon, and a hydroelectric plant the next morning, you can query a database of everyone's cell phone locations, and anyone who fits those characteristics will pop up.

You can also search for anomalous behavior. Here are four examples of how the NSA uses cell phone data.

1. The NSA uses cell phone location information to track people whose movements intersect. For example, assume that the NSA is interested in Alice. If Bob is at the same restaurant as Alice one evening, and then at the same coffee shop as Alice a week later, and at the same airport as Alice a month later, the system will flag Bob as a potential associate of Alice's, even if the two have never communicated electronically.

2. The NSA tracks the locations of phones that are carried around by US spies overseas. Then it determines whether there are any other cell phones that follow the agents' phones around. Basically, the NSA checks whether anyone is tailing those agents.

3. The NSA has a program where it trawls through cell phone metadata to spot phones that are turned on, used for a while, and then turned off and never used again. And it uses the phones' usage patterns to chain them together. This technique is employed to find "burner" phones used by people who wish to avoid detection.

4. The NSA collects data on people who turn their phones off, and for how long. It then collects the locations of those people when they turned their phones off, and looks for others nearby who also turned their phones off for a similar period of time. In other words, it looks for secret meetings.

I've already discussed the government of Ukraine using cell phone location data to find everybody who attended an antigovernment demonstration, and the Michigan police using it to find everyone who was near a planned labor union protest site. The FBI has used this data to find phones that were used by a particular target but not otherwise associated with him.

Corporations do some of this as well. There's a technique called geofencing that marketers use to identify people who are near a particular business so as to deliver an ad to them. A single geofencing company, Placecast, delivers location-based ads to ten million phones in the US and UK for chains like Starbucks, Kmart, and Subway. Microsoft does the same thing to people passing within ten miles of some of its stores; it works with the company Ninth-Decimal. Sense Networks uses location data to create individual profiles.

CORRELATING DIFFERENT DATA SETS

Vigilant Solutions is one of the companies that collect license plate data from cameras. It has plans to augment this system with other algorithms for automobile identification, systems of facial recognition, and information from other databases. The result would be a much more powerful surveillance platform than a simple database of license plate scans, no matter how extensive, could ever be.

News stories about mass surveillance are generally framed in terms of data collection, but miss the story about data correlation: the linking of identities across different data sets to draw inferences from the combined data. It's not just that inexpensive drones with powerful cameras will become increasingly common. It's the drones plus facial recognition software that allows the system to identify people automatically, plus the large databases of tagged photos—from driver's licenses, Facebook, newspapers, high school yearbooks—that will provide reference images for that software. It's also the ability to correlate that identification with numerous other databases, and the ability to store all that data indefinitely.

Ubiquitous surveillance is the result of multiple streams of mass surveillance tied together.

I have an Oyster card that I use to pay for public transport while in London. I've taken pains to keep it cash-only and anonymous. Even so, if you were to correlate the usage of that card with a list of people who visit London and the dates—whether that list is provided by the airlines, credit card companies, cell phone companies, or ISPs—I'll bet that I'm the only person for whom those dates correlate perfectly. So my "anonymous" movement through the London Underground becomes nothing of the sort.

Snowden disclosed an interesting research project from the CSEC—that's the Communications Security Establishment Canada, the country's NSA equivalent—that demonstrates the value of correlating different streams of surveillance information to find people who are deliberately trying to evade detection.

A CSEC researcher, with the cool-sounding job title of "tradecraft developer," started with two weeks' worth of Internet identification data: basically, a list of user IDs that logged on to various websites. He also had a database of geographic locations for different wireless networks' IP addresses. By putting the two databases together, he could tie user IDs logging in from different wireless networks to the physical location of those networks. The idea was to use this data to find people. If you know the user ID of some surveillance target, you can set an alarm when that target uses an airport or hotel wireless network and learn when he is traveling. You can also identify a particular person who you know visited a particular geographical area on a series of dates and times. For example, assume you're looking for someone who called you anonymously from three different pay phones. You know the dates and times of the calls, and the locations of those pay phones. If that person has a smartphone in his pocket that automatically logs into wireless networks, then you can correlate that log-in database with dates and times you're interested in and the locations of those networks. The odds are that there will only be one match.

Researchers at Carnegie Mellon University did something similar. They put a camera in a public place, captured images of people walking past, identified them with facial recognition software and Facebook's public tagged photo database, and correlated the names with other databases. The result was that they were able to display personal information about a person in real time as he or she was walking by. This technology could easily be available to anyone, using smartphone cameras or Google Glass.

Sometimes linking identities across data sets is easy; your cell phone is connected to your name, and so is your credit card. Sometimes it's harder; your e-mail address might not be connected to your name, except for the times people refer to you by name in e-mail. Companies like Initiate Systems sell software that correlates data across multiple data sets; they sell to both governments and corporations. Companies are also correlating your online behavior with your offline actions. Facebook, for example, is partnering with the data brokers Acxiom and Epsilon to match your online profile with in-store purchases.

Once you can correlate different data sets, there is a lot you can do with them. Imagine building up a picture of someone's health without ever looking at his patient records. Credit card records and supermarket affinity cards reveal what food and alcohol he buys, which restaurants he eats at, whether he has a gym membership, and what nonprescription items he buys at a pharmacy. His phone reveals how often he goes to that gym, and his activity tracker reveals his activity level when he's there. Data from websites reveal what medical terms he's searched on. This is how a company like ExactData can sell lists of people who date online, people who gamble, and people who suffer from anxiety, incontinence, or erectile dysfunction.

PIERCING OUR ANONYMITY

When a powerful organization is eavesdropping on significant portions of our electronic infrastructure and can correlate the various surveillance streams, it can often identify people who are trying to hide. Here are four stories to illustrate that.

1. Chinese military hackers who were implicated in a broad set of attacks against the US government and corporations were identified because they accessed Facebook from the same network infrastructure they used to carry out their attacks.

2. Hector Monsegur, one of the leaders of the LulzSec hacker movement under investigation for breaking into numerous commercial networks, was identified and arrested in 2011 by the FBI. Although he usually practiced good computer security and used an anonymous relay service to protect his identity, he slipped up once. An inadvertent disclosure during a chat allowed an investigator to track down a video on YouTube of his car, then to find his Facebook page.

3. Paula Broadwell, who had an affair with CIA director David Petraeus, similarly took extensive precautions to hide her identity. She never logged in to her anonymous e-mail service from her home network. Instead, she used hotel and other public networks when she e-mailed him. The FBI correlated registration data from several different hotels—and hers was the common name.

4. A member of the hacker group Anonymous called "w0rmer," wanted for hacking US law enforcement websites, used an anonymous Twitter account, but linked to a photo of a woman's breasts taken with an iPhone. The photo's embedded GPS coordinates pointed to a house in Australia. Another website that referenced w0rmer also mentioned the name Higinio

Ochoa. The police got hold of Ochoa's Facebook page, which included the information that he had an Australian girlfriend. Photos of the girlfriend matched the original photo that started all this, and police arrested w0rmer aka Ochoa.

Maintaining Internet anonymity against a ubiquitous surveillor is nearly impossible. If you forget even once to enable your protections, or click on the wrong link, or type the wrong thing, you've permanently attached your name to whatever anonymous provider you're using. The level of operational security required to maintain privacy and anonymity in the face of a focused and determined investigation is beyond the resources of even trained government agents. Even a team of highly trained Israeli assassins was quickly identified in Dubai, based on surveillance camera footage around the city.

The same is true for large sets of anonymous data. We might naïvely think that there are so many of us that it's easy to hide in the sea of data. Or that most of our data is anonymous. That's not true. Most techniques for anonymizing data don't work, and the data can be de-anonymized with surprisingly little information.

In 2006, AOL released three months of search data for 657,000 users: 20 million searches in all. The idea was that it would be useful for researchers; to protect people's identity, they replaced names with numbers. So, for example, Bruce Schneier might be 608429. They were surprised when researchers were able to attach names to numbers by correlating different items in individuals' search history.

In 2008, Netflix published 10 million movie rankings by 500,000 anonymized customers, as part of a challenge for people to come up with better recommendation systems than the one the company was using at that time. Researchers were able to de-anonymize people by comparing rankings and time stamps with public rankings and time stamps in the Internet Movie Database.

These might seem like special cases, but correlation opportunities pop up more frequently than you might think. Someone with access to an anonymous data set of telephone records, for example, might partially de-anonymize it by correlating it with a catalog merchant's telephone order database. Or Amazon's online book reviews could be the key to partially de-anonymizing a database of credit card purchase details.

Using public anonymous data from the 1990 census, computer scientist Latanya Sweeney found that 87% of the population in the United States, 216 million of 248 million people, could likely be uniquely identified by their five-digit ZIP code combined with their gender and date of birth. For about half, just a city, town, or municipality name was sufficient. Other researchers reported similar results using 2000 census data.

Google, with its database of users' Internet searches, could de-anonymize a public database of Internet purchases, or zero in on searches of medical terms to de-anonymize a public health database. Merchants who maintain detailed customer and purchase information could use their data to partially de-anonymize any large search engine's search data. A data broker holding databases of several companies might be able to de-anonymize most of the records in those databases.

Researchers have been able to identify people from their anonymous DNA by comparing the data with information from genealogy sites and other sources. Even something like Alfred Kinsey's sex research data from the 1930s and 1940s isn't safe. Kinsey took great pains to preserve the anonymity of his subjects, but in 2013, researcher Raquel Hill was able to identify 97% of them.

It's counterintuitive, but it takes less data to uniquely identify us than we think. Even though we're all pretty typical, we're nonetheless distinctive. It turns out that if you eliminate the top 100 movies everyone watches, our movie-watching habits are all pretty individual. This is also true for our book-reading habits, our Internet-shopping habits, our telephone habits, and our web-searching habits. We can be uniquely identified by our relationships. It's quite obvious that you can be uniquely identified by your location data. With 24/7 location data from your cell phone, your name can be uncovered without too much trouble. You don't even need all that data; 95% of Americans can be identified *by name* from just four time/date/location points.

The obvious countermeasures for this are, sadly, inadequate. Companies have anonymized data sets by removing some of the data, changing the time stamps, or inserting deliberate errors into the unique ID numbers they replaced names with. It turns out, though, that these sorts of tweaks only make de-anonymization slightly harder.

This is why regulation based on the concept of "personally identifying information" doesn't work. PII is usually defined as a name, unique account number, and so on, and special rules apply to it. But PII is also about the amount of data; the more information someone has about you, even anonymous information, the easier it is for her to identify you.

For the most part, our protections are limited to the privacy policies of the companies we use, not by any technology or mathematics. And being identified by a unique number often doesn't provide much protection. The data can still be collected and correlated and used, and eventually we do something to attach our name to that "anonymous" data record.

In the age of ubiquitous surveillance, where everyone collects data on us all the time, anonymity is fragile. We either need to develop more robust techniques for preserving anonymity, or give up on the idea entirely.

4

The Business of Surveillance

One of the most surprising things about today's cell phones is how many other things they also do. People don't wear watches, because their phones have a clock. People don't carry cameras, because they come standard in most smartphones.

That camera flash can also be used as a flashlight. One of the flashlight apps available for Android phones is Brightest Flashlight Free, by a company called GoldenShores Technologies, LLC. It works great and has a bunch of cool features. Reviewers recommended it to kids going trick-or-treating. One feature that wasn't mentioned by reviewers is that the app collected location information from its users and allegedly sold it to advertisers.

It's actually more complicated than that. The company's privacy policy, never mind that no one read it, actively misled consumers. It said that the company would use any information collected, but left out that the information would be sold to third parties. And although users had to click "accept" on the license agreement they also didn't read, the app started collecting and sending location information even before people clicked.

This surprised pretty much all of the app's 50 million users when researchers discovered it in 2012. The US Federal Trade Commission got involved, forcing the company to clean up its deceptive practices and delete the data it had collected. It didn't fine the company, though, because the app was free.

Imagine that the US government passed a law requiring all citizens to carry a tracking device. Such a law would immediately be found unconstitutional. Yet we carry our cell phones everywhere. If the local police department required us to notify it whenever we made a new friend, the nation would rebel. Yet we notify Facebook. If the country's spies demanded copies of all our conversations and correspondence, people would refuse. Yet we provide copies to our e-mail service providers, our cell phone companies, our social networking platforms, and our Internet service providers.

The overwhelming bulk of surveillance is corporate, and it occurs because we ostensibly agree to it. I don't mean that we make an informed decision agreeing to it; instead, we accept it either because we get value from the service or because we are offered a package deal that includes surveillance and don't have any real choice in the matter. This is the bargain I talked about in the Introduction.

This chapter is primarily about Internet surveillance, but remember that everything is—or soon will be—connected to the Internet. Internet surveillance is really shorthand for surveillance in an Internet-connected world.

INTERNET SURVEILLANCE

The primary goal of all this corporate Internet surveillance is advertising. There's a little market research and customer service in there, but those activities are secondary to the goal of more effectively selling you things.

Internet surveillance is traditionally based on something

called a cookie. The name sounds benign, but the technical description "persistent identifier" is far more accurate. Cookies weren't intended to be surveillance devices; rather, they were designed to make surfing the web easier. Websites don't inherently remember you from visit to visit or even from click to click. Cookies provide the solution to this problem. Each cookie contains a unique number that allows the site to identify you. So now when you click around on an Internet merchant's site, you keep telling it, "I'm customer #608431." This allows the site to find your account, keep your shopping cart attached to you, remember you the next time you visit, and so on.

Companies quickly realized that they could set their own cookies on pages belonging to other sites—with their permission and by paying for the privilege—and the third-party cookie was born. Enterprises like DoubleClick (purchased by Google in 2007) started tracking web users across many different sites. This is when ads started following you around the web. Research a particular car or vacation destination or medical condition, and for weeks you'll see ads for that car or city or a related pharmaceutical on every commercial Internet site you visit.

This has evolved into a shockingly extensive, robust, and profitable surveillance architecture. You are being tracked pretty much everywhere you go on the Internet, by many companies and data brokers: ten different companies on one site, a dozen on another. Facebook tracks you on every site with a Facebook Like button (whether you're logged in to Facebook or not), and Google tracks you on every site that has a Google Plus +1 button or that simply uses Google Analytics to monitor its own web traffic.

Most of the companies tracking you have names you've never heard of: Rubicon Project, AdSonar, Quantcast, Pulse 260, Undertone, Traffic Marketplace. If you want to see who's tracking you, install one of the browser plugins that let you monitor cookies. I guarantee you will be startled. One reporter discovered that 105 different companies tracked his Internet use during one 36-hour period. In 2010, a seemingly innocuous site like Dictionary.com installed over 200 tracking cookies on your browser when you visited.

It's no different on your smartphone. The apps there track you as well. They track your location, and sometimes download your address book, calendar, bookmarks, and search history. In 2013, the rapper Jay-Z and Samsung teamed up to offer people who downloaded an app the ability to hear the new Jay-Z album before release. The app required the ability to view all accounts on the phone, track the phone's location, and track who the user was talking to on the phone. And the Angry Birds game even collects location data when you're not playing.

Broadband companies like Comcast also conduct surveillance on their users. These days they're mostly monitoring to see whether you illegally download copyrighted songs and videos, but other applications aren't far behind. Verizon, Microsoft, and others are working on a set-top box that can monitor what's going on in the room, and serve ads based on that information.

It's less Big Brother, and more hundreds of tattletale little brothers.

Today, Internet surveillance is far more insistent than cookies. In fact, there's a minor arms race going on. Your browser—yes, even Google Chrome—has extensive controls to block or delete cookies, and many people enable those features. DoNotTrackMe is one of the most popular browser plug-ins. The Internet surveillance industry has responded with "flash cookies"—basically, cookie-like files that are stored with Adobe's Flash player and remain when browsers delete their cookies. To block those, you can install FlashBlock. But there are other ways to uniquely track you, with esoteric names like evercookies, canvas fingerprinting, and cookie synching. It's not just marketers; in 2014, researchers found that the White House website used evercookies, in violation of its own privacy policy. I'll give some advice about blocking web surveillance in Chapter 15.

Cookies are inherently anonymous, but companies are increasingly able to correlate them with other information that positively identifies us. You identify yourself willingly to lots of Internet services. Often you do this with only a username, but increasingly usernames can be tied to your real name. Google tried to compel this with its "real name policy," which mandated that users register for Google Plus with their legal names, until it rescinded that policy in 2014. Facebook pretty much demands real names. Anytime you use your credit card number to buy something, your real identity is tied to any cookies set by companies involved in that transaction. And any browsing you do on your smartphone is tied to you as the phone's owner, although the website might not know it.

FREE AND CONVENIENT

Surveillance is the business model of the Internet for two primary reasons: people like free, and people like convenient. The truth is, though, that people aren't given much of a choice. It's either surveillance or nothing, and the surveillance is conveniently invisible so you don't have to think about it. And it's all possible because US law has failed to keep up with changes in business practices.

Before 1993, the Internet was entirely noncommercial, and free became the online norm. When commercial services first hit the Internet, there was a lot of talk about how to charge for them. It quickly became clear that, except for a few isolated circumstances like investment and porn websites, people weren't willing to pay even a small amount for access. Much like the business model for television, advertising was the only revenue model that made sense, and surveillance has made that advertising more profitable. Websites can charge higher prices for personally targeted advertising than they can for broadcast advertising. This is how we ended up with nominally free systems that collect and sell our data in exchange for services, then blast us with advertising.

"Free" is a special price, and there has been all sorts of psychological research showing that people don't act rationally around it. We overestimate the value of free. We consume more of something than we should when it's free. We pressure others to consume it. Free warps our normal sense of cost vs. benefit, and people end up trading their personal data for less than its worth.

This tendency to undervalue privacy is exacerbated by companies deliberately making sure that privacy is not salient to users. When you log on to Facebook, you don't think about how much personal information you're revealing to the company; you chat with your friends. When you wake up in the morning, you don't think about how you're going to allow a bunch of companies to track you throughout the day; you just put your cell phone in your pocket.

The result is that Internet companies can improve their product offerings to their actual customers by reducing user privacy. Facebook has done it systematically over the years, regularly updating its privacy policy to obtain more access to your data and give you less privacy. Facebook has also changed its default settings so that more people can see your name, photo, wall posts, photos you post, Likes, and so on. Google has done much the same. In 2012, it announced a major change: Google would link its data about you from search, Gmail, YouTube (which Google owns), Google Plus, and so on into one large data set about you.

Apple is somewhat of an exception here. The company exists to market consumer products, and although it could spy on iCloud users' e-mail, text messages, calendar, address book, and photos, it does not. It uses iTunes purchase information only to suggest other songs and videos a user might want to buy. In late 2014, it started using this as a market differentiator.

Convenience is the other reason we willingly give highly personal data to corporate interests, and put up with becoming objects of their surveillance. As I keep saying, surveillance-based services are useful and valuable. We like it when we can access our address book, calendar, photographs, documents, and everything else on any device we happen to be near. We like services like Siri and Google Now, which work best when they know tons about you. Social networking apps make it easier to hang out with our friends. Cell phone apps like Google Maps, Yelp, Weather, and Uber work better and faster when they know our location. Letting apps like Pocket or Instapaper know what we're reading feels like a small price to pay for getting everything we want to read in one convenient place. We even like it when ads are targeted to exactly what we're interested in. The benefits of surveillance in these and other applications are real, and significant.

We especially don't mind if a company collects our data and uses it within its own service to better serve us. This is why Amazon recommendations are rarely mentioned when people complain about corporate surveillance. Amazon constantly recommends things for you to buy based on the things you've bought and the things other people have bought. Amazon's using your data in the same context it was collected, and it's completely transparent to the user. It's very big business for Amazon, and people largely accept it. They start objecting, though, when their data is bought, sold, and used without their knowledge or consent.

THE DATA BROKER INDUSTRY

Customer surveillance is much older than the Internet. Before the Internet, there were four basic surveillance streams. The first flowed from companies keeping records on their customers. This was a manufacturing supply company knowing what its corporate customers order, and who does the ordering. This was Nordstrom remembering its customers' sizes and the sorts of tailoring they like, and airlines and hotels keeping track of their frequent customers. Eventually this evolved into the databases that enable companies to track their sales leads all the way from initial inquiry to final purchase, and retail loyalty cards, which offer consumers discounts but whose real purpose is to track their purchases. Now lots of companies offer Customer Relationship Management, or CRM, systems to corporations of all sizes.

The second traditional surveillance stream was direct marketing. Paper mail was the medium, and the goal was to provide companies with lists of people who wanted to receive the marketing mail and not waste postage on people who did not. This was necessarily coarse, based on things like demographics, magazine subscriptions, or customer lists from related enterprises.

The third stream came from credit bureaus. These companies collected detailed credit information about people, and sold that information to banks trying to determine whether to give individuals loans and at what rates. This has always been a relatively expensive form of personal data collection, and only makes sense when lots of money is at stake: issuing credit cards, allowing someone to lease an apartment, and so on.

The fourth stream was from government. It consisted of various public records: birth and death certificates, driver's license records, voter registration records, various permits and licenses, and so on. Companies have increasingly been able to download, or purchase, this public data.

Credit bureaus and direct marketing companies combined these four streams to become modern day data brokers like Acxiom. These companies buy your personal data from companies you do business with, combine it with other information about you, and sell it to companies that want to know more about you. And they've ridden the tides of computerization. The more data you produce, the more they collect and the more accurately they profile you.

The breadth and depth of information that data brokers have is astonishing. They collect demographic information: names, addresses, telephone numbers, e-mail addresses, gender, age, marital status, presence and ages of children in household, education level, profession, income level, political affiliation, cars driven, and information about homes and other property. They collect lists of things you've purchased, when you've purchased them, and how you paid for them. They keep track of deaths, divorces, and diseases in your family. They collect everything about what you do on the Internet.

Data brokers use your data to sort you into various marketable categories. Want lists of people who fall into the category of "potential inheritor" or "adult with senior parent," or addresses of households with a "diabetic focus" or "senior needs"? Acxiom can provide you with that. InfoUSA has sold lists of "suffering seniors" and gullible seniors. In 2011, the data broker Teletrack sold lists of people who had applied for nontraditional credit products like payday loans to companies who wanted to target them for bad financial deals. In 2012, the broker Equifax sold lists of people who were late on their mortgage payments to a discount loan company. Because this was financial information, both brokers were fined by the FTC for their actions. Almost everything else is fair game.

PERSONALIZED ADVERTISING

We use systems that spy on us in exchange for services. It's just the way the Internet works these days. If something is free, you're not the customer; you're the product. Or, as Al Gore said, "We have a stalker economy."

Advertising has always suffered from the problem that most

people who see an advertisement don't care about the product. A beer ad is wasted on someone who doesn't drink beer. A car advertisement is largely wasted unless you are in the market for a car. But because it was impossible to target ads individually, companies did the best they could with the data they had. They segmented people geographically, and guessed which magazines and TV shows would best attract their potential customers. They tracked populations as a whole, or in large demographic groups. It was very inefficient. There's a famous quote, most reliably traced to the retail magnate John Wanamaker: "I know half of my advertising is wasted. The trouble is, I don't know which half."

Ubiquitous surveillance has the potential to change that. If you know exactly who wants to buy a lawn mower or is worried about erectile dysfunction, you can target your advertising to the right person at the right time, eliminating waste. (In fact, a national lawn care company uses aerial photography to better market its services.) And if you know the details about that potential customer—what sorts of arguments would be most persuasive, what sorts of images he finds most appealing—your advertising can be even more effective.

This also works in political advertising, and is already changing the way political campaigns are waged. Obama used big data and individual marketing to great effect in both 2008 and 2012, and other candidates across parties are following suit. This data is used to target fund-raising efforts and individualized political messages, and ensure that you actually get to the polls on Election Day—assuming the database says that you're voting for the correct candidate.

A lot of commercial surveillance data is filled with errors, but this information can be valuable even if it isn't very accurate. Even if you ended up showing your ad to the wrong people a third of the time, you could still have an effective advertising campaign. What's important is not perfect targeting accuracy; it's that the data is enormously better than before.

For example, in 2013, researchers were able to determine the physical locations of people on Twitter by analyzing similarities with other Twitter users. Their accuracy rate wasn't perfect—they were only able to predict a user's city with 58% accuracy—but for plenty of commercial advertising that level of precision is good enough.

Still, a lot of evidence suggests that surveillance-based advertising is oversold. There is value in showing people ads for things they want, especially at the exact moment they are considering making a purchase. This is what Google tries to do with Adwords, its service that places ads next to search results. It's what all retailers try to do with "people who bought this also bought this" advertising. But these sorts of things are based on minimal surveillance.

What's unclear is how much more data helps. There is value in knowing broad personal details about people: they're gay, they're getting married, they're thinking about taking a tropical vacation, they have a certain income level. And while it might be very valuable for a car company to know that you're interested in an SUV and not a convertible, it's only marginally more valuable to know that you prefer the blue one to the green one. And it's less valuable to know that you have two kids, one of whom still needs a car seat. Or that one of the kids died in a car crash. Yes, a dealer would push the larger SUV in the first instance and tout safety in the second, but there are diminishing returns. And advertising that's too targeted feels creepy and risks turning customers off.

There's a concept from robotics that's useful here. We tend to be comfortable with robots that obviously look like robots, and with robots that appear fully human. But we're very uncomfortable with robots that look a lot like people but don't appear fully human. Japanese roboticist Masahiro Mori called this phenomenon the "uncanny valley." Technology critic Sara M. Watson suggested that there's a similar phenomenon in advertising. People are okay with sloppily personalized advertising and with seamless and subtle personalized advertising, but are creeped out when they see enough to realize they're being manipulated or when it doesn't match their sense of themselves.

This is all going to change over time, as we become used to personalized advertising. The definition of "creepy" is relative and fluid, and depends a lot on our familiarity with the technologies in question. Right now, ads that follow us around the Internet feel creepy. Creepy is also self-correcting. Google has a long and complex policy of impermissible search ads, because users found some types of advertising too creepy. Other companies are letting people click on a link to find out why they were targeted for a particular ad, hoping that that will make them more comfortable with the process.

On the other hand, some companies just hide it better. After the story ran about Target figuring out that the teenager was pregnant, the company changed the way it sent targeted advertising to people. It didn't stop advertising to women it thought were pregnant, but it embedded those targeted ads among more general ads. Recipients of these mailings didn't feel targeted, so they were less creeped out by the advertisements.

Meanwhile, the prevalence of advertising in our environment is making individual ads less valuable for two reasons. First, as advertising saturates our world, the value of each individual ad falls. This is because the total amount of money we have to spend doesn't change. For example, all automobile manufacturers are fighting for the profit from the one car you will buy. If you see ten times the ads, each one is only worth one tenth the price, because in the end you're only going to buy one car.

Second, we are better at tuning advertising out. Since the popularization of analog video recorders in the mid-1970s, television advertisers have paid attention to how their ads look in fast-forward, because that's how many people watch them. Internet advertising has waged an even more complex battle for our attention. Initially, ads were banners on the top of pages. When we learned how to ignore them, the advertisers placed their ads in the main parts of the pages. When we learned to ignore those, they started blinking and showing video. Now they're increasingly interfering with what we want to read, so we need to deliberately shoo them away. More than 50 million people have installed AdBlock Plus on their browsers to help them do this.

The result is that the value of a single Internet advertisement is dropping rapidly, even as the cost of Internet advertising as a whole is rising. Accordingly, the value of our data to advertisers has been falling rapidly. A few years ago, a detailed consumer profile was valuable; now so many companies and data brokers have the data that it's a common commodity. One analysis of 2013 financial reports calculated that the value of each user to Google is $40 per year, and only $6 to Facebook, LinkedIn, and Yahoo. This is why companies like Google and Facebook keep raising the ante. They need more and more data about us to sell to advertisers and thereby differentiate themselves from the competition.

It's possible that we've already reached the peak, and the profitability of advertising as a revenue source will start falling, eventually to become unsustainable as a sole business model. I don't think anyone knows how the Internet would look if the advertising bubble burst, surveillance-based marketing turned out not to be effective, and Internet companies needed to revert to more traditional business models, like charging their users.

NEW MIDDLEMEN CONSOLIDATE POWER

One of the early tropes of the Internet was that it would eliminate traditional corporate middlemen. No longer would you have to rely on a newspaper to curate the day's news and provide it to you in an easy-to-read paper package. You could go out and design your own newspaper, taking bits from here and there, creating exactly what you wanted. Similarly, no longer would you have to rely on centralized storefronts to accumulate and resell collectibles; eBay connected buyers and sellers directly. It was the same with music promotion and distribution, airline tickets, and—in some cases—advertising. The old gatekeepers' business models relied on inefficiencies of technology, and the Internet changed that dynamic.

It's even more true today. AirBnB allows individuals to compete with traditional hotel chains. TaskRabbit makes it easier to connect people who want to do odd jobs with people who need odd jobs done. Etsy, CafePress, and eBay all bypass traditional flea markets. Zillow and Redfin bypass real estate brokers, eTrade bypasses investment advisors, and YouTube bypasses television networks. Craigslist bypasses newspaper classifieds. Hotwire and Travelocity bypass travel agents.

These new companies might have broken the traditional power blocs of antique stores, newspapers, and taxi companies, but by controlling the information flow between buyers and sellers they have become powerful middlemen themselves. We're increasingly seeing new and old middlemen battle in the marketplace: Apple and its iTunes store versus the music industry, Amazon versus the traditional publishing industry, Uber versus taxi companies. The new information middlemen are winning.

Google CEO Eric Schmidt said it: "We believe that modern technology platforms, such as Google, Facebook, Amazon and Apple, are even more powerful than most people realize . . . , and what gives them power is their ability to grow—specifically, their speed to scale. Almost nothing, short of a biological virus, can scale as quickly, efficiently or aggressively as these technology platforms and this makes the people who build, control, and use them powerful too."

What Schmidt is referring to is the inherently monopolistic nature of information middlemen. A variety of economic effects reward first movers, penalize latecomer competitors, entice people to join the largest networks, and make it hard for them to switch to a competing system. The result is that these new middlemen have more power than those they replaced.

Google controls two-thirds of the US search market. Almost three-quarters of all Internet users have Facebook accounts. Amazon controls about 30% of the US book market, and 70% of the e-book market. Comcast owns about 25% of the US broadband market. These companies have enormous power and control over us simply because of their economic position.

They all collect and use our data to increase their market dominance and profitability. When eBay first started, it was easy for buyers and sellers to communicate outside of the eBay system because people's e-mail addresses were largely public. In 2001, eBay started hiding e-mail addresses; in 2011, it banned e-mail addresses and links in listings; and in 2012, it banned them from user-to-user communications. All of these moves served to position eBay as a powerful intermediary by making it harder for buyers and sellers to take a relationship established inside of eBay and move it outside of eBay.

Increasingly, companies use their power to influence and manipulate their users. Websites that profit from advertising spend a lot of effort making sure you spend as much time on those sites as possible, optimizing their content for maximum addictiveness. The few sites that allow you to opt out of personalized advertising make that option difficult to find. Once companies combine these techniques with personal data, the result is going to be even more insidious.

Our relationship with many of the Internet companies we rely on is not a traditional company–customer relationship. That's primarily because we're not customers. We're products those companies sell to their *real* customers. The relationship is more feudal than commercial. The companies are analogous to feudal lords, and we are their vassals, peasants, and—on a bad day—serfs. We are tenant farmers for these companies, working on their land by producing data that they in turn sell for profit.

Yes, it's a metaphor—but it often really feels like that. Some people have pledged allegiance to Google. They have Gmail accounts, use Google Calendar and Google Docs, and have Android phones. Others have pledged similar allegiance to Apple. They have iMacs, iPhones, and iPads, and let iCloud automatically synchronize and back up everything. Still others of us let Microsoft do it all. Some of us have pretty much abandoned e-mail altogether for Facebook, Twitter, and Instagram. We might prefer one feudal lord to the others. We might distribute our allegiance among several of these companies, or studiously avoid a particular one we don't like. Regardless, it's becoming increasingly difficult to not pledge allegiance to at least one of them.

After all, customers get a lot of value in having feudal lords. It's simply easier and safer for someone else to hold our data and manage our devices. We like having someone else take care of our device configurations, software management, and data storage. We like it when we can access our e-mail anywhere, from any computer, and we like it that Facebook just works, from any device, anywhere. We want our calendar entries to automatically appear on all of our devices. Cloud storage sites do a better job of backing up our photos and files than we can manage by ourselves; Apple has done a great job of keeping malware out of its iPhone app store. We like automatic security updates and automatic backups; the companies do a better job of protecting our devices than we ever did. And we're really happy when, after we lose a smartphone and buy a new one, all of our data reappears on it at the push of a button.

In this new world of computing, we're no longer expected to manage our computing environment. We trust the feudal lords to treat us well and protect us from harm. It's all a result of two technological trends.

The first is the rise of cloud computing. Basically, our data is no longer stored and processed on our computers. That all happens on servers owned by many different companies. The result is that we no longer control our data. These companies access our data—both content and metadata—for whatever profitable purpose they want. They have carefully crafted terms of service that dictate what sorts of data we can store on their systems, and can delete our entire accounts if they believe we violate them. And they turn our data over to law enforcement without our knowledge or consent. Potentially even worse, our data might be stored on computers in a country whose data protection laws are less than rigorous.

The second trend is the rise of user devices that are managed closely by their vendors: iPhones, iPads, Android phones, Kindles, ChromeBooks, and the like. The result is that we no longer control our computing environment. We have ceded control over what we can see, what we can do, and what we can use. Apple has rules about what software can be installed on iOS devices. You can load your own documents onto your Kindle, but Amazon is able to delete books it has already sold you. In 2009, Amazon automatically deleted some editions of George Orwell's *Nineteen Eighty-Four* from users' Kindles because of a copyright issue. I know, you just couldn't write this stuff any more ironically.

Even the two big computer operating systems, Microsoft's Windows 8 and Apple's Yosemite, are heading in this direction. Both companies are pushing users to buy only authorized apps from centralized stores. Our computers look more like smartphones with every operating system upgrade.

It's not just hardware. It's getting hard to just buy a piece of software and use it on your computer in any way you like. Increasingly, vendors are moving to a subscription model—Adobe did that with Creative Cloud in 2013—that gives the vendor much more control. Microsoft hasn't yet given up on a purchase model, but is making its MS Office subscription very attractive. And Office 365's option of storing your documents in the Microsoft cloud is hard to turn off. Companies are pushing us in this direction because it makes us more profitable as customers or users.

Given current laws, trust is our only option. There are no consistent or predictable rules. We have no control over the actions of these companies. I can't negotiate the rules regarding when Yahoo will access my photos on Flickr. I can't demand greater security for my presentations on Prezi or my task list on Trello. I don't even know the cloud providers to whom those companies have outsourced their infrastructures. If any of those companies delete my data, I don't have the right to demand it back. If any of those companies give the government access to my data, I have no recourse. And if I decide to abandon those services, chances are I can't easily take my data with me.

Political scientist Henry Farrell observed, "Much of our life is conducted online, which is another way of saying that much of our life is conducted under rules set by large private businesses, which are subject neither to much regulation nor much real market competition."

The common defense is something like "business is business." No one is forced to join Facebook or use Google search or buy an iPhone. Potential customers are choosing to enter into these quasi-feudal user relationships because of the enormous value they receive from them. If they don't like it, they shouldn't do it.

This advice is not practical. It's not reasonable to tell people that if they don't like the data collection, they shouldn't e-mail, shop online, use Facebook, or have a cell phone. I can't imagine students getting through school anymore without Internet search or Wikipedia, much less finding a job afterwards. These are the tools of modern life. They're necessary to a career and a social life. Opting out just isn't a viable choice for most of us, most of the time; it violates what have become very real norms of contemporary life.

And choosing among providers is not a choice between surveillance or no surveillance, but only a choice of which feudal lords get to spy on you.

5

Government Surveillance and Control

I t can be hard to comprehend the reach of government surveillance. I'll focus on the US government, not because it's the worst offender, but because we know something about its activities—mostly thanks to the actions of Edward Snowden.

The US national security surveillance state is robust politically, legally, and technically. The documents from Snowden disclosed at least three different NSA programs to collect Gmail user data. These programs are based on three different technical eavesdropping capabilities. They rely on three different legal authorities. They involve cooperation from three different companies. And this is just Gmail. The same is almost certainly true for all the other major e-mail providers—also cell phone call records, cell phone location data, and Internet chats.

To understand the role of surveillance in US intelligence, you need to understand the history of the NSA's global eavesdropping mission and the changing nature of espionage. Because of this history, the NSA is the government's primary eavesdropping organization.

The NSA was formed in 1952 by President Truman, who consolidated the US signals intelligence and codebreaking activities into one organization. It was, and still is, part of the US military, and started out as entirely a foreign intelligence-gathering organization. This mission rose in importance during the Cold War. Back then, a voyeuristic interest in the Soviet Union was the norm, and electronic espionage was a big part of that—becoming more important as everything was computerized and electronic communications became more prevalent. We gathered more and more information as both our capabilities and the amount of communications to be collected increased.

Some of this was useful, though a lot of it was not. Secrets of fact—such as the characteristics of the new Soviet tank—are a lot easier to learn than mysteries of intent—such as what Khrushchev was going to do next. But these were our enemies, and we collected everything we could.

This singular mission should have diminished with the fall of Communism in the late 1980s and early 1990s, as part of the peace dividend. For a while it did, and the NSA's other mission, to protect communications from the spying of others, grew in importance. The NSA became more focused on defense and more open. But eavesdropping acquired a new, and more intense, life after the terrorist attacks of 9/11. "Never again" was an impossible mandate, of course, but the only way to have any hope of preventing something from happening is to know everything that is happening. That led the NSA to put the entire planet under surveillance.

Traditional espionage pits government against government. We spy on foreign governments and on people who are their agents. But the terrorist enemy is different. It isn't a bunch of government leaders "over there"; it's some random terrorist cell whose members could be anywhere. Modern government surveillance monitors everyone, domestic and international alike.

This isn't to say that government-on-population surveillance is a new thing. Totalitarian governments have been doing it for decades: in the Soviet Union, East Germany, Argentina, China, Cuba, North Korea, and so on. In the US, the NSA and the FBI spied on all sorts of Americans in the 1960s and 1970s—antiwar activists, civil rights leaders, and members of nonviolent dissident political groups. In the last decade, they've focused again on antiwar activists and members of nonviolent dissident political groups, as well as on Muslim Americans. This latest mission rose in importance as the NSA became the agency primarily responsible for tracking al Qaeda overseas.

Alongside this change in target came an evolution in communications technology. Before the Internet, focusing on foreign communications was easy. A Chinese military network only carried Chinese communications. A Russian system was only used for Russian communications. If the NSA tapped an undersea cable between Petropavlovsk and Vladivostok, it didn't have to worry about accidentally intercepting phone calls between Detroit and Cleveland.

The Internet works differently. Everyone's communications are mixed up on the same networks. Terrorists use the same e-mail providers as everyone else. The same circuits that carry Russian, Iranian, and Cuban government communications could also carry your Twitter feed. Internet phone calls between New York and Los Angeles might end up on Russian undersea cables. Communications between Rio de Janeiro and Lisbon might be routed through Florida. Google doesn't store your data at its corporate headquarters in Mountain View; it's in multiple data centers around the world: in Chile, Finland, Taiwan, the US, and elsewhere. With the development and expansion of global electronic communications networks, it became hard not to collect data on Americans, even if they weren't the targets.

At the same time, everyone began using the same hardware and software. There used to be Russian electronics, radios, and computers that used Russian technology. No more. We all use Microsoft Windows, Cisco routers, and the same commercial security products. You can buy an iPhone in most countries. This means that the technical capability to, for example, break into Chinese military networks or Venezuelan telephone conversations is generalizable to the rest of the world.

The US has the most extensive surveillance network in the world because it has three advantages. It has a larger intelligence budget than the rest of the world combined. The Internet's physical wiring causes much of the world's traffic to cross US borders, even traffic between two other countries. And almost all of the world's largest and most popular hardware, software, and Internet companies are based in the US and subject to its laws. It's the hegemon.

The goal of the NSA's surveillance is neatly captured by quotes from its top-secret presentations: "collect it all," "know it all," and "exploit it all." The agency taps the Internet at the telcos and cable companies, and collects e-mails, text messages, browsing history, buddy lists, address books, location information, and pretty much everything else it can get its hands on. There is no evidence to suggest that the NSA is recording all telephone calls in the US, but we know it is doing so in (at the least) Afghanistan and Bermuda under the SOMALGET program. The agency's 2013 budget was $10.8 billion; it directly employs some 33,000 people, and many more as contractors. One of the Snowden documents was the top-secret "Black Budget" for the NSA and other intelligence agencies; the total for 2013 was $53 billion. Estimates are that the US spends $72 billion annually on intelligence.

Much of the NSA's money for its modern surveillance infrastructure came from the post-9/11 war efforts in Afghanistan and Iraq: the offensive effort to identify and locate enemy targets, and the defensive effort to identify and neutralize improvised explosive devices. That is, the capabilities were developed against networks in those countries, and because everyone else in the world uses the same equipment, they could be more cheaply deployed against systems elsewhere.

One obvious question arises: is this legal? The real answer is that we don't know. The current authority for NSA surveillance comes from three places:

- Executive Order 12333, signed by President Reagan in 1981, permits the NSA to conduct extensive surveillance abroad. It contains some protection for US citizens only, but allows for extensive collection, analysis, and retention of Americans' data.
- Section 215 of the USA PATRIOT Act, enacted in 2001, allows the NSA to collect "any tangible things (including books, records, papers, documents, and other items)"—about anyone, not just foreigners—"for an investigation to protect against international terrorism or clandestine intelligence activities." That last bit might sound like a limitation, but a secret court interpreted this to include the continuing collection of telephone metadata for every American.
- Section 702 of the FISA (Foreign Intelligence Surveillance Act) Amendments Act of 2008 retroactively authorized NSA collection activities that were conducted illegally after 9/11. It expanded the NSA's remit to gather data on foreigners, with minimal protections for US citizens. The NSA used this authority to monitor Internet backbone connections entering the country, harvesting data on both foreigners and Americans.

The reason the discussion doesn't end there is twofold. One, many of the surveillance provisions of those laws are almost certainly unconstitutional, either as illegal searches or illegal seizures. And two, some of the NSA's interpretations of those laws are almost certainly illegal. Challenges along both of those fronts are being debated in the courts right now. I believe that eventually much of what the NSA is currently doing will be stopped by the courts, and more of what the NSA is currently doing will be stopped by new legislation. Of course, by then Americans will have been subject to decades of extensive surveillance already, which might well have been the agency's strategy all along. I'll talk considerably more about this in Chapter 13.

The NSA collects a lot of data about Americans. Some of it is "incidental." That is, if the NSA monitors a telephone network in France, it will collect data on calls between France and the US. If it monitors an Internet cable under the Atlantic, it will sweep up data on Americans whose traffic happens to get routed through that cable. The NSA has minimization rules designed to limit the amount of data on Americans it collects, analyzes, and retains, although much of what we have learned about them indicates that they don't work very well. The rules are different for communications content and metadata, and the rules are different depending on the legal authority the NSA is using to justify the connection. And minimized doesn't mean that Americans' data is deleted; it just means that it's anonymized unless someone actually wants to see it. The NSA does a lot of playing around with the rules here, and even those trying to oversee the NSA's activity admit that they can't figure out what it's really doing.

A 2014 analysis of some of the actual intercepted traffic provided by Snowden found that data about innocent people, both Americans and non-Americans, far exceeded the data about authorized intelligence targets. Some of this reflects the nature of intelligence; even minimized information about someone will contain all sort of communications with innocents, because literally every communication with a target that provides any interesting information whatsoever will be retained.

The NSA might get the headlines, but the US intelligence community is actually composed of 17 different agencies. There's the CIA, of course. You might have heard of the NRO—the National Reconnaissance Office—it's in charge of the country's spy satellites. Then there are the intelligence agencies associated with all four branches of the military. The Departments of Justice (both FBI and DEA), State, Energy, the Treasury, and Homeland Security all conduct surveillance, as do a few other agencies. And there may be a still-secret 18th agency. (It's unlikely, but possible. The details of the NSA's mission remained largely secret until the 1970s, over 20 years after its formation.)

After the NSA, the FBI appears to be the most prolific government surveillance agency. It is tightly connected with the NSA, and the two share data, technologies, and legislative authorities. It's easy to forget that the first Snowden document published by the *Guardian*—the order requiring Verizon to turn over the calling metadata for all of its customers—was an order by the FBI to turn the data over to the NSA. We know there is considerable sharing amongst the NSA, CIA, DEA, DIA, and DHS. An NSA program code-named ICREACH provides surveillance information to over 23 government agencies, including information about Americans.

That said, unlike NSA surveillance, FBI surveillance is traditionally conducted with judicial oversight, through the warrant process. Under the Fourth Amendment to the US Constitution, the government must demonstrate to a judge that a search might reasonably reveal evidence of a crime. However, the FBI has the authority to collect, without a warrant, all sorts of personal information, either targeted or in bulk through the use of National Security Letters (NSLs). These are basically administrative subpoenas, issued by the FBI with no judicial oversight. They were greatly expanded in scope in 2001 under the USA PATRIOT Act (Section 505), although the initial legal basis for these letters originated in 1978. Today, NSLs are generally used to obtain data from third parties: e-mail from Google, banking records from financial institutions, files from Dropbox.

In the US, we have reduced privacy rights over all that data because of what's called the third-party doctrine. Back in 1976, Michael Lee Smith robbed a woman in Baltimore, and then repeatedly harassed her on the phone. After the police identified someone matching Smith's description, they had the phone company place a "pen register" on Smith's phone line to create a record of all the phone numbers Smith dialed. After verifying that Smith called the woman, they got a search warrant for his home and arrested him for the robbery. Smith tried to get the pen register evidence thrown out, because the police hadn't obtained a warrant. In a 1979 decision, the Supreme Court ruled that a warrant was not necessary: "This Court consistently has held that a person has no legitimate expectation of privacy in information he voluntarily turns over to third parties." Basically, because Smith shared those phone numbers with his phone company, he lost any expectation of privacy with respect to that information. That might have made sense in 1979, when almost all of our data was held by us and close to us. But today, all of our data is in the cloud somewhere, held by third parties of undetermined trust.

Technology has greatly enhanced the FBI's ability to conduct surveillance without a warrant. For example, the FBI (and also local police) uses a tool called an IMSI-catcher, which is basically a fake cell phone tower. If you've heard about it, you've heard the code name StingRay, which is actually a particular type of IMSI-catcher sold by Harris Corporation. By putting up the tower, it tricks nearby cell phones into connecting to it. Once that happens, IMSI-catchers can collect identification and location information of the phones and, in some cases, eavesdrop on phone conversations, text messages, and web browsing. The FBI is so scared of explaining this capability in public that the agency makes local police sign nondisclosure agreements before using the technique, and instructs them to lie about their use of it in court. When it seemed possible that local police in Sarasota, Florida, might release documents about StingRay cell phone interception equipment to plaintiffs in civil rights litigation against them, federal marshals seized the documents.

It's hard to keep track of all the US government organizations involved with surveillance. The National Counterterrorism Center keeps track of the Terrorism Identities Datamart Environment, the US government's central repository of international terrorist suspects. The institution maintains a huge database of US citizens, keeping tabs on 700,000 identifiers (sort of like people, but not really) in 2007, and is where the various watch lists come from. The procedures for getting on these lists seem very arbitrary, and of course there's no recourse once someone gets on one. Boston Marathon bomber Tamerlan Tsarnaev was on this list.

There are also Organized Crime Drug Enforcement Task Forces for drug-related investigations, and a Comprehensive National Cybersecurity Initiative for computer threats. The Bureau of Alcohol, Tobacco, and Firearms is building a massive database to track people and their friends. Even the Pentagon has spied on Americans, through a little-known agency called the Counterintelligence Field Activity, closed in 2008. In 2010, the Naval Criminal Investigative Service monitored every computer in the state of Washington running a particular file-sharing program, whether associated with the military or not—a clear violation of the law.

Outside of the federal government, a lot more surveillance and analysis of surveillance data is going on. Since 9/11, the US has set up "fusion centers" around the country. These institutions are generally run by state and local law enforcement, and are meant to serve as an information bridge between those groups and national agencies like the FBI and DHS. They give local police access to previously unavailable surveillance capabilities and data. They were initially supposed to focus on terrorism, but increasingly they're used in broader law enforcement. And because they're run locally, different fusion centers have different rules—and different levels of adherence to those rules. There's minimal oversight, probably illegal military involvement, and excessive secrecy. For example, fusion centers are known to have spied on political protesters.

Joint Terrorism Task Forces are also locally run, nebulously defined, and shrouded in extreme secrecy. They've been caught investigating political activists, spreading anti-Islamic propaganda, and harassing innocent civilians.

Taken as a whole, there's a great deal of overenthusiastic, ideologically driven surveillance going on in the US.

Across the Atlantic, the NSA's UK equivalent is GCHQ. It conducts extensive spying on its own citizens and worldwide, both from its own country and from remote listening posts in Oman, Cyprus, and elsewhere. It has a very close partnership with the NSA, and is increasingly conducting mass surveillance inside its own borders. Other countries listening in on their own citizens and the citizens of other countries include Germany, France, Denmark, Australia, New Zealand, Israel, Canada…and probably every other country with enough money to have an intelligence budget. The government of Australia has claimed that its surveillance of Indonesia helped thwart several terrorist threats in that country.

We know much less about government surveillance in other countries; but don't assume that they aren't doing these same things just because whistleblowers there haven't brought those stories to light. Other governments are doing much the same thing to as much of the Internet as they can get their hands on, often with fewer legal restrictions on their activities.

Russia collects, stores, and analyzes data from phone calls, e-mail, Internet use, social networking, credit card transactions, and more. Russia's System for Operative Investigative Measures, or SORM, is built right into its Internet. We saw a glimpse of how extensive this system is during the 2014 Sochi Olympics, where the Russian authorities monitored pretty much everything that happened online. Crime and terrorism provide justifications for surveillance, but this data is also used against Russian journalists, human rights activists, and political opponents.

China, too, attempts to monitor everything its citizens do on—and, increasingly, off—the Internet. China also uses location information from mobile phones to track people en masse. It turns mobile phones on remotely to eavesdrop on people, and it monitors physical spaces with its 20 to 30 million surveillance cameras. As in Russia, crime is the ostensible excuse for all this snooping, but dissent is a major reason as well. TOM-Skype is a Chinese video and texting service, a joint venture between Microsoft and the Chinese company TOM Online. Messages containing words like "Tiananmen," "Amnesty International," and "Human Rights Watch," as well as references to drugs and pornography, are copied and saved. More than 30,000 Internet police conduct the monitoring.

We got additional glimpses of global Internet monitoring a few years ago, when India, Russia, Saudi Arabia, the UAE, and Indonesia all threatened to ban BlackBerry if the company didn't allow them access to user communications. BlackBerry data is generally encrypted, which prevents eavesdropping. BlackBerry cut a deal with India whereby corporate users were allowed to keep their data secure, but the government would be able to track individual users' e-mails, chats, and website visits. We don't know about the deals it may have struck with the other countries, but we can assume that they're similar.

Smaller countries often turn to larger ones to help them with their surveillance infrastructure. China helped Iran build surveillance into its own Internet infrastructure. I'll say more in Chapter 6 about Western companies helping repressive governments build surveillance systems.

The actions of these and other countries—I could fill a whole book with examples—are often far more oppressive and totalitarian than anything the US or any of its allies do. And the US has far more legal controls and restrictions on government collection than any other country on the planet, including European countries. In countries like Thailand, India, and Malaysia, arresting people on the basis of their Internet conversations and activities is the norm. I'll talk about risks and harms in Chapter 7; right now, I want to stick to capabilities.

GOVERNMENT HACKS

Electronic espionage is different today from what it was in the pre-Internet days of the Cold War. Before the Internet, when surveillance consisted largely of government-on-government espionage, agencies like the NSA would target specific communications circuits: that Soviet undersea cable between Petropavlovsk and Vladivostok, a military communications satellite, a microwave network. This was for the most part passive, requiring large antenna farms in nearby countries.

Modern targeted surveillance is likely to involve actively breaking into an adversary's computer network and installing malicious software designed to take over that network and "exfiltrate" data—that's NSA talk for stealing it. To put it more plainly, the easiest way for someone to eavesdrop on your communications isn't to intercept them in transit anymore; it's to hack your computer.

And there's a lot of government hacking going on.

In 2011, an Iranian hacker broke into the Dutch certificate

authority DigiNotar. This enabled him to impersonate organizations like Google, CIA, MI6, Mossad, Microsoft, Yahoo, Skype, Facebook, Twitter, and Microsoft's Windows Update service. That, in turn, allowed him to spy on users of these services. He passed this ability on to others—almost certainly in the Iranian government—who in turn used it for mass surveillance on Iranians and probably foreigners as well. Fox-IT estimated that 300,000 Iranian Gmail accounts were accessed.

In 2009, Canadian security researchers discovered a piece of malware called GhostNet on the Dalai Lama's computers. It was a sophisticated surveillance network, controlled by a computer in China. Further research found it installed on computers of political, economic, and media organizations in 103 countries: basically a Who's Who of Chinese espionage targets. Flame is a surveillance tool that researchers detected on Iranian networks in 2012; we believe the US and Israel put it there and elsewhere. Red October, which hacked and spied on computers worldwide for five years before it was discovered in 2013, is believed to be a Russian surveillance system. So is Turla, which targeted Western government computers and was ferreted out in 2014. The Mask, also discovered in 2014, is believed to be Spanish. Iranian hackers have specifically targeted US officials. There are many more known surveillance tools like these, and presumably others still undiscovered.

To be fair, we don't have proof that these countries were behind these surveillance networks, nor that they were government sponsored. Governments almost never admit to hacking each other's computers. Researchers generally infer the country of origin from the target list. For example, The Mask target list included almost all the Spanish-speaking countries, and a bunch of computers in Morocco and Gibraltar. That sounds like Spain.

In the US, the group charged with hacking computers is the Tailored Access Operations group (TAO) inside the NSA. We know that TAO infiltrates computers remotely, using programs with cool code names like QUANTUMINSERT and FOXACID. We know that TAO has developed specialized software to hack into everything from computers to routers to smartphones, and that its staff installs hardware "implants" into computer and networking equipment by intercepting and infecting it in transit. One estimate is that the group has successfully hacked into, and is exfiltrating information from, 80,000 computers worldwide.

Of course, most of what we know about TAO and the US's hacking efforts comes from top-secret NSA documents provided by Snowden. There haven't been similar leaks from other countries, so we know much less about their capabilities.

We do know a lot about China. China has been reliably identified as the origin of many high-profile attacks: against Google, against the Canadian government, against the *New York Times*, against the security company RSA and other US corporations, and against the US military and its contractors. In 2013, researchers found presumed–Chinese government malware targeting Tibetan activists' Android phones. In 2014, Chinese hackers breached a database of the US Office of Personnel Management that stored detailed data on up to 5 million US government employees and contractors with security clearances.

Why? A lot of this is political and military espionage, but some of it is commercial espionage. Many countries have a long history of spying on foreign corporations for their own military and commercial advantage. The US claims that it does not engage in commercial espionage, meaning that it does not hack foreign corporate networks and pass that information on to US competitors for commercial advantage. But it does engage in economic espionage, by hacking into foreign corporate networks and using that information in government trade negotiations that directly benefit US corporate interests. Recent examples are the Brazilian oil company

Petrobras and the European SWIFT international bank payment system. In fact, a 1996 government report boasted that the NSA claimed that the economic benefits of one of its programs to US industry "totaled tens of billions of dollars over the last several years." You may or may not see a substantive difference between the two types of espionage. China, without so clean a separation between its government and its industries, does not.

Many countries buy software from private companies to facilitate their hacking. I'll talk more about this kind of business relationship in Chapter 6. For now, consider an Italian cyberweapons manufacturer called Hacking Team that sells hacking systems to governments worldwide for use against computer and smartphone operating systems. The mobile malware installs itself remotely and collects e-mails, text messages, call history, address books, search history data, and keystrokes. It can take screenshots, record audio to monitor either calls or ambient noise, snap photos, and monitor the phone's GPS coordinates. It then surreptitiously sends all of that back to its handlers. Ethiopia used this software to sneak onto the computers of European and American journalists.

It's a reasonable assumption that most countries have these hacking capabilities. Who they use them against, and what legal rules control that use, depends on the country.

GOVERNMENT ATTACKS

When we first started getting reports of the Chinese breaking into US computer networks for espionage purposes, we described it in very strong language. We labeled the Chinese actions "cyberattacks," sometimes invoking the word "cyberwar." After Snowden revealed that the NSA had been doing exactly the same thing as the Chinese to computer networks around the world, the US used much more moderate language to describe its own actions—terms like "espionage," or "intelligence gathering," or "spying"—and stressed that it is a peacetime activity.

When the Chinese company Huawei tried to sell networking equipment to the US, we feared that the government had back-doored the switches and considered it a "national security threat." But, as we eventually learned, the NSA has been doing exactly the same thing, both to Huawei's equipment and to American-made equipment sold in China.

The problem is that, as they occur and from the point of view of the victim, international espionage and attack look pretty much alike. Modern cyberespionage is a form of cyberattack, and both involve breaking into the network of another country. The only difference between them is whether they deliberately disrupt network operations or not. Of course that's a huge difference, but it's a difference that might be delayed months or even years. Because breaking into a foreign network affects the territory of another country, it is almost certainly illegal under that country's laws. Even so, countries are doing it constantly to one another.

Here's an example. In 2012, the NSA repeatedly penetrated Syria's Internet infrastructure. Its intent was to remotely install eavesdropping code in one of the country's core routers, but it accidentally caused a nationwide Internet blackout. Exfiltrating data and taking out a country's Internet involve exactly the same operations.

Governments are getting into cyberwar big time. About 30 countries have cyberwar divisions in their military: US, Russia, China, the major European countries, Israel, India, Brazil, Australia, New Zealand, and a handful of African countries. In the US, this is led by US Cyber Command inside the Department of Defense. Admiral Michael S. Rogers is in charge of both this organization and the NSA. That's how close the missions are.

Few examples have surfaced of cyberattacks that cause actual damage, either to people or to property. In 2007, Estonia was the victim of a broad series of cyberattacks. This is often called the first cyberwar, because it coincided with increased tensions with neighboring Russia. The ex-Soviet republic of Georgia was also the victim of cyberattacks, ones that preceded a land invasion by Russian troops a year later. In 2009, South Korea was the victim of a cyberattack. All of these were denial-of-service attacks, during which selected Internet sites are flooded with traffic and stop working temporarily. They're disruptive, but not very damaging in the long run.

In all of these cases, we don't know for sure who the perpetrator was, or even whether it was a government. In 2009, a pro-Kremlin youth group took credit for the 2007 Estonian attacks, although the only person convicted of them was a 22-year-old Russian living in Tallinn. That sort of identifiability is rare. Like the espionage attacks discussed earlier, cyberattacks are hard to trace. We're left to infer the attacker by the list of victims. Ethnic tensions with Russia: of course Russia is to blame. South Korea gets attacked: who else but North Korea would be motivated?

Stuxnet is the first military-grade cyberweapon known to be deployed by one country against another. It was launched in 2009 by the US and Israel against the Natanz nuclear facility in Iran, and succeeded in causing significant physical damage. A 2012 attack against Saudi Aramco that damaged some 30,000 of the national oil company's computers is believed to have been retaliation by Iran.

A SINGLE GLOBAL SURVEILLANCE NETWORK

There's an interesting monopolistic effect that occurs with surveillance. Earlier in this chapter, I made a distinction between government-on-government espionage and government-on-population surveillance. Espionage basically follows geopolitical lines; a country gets together with its allies to jointly spy on its adversaries. That's how we did it during the Cold War. It's politics.

Mass surveillance is different. If you're truly worried about attacks coming from anyone anywhere, you need to spy on everyone everywhere. And since no one country can do that alone, it makes sense to share data with other countries.

But whom do you share with? You could share with your traditional military allies, but they might not be spying on the countries you're most worried about. Or they might not be spying on enough of the planet to make sharing worthwhile. It makes the best sense to join the most extensive spying network around. And that's the US.

This is what's happening right now. US intelligence partners with many countries. It is part of an extremely close relationship of wealthy, English-language-speaking countries called the Five Eyes: US, UK, Canada, Australia, and New Zealand. Other partnerships include the Nine Eyes, which adds Denmark, France, the Netherlands, and Norway; and the Fourteen Eyes, which adds Germany, Belgium, Italy, Spain, and Sweden. And the US partners with countries that have traditionally been much more standoffish, like India, and even with brutally repressive regimes like Saudi Arabia's.

All of this gives the NSA access to almost everything. In testimony to the European Parliament in 2014, Snowden said, "The result is a European bazaar, where an EU member state like Denmark may give the NSA access to a tapping center on the (unenforceable) condition that NSA doesn't search it for Danes, and Germany may give the NSA access to another on the condition that it doesn't search for Germans. Yet the two tapping sites may be two points on the same cable, so the NSA simply captures the communications of the German citizens as they transit Denmark, and the Danish citizens as they transit Germany, all the while considering it entirely in accordance with their agreements."

In 2014, we learned that the NSA spies on the Turkish government, and at the same time partners with the Turkish government to spy on the Kurdish separatists within Turkey. We also learned that the NSA spies on the government of one of its much closer surveillance partners: Germany. Presumably we spy on all of our partners, with the possible exception of the other Five Eyes countries. Even when the NSA touts its counterterrorism successes, most of them are foreign threats against foreign countries, and have nothing to do with the US.

It should come as no surprise that the US shares intelligence data with Israel. Normally, identities of Americans are removed before this data is shared with another country to protect our privacy, but Israel seems to be an exception. The NSA gives Israel's secretive Unit 8200 "raw SIGINT"—that's signals intelligence.

Even historical enemies are sharing intelligence with the US, if only on a limited basis. After 9/11, Russia rebranded the Chechen separatists as terrorists, and persuaded the US to help by sharing information. In 2011, Russia warned the US about Boston Marathon bomber Tamerlan Tsarnaev. We returned the favor, watching out for threats at the Sochi Olympics.

These partnerships make no sense when the primary goal of intelligence is government vs. government espionage, but are obvious and appropriate when the primary goal is global surveillance of the population. So while the German government expresses outrage at NSA's surveillance of the country's leaders, its BND continues to partner with the NSA to surveil everyone else.

The endgame of this isn't pretty: it's a global surveillance network where all countries collude to surveil everyone on the entire planet. It'll probably not happen for a while—there'll be holdout countries like Russia that will insist on doing it themselves, and rigid ideological differences will never let countries like Iran cooperate fully with either Russia or the US—but most smaller countries will be motivated to join. From a very narrow perspective, it's the rational thing to do.

6

Consolidation of
Institutional Control

Corporate surveillance and government surveillance aren't separate. They're intertwined; the two support each other. It's a public-private surveillance partnership that spans the world. This isn't a formal agreement; it's more an alliance of interests. Although it isn't absolute, it's become a de facto reality, with many powerful stakeholders supporting its perpetuation. And though Snowden's revelations about NSA surveillance have caused rifts in the partnership—we'll talk about those in Chapter 14—it's still strong.

The Snowden documents made it clear how much the NSA relies on US corporations to eavesdrop on the Internet. The NSA didn't build a massive Internet eavesdropping system from scratch. It noticed that the corporate world was already building one, and tapped into it. Through programs like PRISM, the NSA legally compels Internet companies like Microsoft, Google, Apple, and Yahoo to provide data on several thousand individuals of interest. Through other programs, the NSA gets direct access to the Internet backbone to conduct mass surveillance on everyone. Sometimes those corporations work with the NSA willingly. Sometimes they're forced by the courts to hand over data, largely in secret. At other times, the NSA has hacked into those corporations' infrastructure without their permission.

This is happening all over the world. Many countries use corporate surveillance capabilities to monitor their own citizens. Through programs such as TEMPORA, the UK's GCHQ pays telcos like BT and Vodafone to give it access to bulk communications all over the world. Vodafone gives Albania, Egypt, Hungary, Ireland, and Qatar—possibly 29 countries in total—direct access to Internet traffic flowing inside their countries. We don't know to what extent these countries are paying for access, as the UK does, or just demanding it. The French government eavesdrops on France Télécom and Orange. We've already talked about China and Russia in Chapter 5. About a dozen countries have data retention laws—declared unconstitutional in the EU in 2014—requiring ISPs to keep surveillance data on their customers for some months in case the government wants access to it. Internet cafes in Iran, Vietnam, India, and elsewhere must collect and retain identity information of their customers.

Similar things are happening off the Internet. Immediately after 9/11, the US government bought data from data brokers, including air passenger data from Torch Concepts and a database of Mexican voters from ChoicePoint. US law requires financial institutions to report cash transactions of $10,000 or larger to the government; for currency exchangers, the threshold is $1,000. Many governments require hotels to report which foreigners are sleeping there that night, and many more make copies of guests' ID cards and passports. CCTV cameras, license plate capture systems, and cell phone location data are being used by numerous governments.

By the same token, corporations obtain government data for

their own purposes. States like Illinois, Ohio, Texas, and Florida sell driver's license data, including photos, to private buyers. Some states sell voter registration data. The UK government proposed the sale of taxpayer data in 2014, but public outcry has halted that, at least temporarily. The UK National Health Service also plans to sell patient health data to drug and insurance firms. There's a feedback loop: corporations argue for more government data collection, then argue that the data should be released under open government laws, and then repackage the data and sell it back to the government.

The net result is that a lot of surveillance data moves back and forth between government and corporations. One consequence of this is that it's hard to get effective laws passed to curb corporate surveillance—governments don't really want to limit their own access to data by crippling the corporate hand that feeds them.

The "Do Not Track" debate serves as a sterling example of how bad things are. For years, privacy advocates have attempted to pass a law mandating that Internet users have the option of configuring their browsers so that websites would not track them. Several US national laws have been proposed, but have been fought hard by Internet companies and have never been passed. California passed one in 2013, but it was so watered down by lobbyists that it provides little benefit to users. As a user, you can configure your browser to tell websites you don't want to be tracked, but websites are free to ignore your wishes.

It's a bit different in Europe. Laws such as the EU Data Protection Directive put more constraints on corporate surveillance, and it has had an effect. But a "safe harbor" agreement between the US and the EU means personal data can flow from the EU to participating US companies under standards less strict than those that apply in the EU.

THE PUBLIC-PRIVATE SURVEILLANCE PARTNERSHIP

Governments don't conduct surveillance, censorship, and control operations alone. They are supported by a vast public-private surveillance partnership: an array of for-profit corporations. A 2010 investigation found that 1,931 different corporations are working on intelligence, counterterrorism, or homeland security inside the US. In a 2013 story, the *Washington Post* reported that 70% of the US intelligence budget goes to private firms and that 483,000 government contractors hold top-secret clearances: a third of the 1.4 million people cleared at that level. There's a strong revolving door between government and these companies. Admiral Mike McConnell, who directed the NSA from 1992 to 1996, left to become a vice president at the powerhouse government contractor Booz Allen Hamilton, where he continues to work on national intelligence. After retiring from directing the NSA in 2013, Keith Alexander started his own Internet security consulting firm, and filed patents for security technologies he claimed to have invented on his own time. He's hired the NSA's chief technology officer, who continues to work for the NSA as well.

Many cyberweapons manufacturers sell hacking tools to governments worldwide. For example, FinFisher is an "offensive IT Intrusion solution," according to the promotional material from the UK and German company that makes it, Gamma Group. Governments purchase this software to spy on people's computers and smartphones. In 2012, researchers found evidence that the Fin-Fisher toolkit was deployed in Bahrain, Singapore, Indonesia, Mongolia, Turkmenistan, the UAE, Ethiopia, and Brunei, as well as the US and the Netherlands.

In Chapter 5, I mentioned the Italian company Hacking Team. Its computer and cell phone intrusion and monitoring products are used by the governments of Azerbaijan, Colombia, Egypt, Ethiopia, Hungary, Italy, Kazakhstan, Korea, Malaysia, Mexico, Morocco, Nigeria, Oman, Panama, Poland, Saudi Arabia, Sudan, Thailand, Turkey, the UAE, and Uzbekistan. The Moroccan government employed Hacking Team's software to target the citizen journalist group Mamfakinch via an e-mail that purported to be a message from an anonymous citizen in danger; the attached file contained a payload of malware.

In 2011, arrested dissidents in Bahrain were shown transcripts of their private e-mail and chat sessions, collected by the government with tools provided by Nokia and Siemens.

The conference ISS World—which stands for Intelligence Support Systems—has frequent trade shows in cities like Dubai and Brasilia. The 2014 brochure advertised sessions on location surveillance, call record mining, offensive IT intrusion, and defeating encryption, and the sponsor list was a Who's Who of these capabilities. Many countries send representatives to attend. There are similar conferences in the US and Europe.

Most of the big US defense contractors, such as Raytheon, Northrop Grumman, and Harris Corporation, build cyberweapons for the US military. And many big IT companies help build surveillance centers around the world. The French company Bull SA helped the Libyan government build its surveillance center. Nigeria used the Israeli firm Elbit Systems. Syria used the German company Siemens, the Italian company Area SpA, and others. The Gadhafi regime in Libya purchased telephone surveillance technology from China's ZTE and South Africa's VASTech. We don't know who built the Internet surveillance systems used in Azerbaijan and Uzbekistan, but almost certainly some Western companies helped them. There are few laws prohibiting this kind of technology transfer, and the ones that exist are easily bypassed.

These are not only specially designed government eavesdropping systems; much government surveillance infrastructure is built for corporate use. US-based Blue Coat sells monitoring and content filtering systems for corporate networks, which are also used for government surveillance in countries like Burma, China, Egypt, Indonesia, Nigeria, Qatar, Saudi Arabia, Turkey, and Venezuela. Netsweeper is a Canadian corporate filtering product used for censorship by governments in Qatar, Yemen, the UAE, Somalia, and Pakistan. Filtering software from the US company Fortinet is used to censor the Internet in Burma; SmartFilter, from the US company McAfee and normally used in schools, helps the governments of Tunisia and Iran censor the Internet in their countries. Commercial security equipment from the UK company Sophos has been used by Syria and other oppressive regimes to surveil and arrest their citizens.

Technology is value neutral. You can use your phone to call 911 or to plan a bank robbery. There's no technical difference between a government's using a tool to identify criminals or using it to identify dissidents. There's no technical difference between corporate and government uses. Legitimate corporate tools for blocking employees from e-mailing confidential data can be used by repressive governments for surveillance and censorship. Conversely, the same anti-censorship tools that Saudi and Iranian dissidents use to evade their governments can be used by criminals to distribute child porn. Encryption allows the good guys to communicate without being eavesdropped on by the bad guys, and also allows the bad guys to communicate without being eavesdropped on by the good guys. And the same facial recognition technology that Disney uses in its theme parks to pick out photos its patrons might want to buy as souvenirs can identify political protesters in China, and Occupy Wall Street protesters in New York.

GOVERNMENTS SUBVERTING COMMERCIAL SYSTEMS

So far, I have discussed how government surveillance piggybacks on corporate capabilities. While this is mostly true, government are not above forcing corporations to spy for them.

Back in the early 1990s, the FBI started worrying about its ability to conduct telephone surveillance. The FBI could do it with the old analog phone switches: a laborious process involving alligator clips, wires, and a tape recorder. The problem was that digital switches didn't work that way. Isolating individual connections was harder, and the FBI became concerned about the potential loss of its ability to wiretap. So it lobbied Congress hard and got a law passed in 1994 called the Communications Assistance for Law Enforcement Act, or CALEA, requiring telcos to re-engineer their digital switches to have eavesdropping capabilities built in.

Fast-forward 20 years, and the FBI again wants the IT industry to make surveillance easier for itself. A lot of communications no longer happen over the telephone. They're happening over chat. They're happening over e-mail. They're happening over Skype. The FBI is currently lobbying for a legislative upgrade to CALEA, one that covers *all* communications systems: all voice, video, and text systems, including World of Warcraft and that little chat window attached to your online Scrabble game.

The FBI's ultimate goal is government prohibition of truly secure communications. Valerie Caproni, the general counsel for the FBI, put it this way in 2010: "No one should be promising their customers that they will thumb their nose at a US court order. They can promise strong encryption. They just need to figure out how they can provide us plain text." Translation: you can't actually provide security for your customers.

Depending on the system, doing what the FBI wants would

range from easy to impossible. E-mail systems like Gmail are easy. The mail resides unencrypted on Google's servers, and the company has an office full of people who respond to requests for access to individual accounts from governments all over the world. Encrypted chat programs like Off the Record are impossible to undermine; the chat sessions are encrypted on the conversants' computers, and there's no central node from which to eavesdrop. In those cases, the only way to satisfy the FBI's demands would be to add a backdoor to the user software, which would render it insecure for everyone. I'll talk about the stupidity of that idea in Chapter 11.

As draconian as that measure would be, at least the discussion is happening in public. Much government control of corporate communications infrastructure occurs in secret, and we only hear about it occasionally.

Lavabit was an e-mail service that offered more security privacy than the large corporate e-mail services most of us use. It was a small company, owned and operated by a programmer named Ladar Levison, and it was popular among the tech-savvy. It had half a million users, Edward Snowden amongst them.

Soon after Snowden fled to Hong Kong in 2013, Levison received a National Security Letter demanding that the company turn over the master encryption key that protected all of Lavabit's users—and then not tell any of its customers that they could be monitored. Levison fought this order in court, and when it became clear that he had lost, he shut down his service rather than deceive and compromise his customers.

The moral is clear. If you run a business, and the FBI or the NSA wants to turn it into a mass surveillance tool, it believes that it is entitled to do so, solely on its own authority. The agency can force you to modify your system. It can do it all in secret and then force your business to keep that secret. Once it does that, you no longer control that part of your business. If you're a large company, you can't shut it down. You can't realistically terminate part of your service. In a very real sense, it is not your business anymore. It has become an arm of the vast US surveillance apparatus, and if your interest conflicts with the agency's, the agency wins. Your business has been commandeered.

The only reason we know this story is that Levison ran his own company. He had no corporate masters. He had no shareholders. He was able to destroy his own business for moral reasons. Larger, more beholden companies would never do that. We must assume that every other computer company that received a similar demand has eventually complied.

For example, we know that the US government convinced Skype—through bribery, coercion, threat, or legal compulsion—to make changes in how the program operates, to facilitate eavesdropping. We don't know what the changes were, whether they happened before or after Microsoft bought Skype in 2011, or how they satisfied whatever the government demanded, but we know they happened.

In 2008, the US government secretly threatened Yahoo with a $250,000-per-day fine, with the daily amount increasing rapidly if it didn't join the NSA's PRISM program and provide it with user data. And in 2004, the NSA paid RSA Security to make a back-doored random number generator a default in its crypto library.

Other types of government commandeering are going on as well, behind the backs of the companies whose technologies are being subverted. Where the NSA doesn't have agreements with companies to tap into their systems, it does its best to do so surreptitiously. For instance, not satisfied with the amount of data it receives from Google and Yahoo via PRISM, the NSA hacked into the trunk connections between both companies' data centers, probably with the cooperation of their service provider Level 3 Communications. The angry response from one of Google's security engineers, posted on his personal Google Plus page, was "fuck those guys." Google has since encrypted those connections between its data centers in an effort to keep the NSA out. Yahoo claims to be doing the same.

This isn't the only example of the NSA hacking US technology companies. The agency creates fake Facebook pages to hack into people's computers, and its TAO branch intercepts Cisco equipment during shipping to install hardware implants.

We don't know what sort of pressure the US government has put on the major Internet cloud providers to persuade them to give them access to user data, or what secret agreements those companies may have reached with the NSA. We do know the NSA's BULLRUN program to subvert Internet cryptography, and the companion GCHQ program EDGEHILL, were successful against much of the security that's common on the Internet. Did the NSA demand Google's master encryption keys and force it to keep quiet about it, as it tried with Lavabit? Did its Tailored Access Operations group break into Google's overseas servers and steal the keys, or intercept equipment intended for Google's overseas data centers and install backdoors? Those are all documented NSA tactics. In the first case, Google would be prohibited by law from admitting it, in the second it wouldn't want to, and in the third it would not even know about it. In general, we know that in the years immediately after 9/11, the US government received lots of willing cooperation from companies whose leaders believed they were being patriotic.

I believe we're going to see more bulk access to our data by the NSA, because of the type of data it wants. The NSA used to be able to get everything it wanted from Internet backbone companies and broadband providers. This became less true as encryption— specifically a kind called SSL encryption—became more common. It will become even less true as more of the Internet becomes encrypted. To overcome this, the NSA needs to obtain bulk data from service providers, because they're the ones with our data in plaintext, despite any encryption in transit. And to do that it needs to subvert the security protocols used by those sites to secure their data.

Other countries are involved in similar skullduggery. It is widely believed that the Chinese government embeds the capability to eavesdrop into all networking equipment built and sold by its own company Huawei. And we have reason to suspect that British, Russian, Israeli, and French Internet products have also been backdoored by their governments.

We don't know whether governments attempt to surreptitiously insert backdoors into products of companies over which they have no direct political or legal control, but many computer security experts believe that is happening. Are there Chinese nationals working at major US software companies trying to make it easier for the Chinese government to hack that company's products? French programmers? Israeli programmers? Or, at least, are they passing the source code back to their own country so they can find vulnerabilities more easily? Are there US agents inserting backdoors into computer chips designed and manufactured in Asia? We know they have employees secretly embedded in countries like China, Germany, and South Korea to aid in subverting computer and communications systems.

Companies have responded to this situation with caveat-laden pseudo-assurances. At a 2013 technology conference, Google CEO Eric Schmidt tried to reassure the audience by saying that he was "pretty sure that information within Google is now safe from any government's prying eyes." A more accurate statement might be: "Your data is safe from governments, except for the ways we don't know about and the ways we cannot tell you about." That's a lousy marketing pitch, but as long as the NSA is allowed to operate using secret court orders based on secret interpretations of secret law, it will never be any different.

For most Internet companies, this isn't a problem. The other thing Schmidt didn't say is: "And, of course, we still have complete access to it all, and can sell it at will to whomever we want . . . and you have no recourse." As long as these companies are already engaging in massive surveillance of their customers and users, it's easier for them to comply with government demands and share the wealth with the NSA. And as long as governments keep demanding access and refrain from legislating protections, it's easier to design systems to allow it. It's a powerful feedback loop: the business model supports the government effort, and the government effort justifies the business model.

PART TWO
WHAT'S AT STAKE

7

Political Liberty and Justice

I n 2013, the First Unitarian Church of Los Angeles sued the NSA over its domestic spying, claiming that its surveillance of church members' telephone calling habits discouraged them from banding together to advocate for political causes. The church wasn't just being paranoid. In the 1950s and 1960s, the FBI monitored its minister because of his politics. Today, the church is worried that people, both Americans and foreigners, will end up on watch lists because of their association with the church.

Government surveillance is costly. Most obviously, it's extraordinarily expensive: $72 billion a year in the US. But it's also costly to our society, both domestically and internationally. Harvard law professor Yochai Benkler likens NSA surveillance to an autoimmune disease, because it attacks all of our other systems. It's a good analogy.

The biggest cost is liberty, and the risk is real enough that people across political ideologies are objecting to the sheer invasiveness and pervasiveness of the surveillance system. Even the politically conservative and probusiness *Economist* magazine argued, in a 2013 editorial about video surveillance, that it had gone too far: "This is where one of this newspaper's strongly held beliefs that technological progress should generally be welcomed, not feared, runs up against an even deeper impulse, in favour of liberty. Freedom has to include some right to privacy: if every move you make is being chronicled, liberty is curtailed."

ACCUSATION BY DATA

In the 17th century, the French statesman Cardinal Richelieu famously said, "Show me six lines written by the most honest man in the world, and I will find enough therein to hang him." Lavrentiy Beria, head of Joseph Stalin's secret police in the old Soviet Union, declared, "Show me the man, and I'll show you the crime." Both were saying the same thing: if you have enough data about someone, you can find sufficient evidence to find him guilty of *something*. It's the reason many countries' courts prohibit the police from engaging in "fishing expeditions." It's the reason the US Constitution specifically prohibits general warrants—documents that basically allow the police to search for *anything*. General warrants can be extremely abusive; they were used by the British in colonial America as a form of social control.

Ubiquitous surveillance means that anyone could be convicted of lawbreaking, once the police set their minds to it. It is incredibly dangerous to live in a world where everything you do can be stored and brought forward as evidence against you at some later date. There is significant danger in allowing the police to dig into these large data sets and find "evidence" of wrongdoing, especially in a country like the US with so many vague and punitive laws, which give prosecutors discretion over whom to charge with what, and with overly broad material witness laws. This is especially true given the expansion of the legally loaded terms "terrorism," to include conventional criminals, and "weapons of mass destruction," to include almost anything, including a sawed-off shotgun. The US terminology is so broad that someone who donates $10 to Hamas's humanitarian arm could be considered a terrorist.

Surveillance puts us at risk of abuses by those in power, even if we're doing nothing wrong at the time of surveillance. The definition of "wrong" is often arbitrary, and can quickly change. For example, in the US in the 1930s, being a Communist or Socialist was a bit of an intellectual fad, and not considered wrong among the educated classes. In the 1950s, that changed dramatically with the witch-hunts of Senator Joseph McCarthy, when many intelligent, principled American citizens found their careers destroyed once their political history was publicly disclosed. Is someone's reading of Occupy, Tea Party, animal rights, or gun rights websites going to become evidence of subversion in five to ten years?

This situation is exacerbated by the fact that we are generating so much data and storing it indefinitely. Those fishing expeditions can go into the past, finding things you might have done 10, 15, or 20 years ago . . . and counting. Today's adults were able to move beyond their youthful indiscretions; today's young people will not have that freedom. Their entire histories will be on the permanent record.

Another harm of government surveillance is the way it leads to people's being categorized and discriminated against. George Washington University law professor Daniel Solove calls the situation Kafkaesque. So much of this data is collected and used in secret, and we have no right to refute or even see the evidence against us. This will intensify as systems start using surveillance data to make decisions automatically.

Surveillance data has been used to justify numerous penalties, from subjecting people to more intensive airport security to deporting them. In 2012, before his Los Angeles vacation, 26-year-old Irishman Leigh Van Bryan tweeted, "Free this week, for quick gossip/prep before I go and destroy America." The US government had been surveilling the entire Twitter feed. Agents picked up Bryan's message, correlated it with airplane passenger lists, and were waiting for him at the border when he arrived from Ireland. His comment wasn't serious, but he was questioned for five hours and then sent back home. We know that bomb jokes in airports can get you detained; now it seems that you have to be careful making even vague promises of international rowdiness anywhere on the Internet.

In 2013, a Hawaiian man posted a video on Facebook showing himself drinking and driving. Police arrested him for the crime; his defense was that it was a parody and that no actual alcohol was consumed on the video.

It's worse in the UK. There, people have been jailed because of a racist tweet or a tasteless Facebook post. And it's even more extreme in other countries, of course, where people are routinely arrested and tortured for things they've written online.

Most alarming of all, the US military targets drone strikes partly based on their targets' data. There are two types of drone targeting. The first is "targeted killing," where a known individual is located by means of electronic or other surveillance. The second is "signature strikes," where unidentified individuals are targeted on the basis of their behavior and personal characteristics: their apparent ages and genders, their location, what they appear to be doing. At the peak of drone operations in Pakistan in 2009 and 2010, half of all kills were signature strikes. We don't have any information about how accurate the profiling was.

This is wrong. We should be free to talk with our friends, or send a text message to a family member, or read a book or article, without having to worry about how it would look to the government: our government today, our government in five or ten years, or some other government. We shouldn't have to worry about how our actions might be interpreted or misinterpreted, or how they could be used against us. We should not be subject to surveillance that is essentially indefinite.

GOVERNMENT CENSORSHIP

Freedom also depends on the free circulation of ideas. Government censorship, often enabled by surveillance, stifles them both.

China protects its citizens from the "dangers" of outside news and opinions on the Internet by something called the Golden Shield or, more commonly, the Great Firewall of China. It's a massive project that took eight years and cost $700 million to build, and its job is to censor the Internet. The goal is less to banish harmful ideas or squelch speech, and more to prevent effective organization. The firewall works pretty well; those with technical savvy can evade it, but it blocks the majority of China's population from finding all sorts of things, from information about the Dalai Lama to many Western search sites.

There's more government censorship on the Internet today than ever before. And it's not just politics. Countries censor websites because of their sexual nature, the religious views they espouse, their hosting of gambling platforms, and their promotion of drug use or illegal activity. The citizens of most Middle Eastern countries live under pervasive censorship. France, Germany, and Austria censor neo-Nazi content, including online auctions of Nazi memorabilia; other countries censor sites that incite violence. Vietnam's "Decree 72" prohibits people from discussing current affairs online. Many countries censor content that infringes on copyright. The UK censors pornography by default, although you can still opt out of the censorship. In 2010, the US censored WikiLeaks.

Most censorship is enforced by surveillance, which leads to self-censorship. If people know the government is watching everything they say, they are less likely to read or speak about forbidden topics. This is the point behind a 2014 Russian law requiring bloggers to register with the government. This is why the Great Firewall of China works so well as a censorship tool: it's not merely the technical capabilities of the firewall, but the threat that people trying to evade it will be discovered and reported by their fellow citizens. Those who do the reporting don't even necessarily agree with the government; they might face penalties of their own if they do not report. Internet companies in China often censor their users beyond what is officially required.

And the more severe the consequences of getting caught, the more excessively people self-censor.

CHILLING EFFECTS

Surveillance has a potentially enormous chilling effect on society. US Supreme Court Justice Sonia Sotomayor recognized this in her concurring opinion in a 2012 case about the FBI's installing a GPS tracker in someone's car. Her comments were much broader: "Awareness that the Government may be watching chills associational and expressive freedoms. And the Government's unrestrained power to assemble data that reveal private aspects of identity is susceptible to abuse. The net result is that GPS monitoring—by making available at a relatively low cost such a substantial quantity of intimate information about any person whom the Government, in its unfettered discretion, chooses to track—may 'alter the relationship between citizen and government in a way that is inimical to democratic society.'"

Columbia University law professor Eben Moglen wrote that "omnipresent invasive listening creates fear. And that fear is the enemy of reasoned, ordered liberty." Surveillance is a tactic of intimidation.

In the US, we already see the beginnings of this chilling effect. According to a Human Rights Watch report, journalists covering stories on the intelligence community, national security, and law enforcement have been significantly hampered by government surveillance. Sources are less likely to contact them, and they themselves are worried about being prosecuted. Human Rights Watch concludes that stories in the national interest that need to be reported don't get reported, and that the public is less informed as a result. That's the chilling effect right there.

Lawyers working on cases where there is some intelligence interest—foreign government clients, drugs, terrorism—are also affected. Like journalists, they worry that their conversations are monitored and that discussions with their clients will find their way into the prosecution's hands.

Post-9/11 surveillance has caused writers to self-censor. They avoid writing about and researching certain subjects; they're careful about communicating with sources, colleagues, or friends abroad. A Pew Research Center study conducted just after the first Snowden articles were published found that people didn't want to talk about the NSA online. A broader Harris poll found that nearly half of Americans have changed what they research, talk about, and write about because of NSA surveillance. Surveillance has chilled Internet use by Muslim Americans, and by groups like environmentalists, gun-rights activists, drug policy advocates, and human rights workers. After the Snowden revelations of 2013, people across the world were less likely to search personally sensitive terms on Google.

A 2014 report from the UN High Commissioner on Human Rights noted, "Even the mere possibility of communications information being captured creates an interference with privacy, with a potential chilling effect on rights, including those to free expression and association."

This isn't paranoia. In 2012, French president Nicolas Sarkozy said in a campaign speech, "Anyone who regularly consults internet sites which promote terror or hatred or violence will be sentenced to prison."

This fear of scrutiny isn't just about the present; it's about the past as well. Politicians already live in a world where the opposition follows them around constantly with cameras, hoping to record something that can be taken out of context. Everything they've said and done in the past is pored through and judged in the present, with an exactitude far greater than was imaginable only a few years ago. Imagine this being normal for every job applicant.

Of course, surveillance doesn't affect everyone equally. Some of us are unconcerned about government surveillance, and therefore not affected at all. Others of us, especially those of us in religious, social, ethnic, and economic groups that are out of favor with the ruling elite, will be affected more.

Jeremy Bentham's key observation in conceiving his panopticon was that people become conformist and compliant when they believe they are being observed. The panopticon is an architecture of social control. Think of how you act when a police car is driving next to you, or how an entire country acts when state agents are listening to phone calls. When we know everything is being recorded, we are less likely to speak freely and act individually. When we are constantly under the threat of judgment, criticism, and correction for our actions, we become fearful that—either now or in the uncertain future—data we leave behind will be brought back to implicate us, by whatever authority has then become focused upon our once-private and innocent acts. In response, we do nothing out of the ordinary. We lose our individuality, and society stagnates. We don't question or challenge power. We become obedient and submissive. We're less free.

INHIBITING DISSENT AND SOCIAL CHANGE

These chilling effects are especially damaging to political discourse. There is value in dissent. And, perversely, there can be value in lawbreaking. These are both ways we improve as a society. Ubiquitous mass surveillance is the enemy of democracy, liberty, freedom, and progress.

Defending this assertion involves a subtle argument—something I wrote about in my previous book *Liars and Outliers*—but it's vitally important to society. Think about it this way. Across the US, states are on the verge of reversing decades-old laws about homosexual relationships and marijuana use. If the old laws could have been perfectly enforced through surveillance, society would never have reached the point where the majority of citizens thought those things were okay. There has to be a period where they are still illegal yet increasingly tolerated, so that people can look around and say, "You know, that wasn't so bad." Yes, the process takes decades, but it's a process that can't happen without lawbreaking. Frank Zappa said something similar in 1971: "Without deviation from the norm, progress is not possible."

The perfect enforcement that comes with ubiquitous government surveillance chills this process. We need imperfect security—systems that free people to try new things, much the way off-the-record brainstorming sessions loosen inhibitions and foster creativity. If we don't have that, we can't slowly move from a thing's being illegal and not okay, to illegal and not sure, to illegal and probably okay, and finally to legal.

This is an important point. Freedoms we now take for granted were often at one time viewed as threatening or even criminal by the past power structure. Those changes might never have happened if the authorities had been able to achieve social control through surveillance.

This is one of the main reasons all of us should care about the emerging architecture of surveillance, even if we are not personally chilled by its existence. We suffer the effects because people around us will be less likely to proclaim new political or social ideas, or act out of the ordinary. If J. Edgar Hoover's surveillance of Martin Luther King Jr. had been successful in silencing him, it would have affected far more people than King and his family.

Of course, many things that are illegal will rightly remain illegal forever: theft, murder, and so on. Taken to the extreme, though, perfect enforcement could have unforeseen repercussions. What does it mean for society if the police can track your car 24/7, and then mail you a bill at the end of the month itemizing every time you sped, ran a red light, made an illegal left turn, or followed the car in front of you too closely? Or if your township can use aerial surveillance to automatically fine you for failing to mow your lawn or shovel your walk regularly? Our legal systems are largely based on human judgment. And while there are risks associated with biased and prejudiced judgments, there are also risks associated with replacing that judgment with algorithmic efficiency.

Ubiquitous surveillance could lead to the kind of society depicted in the 2002 Tom Cruise movie *Minority Report*, where people can become the subject of police investigations before they commit a crime. Already law enforcement agencies make use of predictive analytic tools to identify suspects and direct investigations. It's a short step from there to the world of Big Brother and thoughtcrime.

This notion of making certain crimes impossible to get away with is new—a potential result of all this new technology—and it's something we need to think about carefully before we implement it. As law professor Yochai Benkler said, "Imperfection is a core dimension of freedom."

SECRECY CREEP

Secrecy generally shrouds government surveillance, and it poses a danger to a free and open society.

In the US, this has manifested itself in several ways. First, the government has greatly expanded what can be considered secret. One of the truisms of national security is that secrecy is necessary in matters of intelligence, foreign policy, and defense. If the government made certain things public—troop movements, weapons capabilities, negotiating positions—the enemy would alter its behavior to its own advantage. This notion of military secrecy has been true for millennia, but recently has changed dramatically. I'm using the US as an example here. In World War I, we were concerned about the secrecy of specific facts, like the location of military units and the precise plans of a battle. In World War II, we extended that secrecy to both large-scale operations and entire areas of knowledge. Not only was our program to build an atomic bomb secret; the entire science of nuclear weaponry was secret. After 9/11, we generalized further, and now almost anything can be a secret.

The result is that US government secrecy has exploded. No one knows the exact number—it's secret, of course—but reasonable estimates are that hundreds of billions of pages of government documents are classified in the US each year. At the same time, the number of people with security clearances has similarly mushroomed. As of October 2012, almost 5 million people in the US had security clearances (1.4 million at the top-secret level), a 50% increase since 1999.

Pretty much all the details of NSA surveillance are classified, lest they tip off the bad guys. (I'll return to that argument in Chapter 13.) Pre-Snowden, you weren't allowed to read the Presidential Policy Directives that authorized much of NSA surveillance. You weren't even allowed to read the court orders that authorized this surveillance. It was all classified, and it still would be if the release of the Snowden documents hadn't resulted in a bunch of government declassifications.

The NSA and the military aren't the only organizations increasing their levels of secrecy. Local law enforcement is starting to similarly cloak its own surveillance actions. For example, police requests for cell phone surveillance are routinely sealed by the courts that authorize them. (The UK police won't even admit that they use the technology.) There are many more examples of this.

This kind of secrecy weakens the checks and balances we have in place to oversee surveillance and, more broadly, to see that we are all treated fairly by our laws. Since the terrorist attacks of 9/11, FBI and NSA National Security Letters demanding surveillance information from various companies have regularly come with gag orders attached. Those who receive such a letter are prohibited from talking, even in general terms, about it. That makes it much harder to fight the letters in court.

Governments are also hiding behind corporate nondisclosure agreements. That's the reason the FBI and local police give for not revealing the details of their StingRay cell phone surveillance system. That's why local police departments refuse to divulge details of the commercially developed predictive policing algorithms they use to deploy officers.

The second way government secrecy has manifested itself is that it is being exerted to an extreme degree. The US has a complex legal framework for classification that is increasingly being ignored. The executive branch abuses its state secrets privilege to keep information out of public view. The executive branch keeps secrets from Congress. The NSA keeps secrets from those who oversee its operations—including Congress. Certain members of Congress keep secrets from the rest of Congress. Secret courts keep their own secrets, and even the Supreme Court is increasingly keeping documents secret. In Washington, knowledge is currency, and the intelligence community is hoarding it.

The third manifestation of government secrecy is that government has dealt very severely with those who expose its secrets: whistleblowers. President Obama has been exceptionally zealous in prosecuting individuals who have disclosed wrongdoing by government agencies. Since his election in 2008, he has pursued prosecutions against eight people for leaking classified information to the press. There had been only three previous prosecutions since the Espionage Act was passed in 1917.

Intelligence-related whistleblowing is not a legal defense in the US; the Espionage Act prohibits the defendant from explaining why he leaked classified information. Daniel Ellsberg, the first person prosecuted under the law, in 1971, was barred from explaining his actions in court. Former NSA senior executive Thomas Drake, an NSA whistleblower who was prosecuted in 2011, was forbidden to say the words "whistleblowing" and "overclassification" in his trial. Chelsea Manning was prohibited from using a similar defense.

Edward Snowden claims he's a whistleblower. Many people, including me, agree; others don't. Secretary of State John Kerry insisted that Snowden should "come back here and stand in our system of justice and make his case," and former secretary of state Hillary Clinton proclaimed, "If he wishes to return knowing he would be held accountable and also able to present a defense, that is his decision to make." Both comments are examples of misleading political smoke-blowing. Current law does not permit Snowden to make his case.

Inasmuch as government surveillance requires secrecy, people lose the power to debate and vote on what their government is doing in their name, or tell their elected officials what they think should be done. It's easy to forget, in the seemingly endless stream of headlines about the NSA and its surveillance programs, that none of it would be known to the public at all if Snowden hadn't, at great personal cost and risk, exposed what the agency is doing.

ABUSE

In early 2014, someone started a parody Twitter account for Jim Ardis, the mayor of Peoria, Illinois. It was a pretty offensive parody, and it really pissed Ardis off. His anger set off a series of events in which the local police illegally obtained an order demanding that Twitter turn over identity information related to the account, then raided the home of Twitter user Jon Daniel. No charges were filed, mostly because Daniel didn't do anything wrong, and the ACLU is currently suing Peoria on his behalf.

All surveillance systems are susceptible to abuse. In recent years, politicians have used surveillance to intimidate the opposition and, as we saw above, harass people who annoy them. One example is from 2014: police in New Jersey routinely photographed protesters at events hosted by Governor Chris Christie until the state attorney general ordered them to stop. Also in 2014, we learned that the CIA illegally hacked into computers belonging to staffers from the Senate Intelligence Committee who were overseeing them. In 2013, we learned that the NSA had been spying on UN communications, in violation of international law. We know that there have been all sorts of other abuses of state and local government surveillance authorities as well.

Abuses happen inside surveillance organizations as well. For example, NSA employees routinely listen to personal phone calls of Americans overseas, and intercept e-mail and pass racy photos around the office. We learned this from two intercept operators in 2008, and again from Snowden in 2014. We learned from the NSA that its agents sometimes spy on people they know; internally, they call this practice LOVEINT. The NSA's own audit documents note that the agency broke its own privacy rules 2,776 times in 12 months, from 2011 to 2012. That's a lot—eight times a day—but the real number is probably much higher. Because of how the NSA polices itself, it essentially decides how many violations it discovers.

This is not a new problem, nor one limited to the NSA. Recent US history illustrates many episodes in which surveillance has been systematically abused: against labor organizers and suspected Communists after World War I, against civil rights leaders, and against Vietnam War protesters. The specifics aren't pretty, but it's worth giving a couple of them.

- Through extensive surveillance, J. Edgar Hoover learned of Martin Luther King's extramarital affairs, and in an anonymous letter he tried to induce him to commit suicide in 1964: "King, look into your heart. You know you are a complete fraud and a great liability to all of us Negroes. White people in this country have enough frauds of their own but I am sure they don't have one at this time anywhere near your equal. You are no clergyman and you know it. I repeat you are a colossal fraud and an evil, vicious one at that. You could not believe in God.... Clearly you don't believe in any personal moral principles.... King, there is only one thing left for you to do. You know what it is. You have just 34 days in which to do it (this exact number has been selected for a specific reason, it has definite practical significance). You are done. There is but one way out for you. You better take it before your filthy, abnormal fraudulent self is bared to the nation."

- This is how a Senate investigation described the FBI's COINTELPRO surveillance program in 1976: "While the declared purposes of these programs were to protect the 'national security' or prevent violence, Bureau witnesses admit that many of the targets were nonviolent and most had no connections with a foreign power. Indeed, nonviolent organizations and individuals were targeted because the Bureau believed they represented a 'potential' for violence—and nonviolent citizens who were against the war in Vietnam were targeted because they gave 'aid and comfort' to violent demonstrators by lending respectability to their cause. . . . But COINTELPRO was more than simply violating the law or the Constitution. In COINTELPRO the Bureau secretly took the law into its own hands, going beyond the collection of intelligence and beyond its law enforcement function to act outside the legal process altogether and to covertly disrupt, discredit and harass groups and individuals."

Nothing has changed. Since 9/11, the US has spied on the Occupy movement, pro- and anti-abortion activists, peace activists, and other political protesters.

- The NSA and FBI spied on many prominent Muslim Americans who had nothing to do with terrorism, including Faisal Gill, a longtime Republican Party operative and onetime candidate for public office who held a top-secret security clearance and served in the Department of Homeland Security under President George W. Bush; Asim Ghafoor, a prominent attorney who has represented clients in terrorism-related cases; Hooshang Amirahmadi, an Iranian American professor of international relations at Rutgers University; and Nihad Awad, the executive director of the largest Muslim civil rights organization in the country.
- The New York Police Department went undercover into minority neighborhoods. It monitored mosques, infiltrated student and political groups, and spied on entire communi-

ties. Again, people were targeted because of their ethnicity, not because of any accusations of crimes or evidence of wrongdoing. Many of these operations were conducted with the help of the CIA, which is prohibited by law from spying on Americans.

There's plenty more. Boston's fusion center spied on Veterans for Peace, the women's antiwar organization Code Pink, and the Occupy movement. In 2013, the city teamed with IBM to deploy a video surveillance system at a music festival. During the same time period, the Pentagon's Counterintelligence Field Activity spied on all sorts of innocent American civilians—something the Department of Defense is prohibited by law from doing.

Echoing Hoover's attempt to intimidate King, the NSA has been collecting data on the porn-viewing habits of Muslim "radicalizers"—not terrorists, but those who through political speech might radicalize others—with the idea of blackmailing them.

In 2010, DEA agents searched an Albany woman's cell phone—with permission—but then saved the intimate photos they found to create a fake Facebook page for her. When they were sued for this abuse, the government speciously argued that by consenting to the search of her phone, the woman had implicitly consented to identity theft.

Local authorities abuse surveillance capabilities, too. In 2009, the Lower Merion School District, near Philadelphia, lent high schoolers laptops to help them with their homework. School administrators installed spyware on the computers, then recorded students' chat logs, monitored the websites they visited, and—this is the creepiest—surreptitiously photographed them, often in their bedrooms. This all came to light when an assistant principal confronted student Blake Robbins with pictures of him popping pills like candy. Turns out they *were* candy—Mike and

Ike, to be exact—and the school was successfully sued for its invasive practices.

Aside from such obvious abuses of power, there's the inevitable expansion of power that accompanies the expansion of any large and powerful bureaucratic system: mission creep. For example, after 9/11, the CIA and the Treasury Department joined forces to gather data on Americans' financial transactions, with the idea that they could detect the funding of future terrorist groups. This turned out to be a dead end, but the expanded surveillance netted a few money launderers. So it continues.

In the US, surveillance is being used more often, in more cases, against more offenses, than ever before. Surveillance powers justified in the PATRIOT Act as being essential in the fight against terrorism, like "sneak and peek" search warrants, are far more commonly used in non-terrorism investigations, such as searches for drugs. In 2011, the NSA was given authority to conduct surveillance against drug smugglers in addition to its traditional national security concerns. DEA staff were instructed to lie in court to conceal that the NSA passed data to the agency.

The NSA's term is "parallel construction." The agency receiving the NSA information must invent some other way of getting at it, one that is admissible in court. The FBI probably got the evidence needed to arrest the hacker Ross Ulbricht, aka Dread Pirate Roberts, who ran the anonymous Silk Road website where people could buy drugs and more, in this way.

Mission creep is also happening in the UK, where surveillance intended to nab terrorists is being used against political protesters, and in all sorts of minor criminal cases: against people who violate a smoking ban, falsify their address, and fail to clean up after their dogs. The country has a lot of cameras, so it "makes sense" to use them as much as possible.

Other countries provide many more examples. Israel, for

instance, gathers intelligence on innocent Palestinians for political persecution. Building the technical means for a surveillance state makes it easy for people and organizations to slip over the line into abuse. Of course, less savory governments abuse surveillance as a matter of course—with no legal protections for their citizens.

All of this matters, even if you happen to trust the government currently in power. A system that is overwhelmingly powerful relies on everyone in power to act perfectly—so much has to go right to prevent meaningful abuse. There are always going to be bad apples—the question is how much harm they are allowed and empowered to do and how much they corrupt the rest of the barrel. Our controls need to work not only when the party we approve of leads the government but also when the party we disapprove of does.

CURTAILING INTERNET FREEDOM

In 2010, then secretary of state Hillary Clinton gave a speech declaring Internet freedom a major US foreign policy goal. To this end, the US State Department funds and supports a variety of programs worldwide, working to counter censorship, promote encryption, and enable anonymity, all designed "to ensure that any child, born anywhere in the world, has access to the global Internet as an open platform on which to innovate, learn, organize, and express herself free from undue interference or censorship." This agenda has been torpedoed by the awkward realization that the US and other democratic governments conducted the same types of surveillance they have criticized in more repressive countries.

Those repressive countries are seizing on the opportunity, pointing to US surveillance as a justification for their own more draconian Internet policies: more surveillance, more censorship, and a more isolationist Internet that gives individual countries more control over what their citizens see and say. For example, one of the defenses the government of Egypt offered for its plans to monitor social media was that "the US listens in to phone calls, and supervises anyone who could threaten its national security." Indians are worried that their government will cite the US's actions to justify surveillance in that country. Both China and Russia publicly called out US hypocrisy.

This affects Internet freedom worldwide. Historically, Internet governance—what little there was—was largely left to the United States, because everyone more or less believed that we were working for the security of the Internet instead of against it. But now that the US has lost much of its credibility, Internet governance is in turmoil. Many of the regulatory bodies that influence the Internet are trying to figure out what sort of leadership model to adopt. Older international standards organizations like the International Telecommunications Union are trying to increase their influence in Internet governance and develop a more nationalist set of rules.

This is the cyber sovereignty movement, and it threatens to fundamentally fragment the Internet. It's not new, but it has been given an enormous boost from the revelations of NSA spying. Countries like Russia, China, and Saudi Arabia are pushing for much more autonomous control over the portions of the Internet within their borders.

That, in short, would be a disaster. The Internet is fundamentally a global platform. While countries continue to censor and control, today people in repressive regimes can still read information from and exchange ideas with the rest of the world. Internet freedom is a human rights issue, and one that the US should support.

Facebook's Mark Zuckerberg publicly took the Obama administration to task on this, writing, "The US government should be the champion for the Internet, not a threat." He's right.

8

Commercial Fairness and Equality

Accretive Health is a debt collection agency that worked for a number of hospitals in Minnesota. It was in charge of billing and collection for those hospitals, but it also coordinated scheduling, admissions, care plans, and duration of hospital stays. If this sounds like a potential conflict of interest, it was. The agency collected extensive patient data and used it for its own purposes, without disclosing to patients the nature of its involvement in their healthcare. It used information about patient debts when scheduling treatment and harassed patients for money in emergency rooms. The company denied all wrongdoing, but in 2012 settled a Minnesota lawsuit by agreeing not to operate in Minnesota for two to six years. On the one hand, the fact that Accretive was caught and punished shows that the system is working. On the other hand, it also shows how easy it is for our data to be mishandled and misused.

Stories like this demonstrate the considerable risk to society in allowing corporations to conduct mass surveillance. It's their surveillance that contributes to all of the offenses against civil liberties, social progress, and freedom that I described in the previous chapter. And in addition to enabling government surveillance, corporate surveillance carries its own risks.

SURVEILLANCE-BASED DISCRIMINATION

In a fundamental way, companies use surveillance data to discriminate. They place people into different categories and market goods and services to them differently on the basis of those categories.

"Redlining" is a term from the 1960s to describe a practice that's much older: banks discriminating against members of minority groups when they tried to purchase homes. Banks would not approve mortgages in minority neighborhoods—they would draw a red line on their maps delineating those zones. Or they would issue mortgages to minorities only if they were buying houses in predominantly minority neighborhoods. It's illegal, of course, but for a long time banks got away with it. More generally, redlining is the practice of denying or charging more for services by using neighborhood as a proxy for race—and it's much easier to do on the Internet.

In 2000, Wells Fargo bank created a website to promote its home mortgages. The site featured a "community calculator" to help potential buyers search for neighborhoods. The calculator collected the current ZIP code of the potential customers and steered them to neighborhoods based on the predominant race of that ZIP code. The site referred white residents to white neighborhoods, and black residents to black neighborhoods.

This practice is called weblining, and it has the potential to be much more pervasive and much more discriminatory than traditional redlining. Because corporations collect so much data about us and can compile such detailed profiles, they can influence us in many different ways. A 2014 White House report on big data concluded, ". . . big data analytics have the potential to eclipse long-standing civil rights protections in how personal information is used in housing, credit, employment, health, education, and the marketplace." I think the report understated the risk.

Price discrimination is also a big deal these days. It's not discrimination in the same classic racial or gender sense as weblining; it's companies charging different people different prices to realize as much profit as possible. We're most familiar with this concept with respect to airline tickets. Prices change all the time, and depend on factors like how far in advance we purchase, what days we're traveling, and how full the flight is. The airline's goal is to sell tickets to vacationers at the bargain prices they're willing to pay, while at the same time extracting from business travelers the much higher amounts that *they're* willing to pay. There is nothing nefarious about the practice; it's just a way of maximizing revenues and profits. Even so, price discrimination can be *very* unpopular. Raising the price of snow shovels after a snowstorm, for example, is considered price-gouging. This is why it is often cloaked in things like special offers, coupons, or rebates.

Some types of price discrimination are illegal. For example, a restaurant cannot charge different prices depending on the gender or race of the customer. But it can charge different prices based on time of day, which is why you see lunch and dinner menus with the same items and different prices. Offering senior discounts and special children's menus is legal price discrimination. Uber's surge pricing is also legal.

In many industries, the options you're offered, the price you pay, and the service you receive depend on information about you: bank loans, auto insurance, credit cards, and so on. Internet surveillance facilitates a fine-tuning of this practice. Online merchants already show you different prices and options based on your history and what they know about you. Depending on who you are, you might see a picture of a red convertible or a picture of a mini-van in online car ads, and be offered different options for financing and discounting when you visit dealer websites. According to a 2010 *Wall Street Journal* article, the price you pay on the Staples website depends on where you are located, and how close a competitor's store is to you. The article states that other companies, like Rosetta Stone and Home Depot, are also adjusting prices on the basis of information about the individual user.

More broadly, we all have a customer score. Data brokers assign it to us. It's like a credit score, but it's not a single number, and it's focused on what you buy, based on things like purchasing data from retailers, personal financial information, survey data, warranty card registrations, social media interactions, loyalty card data, public records, website interactions, charity donor lists, online and offline subscriptions, and health and fitness information. All of this is used to determine what ads and offers you see when you browse the Internet.

In 2011, the US Army created a series of recruiting ads showing soldiers of different genders and racial backgrounds. It partnered with a cable company to deliver those ads according to the demographics of the people living in the house.

There are other ways to discriminate. In 2012, Orbitz highlighted different prices for hotel rooms depending on whether viewers were using Mac or Windows. Other travel sites showed people different offers based on their browsing history. Many sites estimate your income level, and show you different pages based on that. Much of this is subtle. It's not that you can't see certain airfares or hotel rooms, it's just that they're ordered so that the ones the site wants to show you are easier to see and click on. We saw in Chapter 3 how data about us can be used to predict age, gender, race, sexual preference, relationship status, and many other things. This gives corporations a greater advantage over consumers, and as they amass more data, both on individuals and on classes of people, that edge will only increase. For example, marketers know that women feel less attractive on Mondays, and that that's the best time to advertise cosmetics to them. And they know that different ages and genders respond better to different ads. In the future, they might know enough about specific individuals to know you're not very susceptible to offers at 8:00 am because you haven't had your coffee yet and are grouchy, you get more susceptible around 9:30 because you're fully caffeinated, and then are less susceptible again by 11:00 because your blood sugar is low just before lunch.

People are also judged by their social networks. Lenddo is a Philippine company that assesses people's credit risk by looking at the creditworthiness of the people they interact with frequently on Facebook. In another weblining example, American Express has reduced people's credit limits based on the types of stores they shop at.

University of Pennsylvania law professor Oscar Gandy presciently described all this in 1993 as the "panoptic sort": "The collection, processing, and sharing of information about individuals and groups that is generated through their daily lives as citizens, employees, and consumers and is used to coordinate and control their access to the goods and services that define life in the modern capitalist economy." Those who have this power have enormous power indeed. It's the power to use discriminatory criteria to dole out different opportunities, access, eligibility, prices (mostly in terms of special offers and discounts), attention (both positive and negative), and exposure.

This practice can get very intrusive. High-end restaurants are starting to Google their customers, to better personalize their dining experiences. They can't give people menus with different prices, but they can certainly hand them the wine list with either the cheaper side up or the more expensive side up. Automobile insurance compa-

nies are experimenting with usage-based insurance. If you allow
your insurance company to monitor when, how far, and how fast you
drive, you could get a lower insurance rate.

The potential for intrusiveness increases considerably when it's
an employer–employee relationship. At least one company negoti-
ated a significant reduction in its health insurance costs by distributing Fitbits to its employees, which gave the insurance company
an unprecedented view into its subscribers' health habits. Similarly, several schools are requiring students to wear smart heart
rate monitors in gym class; there's no word about what happens to
that data afterwards. In 2011, Hewlett-Packard analyzed employee
data to predict who was likely to leave the company, then informed
their managers.

Workplace surveillance is another area of enormous potential
harm. For many of us, our employer is the most dangerous power
that has us under surveillance. Employees who are regularly surveilled include call center workers, truck drivers, manufacturing
workers, sales teams, retail workers, and others. More of us have
our corporate electronic communications constantly monitored. A
lot of this comes from a new field called "workplace analytics,"
which is basically surveillance-driven human resources management. If you use a corporate computer or cell phone, you have
almost certainly given your employer the right to monitor everything you do on those devices. Some of this is legitimate; employers
have a right to make sure you're not playing Farmville on your computer all day. But you probably use those devices on your own time
as well, for personal as well as work communications.

Any time we're monitored and profiled, there's the potential
for getting it wrong. You are already familiar with this; just think of
all the irrelevant advertisements you've been shown on the Internet, on the basis of some algorithm misinterpreting your interests.
For some people, that's okay; for others, there's low-level psycho-

logical harm from being categorized, whether correctly or incorrectly. The opportunity for harm rises as the judging becomes more important: our credit ratings depend on algorithms; how we're treated at airport security depends partly on corporate-collected data.

There are chilling effects as well. For example, people are refraining from looking up information about diseases they might have because they're afraid their insurance companies will drop them.

It's true that a lot of corporate profiling starts from good intentions. Some people might be denied a bank loan because of their deadbeat Facebook friends, but Lenddo's system is designed to enable banks to give loans to people without credit ratings. If their friends had good credit ratings, that would be a mark in their favor. Using personal data to determine insurance rates or credit card spending limits might cause some people to get a worse deal than they otherwise would have, but it also gives many people a better deal than they otherwise would have.

In general, however, surveillance data is being used by powerful corporations to increase their profits at the expense of consumers. Customers don't like this, but as long as (1) sellers are competing with each other for our money, (2) software systems make price discrimination easier, and (3) the discrimination can be hidden from customers, it is going to be hard for corporations to resist doing it.

SURVEILLANCE-BASED MANIPULATION

Someone who knows things about us has some measure of control over us, and someone who knows everything about us has a lot of control over us. Surveillance facilitates control.

Manipulation doesn't have to involve overt advertising. It can be product placement ensuring you see pictures that have a certain brand of car in the background. Or just an increase in how often you see that car. This is, essentially, the business model of search engines. In their early days, there was talk about how an advertiser could pay for better placement in search results. After public outcry and subsequent guidance from the FTC, search engines visually differentiated between "natural" results by algorithm and paid ones. So now you get paid search results in Google framed in yellow, and paid search results in Bing framed in pale blue. This worked for a while, but recently the trend has shifted back. Google is now accepting money to insert particular URLs into search results, and not just in the separate advertising areas. We don't know how extensive this is, but the FTC is again taking an interest.

When you're scrolling through your Facebook feed, you don't see every post by every friend; what you see has been selected by an automatic algorithm that's not made public. But people can pay to increase the likelihood that their friends or fans will see their posts. Payments for placement represent a significant portion of Facebook's income. Similarly, a lot of those links to additional articles at the bottom of news pages are paid placements.

The potential for manipulation here is enormous. Here's one example. During the 2012 election, Facebook users had the opportunity to post an "I Voted" icon, much like the real stickers many of us get at polling places after voting. There is a documented bandwagon effect with respect to voting; you are more likely to vote if you believe your friends are voting, too. This manipulation had the effect of increasing voter turnout 0.4% nationwide. So far, so good. But now imagine if Facebook manipulated the visibility of the "I Voted" icon on the basis of either party affiliation or some decent proxy of it: ZIP code of residence, blogs linked to, URLs liked, and so on. It didn't, but if it had, it would have had the effect of increasing voter turnout in one direction. It would be hard to detect, and it wouldn't even be illegal. Facebook could easily tilt a close election by selectively manipulating what posts its users see. Google might do something similar with its search results.

A truly sinister social networking platform could manipulate public opinion even more effectively. By amplifying the voices of people it agrees with, and dampening those of people it disagrees with, it could profoundly distort public discourse. China does this with its 50 Cent Party: people hired by the government to post comments on social networking sites supporting, and to challenge comments opposing, party positions. Samsung has done much the same thing.

Many companies manipulate what you see according to your user profile: Google search, Yahoo News, even online newspapers like the *New York Times*. This is a big deal. The first listing in a Google search result gets a third of the clicks, and if you're not on the first page, you might as well not exist. The result is that the Internet you see is increasingly tailored to what your profile indicates your interests are. This leads to a phenomenon that political activist Eli Pariser has called the "filter bubble": an Internet optimized to your preferences, where you never have to encounter an opinion you don't agree with. You might think that's not too bad, but on a large scale it's harmful. We don't want to live in a society where everybody only ever reads things that reinforce their existing opinions, where we never have spontaneous encounters that enliven, confound, confront, and teach us.

In 2012, Facebook ran an experiment in control. It selectively manipulated the newsfeeds of 680,000 users, showing them either happier or sadder status updates. Because Facebook constantly monitors its users—that's how it turns its users into advertising revenue—it could easily monitor the experimental subjects and collect the results. It found that people who saw happier posts tended to write happier posts, and vice versa. I don't want to make too much of this result. Facebook only did this for a week, and the effect was small. But once sites like Facebook figure out how to do this effectively, they will be able to monetize this. Not only do women feel less attractive on Mondays; they also feel less attractive when they feel depressed. We're already seeing the beginnings of systems that analyze people's voices and body language to determine mood; companies want to better determine when customers are getting frustrated, and when they can be most profitably upsold. Manipulating those emotions to market products better is the sort of thing that's acceptable in the advertising world, even if it sounds pretty horrible to us.

Manipulation is made easier because of the centralized architecture of so many of our systems. Companies like Google and Facebook sit at the center of our communications. That gives them enormous power to manipulate and control.

Unique harms can arise from the use of surveillance data in politics. Election politics is very much a type of marketing, and politicians are starting to use personalized marketing's capability to discriminate as a way to track voting patterns and better "sell" a candidate or policy position. Candidates and advocacy groups can create ads and fund-raising appeals targeted to particular categories: people who earn more than $100,000 a year, gun owners, people who have read news articles on one side of a particular issue, unemployed veterans ... anything you can think of. They can target outraged ads to one group of people, and thoughtful policy-based ads to another. They can also fine-tune their get-out-the-vote campaigns on Election Day, and more efficiently gerrymander districts between elections. Such use of data will likely have fundamental effects on democracy and voting.

Psychological manipulation—based both on personal information and on control of the underlying systems—will get better and better. Even worse, it will become so good that we won't know we're being manipulated. This is a hard reality for us to accept, because we all like to believe we are too smart to fall for any such ploy. We're not.

PRIVACY BREACHES

In 1995, the hacker Kevin Mitnick broke into the network of an Internet company called Netcom and stole 20,000 customer credit card numbers. In 2004, hackers broke into the network of the data broker ChoicePoint, stole data on over 100,000 people, and used it to commit fraud. In late 2014, hackers broke into Home Depot's corporate networks and stole over 60 million credit card numbers; a month later, we learned about a heist of 83 million households' contact information from JPMorgan Chase. Two decades of the Internet, and it seems as if nothing has changed except the scale.

One reasonable question to ask is: how well do the Internet companies, data brokers, and our government protect our data? In one way, the question makes little sense. In the US, anyone willing to pay for data can get it. In some cases, criminals have legally purchased and used data to commit fraud.

Cybercrime is older than the Internet, and it's big business. Numbers are hard to come by, but the cost to the US is easily in the tens of billions of dollars. And with that kind of money involved, the business of cybercrime is both organized and international.

Much of this crime involves some sort of identity theft, which is the fancy Internet-era term for impersonation fraud. A criminal hacks into a database somewhere, steals your account information and maybe your passwords, and uses them to impersonate you to secure credit in your name. Or he steals your credit card number and charges purchases to you. Or he files a fake tax return in your name and gets a refund that you're later liable for.

This isn't personal. Criminals aren't really after your intimate details; they just want enough information about your financial accounts to access them. Or sufficient personal information to obtain credit.

A dozen years ago, the risk was that the criminals would hack into your computer and steal your personal data. But the scale of data thefts is increasing all the time. These days, criminals are more likely to hack into large corporate databases and steal your personal information, along with that of millions of other people. It's just more efficient. Government databases are also regularly hacked. Again and again we have learned that our data isn't well-protected. Thefts happen regularly, much more often than the news services report. Privacy lawyers I know tell me that there are many more data vulnerabilities and breaches than get reported—and many companies never even figure out that their networks have been hacked and their data is being stolen. It's actually amazing how bad corporate security can be. And because institutions legitimately have your data, you often have no recourse if they lose it.

Sometimes the hackers aren't after money. Californian Luis Mijangos was arrested in 2010 for "sextortion." He would hack into the computers of his female victims, search them for sexual and incriminating photos and videos, surreptitiously turn on the camera and take his own, then threaten to publish them if they didn't provide him with more racy photos and videos. People who do this are known as "ratters," for RAT, or remote access Trojan. That's the piece of malware they use to take over your computer. The most insidious RATs can turn your computer's camera on without turning the indicator light on. Not all ratters extort their victims; some just trade photos, videos, and files with each other.

It's not just hackers who spy on people remotely. In Chapter 7, I talked about a school district that spied on its students through their computers. In 2012, the Federal Trade Commission successfully prosecuted seven rent-to-own computer companies that spied on their customers through their webcams.

While writing this book, I heard a similar story from two different people. A few years after a friend—or a friend's daughter—applied to colleges, she received a letter from a college she'd never applied to—different colleges in each story. The letter basically said that the college had been storing her personal data and that hackers had broken in and stolen it all; it recommended that she place a fraud alert on her account with the major credit bureaus. In each instance, the college had bought the data from a broker back when she was a high school senior and had been trying to entice her to consider attending. In both cases, she hadn't even applied to the college. Yet the colleges were still storing that data years later. Neither had secured it very well.

As long as our personal data sloshes around like this, our security is at risk.

9

Business Competitiveness

In 1993, the Internet was a very different place from what it is today. There was no electronic commerce; the World Wide Web was in its infancy. The Internet was a communications tool for techies and academics, and we used e-mail, newsgroups, and a chat protocol called IRC. Computers were primitive, as was computer security. For about 20 years, the NSA had managed to keep cryptography software out of the mainstream by classifying it as a munition and restricting its export. US products with strong cryptography couldn't be sold overseas, which meant that US hardware and software companies put weak—and by that I mean easily breakable—cryptography into both their domestic and their international products, because that was easier than maintaining two versions.

But the world was changing. Cryptographic discoveries couldn't be quashed, and the academic world was catching up to the capabilities of the NSA. In 1993, I wrote my first book, *Applied Cryptography*, which made those discoveries accessible to a more general audience. It was a big deal, and I sold 180,000 copies in two editions. *Wired* magazine called it "the book the National Security Agency wanted never to be published," because it taught cryptographic expertise to non-experts. Research was international, and non-US companies started springing up, offering strong cryptography in their products. One study from 1993 found over 250 cryptography products made and marketed outside the US. US companies feared that they wouldn't be able to compete, because of the export restrictions in force.

At the same time, the FBI started to worry that strong cryptography would make it harder for the bureau to eavesdrop on the conversations of criminals. It was concerned about e-mail, but it was most concerned about voice encryption boxes that could be attached to telephones. This was the first time the FBI used the term "going dark" to describe its imagined future of ubiquitous encryption. It was a scare story with no justification to support it, just as it is today—but lawmakers believed it. They passed the CALEA law I mentioned in Chapter 6, and the FBI pushed for them to ban all cryptography without a backdoor.

Instead, the Clinton administration came up with a solution: the Clipper Chip. It was a system of encryption with surveillance capabilities for FBI and NSA access built in. The encryption algorithm was alleged to be strong enough to prevent eavesdropping, but there was a backdoor that allowed someone who knew the special key to get at the plaintext. This was marketed as "key escrow" and was billed as a great compromise; trusted US companies could compete in the world market with strong encryption, and the FBI and NSA could maintain their eavesdropping capabilities.

The first encryption device with the Clipper Chip built in was an AT&T secure phone. It wasn't a cell phone; this was 1993. It was a small box that plugged in between the wired telephone and the wired handset and encrypted the voice conversation. For the time, it was kind of neat. The voice quality was only okay, but it worked.

No one bought it.

In retrospect, it was rather obvious. Nobody wanted encryption with a US government backdoor built in. Privacy-minded individuals didn't want it. US companies didn't want it. And people outside the US didn't want it, especially when there were non-US alternatives available with strong cryptography and no backdoors. The US government was the only major customer for the AT&T devices, and most of those were never even used.

Over the next few years, the government tried other key escrow initiatives, all designed to give the US government backdoor access to all encryption, but the market soundly rejected all of those as well.

The demise of the Clipper Chip, and key escrow in general, heralded the death of US government restrictions on strong cryptography. Export controls were gradually lifted over the next few years, first on software in 1996 and then on most hardware a few years later. The change came not a moment too soon. By 1999, over 800 encryption products from 35 countries other than the US had filled the market.

What killed both the Clipper Chip and crypto export controls were not demands for privacy from consumers. Rather, they were killed by the threat of foreign competition and demands from US industry. Electronic commerce needed strong cryptography, and even the FBI and the NSA could not stop its development and adoption.

GOVERNMENT SURVEILLANCE COSTS BUSINESS

Those of us who fought the crypto wars, as we call them, thought we had won them in the 1990s. What the Snowden documents have shown us is that instead of dropping the notion of getting backdoor government access, the NSA and FBI just kept doing it in secret. Now that this has become public, US companies are losing business overseas because their non-US customers don't want their data collected by the US government.

NSA surveillance is costing US companies business in three different ways: people fleeing US cloud providers, people not buying US computer and networking equipment, and people not trusting US companies.

When the story about the NSA's getting user data directly from US cloud providers—the PRISM program—broke in 2013, businesses involved faced a severe public relations backlash. Almost immediately, articles appeared noting that US cloud companies were losing business and their counterparts in countries perceived as neutral, such as Switzerland, were gaining. One survey of British and Canadian companies from 2014 found that 25% of them were moving their data outside the US, even if it meant decreased performance. Another survey of companies found that NSA revelations made executives much more concerned about where their data was being stored.

Estimates of how much business will be lost by US cloud providers vary. One 2013 study by the Information Technology and Innovation Foundation foresees the loss of revenue at $22 to $35 billion over three years; that's 10% to 20% of US cloud providers' foreign market share. The Internet analysis firm Forrester Research believes that's low; it estimates three-year losses at $180 billion because some US companies will also move to foreign cloud providers.

US computer and networking companies are also taking severe hits. Cisco reported 2013 fourth quarter revenue declines of 8% to 10%. AT&T also reported earnings losses, and had problems with its European expansion plans. IBM lost sales in China. So did Qualcomm. Verizon lost a large German government contract. There's more. I have attended private meetings where large US software companies complained about significant loss of foreign sales. Cisco's CEO John Chambers wrote to the Obama administration, saying that NSA's hacking of US equipment "will undermine confidence in our industry and in the ability of technology companies to deliver products globally."

Chambers's comments echo the third aspect of the competitiveness problem facing US companies in the wake of Snowden: they're no longer trusted. The world now knows that US telcos give the NSA access to the Internet backbone and that US cloud providers give it access to user accounts. The world now knows that the NSA intercepts US-sold computer equipment in transit and surreptitiously installs monitoring hardware. The world knows that a secret court compels US companies to make themselves available for NSA eavesdropping, and then orders them to lie about it in public. Remember the Lavabit story from Chapter 5?

All of this mistrust was exacerbated by the Obama administration's repeated reassurances that only non-Americans were the focus of most of the NSA's efforts. More than half of the revenue of many cloud companies comes from outside the US. Facebook's Mark Zuckerberg said it best in a 2013 interview: "The government response was, 'Oh don't worry, we're not spying on any Americans.' Oh, wonderful: that's really helpful to companies trying to serve people around the world, and that's really going to inspire confidence in American internet companies."

To be fair, we don't know how much of this backlash is a temporary blip because NSA surveillance was in the news, and how much of it will be permanent. We know that several countries—Germany is the big one—are trying to build a domestic cloud infrastructure to keep their national data out of the NSA's hands. German courts have recently ruled against data collection practices by Google, Facebook, and Apple, and the German government is considering banning all US companies that cooperate with the

NSA. Data privacy is shaping up to be the new public safety requirement for international commerce.

It's also a new contractual requirement. Increasingly, large US companies are requiring their IT vendors to sign contracts warranting that there are no backdoors in their IT systems. More specifically, the contractual language requires the vendors to warrant that there is nothing that would allow a third party to access their corporate data. This makes it harder for IT companies to cooperate with the NSA or with any other government agency, because it exposes them to direct contractual liability to their biggest and most sophisticated customers. And to the extent they cannot sign such a guarantee, they're going to lose business to companies who can.

We also don't know what sort of increase to expect in competitive products and services from other countries around the world. Many firms in Europe, Asia, and South America are stepping in to take advantage of this new wariness. If the 1990s crypto wars are any guide, hundreds of non-US companies are going to provide IT products that are beyond the reach of US law: software products, cloud services, social networking sites, networking equipment, everything. Regardless of whether these new products are actually more secure—other countries are probably building backdoors in the products they can control—or even beyond the reach of the NSA, the cost of NSA surveillance to American business will be huge.

CORPORATE SURVEILLANCE COSTS BUSINESS

It's been almost an axiom that no one will pay for privacy. This generalization may have been true once, but the attitudes are changing.

People are now much more cognizant of who has access to their data, and for years there have been indications that they're ready to pay for privacy. A 2000 study found that US Internet spending would increase by $6 billion a year if customers felt their privacy was being protected when they made purchases. And a 2007 study found that customers were willing to pay more to have their privacy protected: $0.60 per $15 item. Post-Snowden, many companies are advertising protection from government surveillance.

Most companies don't offer privacy as a market differentiating feature, but there are exceptions. DuckDuckGo is a search engine whose business model revolves around *not* tracking its users. Wickr offers encrypted messaging. Ello is a social network that doesn't track its users. These are nowhere near as big as their established competitors, but they're viable businesses. And new ones are opening up shop all the time.

We are seeing the rising importance of customer and user privacy in the increasing number of corporations with chief privacy officers: senior executives responsible for managing the legal and reputational risk of the personal data the corporation holds. These executives have their own organization, the International Association of Privacy Professionals, and are establishing rules and regulations even in the absence of government impetus. They're doing this because it's good for business.

10

Privacy

The most common misconception about privacy is that it's about having something to hide. "If you aren't doing anything wrong, then you have nothing to hide," the saying goes, with the obvious implication that privacy only aids wrongdoers.

If you think about it, though, this makes no sense. We do nothing wrong when we make love, go to the bathroom, or sing in the shower. We do nothing wrong when we search for a job without telling our current employer. We do nothing wrong when we seek out private places for reflection or conversation, when we choose not to talk about something emotional or personal, when we use envelopes for our mail, or when we confide in a friend and no one else.

Moreover, even those who say that don't really believe it. In a 2009 interview, Google CEO Eric Schmidt put it this way: "If you have something that you don't want anyone to know, maybe you shouldn't be doing it in the first place." But in 2005, Schmidt banned employees from talking to reporters at CNET because a reporter disclosed personal details about Schmidt in an article. Facebook's Mark Zuckerberg declared in 2010 that privacy is no longer a "social norm," but bought the four houses abutting his Palo Alto home to help ensure his own privacy.

There are few secrets we don't tell *someone*, and we continue to believe something is private even after we've told that person. We write intimate letters to lovers and friends, talk to our doctors about things we wouldn't tell anyone else, and say things in business meetings we wouldn't say in public. We use pseudonyms to separate our professional selves from our personal selves, or to safely try out something new.

Facebook's CEO Mark Zuckerberg showed a remarkable naïveté when he stated, "You have one identity. The days of you having a different image for your work friends or co-workers and for the other people you know are probably coming to an end pretty quickly. Having two identities for yourself is an example of a lack of integrity."

We're not the same to everyone we know and meet. We act differently when we're with our families, our friends, our work colleagues, and so on. We have different table manners at home and at a restaurant. We tell different stories to our children than to our drinking buddies. It's not necessarily that we're lying, although sometimes we do; it's that we reveal different facets of ourselves to different people. This is something innately human. Privacy is what allows us to act appropriately in whatever setting we find ourselves. In the privacy of our home or bedroom, we can relax in a way that we can't when someone else is around.

Privacy is an inherent human right, and a requirement for maintaining the human condition with dignity and respect. It is about choice, and having the power to control how you present yourself to the world. Internet ethnographer danah boyd puts it this way: "Privacy doesn't just depend on agency; being able to achieve privacy is an expression *of* agency."

When we lose privacy, we lose control of how we present ourselves. We lose control when something we say on Facebook to one group of people gets accidentally shared with another, and we lose complete control when our data is collected by the government. "How did he know that?" we ask. How did I lose control of who knows about my traumatic childhood, my penchant for tasteless humor, or my vacation to the Dominican Republic? You may know this feeling: you felt it when your mother friended you on Facebook, or on any other social networking site that used to be just you and your friends. Privacy violations are intrusions.

There's a strong physiological basis for privacy. Biologist Peter Watts makes the point that a desire for privacy is innate: mammals in particular don't respond well to surveillance. We consider it a physical threat, because animals in the natural world are surveilled by predators. Surveillance makes us feel like prey, just as it makes the surveillors act like predators.

Psychologists, sociologists, philosophers, novelists, and technologists have all written about the effects of constant surveillance, or even just the perception of constant surveillance. Studies show that we are less healthy, both physically and emotionally. We have feelings of low self-esteem, depression, and anxiety. Surveillance strips us of our dignity. It threatens our very selves as individuals. It's a dehumanizing tactic employed in prisons and detention camps around the world.

Violations of privacy are not all equal. Context matters. There's a difference between a Transportation Security Administration (TSA) officer finding porn in your suitcase and your spouse finding it. There's a difference between the police learning about your drug use and your friends learning about it. And violations of privacy aren't all equally damaging. Those of us in marginal socioeconomic situations—and marginalized racial, political, ethnic, and religious groups—are affected more. Those of us in powerful positions who are subject to people's continued approval are affected more. The lives of some of us depend on privacy.

Our privacy is under assault from constant surveillance. Understanding how this occurs is critical to understanding what's at stake.

THE EPHEMERAL

Through most of history, our interactions and conversations have been ephemeral. It's the way we naturally think about conversation. Exceptions were rare enough to be noteworthy: a preserved diary, a stenographer transcribing a courtroom proceeding, a political candidate making a recorded speech.

This has changed. Companies have fewer face-to-face meetings. Friends socialize online. My wife and I have intimate conversations by text message. We all behave as if these conversations were ephemeral, but they're not. They're saved in ways we have no control over.

On-the-record conversations are hard to delete. Oliver North learned this way back in 1987, when messages he thought he had deleted turned out to have been saved by the White House PROFS Notes system, an early form of e-mail. Bill Gates learned this a decade later, when his conversational e-mails were provided to opposing counsel as part of Microsoft's antitrust litigation discovery process. And over 100 female celebrities learned it in 2014, when intimate self-portraits—some supposedly deleted—were stolen from their iCloud accounts and shared further and wider than they had ever intended.

It's harder and harder to be ephemeral. Voice conversation is largely still unrecorded, but how long will that last? Retail store surveillance systems register our presence, even if we are doing nothing but browsing and even if we pay for everything in cash. Some bars record the IDs of everyone who enters. I can't even buy a glass of wine on an airplane with cash anymore. Pervasive life recorders will make this much worse.

Science fiction writer Charles Stross described this as the end of prehistory. We won't forget anything, because we'll always be able to retrieve it from some computer's memory. This is new to our species, and will be a boon to both future historians and those of us in the present who want better data for self-assessment and reflection.

Having everything recorded and permanently available will change us both individually and as a society. Our perceptions and memories aren't nearly as sharp as we think they are. We fail to notice things, even important things. We misremember, even things we are sure we recall correctly. We forget important things we were certain we never would. People who keep diaries know this; old entries can read as if they were written by someone else. I have already noticed how having a record of all of my e-mail going back two decades makes a difference in how I think about my personal past.

One-fourth of American adults have criminal records. Even minor infractions can follow people forever and have a huge impact on their lives—this is why many governments have a process for expunging criminal records after some time has passed. Losing the ephemeral means that everything you say and do will be associated with you forever.

Having conversations that disappear as soon as they occur is a social norm that allows us to be more relaxed and comfortable, and to say things we might not say if a tape recorder were running. Over the longer term, forgetting—and misremembering—is how we process our history. Forgetting is an important enabler of forgiving. Individual and social memory fades, and past hurts become less sharp; this helps us forgive past wrongs. I'm not convinced that my marriage would be improved by the ability to produce transcripts of old arguments. Losing the ephemeral will be an enormous social and psychological change, and not one that I think our society is prepared for.

ALGORITHMIC SURVEILLANCE

One of the common defenses of mass surveillance is that it's being done by algorithms and not people, so it doesn't compromise our privacy. That's just plain wrong.

The distinction between human and computer surveillance is politically important. Ever since Snowden provided reporters with a trove of top-secret documents, we've learned about all sorts of NSA word games. The word "collect" has a very special definition, according to the Department of Defense. It doesn't mean collect; it means that a person looks at, or analyzes, the data. In 2013, Director of National Intelligence James Clapper likened the NSA's trove of accumulated data to a library. All those books are stored on the shelves, but very few are actually read. "So the task for us in the interest of preserving security and preserving civil liberties and privacy is to be as precise as we possibly can be when we go in that library and look for the books that we need to open up and actually read."

Think of that friend of yours who has thousands of books in his house. According to this ridiculous definition, the only books he can claim to have collected are the ones he's read.

This is why Clapper asserts he didn't lie in a Senate hearing when he replied "no" to the question "Does the NSA collect any type of data at all on millions or hundreds of millions of Americans?" From the military's perspective, it's not surveillance until a human being looks at the data, even if algorithms developed and implemented by defense personnel or contractors have analyzed it many times over.

This isn't the first time we've heard this argument. It was central to Google's defense of its context-sensitive advertising in the early days of Gmail. Google's computers examine each individual e-mail and insert a content-related advertisement in the footer. But no human reads those Gmail messages, only a computer. As one

Google executive told me privately in the early days of Gmail, "Worrying about a computer reading your e-mail is like worrying about your dog seeing you naked."

But it's not, and the dog example demonstrates why. When you're watched by a dog, you're not overly concerned, for three reasons. The dog can't understand or process what he's seeing in the same way another person can. The dog won't remember or base future decisions on what he's seeing in the same way another person can. And the dog isn't able to tell anyone—not a person or another dog—what he's seeing.

When you're watched by a computer, none of that dog analogy applies. The computer is processing what it sees, and basing actions on it. You might be told that the computer isn't saving the data, but you have no assurance that that's true. You might be told that the computer won't alert a person if it perceives something of interest, but you can't know whether that's true. You have no way of confirming that no person will perceive whatever decision the computer makes, and that you won't be judged or discriminated against on the basis of what the computer sees.

Moreover, when a computer stores your data, there's always a risk of exposure. Privacy policies could change tomorrow, permitting new use of old data without your express consent. Some hacker or criminal could break in and steal your data. The organization that has your data could use it in some new and public way, or sell it to another organization. The FBI could serve a National Security Letter on the data owner. On the other hand, there isn't a court in the world that can get a description of you naked from your dog.

The primary difference between a computer and a dog is that the computer communicates with other people and the dog does not—at least, not well enough to matter. Computer algorithms are written by people, and their output is used by people. And when we think of computer algorithms surveilling us or analyzing our personal data, we need to think about the people behind those algorithms. Whether or not anyone actually looks at our data, the very facts that (1) they could, and (2) they guide the algorithms that do, make it surveillance.

You know this is true. If you believed what Clapper said, then you wouldn't object to a camera in your bedroom—as long as there were rules governing when the police could look at the footage. You wouldn't object to being compelled to wear a government-issued listening device 24/7, as long as your bureaucratic monitors followed those same rules. If you do object, it's because you realize that the privacy harm comes from the automatic collection and algorithmic analysis, regardless of whether or not a person is directly involved in the process.

IDENTIFICATION AND ANONYMITY

We all have experience with identifying ourselves on the Internet. Some websites tie your online identity to your real identity: banks, websites for some government services, and so on. Some tie your online identity to a payment system—generally credit cards—and others to your bank account or cell phone. Some websites don't care about your real identity, and allow you to maintain a unique username just for that site. Many more sites could work that way. Apple's iTunes, for example, could be so designed that it doesn't know who you really are, just that you're authorized to access a particular set of audio and video files.

The means to perform identification and authentication include passwords, biometrics, and tokens. Many people, myself included, have written extensively about the various systems and their relative strengths and weaknesses. I'll spare you the details; the takeaway is that none of these systems is perfect, but all are generally good enough for their applications. Authentication basically works.

It works because the people involved want to be identified. You want to convince Hotmail that it's your account; you want to convince your bank that it's your money. And while you might not want AT&T to be able to tie all the Internet browsing you do on your smartphone to your identity, you do want the phone network to transmit your calls to you. All of these systems are trying to answer the following question: "Is this the person she claims to be?" That is why it's so easy to gather data about us online; most of it comes from sources where we've intentionally identified ourselves.

Attribution of anonymous activity to a particular person is a much harder problem. In this case, the person doesn't necessarily want to be identified. He is making an anonymous comment on a website. Or he's launching a cyberattack against your network. In such a case, the systems have to answer the harder question: "Who is this?"

At a very basic level, we are unable to identify individual pieces of hardware and software when a malicious adversary is trying to evade detection. We can't attach identifying information to data packets zipping around the Internet. We can't verify the identity of a person sitting in front of a random keyboard somewhere on the planet. Solving this problem isn't a matter of overcoming some engineering challenges; this inability is inherent in how the Internet works.

This means that we can't conclusively figure out who left an anonymous comment on a blog. (It could have been posted using a public computer, or a shared IP address.) We can't conclusively identify the sender of an e-mail. (Those headers can be spoofed; spammers do it all the time.) We can't conclusively determine who was behind a series of failed log-ins to your bank account, or a cyberattack against our nation's infrastructure.

We can't even be sure whether a particular attack was criminal or military in origin, or which government was behind it. The 2007 cyberattack against Estonia, often talked about as the first cyber-war, was either conducted by a group associated with the Russian government or by a disaffected 22-year-old.

When we do manage to attribute an attack—be it to a mischievous high schooler, a bank robber, or a team of state-sanctioned cyberwarriors—we usually do so after extensive forensic analysis or because the attacker gave himself away in some other manner. It took analysts months to identify China as the definitive source of the *New York Times* attacks in 2012, and we didn't know for sure who was behind Stuxnet until the US admitted it. This is a very difficult problem, and one we're not likely to solve anytime soon.

Over the years, there have been many proposals to eliminate anonymity on the Internet. The idea is that if everything anyone did was attributable—if all actions could be traced to their source—then it would be easy to identify criminals, spammers, stalkers, and Internet trolls. Basically, everyone would get the Internet equivalent of a driver's license.

This is an impossible goal. First of all, we don't have the real-world infrastructure to provide Internet user credentials based on other identification systems—passports, national identity cards, driver's licenses, whatever—which is what would be needed. We certainly don't have the infrastructure to do that globally.

Even if we did, it would be impossible to make it secure. Every one of our existing identity systems is already subverted by teenagers trying to buy alcohol—and that's a face-to-face transaction. A new one isn't going to be any better. And even if it were, it still wouldn't work. It is always possible to set up an anonymity service on top of an identity system. This fact already annoys countries like China that want to identify everyone using the Internet on their territory.

This might seem to contradict what I wrote in Chapter 3—that it is easy to identify people on the Internet who are trying to stay anonymous. This can be done if you have captured enough data streams to correlate and are willing to put in the investigative time. The only way to effectively reduce anonymity on the Internet is through massive surveillance. The examples from Chapter 3 all relied on piecing together different clues, and all took time. It's much harder to trace a single Internet connection back to its source: a single e-mail, a single web connection, a single attack.

The open question is whether the process of identification through correlation and analysis can be automated. Can we build computer systems smart enough to analyze surveillance information to identify individual people, as in the examples we saw in Chapter 3, on a large-scale basis? Not yet, but maybe soon.

It's being worked on. Countries like China and Russia want automatic systems to ferret out dissident voices on the Internet. The entertainment industry wants similar systems to identify movie and music pirates. And the US government wants the same systems to identify people and organizations it feels are threats, ranging from lone individuals to foreign governments.

In 2012, US Secretary of Defense Leon Panetta said publicly that the US has "made significant advances in . . . identifying the origins" of cyberattacks. My guess is that we have not developed some new science or engineering that fundamentally alters the balance between Internet identifiability and anonymity. Instead, it's more likely that we have penetrated our adversaries' networks so deeply that we can spy on and understand their planning processes.

Of course, anonymity cuts both ways, since it can also protect hate speech and criminal activity. But while identification can be important, anonymity is valuable for all the reasons I've discussed in this chapter. It protects privacy, it empowers individuals, and it's fundamental to liberty.

11

Security

O ur security is important. Crime, terrorism, and foreign aggression are threats both in and out of cyberspace. They're not the only threats in town, though, and I just spent the last four chapters delineating others.

We need to defend against a panoply of threats, and this is where we start having problems. Ignoring the risk of overaggressive police or government tyranny in an effort to protect ourselves from terrorism makes as little sense as ignoring the risk of terrorism in an effort to protect ourselves from police overreach.

Unfortunately, as a society we tend to focus on only one threat at a time and minimize the others. Even worse, we tend to focus on rare and spectacular threats and ignore the more frequent and pedestrian ones. So we fear flying more than driving, even though the former is much safer. Or we fear terrorists more than the police, even though in the US you're nine times more likely to be killed by a police officer than by a terrorist.

We let our fears get in the way of smart security. Defending against some threats at the expense of others is a failing strategy, and we need to find ways of balancing them all.

SECURITY FROM TERRORISTS AND CRIMINALS

The NSA repeatedly uses a connect-the-dots metaphor to justify its surveillance activities. Again and again—after 9/11, after the Underwear Bomber, after the Boston Marathon bombings—government is criticized for not connecting the dots.

However, this is a terribly misleading metaphor. Connecting the dots in a coloring book is easy, because they're all numbered and visible. In real life, the dots can only be recognized after the fact.

That doesn't stop us from demanding to know why the authorities couldn't connect the dots. The warning signs left by the Fort Hood shooter, the Boston Marathon bombers, and the Isla Vista shooter look obvious in hindsight. Nassim Taleb, an expert on risk engineering, calls this tendency the "narrative fallacy." Humans are natural storytellers, and the world of stories is much more tidy, predictable, and coherent than reality. Millions of people behave strangely enough to attract the FBI's notice, and almost all of them are harmless. The TSA's no-fly list has over 20,000 people on it. The Terrorist Identities Datamart Environment, also known as the watch list, has 680,000, 40% of whom have "no recognized terrorist group affiliation."

Data mining is offered as the technique that will enable us to connect those dots. But while corporations are successfully mining our personal data in order to target advertising, detect financial fraud, and perform other tasks, three critical issues make data mining an inappropriate tool for finding terrorists.

The first, and most important, issue is error rates. For advertising, data mining can be successful even with a large error rate, but finding terrorists requires a much higher degree of accuracy than data-mining systems can possibly provide.

Data mining works best when you're searching for a well-defined profile, when there are a reasonable number of events per year, and when the cost of false alarms is low. Detecting credit card fraud is one of data mining's security success stories: all credit card companies mine their transaction databases for spending patterns that indicate a stolen card. There are over a billion active credit cards in circulation in the United States, and nearly 8% of those are fraudulently used each year. Many credit card thefts share a pattern—purchases in locations not normally frequented by the cardholder, and purchases of travel, luxury goods, and easily fenced items—and in many cases data-mining systems can minimize the losses by preventing fraudulent transactions. The only cost of a false alarm is a phone call to the cardholder asking her to verify a couple of her purchases.

Similarly, the IRS uses data mining to identify tax evaders, the police use it to predict crime hot spots, and banks use it to predict loan defaults. These applications have had mixed success, based on the data and the application, but they're all within the scope of what data mining can accomplish.

Terrorist plots are different, mostly because whereas fraud is common, terrorist attacks are very rare. This means that even highly accurate terrorism prediction systems will be so flooded with false alarms that they will be useless.

The reason lies in the mathematics of detection. All detection systems have errors, and system designers can tune them to minimize either false positives or false negatives. In a terrorist-detection system, a false positive occurs when the system mistakenly identifies something harmless as a threat. A false negative occurs when the system misses an actual attack. Depending on how you "tune" your detection system, you can increase the number of false positives to assure you are less likely to miss an attack, or you can reduce the number of false positives at the expense of missing attacks.

Because terrorist attacks are so rare, false positives completely overwhelm the system, no matter how well you tune. And I mean *completely*: millions of people will be falsely accused for every real terrorist plot the system finds, if it ever finds any.

We might be able to deal with all of the innocents being flagged by the system if the cost of false positives were minor. Think about the full-body scanners at airports. Those alert all the time when scanning people. But a TSA officer can easily check for a false alarm with a simple pat-down. This doesn't work for a more general data-based terrorism-detection system. Each alert requires a lengthy investigation to determine whether it's real or not. That takes time and money, and prevents intelligence officers from doing other productive work. Or, more pithily, when you're watching everything, you're not seeing anything.

The US intelligence community also likens finding a terrorist plot to looking for a needle in a haystack. And, as former NSA director General Keith Alexander said, "you need the haystack to find the needle." That statement perfectly illustrates the problem with mass surveillance and bulk collection. When you're looking for the needle, the last thing you want to do is pile lots more hay on it. More specifically, there is no scientific rationale for believing that adding irrelevant data about innocent people makes it easier to find a terrorist attack, and lots of evidence that it does not. You might be adding slightly more signal, but you're also adding much more noise. And despite the NSA's "collect it all" mentality, its own documents bear this out. The military intelligence community even talks about the problem of "drinking from a fire hose": having so much irrelevant data that it's impossible to find the important bits.

We saw this problem with the NSA's eavesdropping program:

the false positives overwhelmed the system. In the years after 9/11, the NSA passed to the FBI thousands of tips per month; every one of them turned out to be a false alarm. The cost was enormous, and ended up frustrating the FBI agents who were obligated to investigate all the tips. We also saw this with the Suspicious Activity Reports—or SAR—database: tens of thousands of reports, and no actual results. And all the telephone metadata the NSA collected led to just one success: the conviction of a taxi driver who sent $8,500 to a Somali group that posed no direct threat to the US— and that was probably trumped up so the NSA would have better talking points in front of Congress.

The second problem with using data-mining techniques to try to uncover terrorist plots is that each attack is unique. Who would have guessed that two pressure-cooker bombs would be delivered to the Boston Marathon finish line in backpacks by a Boston college kid and his older brother? Each rare individual who carries out a terrorist attack will have a disproportionate impact on the criteria used to decide who's a likely terrorist, leading to ineffective detection strategies.

The third problem is that the people the NSA is trying to find are wily, and they're trying to avoid detection. In the world of personalized marketing, the typical surveillance subject isn't trying to hide his activities. That is not true in a police or national security context. An adversarial relationship makes the problem *much* harder, and means that most commercial big data analysis tools just don't work. A commercial tool can simply ignore people trying to hide and assume benign behavior on the part of everyone else. Government data-mining techniques can't do that, because those are the very people they're looking for.

Adversaries vary in the sophistication of their ability to avoid surveillance. Most criminals and terrorists—and political dissidents, sad to say—are pretty unsavvy and make lots of mistakes.

But that's no justification for data mining; targeted surveillance could potentially identify them just as well. The question is whether mass surveillance performs sufficiently better than targeted surveillance to justify its extremely high costs. Several analyses of all the NSA's efforts indicate that it does not.

The three problems listed above cannot be fixed. Data mining is simply the wrong tool for this job, which means that all the mass surveillance required to feed it cannot be justified. When he was NSA director, General Keith Alexander argued that ubiquitous surveillance would have enabled the NSA to prevent 9/11. That seems unlikely. He wasn't able to prevent the Boston Marathon bombings in 2013, even though one of the bombers was on the terrorist watch list and both had sloppy social media trails—and this was after a dozen post-9/11 years of honing techniques. The NSA collected data on the Tsarnaevs before the bombing, but hadn't realized that it was more important than the data they collected on millions of other people.

This point was made in the 9/11 Commission Report. That report described a failure to "connect the dots," which proponents of mass surveillance claim requires collection of more data. But what the report actually said was that the intelligence community had all the information about the plot *without* mass surveillance, and that the failures were the result of inadequate analysis.

Mass surveillance didn't catch underwear bomber Umar Farouk Abdulmutallab in 2006, even though his father had repeatedly warned the US government that he was dangerous. And the liquid bombers (they're the reason governments prohibit passengers from bringing large bottles of liquids, creams, and gels on airplanes in their carry-on luggage) were captured in 2006 in their London apartment not due to mass surveillance but through traditional investigative police work. Whenever we learn about an NSA success, it invariably comes from targeted surveillance rather than from mass surveillance. One analysis showed that the FBI identifies potential terrorist plots from reports of suspicious activity, reports of plots, and investigations of other, unrelated, crimes.

This is a critical point. Ubiquitous surveillance and data mining are not suitable tools for finding dedicated criminals or terrorists. We taxpayers are wasting billions on mass-surveillance programs, and not getting the security we've been promised. More importantly, the money we're wasting on these ineffective surveillance programs is not being spent on investigation, intelligence, and emergency response: tactics that have been proven to work.

Mass surveillance and data mining are much more suitable for tasks of population discrimination: finding people with certain political beliefs, people who are friends with certain individuals, people who are members of secret societies, and people who attend certain meetings and rallies. Those are all individuals of interest to a government intent on social control like China. The reason data mining works to find them is that, like credit card fraudsters, political dissidents are likely to share a well-defined profile. Additionally, under authoritarian rule the inevitable false alarms are less of a problem; charging innocent people with sedition instills fear in the populace.

More than just being ineffective, the NSA's surveillance efforts have actually made us less secure. In order to understand how, I need to explain a bit about Internet security, encryption, and computer vulnerabilities. The following three sections are short but important.

INTERNET ATTACK VERSUS DEFENSE

In any security situation, there's a basic arms race between attack and defense. One side might have an advantage for a while, and then technology changes and gives the other side an advantage. And then it changes back.

Think about the history of military technology and tactics. In the early 1800s, military defenders had an advantage; charging a line was much more dangerous than defending it. Napoleon first figured out how to attack effectively using the weaponry of the time. By World War I, firearms—particularly the machine gun—had become so powerful that the defender again had an advantage; trench warfare was devastating to the attacker. The tide turned again in World War II with the invention of blitzkrieg warfare, and the attacker again gained the advantage.

Right now, both on the Internet and with computers in general, the attacker has the advantage. This is true for several reasons.

- It's easier to break things than to fix them.
- Complexity is the worst enemy of security, and our systems are getting more complex all the time.
- The nature of computerized systems makes it easier for the attacker to find one exploitable vulnerability in a system than for the defender to find and fix *all* vulnerabilities in the system.
- An attacker can choose a particular attack and concentrate his efforts, whereas the defender has to defend against every possibility.
- Software security is generally poor; we simply don't know how to write secure software and create secure computer systems. Yes, we keep improving, but we're still not doing very well.
- Computer security is very technical, and it's easy for average users to get it wrong and subvert whatever security they might have.

This isn't to say that Internet security is useless, far from it. Attack might be easier, but defense is still possible. Good security makes many kinds of attack harder, more costly, and more risky. Against an attacker who isn't sufficiently skilled, good security may protect you completely.

In the security field, we think in terms of risk management. You identify what your risk is, and what reasonable precautions you should take. So, as someone with a computer at home, you should have a good antivirus program, turn automatic updates on so your software is up-to-date, avoid dodgy websites and e-mail attachments from strangers, and keep good backups. These plus several more essential steps that are fairly easy to implement will leave you secure enough against common criminals and hackers. On the other hand, if you're a political dissident in China, Syria, or Ukraine trying to avoid arrest or assassination, your precautions must be more comprehensive. Ditto if you're a criminal trying to evade the police, a businessman trying to prevent corporate espionage, or a government embassy trying to thwart military espionage. If you're particularly concerned about corporations collecting your data, you'll need a different set of security measures.

For many organizations, security comes down to basic economics. If the cost of security is less than the likely cost of losses due to lack of security, security wins. If the cost of security is more than the likely cost of losses, accept the losses. For individuals, a lot of psychology mixes in with the economics. It's hard to put a dollar value on a privacy violation, or on being put on a government watch list. But the general idea is the same: cost versus benefit.

Of critical import to this analysis is the difference between random and targeted attacks.

Most criminal attacks are opportunistic. In 2013, hackers broke into the network of the retailer Target Corporation and stole credit card and other personal information belonging to 40 million people. It was the biggest known breach of its kind at the time, and a catastrophe for the company—its CEO, Gregg Steinhafel, resigned over the incident—but the criminals didn't specifically pick Target for any ideological reasons. They were interested in obtaining credit card numbers to commit fraud, and any company's database would have done. If Target had had better security, the criminals would have gone elsewhere. It's like the typical home burglar. He wants to rob a home. And while he might have some selection criteria as to neighborhood and home type, he doesn't particularly care which one he chooses. Your job as a homeowner is to make your home less attractive to the burglar than your neighbor's home. Against undirected attacks, what entails good security is relative.

Compare this with the 2012 attack against the *New York Times* by Chinese hackers, possibly ones associated with the government. In this case, the attackers were trying to monitor reporters' communications with Chinese dissidents. They specifically targeted the *New York Times'* e-mails and internal network because that's where the information they wanted was located. Against targeted attacks, what matters is your absolute level of security. It is irrelevant what kind of security your neighbors have; you need to be secure against the specific capabilities of your attackers.

Another example: Google scans the e-mail of all Gmail users, and uses information gleaned from it to target advertising. Of course, there isn't a Google employee doing this; a computer does it automatically. So if you write your e-mail in some obscure language that Google doesn't automatically translate, you'll be secure against Google's algorithms—because it's not worth it to Google to manually translate your e-mails. But if you're suddenly under targeted investigation by the FBI, officers will take that time and translate your e-mails.

Keep this security distinction between mass and targeted surveillance in mind; we'll return to it again and again.

THE VALUE OF ENCRYPTION

I just described Internet security as an arms race, with the attacker having an advantage over the defender. The advantage might be major, but it's still an advantage of degree. It's never the case that one side has some technology so powerful that the other side can't possibly win—except in movies and comic books.

Encryption, and cryptography in general, is the one exception to this. Not only is defense easier than attack; defense is so much easier than attack that attack is basically impossible.

There's an enormous inherent mathematical advantage in encrypting versus trying to break encryption. Fundamentally, security is based on the length of the key; a small change in key length results in an enormous amount of extra work for the attacker. The difficulty increases exponentially. A 64-bit key might take an attacker a day to break. A 65-bit key would take the same attacker twice the amount of time to break, or two days. And a 128-bit key—which is at most twice the work to use for encryption—would take the same attacker 2^{64} times longer, or one million billion years to break. (For comparison, Earth is 4.5 billion years old.)

This is why you hear statements like "This can't be broken before the heat death of the universe, even if you assume the attacker builds a giant computer using all the atoms of the planet." The weird thing is that those are not exaggerations. They're just effects of the mathematical imbalance between encrypting and breaking.

At least, that's the theory. The problem is that encryption is just a bunch of math, and math has no agency. To turn that encryption math into something that can actually provide some security for you, it has to be written in computer code. And that code needs to run on a computer: one with hardware, an operating system, and other software. And that computer needs to be operated by a person and be on a network. All of those things will invariably introduce vulnerabilities that undermine the perfection of the mathematics, and put us back in the security situation discussed earlier—one that is strongly biased towards attack.

The NSA certainly has some classified mathematics and massive computation capabilities that let it break some types of encryption more easily. It built the Multiprogram Research Facility in Oak Ridge, Tennessee, for this purpose. But advanced as the agency's cryptanalytic capabilities are, we've learned from Snowden's documents that it largely uses those other vulnerabilities—in computers, people, and networks—to circumvent encryption rather than tackling it head-on. The NSA hacks systems, just as Internet criminals do. It has its Tailored Access Operations group break into networks and steal keys. It exploits bad user-chosen passwords, and default or weak keys. It obtains court orders and demands copies of encryption keys. It secretly inserts weaknesses into products and standards.

Snowden put it like this in an online Q&A in 2013: "Encryption works. Properly implemented strong crypto systems are one of the few things that you can rely on. Unfortunately, endpoint security is so terrifically weak that NSA can frequently find ways around it."

But those other methods the NSA can use to get at encrypted data demonstrate exactly why encryption is so important. By leveraging that mathematical imbalance, cryptography forces an attacker to pursue these other routes. Instead of passively eavesdropping on a communications channel and collecting data on everyone, the attacker might have to break into a specific computer system and grab the plaintext. Those routes around the encryption require more work, more risk of exposure, and more targeting than bulk collection of unencrypted data does.

Remember the economics of big data: just as it is easier to save everything than to figure out what to save, it is easier to spy on everyone than to figure out who deserves to be spied on. Widespread encryption has the potential to render mass surveillance ineffective and to force eavesdroppers to choose their targets. This would be an enormous win for privacy, because attackers don't have the budget to pick everyone.

THE PREVALENCE OF VULNERABILITIES

Vulnerabilities are mistakes. They're errors in design or implementation—glitches in the code or hardware—that allow unauthorized intrusion into a system. So, for example, a cybercriminal might exploit a vulnerability to break into your computer, eavesdrop on your web connection, and steal the password you use to log in to your bank account. A government intelligence agency might use a vulnerability to break into the network of a foreign terrorist organization and disrupt its operations, or to steal a foreign corporation's intellectual property. Another government intelligence agency might take advantage of a vulnerability to eavesdrop on political dissidents, or terrorist cells, or rival government leaders. And a military might use a vulnerability to launch a cyberweapon. This is all hacking.

When someone discovers a vulnerability, she can use it either for defense or for offense. Defense means alerting the vendor and getting it patched—and publishing it so the community can learn from it. Lots of vulnerabilities are discovered by vendors themselves and patched without any fanfare. Others are discovered by researchers and ethical hackers.

Offense involves using the vulnerability to attack others. Unpublished vulnerabilities are called "zero-day" vulnerabilities; they're very valuable to attackers because no one is protected against them, and they can be used worldwide with impunity. Eventually the affected software's vendor finds out—the timing depends on how widely the vulnerability is exploited—and issues a patch to close it.

If an offensive military cyber unit or a cyberweapons manufacturer discovers the vulnerability, it will keep it secret for future use to build a cyberweapon. If used rarely and stealthily, the vulnerability might remain secret for a long time. If unused, it will remain secret until someone else discovers it.

Discoverers can sell vulnerabilities. There's a robust market in zero-days for attack purposes—both governments and cyberweapons manufacturers that sell to governments are buyers—and black markets where discoverers can sell to criminals. Some vendors offer bounties for vulnerabilities to spur defense research, but the rewards are much lower.

Undiscovered zero-day vulnerabilities are common. Every piece of commercial software—your smartphone, your computer, the embedded systems that run nuclear power plants—has hundreds if not thousands of vulnerabilities, most of them undiscovered. The science and engineering of programming just isn't good enough to produce flawless software, and that isn't going to change anytime soon. The economics of software development prioritize features and speed to market, not security.

What all this means is that the threat of hacking isn't going away. For the foreseeable future, it will always be possible for a sufficiently skilled attacker to find a vulnerability in a defender's system. This will be true for militaries building cyberweapons, intelligence agencies trying to break into systems in order to eavesdrop, and criminals of all kinds.

MAINTAINING AN INSECURE INTERNET

In Chapter 6, I discussed how the NSA uses both existing and specially created vulnerabilities to hack into systems. Its actions put surveillance ahead of security, and end up making us all less secure. Here's how the NSA and GCHQ think, according to a *Guardian* article on some of the Snowden documents: "Classified briefings between the agencies celebrate their success at 'defeating network security and privacy. . . .'"

Just how do governments go about defeating security and privacy? We know the NSA uses the following four main practices. Assume that the Russians, Chinese, and various other countries are using similar methods. And cybercriminals aren't far behind.

Stockpiling vulnerabilities in commercial software that we use every day, rather than making sure those security flaws get fixed. When the NSA discovers (or buys) a vulnerability, it can either alert the vendor and get a still-secret vulnerability fixed, or it can hold on to it and use it to eavesdrop on target computer systems. Both tactics support important US policy goals, but the NSA has to choose which one to pursue in each case.

Right now, the US—both at the NSA and at US Cyber Command—stockpiles zero-day vulnerabilities. How many it has is unclear. In 2014, the White House tried to clarify the country's policy on this in a blog post, but didn't really explain it. We know that a single cyberweapon, Stuxnet, used four zero-days. Using up that many for a single cyberattack implies that the government's stockpile is in the hundreds.

In congressional testimony, former NSA director Michael Hayden introduced the agency jargon NOBUS, "nobody but us"— that is, a vulnerability that nobody but us is likely to find or use. The NSA has a classified process to determine what it should do about vulnerabilities. The agency claims that it discloses and closes most of the vulnerabilities it finds, but holds back some—we don't know how many—that it believes are NOBUSes.

This approach seems to be the appropriate general framework, but it's impossible to apply in practice. Many of us in the security field don't know how to make NOBUS decisions, and we worry that the government can't, either.

This stockpiling puts everyone at risk. Unpatched vulnerabilities make us all less safe, because anyone can independently discover them and use them to attack us. They're inherently destabilizing, especially because they are only effective for a limited time. Even worse, each use runs the risk that others will learn about the vulnerability and use it for themselves. And they come in families; keeping one secret might mean that an entire class of vulnerabilities remains undiscovered and unpatched. The US and other Western countries are highly vulnerable to zero-days, because of our critical electronic infrastructure, intellectual property, and personal wealth. Countries like China and Russia are less vulnerable—North Korea much less—so they have considerably less incentive to get vulnerabilities fixed.

Inserting backdoors into widely used computer hardware and software products. Backdoors aren't new. The security industry has long worried about backdoors left in software by hackers, and has spent considerable effort trying to find and fix them. But now we know that the US government is deliberately inserting them into hardware and software products.

One of the NSA documents disclosed by Snowden describes the "SIGINT Enabling Project," one tactic of which is to "insert vulnerabilities into commercial encryption systems, IT systems, networks, and endpoint communications devices used by targets." We don't know much about this project: how much of it is done with the knowledge and consent of the manufacturers involved, and how much is done surreptitiously by either employees secretly working for the government or clandestine manipulation of the company's master source code files. We also don't know how well it has succeeded—the documents don't give us a lot of details—but we know it was funded at $250 million per year. We also don't know which other countries do the same things to systems designed by companies under their political control.

We know of a few examples. In Chapter 6, I talked about Microsoft weakening Skype for the NSA. The NSA also pressured Microsoft to put a backdoor in its BitLocker hard drive encryption software, although the company seems to have resisted. Presumably there have been other efforts involving other products; I've heard about several unsuccessful attempts privately.

Deliberately created vulnerabilities are very risky, because there is no way to implement backdoor access to any system that will ensure that only the government can take advantage of it. Government-mandated access forces companies to make their products and services less secure for everyone.

For example, between June 2004 and March 2005 someone wiretapped more than 100 cell phones belonging to members of the Greek government—the prime minister and the ministers of defense, foreign affairs, and justice—and other prominent Greek citizens. Swedish telecommunications provider Ericsson built this wiretapping capability into Vodafone products, but enabled it only for governments that requested it. Greece wasn't one of those governments, but some still-unknown party—a rival political group? organized crime?—figured out how to surreptitiously turn the feature on.

This wasn't an isolated incident. Something similar occurred in Italy in 2006. In 2010, Chinese hackers exploited an intercept system Google had put into Gmail to comply with US government surveillance requests. And in 2012, we learned that every phone switch sold to the Department of Defense had security vulnerabilities in its surveillance system; we don't know whether they were inadvertent or deliberately inserted.

The NSA regularly exploits backdoors built into systems by other countries for other purposes. For example, it used the wiretap capabilities built in to the Bermuda phone system to secretly intercept *all* the country's phone calls. Why does it believe the same thing won't be done to us?

Undermining encryption algorithms and standards. Another objective of the SIGINT Enabling Project is to "influence policies, standards and specifications for commercial public key technologies." Again, details are few, but I assume these efforts are more focused on proprietary standards like cell phone security than on public standards like encryption algorithms. For example, the NSA influenced the adoption of an encryption algorithm for GSM phones that it can easily break. The one public example we know of is the NSA's insertion of a backdoored random number generator into a common Internet standard, followed by efforts to get that generator used more widely. The intent was to subvert the encryption that people use to protect their Internet communications and web browsing, but it wasn't very successful.

Hacking the Internet. In Chapter 5, I talked about the NSA's TAO group and its hacking mission. Aside from directly breaking into computers and networking equipment, the NSA masquerades as Facebook and LinkedIn (and presumably other websites as well) to infiltrate target computers and redirect Internet traffic to its own dummy sites for eavesdropping purposes. The UK's GCHQ can find your private photos on Facebook, artificially increase traffic to a website, disrupt video from a website, delete computer accounts, hack online polls, and much more.

In addition to the extreme distrust that all these tactics engender amongst Internet users, they require the NSA to ensure that surveillance takes precedence over security. Instead of improving the security of the Internet for everyone's benefit, the NSA is ensuring that the Internet remains insecure for the agency's own convenience.

This hurts us all, because the NSA isn't the only actor out there that thrives on insecurity. Other governments and criminals benefit from the subversion of security. And a surprising number of the secret surveillance technologies revealed by Snowden aren't exclusive to the NSA, or even to other national intelligence organizations. They're just better-funded hacker tools. Academics have discussed ways to recreate much of the NSA's collection and analysis tools with open-source and commercial systems.

For example, when I was working with the *Guardian* on the Snowden documents, the one top-secret program the NSA desperately did not want us to expose was QUANTUM. This is the NSA's program for what is called packet injection—basically, a technology that allows the agency to hack into computers. Turns out, though, that the NSA was not alone in its use of this technology. The Chinese government uses packet injection to attack computers. The cyberweapons manufacturer Hacking Team sells packet injection technology to any government willing to pay for it. Criminals use it. And there are hacker tools that give the capability to individuals as well. All of these existed before I wrote about QUANTUM. By using its knowledge to attack others rather than to build up the Internet's defenses, the NSA has worked to ensure that *anyone* can use packet injection to hack into computers.

Even when technologies are developed inside the NSA, they don't remain exclusive for long. Today's top-secret programs become tomorrow's PhD theses and the next day's hacker tools. Techniques first developed for the military cyberweapon Stuxnet have ended up in criminal malware. The same password-cracking software that Elcomsoft sells to governments was used by hackers to hack celebrity photos from iCloud accounts. And once-secret techniques to monitor people's cell phones are now in common use.

The US government's desire for unfettered surveillance has already affected how the Internet works. When surveillance becomes multinational and cooperative, those needs will increasingly take precedence over others. And the architecture choices network engineers make to comply with government surveillance demands are likely to be around for decades, simply because it's easier to keep doing the same things than to change. By putting surveillance ahead of security, the NSA ensures the insecurity of us all.

COLLATERAL DAMAGE FROM CYBERATTACKS

As nations continue to hack each other, the Internet-using public is increasingly part of the collateral damage. Most of the time we don't know the details, but sometimes enough information bubbles to the surface that we do.

Three examples: Stuxnet's target was Iran, but the malware accidentally infected over 50,000 computers in India, Indonesia, Pakistan, and elsewhere, including computers owned by Chevron, and industrial plants in Germany; it may have been responsible for the failure of an Indian satellite in 2010. Snowden claims that the NSA accidentally caused an Internet blackout in Syria in 2012. Similarly, China's Great Firewall uses a technique called DNS injection to block access to certain websites; this technique regularly disrupts communications having nothing to do with China or the censored links.

The more nations attack each other through the global Internet—whether to gain intelligence or to inflict damage—the more civilian networks will become collateral damage.

HARM TO NATIONAL INTERESTS

In Chapter 9, I discussed how the NSA's activities harm US economic interests. It also harms the country's political interests.

Political scientist Ian Bremmer has argued that public revelations of the NSA's activities "have badly undermined US credibility with many of its allies." US interests have been significantly harmed on the world stage, as one country after another has learned about our snooping on its citizens or leaders: friendly countries in Europe, Latin America, and Asia. Relations between the US and Germany have been particularly strained since it became public that the NSA was tapping the cell phone of German chancellor Angela

Merkel. And Brazil's president Dilma Rousseff turned down an invitation to a US state dinner—the first time any world leader did that—because she and the rest of her country were incensed at NSA surveillance.

Much more is happening behind the scenes, over more private diplomatic channels. There's no soft-pedaling it; the US is undermining its global stature and leadership with its aggressive surveillance program.

PART THREE
WHAT TO DO ABOUT IT

12

Principles

The harms from mass surveillance are many, and the costs to individuals and society as a whole disproportionately outweigh the benefits. We can and must do something to rein it in. Before offering specific legal, technical, and social proposals, I want to start this section with some general principles. These are universal truths about surveillance and how we should deal with it that apply to both governments and corporations.

Articulating principles is the easy part. It's far more difficult to apply them in specific circumstances. "Life, liberty, and the pursuit of happiness" are principles we all agree on, but we only need to look at Washington, DC, to see how difficult it can be to apply them. I've been on many panels and debates where people on all sides of this issue agree on general principles about data collection, surveillance, oversight, security, and privacy, even though they disagree vehemently on how to apply those principles to the world at hand.

SECURITY *AND* PRIVACY

Often the debate is characterized as "security versus privacy." This simplistic view requires us to make some kind of fundamental trade-off between the two: in order to become secure, we must sacrifice our privacy and subject ourselves to surveillance. And if we want some level of privacy, we must recognize that we must sacrifice some security in order to get it.

It's a false trade-off. First, some security measures require people to give up privacy, but others don't impinge on privacy at all: door locks, tall fences, guards, reinforced cockpit doors on airplanes. And second, privacy and security are fundamentally aligned. When we have no privacy, we feel exposed and vulnerable; we feel less secure. Similarly, if our personal spaces and records are not secure, we have less privacy. The Fourth Amendment of the US Constitution talks about "the right of the people to be *secure* in their persons, houses, papers, and effects" (italics mine). Its authors recognized that privacy is fundamental to the security of the individual.

Framing the conversation as trading security for privacy leads to lopsided evaluations. Often, the trade-off is presented in terms of monetary cost: "How much would you pay for privacy?" or "How much would you pay for security?" But that's a false trade-off, too. The costs of insecurity are real and visceral, even in the abstract; the costs of privacy loss are nebulous in the abstract, and only become tangible when someone is faced with their aftereffects. This is why we undervalue privacy when we have it, and only recognize its true value when we don't. This is also why we often hear that no one wants to pay for privacy and that therefore security trumps privacy absolutely.

When the security versus privacy trade-off is framed as a life-and-death choice, all rational debate ends. How can anyone talk about privacy when lives are at stake? People who are scared will more readily sacrifice privacy in order to feel safer. This explains why the US government was given such free rein to conduct mass surveillance after 9/11. The government basically said that we all had to give up our privacy in exchange for security; most of us didn't know better, and thus accepted the Faustian bargain.

The problem is that the entire weight of insecurity is compared with the incremental invasion of privacy. US courts do this a lot, saying things on the order of, "We agree that there is a loss of privacy at stake in this or that government program, but the risk of a nuclear bomb going off in New York is just too great." That's a sloppy characterization of the trade-off. It's not the case that a nuclear detonation is impossible if we surveil, or inevitable if we don't. The probability is already very small, and the theoretical privacy-invading security program being considered could only reduce that number very slightly. That's the trade-off that needs to be considered.

More generally, our goal shouldn't be to find an acceptable trade-off between security and privacy, because we can and should maintain both together.

SECURITY OVER SURVEILLANCE

Security and surveillance are conflicting design requirements. A system built for security is harder to surveil. Conversely, a system built for easy surveillance is harder to secure. A built-in surveillance capability in a system is insecure, because we don't know how to build a system that only permits surveillance by the *right* sort of people. We saw this in Chapter 11.

We need to recognize that, to society as a whole, security is more critical than surveillance. That is, we need to choose a secure information infrastructure that inhibits surveillance instead of an insecure infrastructure that allows for easy surveillance.

The reasoning applies generally. Our infrastructure can be used for both good and bad purposes. Bank robbers drive on highways, use electricity, shop at hardware stores, and eat at all-night restaurants, just like honest people. Innocents and criminals alike use cell phones, e-mail, and Dropbox. It rains on the just and the unjust.

Despite this, society continues to function, because the honest, positive, and beneficial uses of our infrastructure far outweigh the dishonest, negative, and harmful ones. The percentage of the drivers on our highways who are bank robbers is negligible, as is the percentage of e-mail users who are criminals. It makes far more sense to design all of these systems for the majority of us who need security from criminals, telemarketers, and sometimes our own governments.

By prioritizing security, we would be protecting the world's information flows—including our own—from eavesdropping as well as more damaging attacks like theft and destruction. We would protect our information flows from governments, non-state actors, and criminals. We would be making the world safer overall.

Tor is an excellent example. It's free open-source software that you can use to browse anonymously on the Internet. First developed with funding from the US Naval Research Laboratory and then from the State Department, it's used by dissidents all over the world to evade surveillance and censorship. Of course, it's also used by criminals for the same purpose. Tor's developers are constantly updating the program to evade the Chinese government's attempts to ban it. We know that the NSA is continually trying to break it, and—at least as of a 2007 NSA document disclosed by Snowden— has been unsuccessful. We know that the FBI was hacking into computers in 2013 and 2014 because it couldn't break Tor. At the same time, we believe that individuals who work at both the NSA and the GCHQ are anonymously helping keep Tor secure. But this is the quandary: Tor is either strong enough to protect the anonymity of both those we like and those we don't like, or it's not strong enough to protect the anonymity of either.

Of course, there will never be a future in which no one spies. That's naïve. Governments have always spied, since the beginning of history; there are even a few spy stories in the Old Testament. The question is which sort of world we want to move towards. Do we want to reduce power imbalances by limiting government's abilities to monitor, censor, and control? Or do we allow governments to have increasingly more power over us?

"Security over surveillance" isn't an absolute rule, of course. There are times when it's necessary to design a system for protection from the minority of us who are dishonest. Airplane security is an example of that. The number of terrorists flying on planes is negligible compared with the number of nonterrorists, yet we design entire airports around those few, because a failure of security on an airplane is catastrophically more deadly than a terrorist bomb just about anywhere else. We don't (yet) design our entire society around terrorism prevention, though.

There are also times when we need to design appropriate surveillance into systems. We want shipping services to be able to track packages in real time. We want first responders to know where an emergency cell phone call is coming from. We don't use the word "surveillance" in these cases, of course; we use some less emotionally laden term like "package tracking."

The general principle here is that systems should be designed with the minimum surveillance necessary for them to function, and where surveillance is required they should gather the minimum necessary amount of information and retain it for the shortest time possible.

TRANSPARENCY

Transparency is vital to any open and free society. Open government laws and freedom of information laws let citizens know what the government is doing, and enable them to carry out their democratic duty to oversee its activities. Corporate disclosure laws perform similar functions in the private sphere. Of course, both corporations and governments have some need for secrecy, but the more they can be open, the more we can knowledgeably decide whether to trust them. Right now in the US, we have strong open government and freedom of information laws, but far too much information is exempted from them.

For personal data, transparency is pretty straightforward: people should be entitled to know what data is being collected about them, what data is being archived about them, and how data about them is being used—and by whom. And in a world that combines an international Internet with country-specific laws about surveillance and control, we need to know where data about us is being stored. We are much more likely to be comfortable with surveillance at any level if we know these things. Privacy policies should provide this information, instead of being so long and deliberately obfuscating that they shed little light.

We also need transparency in the algorithms that judge us on the basis of our data, either by publishing the code or by explaining how they work. Right now, we cannot judge the fairness of TSA algorithms that select some of us for "special screening." Nor can we judge the IRS's algorithms that select some of us for auditing. It's the same with search engine algorithms that determine what Internet pages we see, predictive policing algorithms that decide whom to bring in for questioning and what neighborhoods to patrol, or credit score algorithms that determine who gets a mortgage. Some of this secrecy is necessary so people don't figure out how to game the system, but much of it is not. The EU Data Protection Directive already requires disclosure of much of this information.

It may seem as if I am contradicting myself. On one hand, I am advocating for individual privacy over forced surveillance. On the other, I am advocating for government and corporate transparency over institutional secrecy. The reason I say yes to both lies in the existing power imbalance between people and institutions. Institutions naturally wield more power than people. Institutional secrecy increases institutional power, and that power differential grows. That's inherently bad for personal liberty. Individual privacy increases individual power, thereby reducing that power differential. That's good for liberty. It's exactly the same with transparency and surveillance. Institutional transparency reduces the power imbalance, and that's good. Institutional surveillance of individuals increases the power imbalance, and that's bad.

Transparency doesn't come easily. The powerful do not like to be watched. For example, the police are increasingly averse to being monitored. All over the US, police harass and prosecute people who videotape them, and some jurisdictions have ruled it illegal. Cops in Chicago have deliberately obscured cameras, apparently attempting to conceal their own behavior. The San Diego Police Department denies all requests for police videos, claiming that they're part of ongoing investigations. During the 2014 protests in Ferguson, Missouri, after the police killed an unarmed black man, police routinely prevented protesters from recording them, and several reporters were arrested for documenting events. Los Angeles police even went so far as to sabotage court-mandated voice recorders in their patrol cars.

Governments and corporations routinely resist transparency laws of all kinds. But the world of secrecy is changing. Privacy-law scholar Peter Swire writes about a declining half-life of secrets. What he observed is that, in general, secrets get exposed sooner than they used to. Technology is making secrets harder to keep, and the nature of the Internet makes secrets much harder to keep long-term. The push of a "send" button can deliver gigabytes across the Internet in a trice. A single thumb drive can hold more data every year. Both governments and organizations need to assume that their secrets are more likely to be exposed, and sooner, than ever before.

One of the effects of a shrinking half-life for secrets is that their disclosure is more damaging. One of Snowden's documents indicated that the NSA spied on the cell phone of German chancellor Angela Merkel. The document is undated, but it's obviously from the last few years. If that document had become public 20 years from now, the reaction in Germany would have been very different from the public uproar that occurred in 2013, when Merkel was still in office and the incident was current events rather than historical.

Cultural changes are also making secrets harder to keep. In the old days, guarding institutional secrets was part of a lifelong culture. The intelligence community would recruit people early in their careers and give them jobs for life. It was a private men's club, one filled with code words and secret knowledge. The corporate world, too, was filled with lifers. Those days are gone. Many jobs in intelligence are now outsourced, and there is no job-for-life culture in the corporate world anymore. Workforces are flexible, jobs are outsourced, and people are expendable. Moving from employer to employer is now the norm. This means that secrets are shared with more people, and those people care less about them. Recall that five million people in the US have a security clearance, and that a majority of them are contractors rather than government employees.

There is also a greater belief in the value of openness, especially among younger people. Younger people are much more comfortable with sharing personal information than their elders. They believe that information wants to be free, and that security comes from public knowledge and debate. They have said very personal things online, and have had embarrassing photographs of themselves posted on social networking sites. They have been dumped by lovers in public online forums. They have overshared in the most compromising ways—and they survived intact. It is a tougher sell convincing this crowd that government secrecy trumps the public's right to know.

These technological and social trends are a good thing. Whenever possible, we should strive for transparency.

OVERSIGHT AND ACCOUNTABILITY

In order for most societies to function, people must give others power over themselves. Ceding power is an inherently risky thing to do, and over the millennia we have developed a framework for protecting ourselves even as we do this: transparency, oversight, and accountability. If we know how people are using the power we give them, if we can assure ourselves that they're not abusing it, and if we can punish them if they do, then we can more safely entrust them with power. This is the fundamental social contract of a democracy.

There are two levels of oversight. The first is strategic: are the rules we're imposing the correct ones? For example, the NSA can implement its own procedures to ensure that it's following the rules, but it should not get to decide what rules it should follow. This was nicely explained by former NSA director Michael Hayden: "Give me the box you will allow me to operate in. I'm going to play to the very edges of that box.... You, the American people, through your elected representatives, give me the field of play and I will play very aggressively in it." In one sense he's right; it's not his job to make the rules. But in another he's wrong, and I'll talk about that in Chapter 13.

In either case, we need to get much better at strategic oversight. We need more open debate about what limitations should be placed on government and government surveillance. We need legislatures conducting meaningful oversight and developing forward-looking responses. We also need open, independent courts enforcing laws rather than rubber-stamping agency practices, routine reporting of government actions, vibrant public-sector press and watchdog groups analyzing and debating the actions of those who wield power, and—yes—a legal framework for whistleblowing. And a public that cares. I'll talk about that in Chapter 13, too.

The other kind of oversight is tactical: are the rules being followed? Mechanisms for this kind of oversight include procedures, audits, approvals, troubleshooting protocols, and so on. The NSA, for example, trains its analysts in the regulations governing their work, audits systems to ensure that those regulations are actually followed, and has instituted reporting and disciplinary procedures for occasions when they're not.

Different organizations provide tactical oversight of one another. The warrant process is an example of this. Sure, we could trust the police forces to only conduct searches when they're supposed to, but instead we require them to bring their requests before a neutral third party—a judge—who ensures they're following the rules before issuing a court order.

The key to robust oversight is independence. This is why we're always suspicious of internal reviews, even when they are conducted by a vigorous advocate. This was a key issue with the chief privacy officer at the DHS. I remember Mary Ellen Callahan, who held that job from 2009 to 2012. She was a great advocate for privacy, and recommended that the agency cancel several programs because of privacy concerns. But she reported to Janet Napolitano, the DHS secretary, and all she could do was make suggestions. If Callahan had been outside of DHS, she would have had more formal regulatory powers. Oversight is much better conducted by well-staffed and knowledgeable outside evaluators.

You can think of the difference between tactical and strategic oversight as the difference between doing things right and doing the right things. Both are required.

Neither kind of oversight works without accountability. Those entrusted with power can't be free to abuse it with impunity; there must be penalties for abuse. Oversight without accountability means that nothing changes, as we've learned again and again. Or, as risk analyst Nassim Taleb points out, organizations are less likely to abuse their power when people have skin in the game.

It's easy to say "transparency, oversight, and accountability," but much harder to make those principles work in practice. Still, we have to try—and I'll get to how to do that in the next chapter. These three things give us the confidence to trust powerful institutions. If we're going to give them power over us, we need reassurance that they will act in our interests and not abuse that power.

RESILIENT DESIGN

Designing for resilience is an important, almost philosophical, principle in systems architecture. Technological solutions are often presumed to be perfect. Yet, as we all know, perfection is impossible—people, organizations, and systems are inherently flawed. From government agencies to large multinational corporations, all organizations suffer imperfections.

These imperfections aren't just the result of bad actors inside otherwise good systems. Imperfections can be mundane, run-of-the-mill, bureaucratic drift. One form of imperfection is mission creep. Another comes from people inside organizations focusing on the narrow needs of that organization and not on the broader implications of their actions. Imperfections also come from social change: changes in our values over time. Advancing technology adds new perturbations into existing systems, creating instabilities.

If systemic imperfections are inevitable, we have to accept them—in laws, in government institutions, in corporations, in individuals, in society. We have to design systems that expect them and can work despite them. If something is going to fail or break, we need it to fail in a predictable way. That's resilience.

In systems design, resilience comes from a combination of elements: fault-tolerance, mitigation, redundancy, adaptability, recoverability, and survivability. It's what we need in the complex and ever-changing threat landscape I've described in this book.

I am advocating for several flavors of resilience for both our systems of surveillance and our systems that control surveillance: resilience to hardware and software failure, resilience to technological innovation, resilience to political change, and resilience to coercion. An architecture of security provides resilience to changing political whims that might legitimize political surveillance. Multiple overlapping authorities provide resilience to coercive pressures. Properly written laws provide resilience to changing technological capabilities. Liberty provides resilience to authoritarianism. Of course, full resilience against any of these things, let alone all of them, is impossible. But we must do as well as we can, even to the point of assuming imperfections in our resilience.

ONE WORLD, ONE NETWORK, ONE ANSWER

Much of the current surveillance debate in the US is over the NSA's authority, and whether limiting the NSA somehow empowers others. That's the wrong debate. We don't get to choose a world in which the Chinese, Russians, and Israelis will stop spying if the NSA does. What we have to decide is whether we want to develop an information infrastructure that is vulnerable to all attackers, or one that is secure for all users.

Since its formation in 1952, the NSA has been entrusted with dual missions. First, signals intelligence, or SIGINT, involved intercepting the communications of America's enemies. Second, communications security, or COMSEC, involved protecting

American military—and some government—communications from interception. It made sense to combine these two missions, because knowledge about how to eavesdrop is necessary to protect yourself from eavesdropping, and vice versa.

The two missions were complementary because different countries used different communications systems, and military personnel and civilians used different ones as well. But as I described in Chapter 5, that world is gone. Today, the NSA's two missions are in conflict.

Laws might determine what methods of surveillance are legal, but technologies determine which are possible. When we consider what security technologies we should implement, we can't just look at our own countries. We have to look at the world.

We cannot simultaneously weaken the enemy's networks while still protecting our own. The same vulnerabilities used by intelligence agencies to spy on each other are used by criminals to steal your financial passwords. Because we all use the same products, technologies, protocols, and standards, we either make it easier for everyone to spy on everyone, or harder for anyone to spy on anyone. It's liberty versus control, and we all rise and fall together. Jack Goldsmith, a Harvard law professor and former assistant attorney general under George W. Bush, wrote, "every offensive weapon is a (potential) chink in our defense—and vice versa."

For example, the US CALEA law requires telephone switches to enable eavesdropping. We might be okay with giving police in the US that capability, because we generally trust the judicial warrant process and assume that the police won't abuse their authority. But those telephone switches are sold worldwide—remember the story about cell phone wiretapping in Greece in Chapter 11—with that same technical eavesdropping capability. It's our choice: either everyone gets that capability, or no one does.

It's the same with IMSI-catchers that intercept cell phone calls and metadata. StingRay might have been the FBI's secret, but the technology isn't secret anymore. There are dozens of these devices scattered around Washington, DC, and the rest of the country run by who-knows-what government or organization. Criminal uses are next. By ensuring that the cell phone network is vulnerable to these devices so we can use them to solve crimes, we necessarily allow foreign governments and criminals to use them against us.

I gave more examples in Chapter 11. In general, we get to decide how we're going to build our communications infrastructure: for security or not, for surveillance or not, for privacy or not, for resilience or not. And then *everyone* gets to use that infrastructure.

13

Solutions for Government

In the wake of Snowden's disclosures about NSA surveillance, there has been no shortage of recommendations on how to reform national intelligence. In 2013, President Obama set up a review commission on surveillance and national intelligence; that commission came up with 46 NSA policy recommendations. In 2014, 500 organizations, experts, and officials worldwide, including me, signed the International Principles on the Application of Human Rights to Communications Surveillance, often called the "Necessary and Proportionate" principles. The US Congress has debated several bills offering minor reforms; one or two might have passed by the time you read this.

In this chapter, I look at both national security and law enforcement, and make general policy recommendations, rather than detailed legislative prescriptions. Some of these are easily doable, and others are more aspirational. All of them are where I think government needs to go in the long term.

I am not arguing that governments should never be allowed to conduct surveillance or sabotage. We already give the police broad

International Principles on the Application of Human Rights to Communications Surveillance—Summary (2014)

LEGALITY: Limits on the right to privacy must be set out clearly and precisely in laws, and should be regularly reviewed to make sure privacy protections keep up with rapid technological changes.

LEGITIMATE AIM: Communications surveillance should only be permitted in pursuit of the most important state objectives.

NECESSITY: The State has the obligation to prove that its communications surveillance activities are necessary to achieving a legitimate objective.

ADEQUACY: A communications surveillance mechanism must be effective in achieving its legitimate objective.

PROPORTIONALITY: Communications surveillance should be regarded as a highly intrusive act that interferes with the rights to privacy and freedom of opinion and expression, threatening the foundations of a democratic society. Proportionate communications surveillance will typically require prior authorization from a competent judicial authority.

COMPETENT JUDICIAL AUTHORITY: Determinations related to communications surveillance must be made by a competent judicial authority that is impartial and independent.

DUE PROCESS: Due process requires that any interference with human rights is governed by lawful procedures which are publicly available and applied consistently in a fair and public hearing.

USER NOTIFICATION: Individuals should be notified of a decision authorizing surveillance of their communications. Except when a competent judicial authority finds that notice will harm an investigation, individuals should be provided an opportunity to challenge such surveillance before it occurs.

TRANSPARENCY: The government has an obligation to make enough information publicly available so that the general public can understand the scope and nature of its surveillance activities. The government should not generally prevent service providers from publishing details on the scope and nature of their own surveillance-related dealings with State.

PUBLIC OVERSIGHT: States should establish independent oversight mechanisms to ensure transparency and accountability of communications surveillance. Oversight mechanisms should have the authority to access all potentially relevant information about State actions.

INTEGRITY OF COMMUNICATIONS AND SYSTEMS: Service providers or hardware or software vendors should not be compelled to build surveillance capabilities or backdoors into their systems or to collect or retain particular information purely for State surveillance purposes.

SAFEGUARDS FOR INTERNATIONAL COOPERATION: On occasion, states may seek assistance from foreign service providers to conduct surveillance. This must be governed by clear and public agreements that ensure the most privacy-protective standard applicable is relied upon in each instance.

SAFEGUARDS AGAINST ILLEGITIMATE ACCESS: There should be civil and criminal penalties imposed on any party responsible for illegal electronic surveillance and those affected by surveillance must have access to legal mechanisms necessary for effective redress. Strong protection should also be afforded to whistleblowers who expose surveillance activities that threaten human rights.

powers to invade citizens' privacy and access our data. We do this knowingly—and willingly—because it helps to solve crimes, which in turn makes us safer. The trick is to give government agencies this power without giving them the ability to abuse it. We need the security provided by government as well as security *from* government. This is what documents like the US Constitution and the European Charter try to do, it's what the warrant process does, and it's what fell out of balance in our mad scramble for security against terrorists after the 9/11 attacks.

I'm largely addressing the US, although the recommendations in this chapter are applicable elsewhere. In the US, the president can implement some of these recommendations unilaterally by executive order, some require congressional approval, and others require the passage of new legislation. Other countries have their own separation of powers with their own rules. In many countries, of course, implementing any of these recommendations would require radical changes in the government.

LESS SECRECY, MORE TRANSPARENCY

Since 9/11, the Bush and Obama administrations have repeatedly maintained that an extreme level of secrecy is necessary to prevent the enemy from knowing what we're doing. The levels of secrecy we saw during World War I still make sense. Tactical facts can be very valuable for a limited time, and important to keep secret for that duration. And sometimes we need to keep larger secrets: our negotiating positions with other countries, the identities of foreign agents, military planning, and some areas of national intelligence. Getting back to the important difference between espionage and surveillance, our systems of espionage require a lot more secrecy than our systems of surveillance do.

However, we can be more transparent in many areas. Compare the intense secrecy surrounding NSA surveillance with a very similar domain where we routinely manage quite well without a lot of secrecy: police and crime-fighting. The Fourth Amendment regulates the police's ability to conduct surveillance, and all the court rulings surrounding it are public. Criminals can read up on all of this, or hire a lawyer who understands it, and then create a detailed manual on how to precisely exploit any loopholes in the law. There are many loopholes, and plenty of defense attorneys who know their way through them. Yet police work continues undeterred, and criminals are routinely arrested and convicted.

More generally, almost everything about police and crime-fighting is public. We know the budgets of all our nation's police forces. We know their capabilities. We know how effective they are. We know what they do, and how well they do it. We don't know the identities of undercover police officers, but we know generally how they're used and what they can and cannot do. All of this is public, known by those of us who grant the police powers over us as well as those of us who want to commit crimes. Yet the police regularly manage to solve crimes.

This demonstrates that the current level of secrecy we have in counterterrorism is excessive. It applies a military level of secrecy to what has always been a domestic matter. Terrorists are not smarter and more formidable than organized crime. Terrorists don't cause more damage or kill more people; we just fear them more. We need to transfer the traditional law enforcement trans-parency principles to national security, instead of increasing the secrecy surrounding law enforcement, as we have unfortunately begun to do. We have to design systems that keep us safe even if their details are public and known by the enemy. Secrets are harder to keep today, so we're better off limiting their numbers.

In the 1980s, the US gave up trying to keep cryptography research secret, because all that did was put our mathematicians and engineers at a disadvantage with respect to their peers in other countries. More recently, the US has abandoned attempting to block research on creating biological viruses, because someone somewhere will publish the information regardless of what we do. Military thinkers now realize that many strategic military secrets are harder to keep because of the ubiquity of satellite imagery and other technologies. We need to think the same way about government secrecy surrounding surveillance.

Transparency laws for surveillance already exist in the US. The original 1968 wiretap law mandated extensive public reporting on the government's use of wiretaps. The annual wiretap reports are over 200 pages long, and contain an enormous amount of detail. This made it possible for people to verify what the FBI was doing, and ensure that the agency wasn't abusing its authority. The problem is that when other surveillance authorities were expanded after 9/11, no similar reporting requirements were established. We need to fix this.

The US government should publish detailed, unclassified descriptions of the scope and scale of intelligence gathering. It should publish the legal justifications for all intelligence programs. It should publish information on the type and amount of data collected under those different authorities, as well as details of minimization procedures and data retention rules. And it should declassify all general opinions of the FISA Court, which oversees NSA surveillance under FISA and the FISA Amendments Act. The names of the people and organizations being monitored are legitimately secret; the rules under which organizations operate are not.

MORE—AND BETTER—OVERSIGHT

To rein in NSA surveillance, we need much better oversight over both national intelligence and law enforcement.

Strategic oversight comes first. The NSA has justified its actions by pointing to congressional oversight. Its leaders claim that agency staff merely follow the laws that Congress passes or the orders the president signs. According to one official press release, "NSA conducts all of its activities in accordance with applicable laws, regulations, and policies." This is not true. In fact, it is deeply disingenuous. We know from recently declassified FISA Court opinions, especially those written by Judge John Bates, that the NSA frequently made misrepresentations to the court, did not follow minimization requirements, and regularly exceeded its legal authorizations.

The NSA has gamed the rules governing congressional oversight to ensure that no actual understanding or critical review happens. Documents the NSA provides to Congress are either propaganda pieces designed to convince or jargon-laden documents designed to confuse. Members of Congress can't remove those documents from the secure room they're stored in, nor can they remove any notes they make. They can only bring along security-cleared staffers to help them understand the meaning and significance of the material, but few lawmakers employ staffers with both a top-secret clearance level and appropriate expertise. Additionally, they're lobbied heavily by the NSA. Senator Ron Wyden has stated that senior intelligence officials repeatedly made "misleading and deceptive statements" in congressional hearings. Senator Dianne Feinstein, chair of the Senate Select Committee on Intelligence and a longstanding supporter of government surveillance, regretfully concluded that her committee "was not satisfactorily informed" by the intelligence community about its activities. Congressman Alan Grayson of Florida called congressional oversight of the NSA a "joke."

In 2014, I was invited by six members of Congress—members from both parties—to brief them on the NSA's activities. Because I had reviewed many of the unpublished Snowden documents, I knew more about the NSA's activities than they did. How can our democracy survive when the best information Congress can get about what the NSA was really doing comes from me?

On the other hand, many legislators don't want to perform

the oversight function assigned to Congress. Some of this reluctance stems from a desire for plausible deniability. It's politically safer to let the executive branch make the decisions, then let it take the heat when something goes wrong. There's also political risk in standing up to law enforcement. Few congressional committee members actually venture into that secure room.

The NSA interprets its authority very aggressively and self-servingly. In Chapter 5, I discussed the three different authorities the NSA uses to justify its surveillance activities: Executive Order 12333, Section 215 of the PATRIOT Act, and Section 702 of the FISA Amendments Act.

Executive Order 12333, the 1981 presidential document authorizing most of NSA's surveillance, is incredibly permissive. It is supposed to primarily allow the NSA to conduct surveillance outside the US, but it gives the agency broad authority to collect data on Americans. It provides minimal protections for Americans' data collected outside the US, and even less for the hundreds of millions of innocent non-Americans whose data is incidentally collected. Because this is a presidential directive and not a law, courts have no jurisdiction, and congressional oversight is minimal. Additionally, at least in 2007, the president believed he could modify or ignore it at will and in secret. As a result, we know very little about how Executive Order 12333 is being interpreted inside the NSA.

Section 215 of the PATRIOT Act was never intended to authorize mass surveillance, and strong arguments can be made that the act's language doesn't allow it. The idea was that the FBI would be able to get information "relevant to an authorized [national security] investigation"—that is, about a specific subject of investigation— from a wider set of sources than it could previously. The example the administration talked about was information about what books a suspect checked out of the library; maybe he was reading *The Anarchist's Cookbook* or something. In fact, when the bill was being debated, it was known as the "library provision." It only empowered the FBI to demand information that it could have obtained with a grand jury subpoena—all metadata, no content— but it allowed it to do this without having to convene a grand jury. That made sense; there aren't really grand juries in national security investigations.

However, after the PATRIOT Act was passed in 2001, the Department of Justice's national security lawyers combed through the law looking for loopholes. Even though the law was intended to facilitate targeted surveillance, they decided it could be stretched to authorize mass surveillance. Even though it only empowered the FBI, they decided that the FBI could demand that information be sent to the NSA. At first they did this without any court approval at all. Eventually they decided to argue their case in front of the secret FISA Court. Because there was no one arguing the opposing position, they were able to convince a judge that *everything* was "relevant" to an investigation. This was a new interpretation of the word "relevant," and one that doesn't even pass the sniff test. If "relevant" doesn't restrict collection because everything is relevant, then why was the limitation put into the law in the first place? Even Congressman Jim Sensenbrenner, the person who wrote the USA PATRIOT Act, was surprised when he learned that the NSA used it as a legal justification for collecting mass-surveillance data on Americans. "It's like scooping up the entire ocean to guarantee you catch a fish," he said.

Section 702 of the FISA Amendments Act was a little different. The provision was supposed to solve a very specific problem. Administration officials would draw diagrams: a terrorist in Saudi Arabia was talking to a terrorist in Cuba, and the data was flowing through the US, but the NSA had to eavesdrop outside of the US. This was inefficient, it argued, and Section 702 allowed it to grab that conversation from taps inside the US.

Again, there's nothing in Section 702 that authorizes mass surveillance. The NSA justifies the use by abusing the word "incidental." Everything is intercepted, both metadata and content, and automatically searched for items of interest. The NSA claims that only the things it wants to save count as searching. Everything else is incidental, and as long as its intended "target" is outside the US, it's all okay. A useful analogy would be allowing police officers to search every house in the city without any probable cause or warrant, looking for a guy who normally lives in Bulgaria. They would save evidence of any crimes they happened to find, and then argue that none of the other searches counted because they hadn't found anything, and what they found was admissable as evidence because it was "incidental" to the search for the Bulgarian. The Fourth Amendment specifically prohibits that sort of search as unreasonable, and for good reason.

My guess is that by the time the FISA Amendments Act came around in 2008, the NSA knew what it was doing and deliberately wordsmithed the bill to allow for its preferred interpretation. Its leadership might have even briefed the Senate and House intelligence committees on how it was going to interpret that language. But they certainly didn't brief all of Congress, and they never told the American people.

I believe that much of this will eventually be found to be unconstitutional. The Fourth Amendment protects not only against unreasonable searches but also against unreasonable seizures. I argued in Chapter 10 that computer searches are searches. The mere act of obtaining a copy of the data in bulk from companies like Verizon is an illegal seizure as well.

The problem is that all three branches of government have abrogated their responsibilities for oversight. The normal democratic process of taking a law, turning it into rules, and then turning those rules into procedures is open to interpretation every step of the way, and therefore requires oversight every step of the way. Without it, agencies abuse their power. We saw this in the 1970s, when the FBI and NSA illegally spied on Americans under projects SHAMROCK and MINARET, as well as under an unnamed program that was part of the war on drugs. And we're seeing it again today.

Lest you think this is solely a US phenomenon, the same thing happened in the UK in 2000 around the passage of the Regulation of Investigatory Powers Act. Section 16(3), largely unnoticed when the bill was debated, has been used by GCHQ to spy on British citizens. It was intentionally drafted that way, with some members of Parliament in on it and stubbornly defending the obscure and convoluted language that didn't actually legalize mass surveillance but nonetheless ended up being used to justify it. I believe the idea for FAA Section 702 came from RIPA Section 16(3).

In 2013, President Obama tried to reassure Americans that NSA surveillance programs are reviewed and approved by all three branches of government. His statement was deeply misleading. Before Snowden, the full range of government surveillance activity was known by only a few members of the executive branch, partially disclosed to a few senior members of the legislative branch, and approved by a single judge on the FISA Court—a court that rejected a mere 11 out of 34,000 warrant requests between its formation in 1979 and 2013. That's not real oversight. However, to be fair, it's much more oversight than you'll find in other countries, including European democracies like France, Germany, and the UK.

Some members of Congress are trying to impose limits on the NSA, and some of their proposals have real teeth and might make a difference. Even so, I don't have any hope of meaningful congressional reform right now, because all of the proposals focus on specific programs and authorities: the telephone metadata collection program under Section 215, bulk records collection under Section 702, and so on. It's a piecemeal approach that can't work. We are now beyond the stage where simple legal interventions can make a difference. There's just too much secrecy, and too much shifting of programs amongst different legal justifications. When companies refuse National Security Letters, the government comes back with a Section 215 order. And the NSA has repeatedly threatened that if Congress limits its authority under Sections 215 and 702, it will shift curtailed programs to the more permissive, less regulated, and more secret EO 12333 authority.

There are other attempts at oversight. The president's 2013 NSA review group had broad access to the agency's capabilities and activities. They produced an excellent report outlining 46 policy recommendations, and President Obama agreed to implement many of them. The key question now is whether he will do so. In 2004, Congress created the Privacy and Civil Liberties Oversight Board on the recommendation of the 9/11 Commission to oversee national security issues. It was mostly unstaffed and unfunded until 2012, and has limited powers. (The group's 2014 report only discussed NSA collection under Section 702. It was widely panned as inadequate.)

More members of Congress must commit to meaningful NSA reform. We need comprehensive strategic oversight by independent government agencies, based on full transparency. We need meaningful rules for minimizing data gathered and stored about Americans, rules that require the NSA to delete data to which it should not have access. In the 1970s, the Church Committee investigated intelligence gathering by the NSA, CIA, and FBI. It was able to reform these agencies only after extensive research and discovery. We need a similar committee now. We need to convince President Obama to adopt the recommendations of his own NSA review group. And we need to give the Privacy and Civil Liberties Oversight Board real investigative powers.

Those recommendations all pertain to strategic oversight of mass surveillance. Next, let's consider tactical oversight. One primary mechanism for tactical oversight of government surveillance is the warrant process. Contrary to what many government officials argue, warrants do not harm security. They are a security mechanism, designed to protect us from government overreach.

Secret warrants don't work nearly as well. The judges who oversee NSA actions are from the secret FISA Court. Compared with a traditional court, the FISA Court has a much lower standard of evidence before it issues a warrant. Its cases are secret, its rulings are secret, and no one from the other side ever presents in front of it. Given how unbalanced the process it is, it's amazing that the FISA Court has shown as much backbone as it has in standing up to the NSA (despite almost never rejecting a warrant request).

Some surveillance orders bypass this process entirely. We know, for example, that US Cellular received only two judicially approved wiretap orders in 2012—and another 10,801 subpoenas for the same types of information without any judicial oversight whatsoever. All of this needs to be fixed.

Start with the FISA Court. It should be much more public. The FISA Court's chief judge should become a position that requires Senate confirmation. The court should publish its opinions to the extent possible. An official public interest advocate should be assigned the task of arguing against surveillance applications. Congress should enact a process for appealing FISA rulings, either to some appellate court or to the Supreme Court.

But more steps are needed to put the NSA under credible tactical oversight. Its internal procedures are better suited to detecting activities such as inadvertent and incorrect surveillance targeting than they are to detecting people who deliberately circumvent surveillance controls, either individually or for the organization as a whole. To rectify this, an external auditor is essential. Making government officials personally responsible for overreaching and illegal behavior is also important. Not a single one of those NSA

LOVEINT snoops was fired, let alone prosecuted. And Snowden was rebuffed repeatedly when he tried to express his concern internally about the extent of the NSA's surveillance on Americans.

Other law enforcement agencies, like the FBI, have their own internal oversight mechanisms. Here, too, the more transparency, the better. We have always given the police extraordinary powers to investigate crime. We do this knowingly, and we are safer as a society because of it, because we regulate these actions and have some recourse to ensure that the police aren't abusing them. We can argue about how well these are working in the US and other countries, but the general idea is a sound one.

PROTECT WHISTLEBLOWERS

Columbia law professor David Pozen contends that democracies need to be leaky—leaks and whistleblowing are themselves security mechanisms **against** an overreaching government. In his view, leaks serve as a counterpoint to the trend of overclassification and, ultimately, as a way for governments to win back the trust lost through excessive secrecy.

Ethnographer danah boyd has called whistleblowing the civil disobedience of the information age; it enables individuals to fight back against abuse by the powerful. The NGO Human Rights Watch wrote that "those who disclose official wrongdoing . . . perform an important service in a democratic society. . . ."

In this way of thinking, whistleblowers provide another oversight mechanism. You can think of them as a random surprise inspection. Just as we have laws to protect corporate whistleblowers, we need laws to protect government whistleblowers. Once they are in place, we could create a framework and rules for whistleblowing legally.

This would not mean that anyone is free to leak government

secrets by claiming that he's a whistleblower. It just means that conscience-driven disclosure of official wrongdoing would be a valid defense that a leaker could use in court—juries would have to decide whether it was justified—and that reporters would legally be able to keep their sources secret. The clever thing about this is that it sidesteps the difficult problem of defining "whistleblower," and allows the courts to decide on a case-by-case basis whether someone's actions qualify as such or not. Someone like Snowden would be allowed to return to the US and make his case in court, which—as I explained in Chapter 7—currently he cannot.

Additionally, we need laws that protect journalists who gain access to classified information. Public disclosure in itself is not espionage, and treating journalism as a crime is *extraordinarily* harmful to democracy.

In Chapter 7, I mentioned the Obama administration's overzealous prosecution of whistleblowers. That policy is both hypocritical and dangerous. We encourage individuals to blow the whistle on violations of law by private industry; we need to protect whistleblowing in government as well.

TARGET MORE NARROWLY, AND ONLY WITH JUDICIAL APPROVAL

Electronic surveillance is a valuable tool for both law enforcement and intelligence gathering, and one we should continue to use. The problem is electronic surveillance on the entire population, especially mass surveillance conducted outside of a narrow court order. As we saw in Chapter 11, it doesn't make us any safer. In fact, it makes us less safe by diverting resources and attention from things that actually do make us safer. The solution is to limit data collection and return to targeted—and only targeted—surveillance.

Cybersecurity and information law researcher Axel Arnbak said about government surveillance, "The front door governed by law; the backdoor governed by game theory." What he meant is that the targeted surveillance process is subject to probable cause, warrants, limits in scope, and other laws designed to protect our security and privacy. Mass surveillance is subject to an organization's cold analyses of what it can collect and how likely it is to get away with it. When we give the NSA the ability to conduct mass surveillance by evading the warrant process, we allow NSA staff to think more in terms of what's possible than in terms of what's legal. We let them grow arrogant and greedy, and we pay the price.

Bulk surveillance turns the traditional investigative process on its head. Under a normal sequence of operations, law enforcement has reason to suspect an individual, and applies for a warrant to surveil that person. Bulk surveillance allows law enforcement to surveil everyone—to develop grounds for suspicion. This is expressly prohibited by the US Constitution, and with good reason. That's why a 2014 UN report concluded that mass surveillance threatens international law.

We need legislation that compels intelligence agencies and law enforcement to target their surveillance: both new legislation and new enforcement of existing legislation. That combination will give law enforcement only the information it needs, and prevent abuse.

The US Supreme Court took a baby step in this direction in 2013 when it required police officers to obtain a warrant before attaching a GPS tracking device to a suspect's car, and another in 2014 when it required police officers to obtain a warrant before searching the cell phones of people they stopped or arrested.

In the US, we need to overturn the antiquated third-party doctrine and recognize that information can still be private even if we have entrusted it to an online service provider. The police should need a warrant to access my mail, whether it is on paper in my home, on a computer at my work, or on Google's servers somewhere in the world.

Many of these issues are international. Making this work is going to mean recognizing that governments are obligated to protect the rights and freedoms not just of their own citizens but of every citizen in the world. This is new; US legal protections against surveillance don't apply to non-US citizens outside the US. International agreements would need to recognize that a country's duties don't entirely stop at its borders. There are fundamental moral arguments for why we should do this, but there are also pragmatic ones. Protecting foreigners' privacy rights helps protect our own, and the economic harms discussed in Chapter 9 stem from trampling on them.

FIX ALMOST ALL VULNERABILITIES

As I discussed in Chapter 11, a debate is going on about whether the US government—specifically, the NSA and US Cyber Command—should stockpile Internet vulnerabilities or disclose and fix them. It's a complicated problem, and one that starkly illustrates the difficulty of separating attack and defense in cyberspace.

An arms race is raging in cyberspace right now. The Chinese, the Russians, and many other countries are also hoarding vulnerabilities. If we leave a vulnerability unpatched, we run the risk that another country will independently discover it and use it in a cyberweapon against us and our allies. But if we patch all the vulnerabilities we find, there goes our armory.

Some people believe the NSA should disclose and fix *every* bug it finds. Others claim that this would amount to unilateral disarmament. President Obama's NSA review group recommended something in the middle: that vulnerabilities should only be hoarded in rare instances and for short periods of time. I have made this point myself. This is what the NSA, and by extension US Cyber Command, claims it is doing: balancing several factors, such as whether anyone else is likely to discover the vulnerability—remember NOBUS from Chapter 11—and how strategic it is for the US. The evidence, though, indicates that it hoards far more than it discloses.

This is backwards. We have to err on the side of disclosure. It will especially benefit countries that depend heavily on the Internet's infrastructure, like the US. It will restore trust by demonstrating that we're putting security ahead of surveillance. While stockpiled vulnerabilities need to be kept secret, the more we can open the process of deciding what kind of vulnerabilities to stockpile, the better. To do this properly, we require an independent government organization with appropriate technical expertise making the decisions.

In today's cyberwar arms race, the world's militaries are investing more money in finding and purchasing vulnerabilities than the commercial world is investing in fixing them. Their stockpiles affect the security of us all. No matter what cybercriminals do, no matter what other countries do, we in the US need to err on the side of security by fixing almost all the vulnerabilities we find and making the process for disclosure more public. This will keep us safer, while engendering trust both in US policy and in the technical underpinnings of the Internet.

DON'T SUBVERT PRODUCTS OR STANDARDS

Trust is vitally important to society. It is personal, relative, situational, and fluid. It underpins everything we have accomplished as a species. We have to be able to trust one another, our institutions—both government and corporate—and the technological systems that make society function. As we build systems, we need to ensure they are trustworthy as well as effective.

The exact nature of Internet trust is interesting. Those of us who are techies never had any illusions that the Internet was secure, or that governments, criminals, hackers, and others couldn't break into systems and networks if they were sufficiently skilled and motivated. We never trusted that the programmers were perfect, that the code was bug-free, or even that our crypto math was unbreakable. We knew that Internet security was an arms race and that the attackers had most of the advantages.

What we did trust was that the technologies would stand or fall on their own merits. Thanks to Snowden's revelations, we now know that trust was misplaced. This is why the NSA's and GCHQ's surveillance programs have generated so much outcry around the world, and why the technical community is particularly outraged about the NSA's subversion of Internet products, protocols, and standards. Those agencies' actions have weakened the world's trust in the technology behind the Internet.

I discussed in Chapter 6 that the FBI is continually trying to get laws passed to mandate backdoors into security. I discussed in Chapter 11 how the NSA is surreptitiously inserting backdoors into Internet products and protocols so it can spy. We also have to assume that other countries have been doing the same thing to their own products (and to each other's). A number of observers have concluded that companies with Israeli development teams, such as Verint, Narent, and Amdocs, are in bed with the Israeli government, and that Huawei equipment is backdoored by the Chinese government. Do we trust US products made in China? Do we trust Israeli nationals working at Microsoft? Or hardware and software from Russia? France? Germany? Anything from anywhere?

This mistrust is poison. Security has to come first, eavesdropping second. Law enforcement can obtain a warrant and attempt to eavesdrop, but should not be able to force communications companies to guarantee that eavesdropping attempts will be successful. What we actually need to do is repeal CALEA and get back into the business of securing telephone networks and the Internet.

The response to this from law enforcement people is to try to frighten us with visions of kidnappers, pedophiles, drug dealers, and terrorists going scot-free because they can't decrypt their computer and communications. We saw this in late 2014 when Apple finally encrypted iPhone data; one after the other, law enforcement officials raised the specter of kidnappers and child predators. This is a common fearmongering assertion, but no one has pointed to any actual cases where this was an issue. Of the 3,576 major offenses for which warrants were granted for communications interception in 2013, exactly one involved kidnapping—and the victim wasn't a child. More importantly, there's no evidence that encryption hampers criminal investigations in any serious way. In 2013, encryption foiled the police nine times, up from four in 2012—and the investigations proceeded in some other way.

Law enforcement organizations have a huge array of investigative tools at their disposal. They can obtain warrants for data stored in the cloud and for an enormous array of metadata. They have the right and ability to infiltrate targeted suspects' computers, which can give them the data they need without weakening security for everyone. Good security does not put us at risk.

Our intelligence agencies should not deliberately insert vulnerabilities into anything other than specialized foreign military and government systems, either openly or surreptitiously; and they should work with the academic and business communities to ensure that any vulnerabilities inserted by more hostile parties are discovered, revealed, and disabled.

We'll never get every power in the world to agree not to subvert the parts of the Internet it controls, but we can stop subverting the parts we control. Most of the high-tech companies that make the Internet work are US-based, so our influence is disproportionate.

And once we stop playing the subversion game, we can credibly devote our resources to detecting and preventing subversion by others—thereby increasing trust worldwide.

SEPARATE ESPIONAGE FROM SURVEILLANCE

In 2013, we learned that the NSA eavesdropped on German chancellor Angela Merkel's cell phone. We learned that the NSA spied on embassies and missions all over the world: Brazil, Bulgaria, Colombia, the European Union, France, Georgia, Greece, India, Italy, Japan, Mexico, Slovakia, South Africa, South Korea, Taiwan, Venezuela, and Vietnam. We learned that the NSA spied on the UN. Naturally, these revelations strained international relations, but was anyone really surprised? Spying on foreign governments is what the NSA is supposed to do.

Government-on-government espionage is as old as government itself. It's an important military mission, in both peacetime and wartime, and it's not going to go away. It's targeted. It's focused. It's actually stabilizing, reducing the uncertainty countries have about each other's intentions.

Espionage is fundamentally different from the NSA's mass-surveillance programs, both in the US and internationally. In Chapter 5, I noted that this shift in the NSA's activities was a result of a shift in its mission to terrorism prevention. After 9/11, the primary mission of counterterrorist surveillance was given to the NSA because it had existing capabilities that could easily be repurposed, though the mission could have gone to the FBI instead.

Because the NSA was given the counterterrorist surveillance mission, both the military norms and the legal framework from its espionage activities carried over. Our surveillance efforts against entire populations (including our own) were kept as secret as our espionage efforts against governments.

We need to separate these two missions. Government espionage should stay within the purview of the State Department and the military. The president, as commander in chief, should determine which embassies and whose cell phones to eavesdrop on, and the NSA should carry out those orders. Mass surveillance, whether domestic or foreign, is almost never justified. Government surveillance of private citizens sometimes is, but only as a criminal investigative activity. These surveillance activities should move outside the NSA and the military. They should instead come under the auspices of the FBI and Justice Department, which will apply the police rules of probable cause, due process, and oversight to surveillance activities—in regular open courtrooms.

This isn't to say that we don't need major police reform in the US. We've already discussed police secrecy in Chapter 7. The increasing militarization of the police and many departments' tendency toward racially discriminatory practices are also serious problems. But that's a topic for another book. Counterterrorism was, and still is, primarily the mission of the FBI.

In January 2014, President Obama gave a speech about the NSA in which he made two very important points. He promised that the NSA would no longer spy on Angela Merkel's cell phone. And while he didn't extend that courtesy to the other 82 million citizens of Germany, he did say that he would extend some of the US's constitutional protections against warrantless surveillance to the rest of the world. Putting government-on-population surveillance under a civilian head and police rules would go a long way towards achieving that ideal.

LIMIT THE MILITARY'S ROLE IN CYBERSPACE

One of the great political achievements of the late nineteenth century was the separation of civilian government from the military. Both history and current politics have demonstrated the enormous social damage that occurs when generals are in charge of a country. Separating the two, as many free and democratic countries worldwide do, has provided space for liberty and democracy to flourish.

The problem is that cyberspace doesn't easily lend itself to the traditional separation into civilian and military domains. When you're being physically attacked, you can call on a variety of organizations to defend you: the police, the military, whoever does antiterrorism security in your country, your lawyers. The legal regime justifying that defense depends on two things: who's attacking you, and why. Unfortunately, when you're being attacked in cyberspace, the two things you don't know are who's attacking you, and why.

Additionally, the Internet doesn't have borders comparable to real-world ones—you can argue that it has no borders at all—so the distinction between foreign and domestic is much harder to apply. Attackers can range from bored teenagers to professional criminals to nation-states, perhaps using the same tactics and weaponry, so the distinction between types of attackers is hard to determine. Attacks occur in milliseconds and can have wide-ranging effects.

The easy reaction is to lump all of these unknown attacks under the rubric of "cyberwar," and it's the hot new thing in military planning. I've already mentioned that about 30 countries have cyberwarfare divisions in their militaries. A "cybersiege" mentality is becoming the new norm.

Given that this theater of war is so new and unknown, given that everything happens so fast, and given the military's default belief in the righteousness of its mission, however it is framed, militaries have tended to rush in and fill what they regard as a void in security. The corresponding danger is the perception that we have military problems, which beg for military solutions. These tend to be totalitarian at worst, and extralegal at best.

We need to fix this.

In the US, a series of laws prevents the military from playing a role in normal peacetime domestic affairs, while ensuring they are prepared to counter foreign threats. The 1878 Posse Comitatus Act and other directives prevent the military from engaging in domestic security matters. Because we limit the military's role to making war against foreign powers, we have felt confident in allowing it to operate with more latitude. For example, the normal rules of search and seizure that apply to law enforcement don't apply to the military, because such rules just don't make sense in the middle of a war.

Offensive military operations in cyberspace, be they espionage or attack, should remain within the purview of the military. In the US, that's Cyber Command. If we're going to attack another country's electronic infrastructure, we should treat it like any other attack on a foreign country. Not simple espionage (cyber or real world), but as an attack. Such operations should be recognized as offensive military actions, correspondingly approved at the highest levels of the executive branch, and should be subject to the same international law standards that govern acts of war in the offline world.

BREAK UP THE NSA

I have just proposed that the NSA's espionage mission be separated from its surveillance mission, and that the military's role in cyberspace be restricted to actions against foreign military targets. To accomplish this, I advocate breaking up the NSA and restoring and strengthening the various agencies' responsibilities that existed prior to 9/11:

- As part of the Department of Defense, the NSA should focus on espionage against foreign governments.
- The Department of Justice should be responsible for law enforcement and terrorism investigations. To that end, it should conduct only targeted and legally permissible surveillance activities, domestic and foreign, and should pursue leads based on the expertise of FBI agents and not NSA databases.
- The NSA's defensive capabilities in cryptography, computer security, and network defense should be spun off and become much more prominent and public. The National Institute of Standards and Technology (NIST), a civilian agency outside the Department of Defense, should reassert control over the development of technical standards for network security. The Computer Security Act of 1987 attempted to keep the NSA out of domestic security by making it clear that NIST—then called the National Bureau of Standards—had the lead in establishing technical security standards. We need to strengthen that law and ensure it's obeyed.
- The US's offensive cyber capabilities should remain with US Cyber Command. That organization should subsume the NSA's hacking capabilities (that's TAO). The general in charge of US Cyber Command should not also be the director of the NSA.

This is a long-range plan, but it's the right one. In the meantime, we should reduce the NSA's funding to pre-9/11 levels. That in itself would do an enormous amount of good.

FIGHT THE CYBER SOVEREIGNTY MOVEMENT

Twenty years ago, few governments had any policies regulating the Internet. Today, every country does, and some of them are pretty draconian. This shouldn't come as a surprise; the Internet became too big a deal for governments to ignore. But this change took many Internet watchers by surprise, and continues to do so.

Increasingly, the world's governments are fighting against the Internet's inherently international nature. If a regime wants to surveil its people, limit what they can read, and censor what they can say, the international free-and-open nature of the Internet presents a problem.

For this reason, countries like Russia, China, and Saudi Arabia have pushed for years for more national control over their domestic Internet. Through international organizations like the International Telecommunications Union—that's the UN agency that controls telephony standards—they are trying to wrest control of the Internet from the more informal multi-stakeholder international organizations that are currently in charge. Their arguments sound benign, but their motivations are not. They want an Internet that recognizes both national borders and the rights of governments to exert control within those borders: in this case, resulting in more surveillance and censorship.

The disclosure of the NSA's surveillance activities has given this position a huge boost. Several governments have pushed back against US dominance of the Internet because they're concerned about their citizens' privacy. Countries like Brazil and Germany have called for more of their citizens' data to be stored within their own borders. Other countries, with the opposite agenda, have seized on the same rhetoric. Russia passed a law in 2014 mandating that online businesses store data on its citizens within the country, beyond the reach of the NSA but within easy reach of the Russian government.

I hold conflicting views about this. On one hand, I want countries with stronger privacy laws to protect their citizens' data by demanding that it be subject to their jurisdiction. On the other hand, I don't think this will protect such data against NSA surveillance. At least the NSA has some constraints on what it may access within the US. If that same data were stored in Brazilian and German servers, those legal restrictions would not apply. And given what we know about the NSA's technical capabilities, I have no doubt that the agency will gain access in any case.

The fundamentally international nature of the Internet is an enormous benefit for people living in countries that engage in surveillance and censorship. Cyber sovereignty is often a smoke screen for the desires of political leaders to monitor and control their citizens without interference from foreign governments or corporations. And the fight against cyber sovereignty is often viewed as a smoke screen for the NSA's efforts to gain access to more of the world's communications. We need to reaffirm our support for a free, open, and global Internet, and then work to ensure its continued existence.

PROVIDE FOR COMMONS

Unowned public spaces have enormous social value. Our public parks, our sidewalks, our roads are not owned by any private concern, and we have laws that reflect that public ownership. On the Internet, everything is owned by some private entity; even that website independently run by your friend is hosted on some corporate server somewhere. There is no commons.

We don't perceive our online experience this way. Chatting on Facebook feels like chatting in person, and we're surprised when the company exercises its right to delete posts and ban people. We're even more surprised when we learn that we have no right to appeal—or even to our data. Yes, we agreed to hand over all those rights when we clicked that end-user license agreement. But because we didn't bother reading it, we weren't aware of it.

The concept of public space is important because a lot of our freedoms in the offline world are based on that notion. In the US, the First Amendment protects free speech in public places. Other laws limit behaviors like public drunkenness and lewdness. These laws don't apply to the Internet, because everything there is private space. The laws don't apply to things we say on Facebook, Twitter, Instagram, or Medium—or to comments we make on news sites—even if they are publicly readable.

Back in the dawn of the Internet, public discussion forums were conducted on something called Usenet. It was a decentralized system, and no one company could control who could speak and what they could say. As discussion forums moved to websites and corporate-owned platforms, that freedom disappeared.

We need places on the Internet that are not controlled by private parties—places to speak, places to converse, places to gather, places to protest. They could be government-run, or they could be corporate-run with special rules treating them as a true commons. Similar to common-carrier rules by which telcos are not allowed to discriminate amongst different types of traffic, there could be common-carrier social networking areas that the owners are not allowed to monitor or censor.

Whatever the solution, commons are vital to society. We should deliberately work to ensure that we always have them in cyberspace.

14

Solutions for Corporations

A s we look to limit corporate surveillance, it's important to remember that we all reap enormous benefits from data collection and use. Data collection gives us many benefits and conveniences that just weren't possible before: real-time driving directions based on actual congestion data, grocery lists that remember what we bought last time, the ability to get a store refund even if you don't save your receipts, the ability to remotely verify that you turned out the lights and locked the door, instant communication with anyone anywhere in the world. There's more coming. Watch any science fiction movie or television show and pay attention to the marvels of a fully computerized world; much of it assumes that computers know, respond to, and remember what people are doing. This sort of surveillance is our future, and it's a future filled with things that make our lives better and more enjoyable.

Similarly, there is value to unfettered access to technology. Although much of this book focuses on the dark side of technology, we must remember that technology has been an enormous benefit to us all. Technology enables us to accomplish complex tasks more quickly, easily, and accurately for many purposes: to develop more durable construction materials; to find and disseminate information; to precisely depict physical phenomena; to communicate with others free of geographical constraints; to document events; to grow more food; to live longer. I could not have written this book without the Internet. It's not perfect, of course. Technology is unevenly distributed on the planet, and there are haves and have-nots, but—in general—more technology is better.

The last thing we want to do is derail that future. We simply don't know what sorts of inventions are coming, or what major human problems they will be able to solve. We need to be able to experiment with new technologies and with new businesses based on those technologies, and this includes surveillance technologies. The trick will be maximizing the benefits that come from companies collecting, storing, and analyzing our data, while minimizing the harms.

There are lots of solutions out there to consider. The 1980 OECD Privacy Framework is a great place to start; it lays out limitations on data collection, data storage, and data use. In 1995, the European Union passed the EU Data Protection Directive, which regulated personal data collected by corporations. American corporations, accustomed to the much more permissive legal regime in the US, are constantly running afoul of European law. And reforms, bringing that law up to date with modern technology, are currently being debated.

The solutions offered in this chapter are all directed at the private collection and use of our data. Sometimes these changes can be spurred by the market, but most of the time they will be facilitated by laws. This is really a list of things governments need to do, which in turn is really a list of things citizens need to demand that their governments do. Since they affect corporations, they're in this chapter.

MAKE VENDORS LIABLE FOR PRIVACY BREACHES

One way to improve the security of collected data is to make companies liable for data breaches.

Corporations are continually balancing costs and benefits. In this case, the costs consist of the cost of securing the data they collect and save, the cost of insecurity if there's a breach, and the value of the data they collect. Right now, the cost of insecurity is low. A few very public breaches aside—Target is an example here—corporations find it cheaper to spend money on PR campaigns touting good security, weather the occasional press storm and round of lawsuits when they're proven wrong, and fix problems after they become public.

This is because most of the cost of privacy breaches falls on the people whose data is exposed. In economics, this is known as an externality: an effect of a decision not borne by the decision maker. Externalities limit the incentive for companies to improve their security.

You might expect users to respond by favoring secure services over insecure ones—after all, they're making their own buying decisions on the basis of the same market model. But that's not generally possible. In some cases, software monopolies limit the available product choice. In other cases, the "lock-in effect" created by proprietary file formats, existing infrastructure, compatibility requirements, or software-as-a-service makes it harder to switch. In many cases, we don't know who is collecting our data; recall the discussion of hidden surveillance in Chapter 2. In all cases, it's hard for buyers to assess the security of any data service. And it's not just nontechnical buyers; even I can't tell you whether or not to entrust your privacy to any particular service provider.

Liabilities change this. By raising the cost of privacy breaches, we can make companies accept the costs of the externality and

OECD Privacy Framework (1980)

COLLECTION LIMITATION PRINCIPLE: There should be limits to the collection of personal data and any such data should be obtained by lawful and fair means and, where appropriate, with the knowledge or consent of the data subject.

DATA QUALITY PRINCIPLE: Personal data should be relevant to the purposes for which they are to be used, and, to the extent necessary for those purposes, should be accurate, complete and kept up-to-date.

PURPOSE SPECIFICATION PRINCIPLE: The purposes for which personal data are collected should be specified not later than at the time of data collection and the subsequent use limited to the fulfilment of those purposes or such others as are not incompatible with those purposes and as are specified on each occasion of change of purpose.

USE LIMITATION PRINCIPLE: Personal data should not be disclosed, made available or otherwise used for purposes other than those specified in accordance with Paragraph 9 except: a) with the consent of the data subject; or b) by the authority of law.

SECURITY SAFEGUARDS PRINCIPLE: Personal data should be protected by reasonable security safeguards against such risks as loss or unauthorized access, destruction, use, modification or disclosure of data.

OPENNESS PRINCIPLE: There should be a general policy of openness about developments, practices and policies with respect to personal data. Means should be readily available of establishing the existence and nature of personal data, and the main purposes of their use, as well as the identity and usual residence of the data controller.

INDIVIDUAL PARTICIPATION PRINCIPLE: Individuals should have the right: a) to obtain from a data controller, or otherwise, confirmation of whether or not the data controller has data relating to them; b) to have communicated to them, data relating to them i. within a reasonable time; ii. at a charge, if any, that is not excessive; iii. in a reasonable manner; and iv. in a form that is readily intelligible to them; c) to be given reasons if a request made under subparagraphs (a) and (b) is denied, and to be able to challenge such denial; and d) to challenge data relating to them and, if the challenge is successful to have the data erased, rectified, completed or amended

ACCOUNTABILITY PRINCIPLE: A data controller should be accountable for complying with measures which give effect to the principles stated above.

force them to expend more effort protecting the privacy of those whose data they have acquired. We're already doing this in the US with healthcare data; privacy violations in that industry come with serious fines.

And it's starting to happen here with data from stores, as well. Target is facing several lawsuits as a result of its 2013 breach. In other cases, banks are being sued for inadequately protecting the privacy of their customers. One way to help would be to require companies to inform users about *all* the information they possess that might have been compromised.

These cases can be complicated, with multiple companies involved in a particular incident, and apportioning liability will be hard. Courts have been reluctant to find a value in privacy, because people willingly give it away in exchange for so little. And because it is difficult to link harms from loss of privacy to specific actions that caused those harms, such cases have been very difficult to win.

There's a better way to approach this: make the point of harm the privacy breach, not any ensuing harms. Companies must be compelled to comply with regulations like the 1973 Code of Fair Information Practices and other similar privacy regulations that are currently not mandatory; then the violation becomes failure to adhere to the regulations.

There's a parallel with how the EPA regulates environmental pollutants. Factories have a legal obligation to limit the amount of particulates they emit into the environment. If they exceed these limits, they are subject to fines. There's no need to wait until there is an unexpected surge of cancer cases. The problem is understood, the regulations are in place, companies can decide whether to build factories with coal furnaces or solar panels, and sanctions are waiting if they fail to comply with what are essentially best practices. That is the direction we need to go.

To be sure, making systems more secure will cost money, and corporations will pass those costs on to users in the form of higher prices if they can. But users are already paying extra costs for inse-

---

The US Code of Fair Information Practices (1973)

The Code of Fair Information Practices is based on five principles:

1. There must be no personal data record-keeping systems whose very existence is secret.
2. There must be a way for a person to find out what information about the person is in a record and how it is used.
3. There must be a way for a person to prevent information about the person that was obtained for one purpose from being used or made available for other purposes without the person's consent.
4. There must be a way for a person to correct or amend a record of identifiable information about the person.
5. Any organization creating, maintaining, using, or disseminating records of identifiable personal data must assure the reliability of the data for their intended use and must take precautions to prevent misuses of the data.

cure systems: the direct and indirect costs of privacy breaches. Making companies liable for breaches moves those costs to them and, as a by-product, causes the companies to improve their security. The relevant term from economics is "least cost avoider": it is economically efficient to assign liability to the entity in possession of the data because it is best positioned to minimize risk. Think about it—what can you do if you want Facebook to better secure your data? Not much. Economic theory says that's why the company should bear the cost of poor security practices.

REGULATE DATA USE

Unlike in the EU, in the US today personal information about you is not your property; it's owned by the collector. Laws protect specific categories of personal data—financial data, healthcare information, student data, videotape rental records—but we have nothing like the broad privacy protection laws you find in European countries. But broad legal protections are really the only solution; leaving the market to sort this out will lead to even more invasive mass surveillance.

Here's an example. Dataium is a company that tracks you as you shop for a car online. It monitors your visits to different manufacturers' websites: what types of cars you're looking at, what options you click on for more information, what sorts of financing options you research, how long you linger on any given page. Dealers pay for this information about you—not just information about the cars they sell, but the cars you looked at that are sold by other manufacturers. They pay for this information so that when you walk into a showroom, they can more profitably sell you a car.

Think about the economics here. That information might cost you (ballpark estimate) $300 extra on the final price when you buy your car. That means it's worth no more than $300 to protect yourself from Dataium's tactics. But there are 16 million cars sold annually in the US. Even if you assume that Dataium has customer information relevant to just 2% of them, that means it's worth about $100 million to the company to ensure that its tactics work.

This asymmetry is why market solutions tend to fail. It's a collective action problem. It's worth $100 million to all of us collectively to protect ourselves from Dataium, but we can't coordinate effectively. Dataium naturally bands the car dealers together, but the best way for us customers to band together is through collective political action.

The point of use is a sensible place to regulate, because much of the information that's collected about us is collected because we want it to be. We object when that information is being used in ways we didn't intend: when it is stored, shared, sold, correlated, and used to manipulate us in some stealthy way. This means that we need restrictions on how our data can be used, especially restrictions on ways that differ from the purposes for which it was collected.

Other problems arise when corporations treat their underlying algorithms as trade secrets: Google's PageRank algorithm, which determines what search results you see, and credit-scoring systems are two examples. The companies have legitimate concerns about secrecy. They're worried both that competitors will copy them and that people will figure out how to game them. But I believe transparency trumps proprietary claims when the algorithms have a direct impact on the public. Many more algorithms can be made public—or redesigned so they can be made public—than currently are. For years, truth in lending and fair lending laws have required financial institutions to ensure that the algorithms they use are both explainable and legally defensible. Mandated transparency needs to be extended into other areas where algorithms hold power over people: they have to be open. Also, there are ways of auditing algorithms for fairness without making them public.

Corporations tend to be rational risk assessors, and will abide by regulation. The key to making this work is oversight and accountability. This isn't something unusual: there are many regulated industries in our society, because we know what they do is both important and dangerous. Personal information and the algorithms used to analyze it are no different. Some regular audit mechanism would ensure that corporations are following the rules, and would penalize them if they don't.

This all makes sense in theory, but actually doing it is hard. The last thing we want is for the government to start saying, "You can only do this and nothing more" with our data. Permissions-based regulation would stifle technological innovation and change. We want rights-based regulation—basically, "You can do anything you want unless it is prohibited."

REGULATE DATA COLLECTION AS WELL

Regulating data use isn't enough. Privacy needs to be regulated in many places: at collection, during storage, upon use, during disputes. The OECD Privacy Framework sets them out nicely, and they're all essential.

There's been a concerted multi-year effort by US corporations to convince the world that we don't need regulations on data collection, only on data use. Companies seek to eradicate any limitations on data collection because they know that any use limitations will be narrowly defined, and that they can slowly expand them once they have our data. (A common argument against any particular data-use regulation is that it's a form of censorship.) They know that if collection limitations are in place, it's much harder to change them. But as with government mass surveillance, the privacy harms come from the simple collection of the data, not only from its use. Remember the discussion of algorithmic surveillance from Chapter 10. Unrestricted corporate collection will result in broad collection, expansive sharing with the government, and a slow chipping away at the necessarily narrowly defined use restrictions.

We need to fight this campaign. Limitations on data collection aren't new. Prospective employers are not allowed to ask job applicants whether they're pregnant. Loan applications are not allowed to ask about the applicants' race. "Ban the Box" is a campaign to make it illegal for employers to ask about applicants' criminal pasts. The former US gays-in-the-military compromise, "Don't Ask Don't Tell," was a restriction on data collection. There are restrictions on what questions can be asked by the US Census Bureau.

Extending this to a world where everything we do is mediated by computers isn't going to be easy, but we need to start discussing what sorts of data should never be collected. There are some obvious places to start. What we read online should be as private as it is in the paper world. This means we should legally limit recording the webpages we read, the links we click on, and our search results. It's the same with our movements; it should not be a condition of having a cell phone that we subject ourselves to constant surveillance. Our associations—to whom we communicate, whom we meet on the street—should not be continually monitored. Maybe companies can be allowed to use some of this data immediately and then must purge it. Maybe they'll be allowed to save it for a short period of time.

One intriguing idea has been proposed by University of Miami Law School professor Michael Froomkin: requiring both government agencies and private companies engaging in mass data collection to file Privacy Impact Notices, modeled after Environmental Impact Reports. This would serve to inform the public about what's being collected and why, and how it's being stored and used. It would encourage decision makers to think about privacy early in any project's development, and to solicit public feedback.

One place to start is to require opt-in. Basically, there are two ways to obtain consent. Opt-in means that you have to explicitly consent before your data is collected and used. Opt-out is the opposite; your data will be collected and used unless you explicitly object. Companies like Facebook prefer opt-out, because they can make the option difficult to find and know that most people won't bother. Opt-in is more fair, and the use of service shouldn't be contingent on allowing data collection.

Right now, there's no downside to collecting and saving everything. By limiting what companies can collect and what they can do with the data they collect, by making companies responsible for the data under their control, and by forcing them to come clean with customers about what they actually collect and what they do with it, we will influence them to collect and save only the data about us they know is valuable.

Congress needs to begin the hard work of updating US privacy laws and stop making excuses for inaction. Courts can also play a significant role safeguarding consumer privacy by enforcing current privacy laws. The regulatory agencies, such as the FTC and the FCC, have some authority to protect consumer privacy in certain domains. But what the United States needs today is an independent data protection agency comparable to those in other countries around the world. And we have to do better than patching problems only after they become sufficiently harmful. These challenges are big and complex, and we require an agency with the expertise and resources to have a meaningful impact.

MAKE DO WITH LESS DATA

By and large, organizations could make do collecting much less data, and storing it for shorter periods of time, than they do now. The key is going to be understanding how much data is needed for what purpose.

For example, many systems that collect identifications don't really need that information. Often, authorization is all that's required. A social networking site doesn't need to know your real identity. Neither does a cloud storage company.

Some types of data analysis require you to have data on a lot of people, but not on everyone. Think about Waze. It uses surveillance data to infer traffic flow, but doesn't need everyone's data to do that. If it has enough cars under surveillance to get a broad coverage of major roads, that's good enough. Many retailers rely on ubiquitous surveillance to measure the effectiveness of advertisements, infer buying patterns, and so on; but again, they do not need everyone's data. A representative sample is good enough for those applications, and was common when data collection was expensive.

Other applications prefer having everyone's data simply because it makes them more effective. Sure, Google could do well if it only had data on half of its users, or saved only half of the search queries on all of its users, but it would be a less profitable business. Still other applications actually need all of the data. If you're a cell phone company trying to deliver mobile phone calls, you need to know where each user is located—otherwise the system won't work.

There are also differences in how long a company needs to store data. Waze and your cell phone company only need location data in real time. Advertisers need some historical data, but newer data is more valuable. On the other hand, some data is invaluable for research. Twitter, for example, is giving its data to the Library of Congress.

We need laws that force companies to collect the minimum data they need and keep it for the minimum time they need it, and to store it more securely than they currently do. As one might expect, the German language has a single word for this kind of practice: *Datensparsamkeit*.

GIVE PEOPLE RIGHTS TO THEIR DATA

The US is the only Western country without basic data protection laws. We do have protections for certain types of information, but those are isolated areas. In general, our rights to our data are spotty. Google "remembers" things about me that I have long forgotten. That's because Google has my lifelong search history, but I don't have access to it to refresh my memory. Medtronic maintains that data from its cardiac defibrillators is proprietary to the company, and won't let patients in whom they're implanted have access to it. In the EU, people have a right to know what data companies have about them. This was why the Austrian Max Schrems was able to force Facebook to give him all his personal information the company had. Those of us in the US don't enjoy that right.

Figuring out how these rights *should* work is not easy. For example, here is a list of different types of data you produce on a social networking site.

- Service data: the data you give to a social networking site in order to use it. Depending on the site, such data might include your legal name, your age, and your credit card number.
- Disclosed data: what you post on your own pages, such as blog entries, photographs, messages, and comments.
- Entrusted data: what you post on other people's pages. It's basically the same stuff as disclosed data, but the difference is that you don't have control over the data once you post it— another user does.
- Incidental data: what other people post about you. Maybe it's a paragraph about you that someone else writes, or a picture of you that someone else takes and posts. Not only do you not have any control over it, you didn't even create it.

- Behavioral data: data the site collects about your habits by monitoring what you do and whom you do it with.
- Derived data: data about you that is inferred from all the other data. For example, if 80% of your friends self-identify as gay, you're probably gay, too.

What rights should you have regarding each of those types of data? Today, it's all over the map. Some types are always private, some can be made private, and some are always public. Some can be edited or deleted—I know one site that allows entrusted data to be edited or deleted within a 24-hour period—and some cannot. Some can be viewed and some cannot. In the US there are no rules; those that hold the data get to decide—and of course they have complete access.

Different platforms give you different abilities to restrict who may see your communications. Until 2011, you could either make your Facebook posts readable by your friends only or by everyone; at that point, Facebook allowed you to have custom friends groups, and you could make posts readable by some of your friends but by not all of them. Tweets are either direct messages or public to the world. Instagram posts can be either public, restricted to specific followers, or secret. Pinterest pages have public or secret options.

Standardizing this is important. In 2012, the White House released a "Consumer Privacy Bill of Rights." In 2014, a presidential review group on big data and privacy recommended that this bill of rights be the basis for legislation. I agree.

It's easy to go too far with this concept. Computer scientist and technology critic Jaron Lanier proposes a scheme by which anyone who uses our data, whether it be a search engine using it to serve us ads or a mapping application using it to determine real-time road congestion, automatically pays us a royalty. Of course, it would be a micropayment, probably even a nanopay-

---

US Consumer Privacy Bill of Rights (2012)

INDIVIDUAL CONTROL: Consumers have a right to exercise control over what personal data companies collect from them and how they use it.

TRANSPARENCY: Consumers have a right to easily understandable and accessible information about privacy and security practices.

RESPECT FOR CONTEXT: Consumers have a right to expect that companies will collect, use, and disclose personal data in ways that are consistent with the context in which consumers provide the data.

SECURITY: Consumers have a right to secure and responsible handling of personal data.

ACCESS AND ACCURACY: Consumers have a right to access and correct personal data in usable formats, in a manner that is appropriate to the sensitivity of the data and the risk of adverse consequences to consumers if the data is inaccurate.

FOCUSED COLLECTION: Consumers have a right to reasonable limits on the personal data that companies collect and retain.

ACCOUNTABILITY: Consumers have a right to have personal data handled by companies with appropriate measures in place to assure they adhere to the Consumer Privacy Bill of Rights.

---

ment, but over time it might add up to a few dollars. Making this work would be extraordinarily complex, and in the end would require constant surveillance even as it tried to turn that surveillance into a revenue stream for everyone. The more fundamental problem is the conception of privacy as something that should be subjected to commerce in this way. Privacy needs to be a fundamental right, not a property right.

We should have a right to delete. We should be able to tell any company we're entrusting our data to, "I'm leaving. Delete all the data you have on me." We should be able to go to any data broker and say, "I'm not your product. I never gave you permission to gather information about me and sell it to others. I want my data out of your database." This is what the EU is currently grappling with: the right to be forgotten. In 2014, the European Court of Justice ruled that in some cases search engines need to remove information about individuals from their results. This caused a torrent of people demanding that Google remove search results that reflected poorly on them: politicians, doctors, pedophiles. We can argue about the particulars of the case, and whether the court got the balance right, but this is an important right for citizens to have with respect to their data that corporations are profiting from.

MAKE DATA COLLECTION AND PRIVACY SALIENT

We reveal data about ourselves all the time, to family, friends, acquaintances, lovers, even strangers. We share with our doctors, our investment counselors, our psychologists. We share a lot of data. But we think of that sharing transactionally: I'm sharing data with *you*, because I need you to know things/trust you with my secrets/am reciprocating because you've just told me something personal.

As a species, we have evolved all sorts of psychological systems to navigate these complex privacy decisions. And these systems are extraordinarily complex, highly attuned, and delicately social. You can walk into a party and immediately know how to behave. Whom you talk to, what you tell to whom, who's around you, who's listening: most of us can navigate that beautifully. The problem is that technology inhibits that social ability. Move that same party onto Facebook, and suddenly our intuition starts failing. We forget who's reading our posts. We accidentally send something private to a public forum. We don't understand how our data is monitored in the background. We don't realize what the technologies we're using can and cannot do.

In large part that's because the degree of privacy in online environments isn't salient. Intuition fails when thoughts of privacy fade into the background. Once we can't directly perceive people, we don't do so well. We don't think, "There's a for-profit corporation recording everything I say and trying to turn that into advertising." We don't think, "The US and maybe other governments are recording everything I say and trying to find terrorists, or criminals, or drug dealers, or whoever is the bad guy this month." That's not what's obvious. What's obvious is, "I'm at this virtual party, with my friends and acquaintances, and we're talking about personal stuff."

And so we can't use people's continual exposure of their private data on these sites as evidence of their consent to be monitored. What they're consenting to is the real-world analogue they have in their heads, and they don't fully understand the ramifications of moving that system into cyberspace.

Companies like Facebook prefer it this way. They go out of their way to make sure you're not thinking about privacy when you're on their site, and they use cognitive tricks like showing you pictures of your friends to increase your trust. Governments go even further, making much of their surveillance secret so people don't even know it's happening. This explains the disconnect between people's claims that privacy is important and their actions demonstrating that it isn't: the systems we use are deliberately designed so that privacy issues don't arise.

We need to give people the option of true online privacy, and the ability to understand and choose that option. Companies will be less inclined to do creepy things with our data if they have to justify themselves to their customers and users. And users will be less likely to be seduced by "free" if they know the true costs. This is going to require "truth in product" laws that will regulate corporations, and similar laws to regulate government.

For starters, websites should be required to disclose what third parties are tracking their visitors, and smartphone apps should disclose what information they are recording about their users. There are too many places where surveillance is hidden; we need to make it salient as well.

Again, this is hard. Notice, choice, and consent is the proper way to manage this, but we know that lengthy privacy policies written in legalese—those notice-and-consent user agreements you click "I agree" to without ever reading—don't work. They're deliberately long and detailed, and therefore boring and confusing; and they don't result in any meaningful consent on the part of the user. We can be pretty sure that a pop-up window every time you post something to Facebook saying, "What you've written will be saved by Facebook and used for marketing, and will be given to the government on demand," won't work, either. We need some middle way. My guess is that it will involve standardized policies and some sort of third-party certification.

ESTABLISH INFORMATION FIDUCIARIES

In several areas of our lives we routinely give professionals access to very personal information about ourselves. To ensure that they only use that information in our interests, we have established the notion of fiduciary responsibility. Doctors, lawyers, and accountants are all bound by rules that require them to put the interests of their clients above their own. These rules govern when and how they can use the information and power we give them, and they are generally not allowed to use it for unrelated purposes. The police have rules about when they can demand personal information from fiduciaries. The fiduciary relationship creates a duty of care that trumps other obligations.

We need information fiduciaries. The idea is that they would become a class of organization that holds personal data, subject to special legal restrictions and protections. Companies could decide whether or not to become part of this class or not. That is comparable to investment advisors, who have fiduciary duties, and brokers, who do not. In order to motivate companies to become fiduciaries, governments could offer certain tax breaks or legal immunities for those willing to accept the added responsibility. Perhaps some types of business would be automatically classified as fiduciaries simply because of the large amount of personal information they naturally collect: ISPs, cell phone companies, e-mail providers, search engines, social networking platforms.

Fiduciary regulation would give people confidence that their information wasn't being handed to the government, sold to third parties, or otherwise used against them. It would provide special protections for information entrusted to fiduciaries. And it would require certain duties of care on the part of providers: a particular level of security, regular audits, and so on. It would enable trust.

Along similar lines, Internet security expert Dan Geer proposed that Internet service providers choose whether they were content companies or communications companies. As content companies, they could use and profit from the data but would also be liable for the data. As communications companies, they would not be liable for the data but could not look at it.

In the Middle Ages, the Catholic Church imposed a strict obligation of confidentiality regarding all sins disclosed in confession, recognizing that no one would partake of the sacrament if they feared that their trust might be betrayed by the priest. Today we need a similar confidence online.

INCENT NEW BUSINESS MODELS

Surveillance became the business model of the Internet because it was the easiest thing that made money and there were no rules regulating it. It has remained the business model of the Internet because the costs are low, the potential gains are enormous, and (at least in the US) there are *still* no rules regulating it.

By both regulating the collection and use of our data, and raising the costs of retaining our data, we will naturally incent new business models that don't rely on surveillance. The technical capabilities already exist. There's a lot of research on building privacy into products and services from the start: privacy by design. Credit card companies don't have to track our every purchase in order to bill us and prevent fraud. Cell phone providers don't have to permanently record our locations in order to let us make phone calls and send text messages. The Internet can be built with strong anonymity protections. Electronic cash can be both secure and anonymous. All of these things are possible; we just have to want them.

Admittedly, this will be a slow process. The companies that most extensively collect our data believe in the potential for massive increases in advertising revenue. Internet advertising might be a $125 billion business worldwide, but it's still only 25% of the advertising market. Companies like Google and Facebook have their eyes on the advertising money spent on television (40%) and in newspapers and magazines (36%). They have a lot of money invested in the value of big data—collecting everything and then figuring out what to do with it later—and will not switch gears easily. Journalist James Kunstler calls this the "psychology of previous investment," and it's why we so often throw bad money after good. Admitting you're wrong is hard, especially because the cost of data collection and storage is so low.

In a market economy, if a company can't figure out a profitable business model, others that do will emerge. If we succeed in raising the cost of surveillance and data collection, new businesses that don't rely on it will rise up and take the place of the current ones that do.

FIGHT GOVERNMENT SURVEILLANCE

So far, the most important effect of the Snowden revelations is that they have ruptured the public-private surveillance partnership I discussed in Chapter 6. Pre-Snowden, there was no downside for a company cooperating with the NSA. If the NSA asked you to supply copies of all your Internet traffic, or to put backdoors into your security software, you could assume that your assistance would forever remain secret. To be fair, not everyone cooperated willingly. Some fought in court. But it seems that a lot of them, government-regulated monopoly telcos and backbone providers especially, were happy to give the NSA unfettered access to everything it demanded. It was easy, and they did it all through the Cold War, and then immediately after 9/11, without fuss.

This is changing. There is now business value in championing privacy and fighting the NSA, and business harm in cooperation. There are basically four means by which corporations can fight: transparency, technology, litigation, and lobbying.

Many computer companies—Yahoo, Google, Microsoft, and others—are now regularly publishing "transparency reports," giving us a general idea how many government data requests the companies have received and how many they have complied with. It's largely PR motivated, to reassure us that only a very small percentage of users' data is being sent to the government. For example, in 2013 Google says it turned over the Internet metadata of somewhere between 1 and 2,000 users, and the contents of communications from between 18,000 and 20,000 users, to the US government. Those ranges are regulated; the companies are not allowed to report exact numbers, although many are pressing the government for the ability to reveal more precise information. (Google already reports more precisely on requests from other governments around the world.)

Even some of the telcos and cable companies are releasing transparency reports, starting with CREDO Mobile in early 2014. These have less value. Verizon, for example, reports that it received 320,000 "law enforcement demands" for data in 2013. We know that every three months Verizon is served with a single National Security Letter that requires it to turn over the metadata of all 290 million of its customers, so what does that 320,000 mean?

Some companies are trying to go further. In 2014, Apple announced that it would inform individual users about all government demands for its data that it was not specifically legally prohibited from disclosing. Microsoft and Google have teamed up to sue the US government, demanding more transparency. Yahoo is doing the same.

Other companies are employing "warrant canaries" to try to get around legal gag orders. Starting in 2013, Apple's transparency reports contain this sentence: "Apple has never received an order under Section 215 of the USA Patriot Act." The idea is that if it ever receives such an order it will be prohibited from disclosing it, but it could remove the sentence as a signal to watchful readers. The courts have never ruled on the legality of this practice, and I personally am skeptical that it would work, but it's a valiant and clever effort.

On the technology front, many companies are stepping up their use of encryption: of their Internet connections with their users and customers, of their own networks, and of their databases. After Google learned that the NSA was eavesdropping on its trunk communications links between data centers, it encrypted those links. After Yahoo learned that the NSA was eavesdropping on the web connections between its users and Yahoo websites, both Yahoo and Microsoft (which assumed its users were being eavesdropped on, too) began encrypting them. Several large e-mail providers are now encrypting e-mail as it flows between their data centers. Other companies are doing more to encrypt communications between them and their users and customers. Both iPhones and Android phones are encrypted by default. Google is now offering end-to-end Gmail encryption, although my guess is that it will be a little-used option because users won't be able to search and sort their e-mail if it remains encrypted.

In the courts, companies should litigate on their users' behalf. They should demand court orders for all access, and fight back against any court orders that seem overly broad. Some of this is already going on. In 2008, Yahoo secretly fought the NSA in court long and hard before being forced to join the PRISM program. In 2012, Twitter unsuccessfully fought a government demand to turn over information related to an Occupy Wall Street protester. As of 2014, Facebook is fighting a court order to hand over 400 users' private messages, photos, and the like to a New York district attorney looking for evidence of Social Security fraud.

Companies can do more to support litigation efforts. They should file amicus briefs in any cases whose precedents affect them. In 2013, when the FBI demanded the master key for all Lavabit users in an attempt to get at one person's e-mail, none of the big e-mail providers—Google, Microsoft, Yahoo, anyone—filed briefs in that case. Why not? They need to recognize that we're all in this together.

The Internet's international nature again creates a complicated wrinkle in this. It's one thing for a corporation to comply with lawful requests for data from its own country, but what about other countries? On four occasions in the early 2000s, Yahoo complied with Chinese government requests for data about individual users that led to those people's arrest and imprisonment on charges of "subversion" and "divulging state secrets." Should Yahoo have done that? Does it make a difference if the repressive regime is, like Saudi Arabia, on friendly terms with the US? Many US Internet companies argue that they are not subject to the jurisdiction of countries in which they do not maintain offices. A US company probably can't resist Chinese law, but it probably can resist those of smaller and less powerful countries. In a lot of ways, these companies can choose which foreign laws they want to follow or not. They should choose to maximize their users' privacy.

In the halls of politics, corporations should use their political influence. Google, Facebook, Microsoft, and others are actively lobbying for legislative restrictions on how the US government conducts surveillance. This is good, but we need more. Often the most persuasive arguments in Washington come from corporations concerned about their bottom line.

It's important not to make too much of all this. Corporate interests may temporarily overlap with their users' privacy interests, but they're not permanently aligned. For years, corporations fought any laws limiting their ability to collect and use data. The EU has been trying to pass an updated and stricter data protection regulation, but faces furious lobbying from US Internet companies that don't want to stop data collection. This newfound backbone to stand up to the NSA is more about managing user perceptions than about solving privacy problems. This is why we need strong regulations on corporations as well.

A NEW MAGNA CARTA

Tim Berners-Lee, the inventor of the World Wide Web, has called for a new Magna Carta—one that restricts the actions of both governments and corporations, and that imposes responsibilities on information-age corporations rather than just rights. The historical analogy is actually not that great, but the general idea is worth exploring. It's basically what I'm calling for in this book.

Recall Chapter 4, when I characterized the corporation–user relationship as feudal? That's because it's ad hoc and one-sided: based on an end-user license agreement that's written in mind-numbing legalese and that the company can change at whim. Historical feudalism was a lot like that; the lords had the power to force the peasants into relationships whereby the lords possessed all the rights and were burdened with few enforceable responsibilities. In medieval Europe, the rise of the centralized state and the rule of law provided the flexibility that feudalism lacked. In 1215, the Magna Carta became the first modern document enshrining the idea that the legitimacy of a ruler comes from his subjects, and subjected the king to the rule of law. The document first imposed responsibilities on kings with respect to the lesser lords, and over time put society on the long road towards government of the people, by the people, and for the people.

In the 1700s, when countries were beginning to recognize that their governing power derived from *all* the people, the prevailing political philosophy was that of Thomas Hobbes, who argued that the people sacrifice power and freedom to a benevolent sovereign, who in return provides them with various services, including security. John Locke argued that this relationship is unfair and unbalanced, and that governments derive their authority from the "consent of the governed." This notion fueled the English, French, and American revolutions, and led to the French Declaration of the Rights of Man and the Citizen and the US Bill of Rights.

In her book *Consent of the Networked*, journalist and digital rights advocate Rebecca MacKinnon makes this point: "No company will ever be perfect—just as no sovereign will ever be perfect no matter how well intentioned and virtuous a king, queen, or benevolent dictator might be. But that is the point: right now our

Madrid Privacy Declaration (2009)

Civil Society takes the occasion of the 31st annual meeting of the International Conference of Privacy and Data Protection Commissioners to:

1. Reaffirm support for a global framework of Fair Information Practices that places obligations on those who collect and process personal information and gives rights to those whose personal information is collected;
2. Reaffirm support for independent data protection authorities that make determinations, in the context of a legal framework, transparently and without commercial advantage or political influence;
3. Reaffirm support for genuine Privacy Enhancing Techniques that minimize or eliminate the collection of personally identifiable information and for meaningful Privacy Impact Assessments that require compliance with privacy standards;
4. Urge countries that have not ratified Council of Europe Convention 108 together with the Protocol of 2001 to do so as expeditiously as possible;
5. Urge countries that have not yet established a comprehensive framework for privacy protection and an independent data protection authority to do so as expeditiously as possible;
6. Urge those countries that have established legal frameworks for privacy protection to ensure effective implementation and enforcement, and to cooperate at the international and regional level;
7. Urge countries to ensure that individuals are promptly notified when their personal information is improperly disclosed or used in a manner inconsistent with its collection;
8. Recommend comprehensive research into the adequacy of techniques that deidentify; data to determine whether in practice such methods safeguard privacy and anonymity;
9. Call for a moratorium on the development or implementation of new systems of mass surveillance, including facial recognition, whole body imaging, biometric identifiers, and embedded RFID tags, subject to a full and transparent evaluation by independent authorities and democratic debate; and

> 10. Call for the establishment of a new international framework for privacy protection, with the full participation of civil society, that is based on the rule of law, respect for fundamental human rights, and support for democratic institutions.

social contract with the digital sovereigns is at a primitive, Hobbesian, royalist level. If we are lucky we get a good sovereign, and we pray that his son or chosen successor is not evil. There is a reason most people no longer accept that sort of sovereignty. It is time to upgrade the social contract over the governance of our digital lives to a Lockean level, so that the management of our identities and our access to information can more genuinely and sincerely reflect the consent of the networked."

The idea is that a new Magna Carta, one more focused on the institutions that abuse power in the 21st century, will do something similar. A few documents come close. The Madrid Privacy Declaration, signed by about 100 organizations in 2009, is still the most robust articulation of privacy rights in the modern age.

15

Solutions for the Rest of Us

Surveillance is both a technological and a legal problem. Technological solutions are often available to the user. We can use various privacy and anonymity technologies to protect our data and identities. These are effective, but can be thwarted by secret government orders. We need to fight the political battle as well.

Political solutions require group effort, but are generally limited to specific countries. Technological solutions have the potential to be global. If Microsoft designs its Windows operating system with ubiquitous file encryption, or if the Internet Engineering Task Force decides that all Internet traffic will be encrypted by default, then those changes will affect everyone in the world who uses those products and protocols.

The point is that politics can undermine technology, and also that technology can undermine politics. Neither trumps the other. If we are going to fix things, we need to fight on both the technological and the political fronts. And it's not just up to governments and corporations. We the people have a lot of work to do here.

DEFEND AGAINST SURVEILLANCE

Law professor Eben Moglen wrote, "If we are not doing anything wrong, then we have a right to do everything we can to maintain the traditional balance between us and power that is listening. We have a right to be obscure. We have a right to mumble. We have a right to speak languages they do not get. We have a right to meet when and where and how we please." If a policeman sits down within earshot, it's within your rights to move your conversation someplace else. If the FBI parks a van bristling with cameras outside your house, you are perfectly justified in closing your blinds.

Likewise, there are many ways we personally can protect our data and defend ourselves against surveillance. I'm going to break them down into categories.

Avoid Surveillance. You can alter your behavior to avoid surveillance. You can pay for things in cash instead of using a credit card, or deliberately alter your driving route to avoid traffic cameras. You can refrain from creating Facebook pages for your children, and tagging photos of them online. You can refrain from using Google Calendar, or webmail, or cloud backup. You can use DuckDuckGo for Internet searches. You can leave your cell phone at home: an easy, if inconvenient, way to avoid being tracked. More pointedly, you can leave your computer and cell phone at home when you travel to countries like China and Russia, and only use loaner equipment.

You can avoid activating automatic surveillance systems by deliberately not tripping their detection algorithms. For example, you can keep your cash transactions under the threshold over which financial institutions must report the transaction to the feds. You can decline to discuss certain topics in e-mail. In China, where automatic surveillance is common, people sometimes write messages on paper, then send photographs of those messages over the Internet. It won't help at all against targeted surveillance, but it's much harder for automatic systems to monitor. Steganography—hiding messages in otherwise innocuous image files—is a similar technique.

Block Surveillance. This is the most important thing we can do to defend ourselves. The NSA might have a larger budget than the rest of the world's national intelligence agencies combined, but it's not made of magic. Neither are any of the world's other national intelligence agencies. Effective defense leverages economics, physics, and math. While the national security agencies of the large powerful countries are going to be able to defeat anything you can do if they want to target you personally, mass surveillance relies on easy access to our data. Good defense will force those who want to surveil us to choose their targets, and they simply don't have the resources to target everyone.

Privacy enhancing technologies, or PETs, can help you block mass surveillance. Lots of technologies are available to protect your data. For example, there are easy-to-use plug-ins for browsers that monitor and block sites that track you as you wander the Internet: Lightbeam, Privacy Badger, Disconnect, Ghostery, FlashBlock, and others. Remember that the private browsing option on your browser only deletes data locally. So while it's useful for hiding your porn viewing habits from your spouse, it doesn't block Internet tracking.

The most important PET is encryption. Encrypting your hard drive with Microsoft's BitLocker or Apple's FileVault is trivially easy and completely transparent. (Last year, I recommended True-Crypt, but the developers stopped maintaining the program in 2014 under mysterious circumstances, and no one knows what to think about it.) You can use a chat encryption program like Off the Record, which is user-friendly and secure. Cryptocat is also worth looking at. If you use cloud storage, choose a company that provides encryption. I like Spideroak, but there are others. There are encryption programs for Internet voice: Silent Circle, TORFone, RedPhone, Blackphone.

Try to use an e-mail encryption plug-in like PGP. Google is now offering encrypted e-mail for its users. You'll lose some search and organization functionality, but the increased privacy might be worth it.

TLS—formerly SSL—is a protocol that encrypts some of your web browsing. It's what happens automatically, in the background, when you see "https" at the beginning of a URL instead of "http." Many websites offer this as an option, but not as a default. You can make sure it's always on wherever possible by running a browser plug-in called HTTPS Everywhere.

This is not meant to be a comprehensive list. That would take its own book, and it would be obsolete within months. Technology is always changing; go on the Internet to find out what's being recommended.

I'm not going to lead you on; many PETs will be beyond the capabilities of the average reader of this book. PGP e-mail encryption, especially, is very annoying to use. The most effective encryption tools are the ones that run in the background even when you're not aware of them, like HTTPS Everywhere and hard-drive encryption programs. In Chapter 14, I discussed some things companies are doing to secure the data of their users. Much more is going on behind the scenes. The standards bodies that run the Internet are sufficiently incensed at government surveillance that they're working to make encryption more ubiquitous online. Hopefully there will be more options by the time this book is published.

Also remember that there's a lot that encryption can't protect. Google encrypts your connection to Gmail by default, and encrypts your mail as it sits on its servers and flows around its network. But Google processes your mail, so it has a copy of the keys. The same is true for anything you send to any social networking site.

Most metadata can't be encrypted. So while you can encrypt the contents of your e-mail, the To and From lines need to be unencrypted so the e-mail system can deliver messages. Similarly, your cell phone can encrypt your voice conversations, but the phone numbers you dial, the location of your phone, and your phone's ID number all need to be unencrypted. And while you can encrypt your credit card data when you send it over the Internet to an online retailer, that company needs your name and address so it can mail your purchases to you.

And finally, encryption doesn't protect your computer while in use. You can still be hacked, either by criminals or governments. But, again, this is likely to be targeted surveillance rather than mass. All this means that while encryption is an important part of the solution, it's not the whole of it.

The current best tool to protect your anonymity when browsing the web is Tor. It's pretty easy to use and, as far as we know, it's secure. Similarly, various proxies can be used to evade surveillance and censorship. The program Onionshare anonymously sends files over the Internet using Tor. Against some adversaries, web proxies are adequate anonymity tools.

There are more low-tech things you can do to block surveillance. You can turn location services off on your smartphone when you don't need it, and try to make informed decisions about which apps may access your location and other data. You can refrain from posting identifying details on public sites. When Snowden first met journalists in Hong Kong, he made them all put their cell phones in a refrigerator to block all signals to and from the devices, so they couldn't be remotely turned into listening devices.

Sometimes surveillance blocking is remarkably simple. A sticker placed over a computer's camera can prevent someone who controls it remotely from taking pictures of you. You can leave the return address off an envelope to limit what data the post office can collect. You can hire someone to walk behind your car to obscure your license plate from automatic scanners, as people do in Tehran. Sometimes it is as easy as saying "no": refusing to divulge personal information on forms when asked, not giving your phone number to a sales clerk at a store, and so on.

Some sorts of blocking behaviors are illegal: you're not allowed to actually cover your car's license plate. Others are socially discouraged, like walking around town wearing a mask. And still others will get you funny looks, like wearing face paint to fool facial recognition cameras or special clothing to confuse drones.

Distort Surveillance. I have my browser configured to delete my cookies every time I close it, which I do multiple times a day. I am still being surveilled, but now it's much harder to tie all those small surveillances back to me and ads don't follow me around. When I shop at Safeway, I use a friend's frequent shopper number. That ends up distorting the store's surveillance of her.

Sometimes this is called obfuscation, and there are lots of tricks, once you start thinking about it. You can swap retailer affinity cards with your friends and neighbors. You can dress in drag. In Cory Doctorow's 2008 book, *Little Brother*, the lead character puts rocks in his shoes to alter the way he walks, to fool gait recognition systems.

There is also safety in numbers. As long as there are places in the world where PETs keep people alive, the more we use them, the more secure they are. It's like envelopes. If everyone used postcards by default, the few who used envelopes would be suspect. Since almost everyone uses envelopes, those who really need the privacy of an envelope don't stand out. This is especially true for an anonymity service like Tor, which relies on many people using it to obscure the identities of everyone.

You can also, and I know someone who does this, search for random names on Facebook to confuse it about whom you really know. At best, this is a partial solution; data analysis is a signal-to-noise problem, and adding random noise makes the analysis harder.

You can give false information on web forms or when asked. (Your kids do it all the time.) For years, well before consumer tracking became the norm, Radio Shack stores would routinely ask their customers for their addresses and phone numbers. For a while I just refused, but that was socially awkward. Instead, I got in the habit of replying with "9800 Savage Road, Columbia, MD, 20755": the address of the NSA. When I told this story to a colleague some years ago, he said that he always gave out the address "1600 Pennsylvania Avenue, Washington, DC." He insisted that no one recognized it.

You can also get a credit card in another name. There's nothing shady about it, just ask your credit card company for a second card in another name tied to your account. As long as the merchant doesn't ask for ID, you can use it.

Deception can be extremely powerful if used sparingly. I remember a story about a group of activists in Morocco. Those who didn't carry cell phones were tracked physically by the secret police and occasionally beaten up. Those who did weren't, and could therefore leave their phones home when they really needed to hide their movements. More generally, if you close off all the enemy's intelligence channels, you close off your ability to deceive him.

Break Surveillance. Depending on the technology, you can break some surveillance systems. You can sever the wires powering automatic speed traps on roads. You can spray-paint the lenses of security cameras. If you're a good enough hacker, you can disable Internet surveillance systems, delete or poison surveillance databases, or otherwise monkey wrench. Pretty much everything in this category is illegal, so beware.

Some of these methods are harder than others. Some of us will be able to do more than others. Many people enter random information into web forms. Far fewer people—I've only ever met one who did this—search for random things on Google to muddle up their profiles. Many of these behaviors carry social, time, or monetary costs, not to mention the psychological burden of constant paranoia. I rarely sign up for retail affinity cards, and that means I miss out on discounts. I don't use Gmail, and I never access my e-mail via the web. I don't have a personal Facebook account, and that means I'm not as connected with my friends as I might otherwise be. But I do carry a cell phone pretty much everywhere I go, and I collect frequent flier miles whenever possible, which means I let those companies track me. You'll find your own sweet spot.

We should all do what we can, because we believe that our privacy is important and that we need to exercise our rights lest we lose them. But for Pete's sake, don't take those silly online surveys unless you know where your data is going to end up.

AID GOVERNMENT SURVEILLANCE

A call to help the government in its surveillance efforts might seem out of place in this book, but hear me out.

There are legitimate needs for government surveillance, both law enforcement and intelligence needs, and we should recognize that. More importantly, we need to support legitimate surveillance, and work on ways for these groups to do what they need to do without violating privacy, subverting security, and infringing upon citizens' right to be free of unreasonable suspicion and observation. If we can provide law enforcement people with new ways to investigate crime, they'll stop demanding that security be subverted for their benefit.

Geopolitical conflicts aren't going away, and foreign intelligence is a singular tool to navigate these incidents. As I write this in the late summer of 2014, Russia is amassing forces against Ukraine, China is bullying Japan and Korea in the South China Sea, Uighur terrorists are killing Han Chinese, Israel is attacking Gaza, Qatar and Turkey are helping Gaza defend itself, Afghanistan is a chaotic mess, Libya is in decline, Egypt is back to a dictatorship, Iran's nuclear program might be resuming, Ebola is sweeping West Africa, North Korea is testing new missiles, Syria is killing its own people, and much of Iraq is controlled by a nominally Islamic extremist organization known as ISIS. And this is just the stuff that makes the news. When you read this book, the list will be different but no less serious. I assure you that no one in the White House is calling for the NSA to minimize collection of data on these and similar threats. Nor should they.

Additionally, governments around the world have a pervasive fear of cyberattack. A lot of this is overreaction, but there are real risks. And cyberdefense is mired in a classic collective action problem. Most of the infrastructure of cyberspace is in private hands, but most of the harm of a major cyberattack will be felt by the population as a whole. This means that it's not going to work long-term to trust the companies that control our infrastructure to adequately protect that infrastructure. Some sort of government involvement is necessary. In 2013, NSA director General Keith Alexander said, "I can't defend the country until I'm into all the networks." That's the prevailing view in Washington.

Yes, we need to figure out how much we want the NSA in all of our networks. But we also need to help the NSA not want to get into all of our networks. If we can give governments new ways to collect data on hostile nations, terrorist groups, and global criminal elements, they'll have less need to go to the extreme measures I've detailed in this book. This is a genuine call for new ideas, new tools, and new techniques. Honestly, I don't know what the solutions will look like. There's a middle road, and it's up to us to find it.

This isn't a task for everyone. It's something for industry, academia, and those of us who understand and work with the technologies. But it's an important task, and not one that either the intelligence or the law enforcement communities will do for us. If we want organizations like the NSA to protect our privacy, we're going to have to give them new ways to perform their intelligence jobs.

CHOOSE YOUR ALLIES AND ENEMIES

Our laws are based on geographical location. For most of human history, this made a lot of sense. It makes less sense when it comes to the Internet; the Internet is just too international.

You're obviously subject to the legal rules of the country you live in, but when you're online, things get more complicated. You're going to be affected by the rules of the country your hardware manufacturer lives in, the rules of the country your software vendor lives in, and the rules of the country your online cloud application provider lives in. You're going to be affected by the rules of the country where your data resides, and the rules of whatever countries your data passes through as it moves around the Internet.

The PATRIOT Act, for example, compels US companies to turn data over to the US government when asked, no matter where it is stored. You might be a French citizen living in France, and Microsoft might store your e-mail solely on servers in Ireland. But because Microsoft is a US company, the US maintains that it is compelled to produce your data on demand. The UK wants similar access.

This means you have to decide: which countries do you trust with your data, and which companies do you trust with your data?

Corporations are not all equally bad. You can get your e-mail, calendar, and address book from either Google or Apple. They will both protect your data from bulk government collection, but will give your data to many of the world's governments when legally compelled. Google is embarking on a major project to improve the security of its users against government surveillance. But Google is in the business of collecting your data and using it for advertising, whereas Apple's business model protects its customers' privacy.

Do you trust a company in the US that is unfettered in what it can do with your data and is also subject to NSA and FBI legal requests? Or do you trust a company in Europe that is tightly regulated by the government with regard to corporate surveillance, but is also subject to unfettered surveillance by both its own government and that of the US, and whose use means your data crosses international borders? If you don't buy networking equipment from Cisco because you are concerned about NSA backdoors, whom will you buy it from? Huawei? Remember my feudal analogy from Chapter 4; which lord do you trust more?

It is hard to know where to start. In today's cloud computing world, we often have no idea which companies actually host our data. An Internet company like Orbitz might host its infrastructure on a provider like Atlassian, which in turn hosts its infrastructure on a provider like Rackspace. Do you have any idea where your Orbitz data actually is?

We need to be able to know where our data is stored, and to specify which countries we want our data stored in, and which countries we want our data never to go near. In the meantime, we have to do the best we can. And recognize that in most cases we simply don't know.

But when it comes to governments, unhappy as I am to say it, I would rather be eavesdropped on by the US government than by many other regimes.

AGITATE FOR POLITICAL CHANGE

In 2014, the European Court of Justice struck down the EU's data retention rules, which required service providers to save e-mail and information about phone calls for two years. In response, the UK government rushed through a new law that reinstated the data retention requirement and also gave the police new surveillance powers over its citizens. It was an ugly political railroad job, but what's interesting is how Prime Minister David Cameron justified the law on a radio program: "I am simply not prepared to be a prime minister who has to address the people after a terrorist incident and explain that I could have done more to prevent it."

That's fear talking, but it's not fear of terrorists. It's political fear of being blamed when there's a terrorist attack. The career politician wants to do everything possible, regardless of the cost, regardless of whether it actually makes anyone safer, regardless of the side effects, to avoid blame for not having done enough. This fear explains most post-9/11 anti-terrorism policy, and much of the NSA's mass-surveillance programs. Our politicians are scared that we'll blame them because they didn't do everything the intelligence agencies said they could have done to prevent further terrorism.

We have to convince them—and our fellow voters—that they should do the right thing anyway.

Most of the solutions offered in the preceding two chapters require the government to either enforce existing laws or change the law. By and large, neither of these things will happen unless we demand them. Politicians are reluctant to engage in these debates, and even more reluctant to enact meaningful constraints on government surveillance. Legislatures are naturally deferential to law enforcement demands, and the vast surveillance-industrial complex employs a powerful lobbying force to back them up. No one wants to be painted as being soft on crime or terrorism. And today, when US intelligence agencies are caught breaking the law, the only ones threatened with jail time are the whistleblowers.

On the corporate side, throngs of lobbyists are doing their best to ensure that there's no meaningful reform of corporate surveillance. Free markets are held up as a justification to continue to do nothing. And the police and the national security apparatus are also pushing to ensure that all of our data remains available to them for their own use.

If we want our legislators to vote against the powerful interests of the military, law enforcement, and lobbyist-laden corporations (both the ones that supply the government and the ones that spy on us directly), we're going to have to make ourselves even more powerful. And that means we have to engage in the political process. I have three specific recommendations here.

Notice Surveillance. This is the first step. Lots of surveillance is hidden, but not completely invisible. The cameras might be small, but you can still see most of them if you look. You can notice when someone scans your ID when you enter a bar. You can install a browser plug-in and see who's tracking you online. You can pay attention to news stories about surveillance. There are online sites that identify surveillance cameras. The more you know, the more you'll understand what's going on.

Talk about Surveillance. This is the next step. The more we talk about it, the more people realize what's going on. And the more they realize what's going on, the more they're going to care about it. And the more we talk about it publicly, the more our elected representatives will realize that we care about it.

I mean this very generally. Talk about surveillance with your family, friends, and colleagues. Don't be one of those annoying people who never posts about anything else, but share interesting news stories on social media. Attend rallies and sign petitions. Write to your elected representatives. Give copies of this book to all your friends as gifts. Make your opinions known. This is important.

Talk about the laws in your country. What kinds of government surveillance are legal in your country? How are your country's businesses complicit in this, and what sorts of surveillance are legal for them to conduct? What rights do people have to use privacy enhancing technologies? Find out.

One of the most surreal aspects of the NSA stories based on the Snowden documents is how they made even the most paranoid conspiracy theorists seem like paragons of reason and common sense. It's easy to forget the details and fall back into complacency; only continued discussion of the details can prevent this.

Organize Politically. This is our most effective strategy. There are many good recent examples of people organizing against surveillance: South Korean teachers objecting to new student databases, German consumers opposing RFID-enabled shopping carts, Facebook users objecting to new terms of service, US airline travelers objecting to airport full-body scanners. The campaigns are not always successful and the outcomes are imperfect, but the significance of collective action can't be overstated. We need to see these problems as common to us all, and the solutions as general.

This isn't a book about political organizing, and there are far better people than me at advising how to agitate for political change. I do know that politics isn't just something that happens at election times. It's a continual process that involves engaging with legislators, protesting in public, and supporting relevant nonprofit groups. Look at the Electronic Frontier Foundation, the Electronic Privacy Information Center, the Center for Democracy and Technology, Privacy International, the Open Technology Institute, and others. They're all fighting for more privacy and less surveillance. Help them.

There's nothing we can do about much of the world, of course, but we can push for change where we can. And then we can slowly move outwards. It's how worldwide change happens.

DON'T GIVE UP

Fatalism is the enemy of change. Fatalism as in: governments and large corporations are both all-powerful, and the majority of politicians have no desire to restrain either of them, so there's nothing we can do to change things. And fatalism as in: mass surveillance is so ubiquitous that there's nothing we can do to resist it, and resistance only makes us more interesting to them anyway.

The assertions have some truth to them, but the conclusions are false. Good computer security and pervasive encryption make mass surveillance difficult. Choosing companies to do business with on the basis of their privacy policies makes companies more likely to have good privacy policies. Political organization is effective. Our infatuation with big data and our irrational fear of terrorism will both wane over time. Laws will eventually constrain both government and corporate power on the Internet.

The policy shifts I advise are major, and they're going to take work. Every major policy shift in history looked futile in the beginning. That's just the way of it. We need to fight for political change, and we need to keep fighting until we prevail. And until then, there are lots of little battles we can win along the way.

There is strength in numbers, and if the public outcry grows, governments and corporations will be forced to respond. We are trying to prevent an authoritarian government like the one portrayed in Orwell's *Nineteen Eighty-Four*, and a corporate-ruled state like the ones portrayed in countless dystopian cyberpunk science fiction novels. We are nowhere near either of those endpoints, but the train is moving in both those directions, and we need to apply the brakes.

16

Social Norms and the Big Data Trade-off

I n the preceding three chapters, I outlined a lot of changes that need to happen: changes in government, corporate, and individual behavior. Some of them are technical, but most of them require new laws or at least new policies. At this point many of them are unrealistic, at least in the US. I'm not yet living in a country where the majority of people want these changes, let alone a country where the will of the people easily translates into legislative action.

Most people don't seem to care whether their intimate details are collected and used by corporations; they think that surveillance by the governments they trust is a necessary prerequisite to keeping them safe. Most people are still overly scared of terrorism. They don't understand the extent of the surveillance capabilities available to both governments and private parties. They underestimate the amount of surveillance that's going on and don't realize that mass government surveillance doesn't do much to keep us safe. Most people are happy to exchange sensitive personal information for free e-mail, web search, or a platform on which to chat with their friends.

Europe is somewhat different—it regulates corporate surveillance more heavily and government surveillance much less so—but for most purposes the public sentiments are the same.

Before we get meaningful political change, some of our social norms are going to have to change. We need to get to the point where people comprehend the vast extent of surveillance and the enormous concentration of power that flows from it. Once they do, most people will probably say, "That's just not okay." We need to summon the political will to fight both the law enforcement and national intelligence communities on the government side, and the government contractors and surveillance industry on the corporate side. And before any of that can happen, there must be some major changes in the way society views and values privacy, security, liberty, trust, and a handful of other abstract concepts that are defining this debate.

This is hard. Public sentiment tends to move towards actual practice. We're good at accepting the status quo—whatever that is and however recently it has emerged. (Honestly, it blows me away that most of this surveillance has emerged in less than two decades.) We're growing accustomed to the panopticon. You can see it writ large, when people shrug and say, "What are you going to do?" You can see it in a microcosm every time Facebook degrades its users' privacy options; people complain in the beginning, but soon get used to it.

What follows in this chapter are all changes in attitude. They're ways in which we are going to have to modify our feelings and thoughts if we are ever going to get beyond the surveillance society.

RECALIBRATE OUR FEAR

The PATRIOT Act was signed into law on October 26, 2001, just 45 days after the terrorist attacks against the World Trade Center and the Pentagon. It was a wish list of police and intelligence powers and authorities, passed overwhelmingly in both houses with minimal debate. No one in Congress read it before voting. And almost everyone in the country wanted the law to pass, despite not understanding its provisions.

In 2014, I attended a talk in which Tim Duffy, the chairman and chief executive of the advertising agency M&C Saatchi, tried to improve the messaging of privacy. He suggested "Where do you draw the line?" as a possible framing. But if listeners are scared of terrorists, they will draw the line in such a way as to allow a whole lot of surveillance. Harvard Law School professor Jack Goldsmith pointed out that when we're scared, more congressional oversight yields more NSA authority.

Fear trumps privacy. Fear of terrorism trumps fear of tyranny. If strong enough, it trumps all the concerns in this book piled together. In the people, it's fear of the next terrorist attack. In politicians, it's that and also fear of being *blamed* for the next terrorist attack. But it's fear, nonetheless. Recall Prime Minister Cameron in the preceding chapter. This is what I hear again and again from government officials when I ask about the obvious ineffectiveness of mass surveillance against the terrorist threat. Yes, they admit, it hasn't resulted in any successes; but it's an insurance policy. They know that their targeted surveillance efforts will fail at some point, and they hope that mass surveillance will be there for backup. True, the odds are low that it will work like that, but they believe they have to do everything possible—both for the security of the country and for the security of their jobs.

Regardless of the magnitude of the threat, mass surveillance is not an effective countermeasure; conventional police and intelligence work is. We need to resist the urge to *do something*, regardless of whether or not the proposed action is effective.

Keeping the fear stoked is big business. Those in the intelligence community know it's the basis of their influence and power. And government contractors know it's where the money for their contracts comes from. Writer and Internet activist Clay Shirky has noted that "institutions will try to preserve the problem to which they are the solution." Fear is that problem.

It's a fear that's stoked by the day's news. As soon as there's a horrific crime or a terrorist attack that supposedly could have been prevented if only the FBI or DHS had had access to some data stored by Facebook or encrypted in an iPhone, people will demand to know why the FBI or DHS didn't have access to that data—why they were prevented from "connecting the dots." And then the laws will change to give them even more authority. Jack Goldsmith again: "The government will increase its powers to meet the national security threat fully (because the People demand it)."

We need a better way to handle our emotional responses to terrorism than by giving our government carte blanche to violate our freedoms, in some desperate attempt to feel safe again. If we don't find one, then, as they say, the terrorists will truly have won. One goal of government is to provide security for its people, but in democracies, we need to take risks. A society that refuses risk—in crime, terrorism, or elsewhere—is by definition a police state. And a police state brings with it its own dangers.

It's not just politicians who are to blame for this. The media are culpable, too. By fixating on rare and spectacular events, they condition us to behave as if terrorism were much more common than it is and to fear it far out of proportion to its actual incidence. And we are also at fault, if we buy the propaganda the media are selling.

We also need to counter the notion that modern technology makes everything different. In the days and weeks after the 9/11 terrorist attacks, as we debated new laws and new police powers, we heard this sentence: "The Constitution is not a suicide pact." It expresses a sentiment based in fear, and its meaning is worth unpacking. What it says is something like this: "The people who wrote our laws couldn't possibly have anticipated the situation we now face. Therefore, the limits they put on police power and the prohibitions they enacted against surveillance should not apply to us. Our situation is unique, and we must ignore all of that." The primary reason for succumbing to these notions was that we believed that the damage terrorists could cause was so great that we could not conceivably rely on conventional law enforcement means and after-the-fact prosecutions.

It's just not true. It's a common psychological fallacy to believe that we live in unique times, that our challenges are totally unlike anything that came before and necessitate ignoring any of the societal controls we previously put in place to check the powers of governmental authorities. President Lincoln succumbed to the fallacy when he suspended habeas corpus during the Civil War. President Wilson did so when he arrested and deported Socialists and labor leaders just after World War I. President Roosevelt did so when he interned Americans of Japanese, German, and Italian descent during World War II. We did it during the Cold War's McCarthy era. And we are doing it again after 9/11.

Fear isn't the only way we can react to these threats, and there are many instances in history where society did not give up its rights in an effort to remain safe. In the wake of the horrific 2011 massacre in Norway by Anders Breivik, that country has largely preserved its core values of liberty and openness. And, of course, there's FDR's famous line "The only thing we have to fear is fear itself." Indomitability is the correct response to terrorism.

There's hope for the US. We don't always respond to terrorism with fear. Looking back through recent history, the presidents who stood up to terrorism—Truman, Eisenhower, Nixon, Reagan some of the time, Bush the elder—achieved better operational and political results than those who used terrorism as an opportunity for political grandstanding: Carter, Reagan the rest of the time, Bush the younger. We need to recognize the strength of politicians who protect our freedoms in the face of risk, and the weakness of those who cannot solve problems and choose to sacrifice our freedoms instead. More than a decade after 9/11, it's well past time to move beyond fear and return to our core American values of freedom, liberty, and justice. And there are indications that we are doing so. In 2013, we started seeing a significant shift in Americans' perceptions regarding the trade-off between civil liberties and national security.

RECALIBRATE PRIVACY

Our personal definitions of privacy are both cultural and situational. They were different 100 years ago than they are today, and they'll be different 100 years from now. They're different in the US than they are in Europe, Japan, and elsewhere. They're different across generations.

Right now, the Internet is forcing our attitudes about privacy to shift as never before. That's because one of the main ways we use it is to learn about each other. Lawyers look up potential jurors. Job seekers look up company executives; company HR departments look up potential employees. Before a first date, people look up each other. This sort of thing even has a name: Google stalking.

Online, we are constantly probing, and occasionally violating, one another's privacy. This can be pretty uncomfortable. The semi-permanent nature of Internet communications provides all sorts of opportunities for someone to embarrass you. E-mails you send to someone in private can easily be forwarded to others. Kids do this to each other all the time: forwarding private chats, photos, and messages, or showing each other private postings on social networking sites. One of the reasons apps that delete messages and photos after a few seconds are so popular among teenagers is that they help prevent this sort of thing. Old web pages have a way of sticking around. In 2010, WikiLeaks founder Julian Assange's old OKCupid dating profile was dug up for public discussion.

Even worse are people who use the Internet to shame and harass. Revenge porn—for the most part, ex-boyfriends posting compromising photographs of former girlfriends—is an extreme example. Mug shot extortion sites turn this sort of thing into a business. Mug shots are public record, but they're not readily available. Owners of mug shot sites acquire the photos in bulk and publish them online, where everybody can find them, then charge individuals to remove their photos from the sites. It is extortion, although technically legal. None of this is going away, even if some instances of it are outlawed in some jurisdictions.

We need to figure this out. Everyone has the ability to buy sophisticated surveillance gear, so we need social norms that tell us when not to use it. We know more about one another than any one of us is comfortable with, so we need to develop social norms around acknowledging what we do know or pretending we don't. This is essentially the point of David Brin's 1998 book, *The Transparent Society*; ubiquitous surveillance is coming and we have to adapt.

The Internet has engendered the greatest generation gap since rock and roll. As Clay Shirky pointed out, it's not that the elders were wrong about all the changes rock and roll would bring; it's that they were wrong about how harmful they would be. People adapt. When everyone leaves a public digital trail of their personal thoughts since birth, no one will think twice about its being there. If technology means that everything we say—the regrettable accusations, the banalities, all of it—will be recorded and preserved eternally, we're going to have to learn to live with that.

The problem is that we're too good at adapting, at least in the short term. People who grow up with more surveillance will be more comfortable with it. Some of us went to schools with ID checks and metal detectors. Some of us work at buildings that demand daily badge checks. Most of us who fly in the US now accept TSA searches. And all of us who shop are no longer surprised about massive thefts of credit card numbers. These are all ways in which we have accustomed ourselves to having less privacy. Like many fundamental rights, privacy is one of those things that becomes noticed only when it's gone. That's unfortunate, because after it's gone it's much harder to regain.

We have to stop the slide. Fundamentally, the argument for privacy is a moral one. It is something we ought to have—not because it is profitable or efficient, but because it is moral. Mass surveillance should be relegated to the dustbin of history, along with so many other practices that humans once considered normal but are now universally recognized as abhorrent. Privacy is a human right.

Charter of Fundamental Rights of the European Union (2000)

ARTICLE 7: Respect for private and family life. Everyone has the right to respect for his or her private and family life, home and communications.

ARTICLE 8: Protection of personal data. 1. Everyone has the right to the protection of personal data concerning him or her. 2. Such data must be processed fairly for specified purposes and on the basis of the consent of the person concerned or some other legitimate basis laid down by law. Everyone has the right of access to data which has been collected concerning him or her, and the right to have it rectified. 3. Compliance with these rules shall be subject to control by an independent authority.

This isn't a new idea. Privacy is recognized as a fundamental right in the Universal Declaration of Human Rights (1948) and the European Convention on Human Rights (1970).

It's in the US Constitution—not explicitly, but it's implied in the Fourth, Fifth, and Ninth Amendments. It's part of the 2000 Charter of Fundamental Rights of the European Union. In 2013, the UN General Assembly approved a resolution titled "The right to privacy in the digital age," affirming that our fundamental right to privacy applies online as well as offline, and the risk of mass surveillance undermines this right.

The principles are enshrined in both national and international law. We need to start following them. Privacy is not a luxury that we can only afford in times of safety. Instead, it's a value to be preserved. It's essential for liberty, autonomy, and human dignity. We must understand that privacy is not something to be traded away in some fearful attempt to guarantee security, but something to maintain and protect in order to have real security.

None of this will happen without a change of attitude. In the end, we'll get the privacy we as a society demand and not a bit more.

DON'T WAIT

The longer we wait to make changes, the harder it will become. On the corporate side, ubiquitous tracking and personalized advertising are already the norm, and companies have strong lobbying presences to stymie any attempt to change that. California's Do Not Track law is an example of that: it started out as a good idea, but was completely defanged by the time it passed. The natural trajectory of surveillance technology (remember the declining cost from Chapter 2?) and the establishment of a new status quo will make changes much harder to achieve in the future, especially in the US.

It's not just corporations that oppose change. Politicians like the same data that commercial advertisers do: demographic data, information about individual consumer preferences, political and religious beliefs. They use it in their campaigns, and won't want to give it up. Convincing them to forgo access to data that helps them with targeted messaging and get-out-the-vote campaigns will be tough. And once someone figures out how to use this data to make elections permanently unfair, as gerrymandering does, change will be even harder.

At a conference last year, I overheard someone saying, "Google Analytics is the crack cocaine of Internet surveillance. Once you see it, you never want to give it up." More generally, data becomes its own justification. The longer we wait, the more people and organizations become used to having broad access to our data and the more they will fight to maintain that access.

We're at a unique time to make the sorts of changes I recommend in this book.

The industries that collect and resell our data are powerful, but they're still relatively new. As they mature and become more entrenched, it will be much harder to make major changes in how they do business.

Snowden has forced government surveillance into the spotlight by revealing the actions of the NSA and GCHQ. This has produced some singular tensions amongst the world's countries, between Germany and the US in particular. And in the US, this political tension cuts across the traditional partisan divide. There's an opportunity for real change here. As Chicago mayor and former Obama chief of staff Rahm Emanuel said, "You never want a serious crisis to go to waste." That's true here, even if most people don't realize that this is a crisis.

We're at a unique moment in the relationship between the US and the EU. Both sides want to harmonize rules about this sort of thing, to make cross-border commerce easier. Things could go one of two ways: Europe could become more permissive to match the US, or the US could become more restrictive to match Europe. Once those rules get equalized, they'll be harder to change.

We're also in a unique time in the development of the information age. The Internet is being integrated into everything. We have temporary visibility of these systems. We can make changes now that will stand for decades.

Even so, we need to be prepared to do this all over again.

Technology constantly changes, making new things possible and old laws obsolete. There's no reason to think that the security, privacy, and anonymity technologies that protect us against today's threats will work against tomorrow's.

Political realities also change, and laws change with them. It's folly to believe that any set of solutions we establish today will hold forever, or even for half a century. A look back at recent US history suggests that gross abuses of executive power—and the resulting big public scandals and mitigating reforms—have occurred every 25 to 30 years. Consider the Palmer Raids in the 1920s, McCarthyism in the 1950s, abuses by the NSA and the FBI in the 1970s, and the ongoing post-9/11 abuses in the 2000s.

If you think about it, 30 years is about the career length of a professional civil servant. My guess is that's not a coincidence. What seems to be going on is that we reform, we remember for a while why we implemented those reforms, and then eventually enough people change over in government that we begin to forget. And then we roll back the reforms and have to do the whole thing over again in a new technological context.

The next set of abuses is for another generation to reckon with, though. This one is ours.

I worry that we're not up to it: that this is generational, and that it will be up to the next generation to make the social shifts necessary to enact policy changes that protect our fundamental privacy.

I worry that the generation currently in charge is too scared of the terrorists, and too quick to give corporations anything they want. I hope I'm wrong.

THE BIG DATA TRADE-OFF

Most of this book is about the misuse and abuse of our personal data, but the truth is, this data also offers incredible value for society.

Our data has enormous value when we put it all together. Our movement records help with urban planning. Our financial records enable the police to detect and prevent fraud and money laundering. Our posts and tweets help researchers understand how we tick as a society. There are all sorts of creative and interesting uses for personal data, uses that give birth to new knowledge and make all of our lives better.

Our data is also valuable to each of us individually, to conceal or disclose as we want. And there's the rub. Using data pits group interest against self-interest, the core tension humanity has been struggling with since we came into existence.

Remember the bargains I talked about in the Introduction. The government offers us this deal: if you let us have all of your data, we can protect you from crime and terrorism. It's a rip-off. It doesn't work. And it overemphasizes group security at the expense of individual security.

The bargain Google offers us is similar, and it's similarly out of balance: if you let us have all of your data and give up your privacy, we will show you advertisements you want to see—and we'll throw in free web search, e-mail, and all sorts of other services. Companies like Google and Facebook can only make that bargain when enough of us give up our privacy. The group can only benefit if enough individuals acquiesce.

Not all bargains pitting group interest against individual interest are such raw deals. The medical community is about to make a similar bargain with us: let us have all your health data, and we will use it to revolutionize healthcare and improve the lives of everyone. In this case, I think they have it right. I don't think anyone can comprehend how much humanity will benefit from putting all of our health data in a single database and letting researchers access it. Certainly this data is incredibly personal, and is bound to find its way into unintended hands and be used for unintended purposes. But in this particular example, it seems obvious to me that the communal use of the data should take precedence. Others disagree.

Here's another case that got the balance between group and individual interests right. Social media researcher Reynol Junco analyzes the study habits of his students. Many textbooks are online, and the textbook websites collect an enormous amount of data about how—and how often—students interact with the course material. Junco augments that information with surveillance of his students' other computer activities. This is incredibly invasive research, but its duration is limited and he is gaining new understanding about how both good and bad students study—and has developed interventions aimed at improving how students learn. Did the group benefit of this study outweigh the individual privacy interest of the subjects who took part in it?

Junco's subjects consented to being monitored, and his research was approved by a university ethics board—but what about experiments performed by corporations? The dating site OKCupid has been experimenting on its users for years, selectively showing or hiding photos, inflating or deflating compatibility measures, to see how such changes affect people's behavior on the site. You can argue that we've learned from this experimentation, but it's hard to justify manipulating people in this way without their knowledge or permission.

Again and again, it's the same tension: group value versus individual value. There's value in our collective data for evaluating the efficacy of social programs. There's value in our collective data for market research. There's value in it for improving government services. There's value in studying social trends, and predicting future ones. We have to weigh each of these benefits against the risks of the surveillance that enables them.

The big question is this: how do we design systems that make use of our data collectively to benefit society as a whole, while at the same time protecting people individually? Or, to use a term from game theory, how do we find a "Nash equilibrium" for data collection: a balance that creates an optimal overall outcome, even while forgoing optimization of any single facet?

This is it: this is the fundamental issue of the information age. We can solve it, but it will require careful thinking about the specific issues and moral analysis of how the different solutions affect our core values.

I've met hardened privacy advocates who nonetheless think it should be a crime not to put your medical data into a society-wide database. I've met people who are perfectly fine with permitting the most intimate surveillance by corporations, but want governments never to be able to touch that data. I've met people who are fine with government surveillance, but are against anything that has a profit motive attached to it. And I've met lots of people who are fine with any of the above.

As individuals and as a society, we are constantly trying to balance our different values. We never get it completely right. What's important is that we deliberately engage in the process. Too often the balancing is done for us by governments and corporations with their own agendas.

Whatever our politics, we need to get involved. We don't want the FBI and NSA to secretly decide what levels of government surveillance are the default on our cell phones; we want Congress to decide matters like these in an open and public debate. We don't want the governments of China and Russia to decide what censorship capabilities are built into the Internet; we want an international standards body to make those decisions. We don't want Facebook to decide the extent of privacy we enjoy amongst our friends; we want to decide for ourselves. All of these decisions are bigger and more important than any one organization. They need to be made by a greater and more representative and inclusive institution. We want the public to be able to have open debates about these things, and "we the people" to be able to hold decision makers accountable.

I often turn to a statement by Rev. Martin Luther King Jr: "The arc of history is long, but it bends toward justice." I am long-term optimistic, even if I remain short-term pessimistic. I think we will overcome our fears, learn how to value our privacy, and put rules in place to reap the benefits of big data while securing ourselves from some of the risks. Right now, we're seeing the beginnings of a very powerful worldwide movement to recognize privacy as a fundamental human right, not just in the abstract sense we see in so many public pronouncements, but in a meaningful and enforceable way. The EU is leading the charge, but others will follow. The process will take years, possibly decades, but I believe that in half a century people will look at the data practices of today the same way we now view archaic business practices like tenant farming, child labor, and company stores. They'll look immoral. The start of this movement, more than anything else, will be Edward Snowden's legacy.

I started this book by talking about data as exhaust: something we all produce as we go about our information-age business. I think I can take that analogy one step further. Data is the pollution problem of the information age, and protecting privacy is the environmental challenge. Almost all computers produce personal information. It stays around, festering. How we deal with it—how we contain it and how we dispose of it—is central to the health of our information economy. Just as we look back today at the early decades of the industrial age and wonder how our ancestors could have ignored pollution in their rush to build an industrial world, our grandchildren will look back at us during these early decades of the information age and judge us on how we addressed the challenge of data collection and misuse.

We should try to make them proud.

Acknowledgments

For me, writing a book is an exploration of a topic. I don't know where I'll end up until I'm done writing. This makes it very hard for me to sell a book. I can't provide an outline. I can't even say for sure what the book is about. Publishers don't tend to go for that.

First, I need to thank my agent, Eric Nelson at the Susan Rabiner Literary Agency, for representing my book before there was a book. He believed that he could sell "the next Schneier book" to a mainstream publisher, and believed it so much that he didn't ask for any formal agreement before he started.

Second, I need to thank my editor, Jeff Shreve, at Norton. He was willing to buy "the next Schneier book" with only vague assurances as to what it was about. And he was willing to accept my writing process.

I don't write books from beginning to end. I write them from bottom to top. What I mean is that at every moment I am working on the entire book at once. This has two curious effects. One, the book is complete very soon after I start writing. It's just not very good, and improves as I keep writing. It just continues to improve as I keep writing. And two, I would keep writing and improving the book forever if allowed to. What I do is arbitrarily define "done" as the moment the book is due.

This process allows me to get detailed feedback on the book throughout the process. Many people read all or parts of the manuscript: Ross Anderson, Steve Bass, Caspar Bowden, Cody Charette, David Campbell, Karen Cooper, Dorothy Denning, Cory Doctorow, Ryan Ellis, Addison Fischer, Camille François, Naomi Gilens, John Gilmore, Jack Goldsmith, Bob Gourley, Bill Herdle, Deborah Hurley, Chrisma Jackson, Reynol Junco, John Kelsey, Alexander Klimburg, David Levari, Stephen Leigh, Harry Lewis, Jun Li, Ken Liu, Alex Loomis, Sascha Meinrath, Aleecia M. McDonald, Pablo Molina, Ramez Naam, Peter Neumann, Joseph Nye, Cirsten Paine, David M. Perry, Leah Plunkett, David Prentiss, Barath Raghavan, Marc Rotenberg, Martin Schneier, Seth David Schoen, Adam Shostack, Peter Swire, Kit Walsh, Sara M. Watson, David Weinberger, Dustin Wenzel, Marcy Wheeler, Richard Willey, Ben Wizner, Josephine Wolff, Jonathan Zittrain, and Shoshana Zuboff. Every one of these people gave me suggestions that I incorporated into the book.

A few people were invaluable in writing this book. Kathleen Seidel is the best researcher I have ever found, and I can no longer imagine writing a book without her help. Same with Rebecca Kessler, who edited the book twice during my writing process and gave me critical suggestions each time. Beth Friedman, who has copyedited everything I have written for over a decade, continues to be irreplaceable.

I would also like to thank Edward Snowden, whose courageous actions resulted in the global conversation we are now having about surveillance. It's not an exaggeration to say that I would not have written this book had he not done what he did. Also, as a longtime NSA watcher, reading those top-secret documents is pretty cool.

A note about the title. Both my editor and I immediately liked *Data and Goliath*, but there was a problem. Malcolm Gladwell had recently published a book titled *David and Goliath*. That wasn't so bad, but my previous book was titled *Liars and Outliers*; it was published immediately after Gladwell's previous book *Outliers*. Aping him twice seemed too much. In April, I explained my dilemma on my blog, and received an e-mail out of the blue from Gladwell, saying, "i LOVE data and goliath! :-)" So with his blessing—and blurb— the title stayed.

I wrote this book while a fellow at the Berkman Institute for Internet and Society at Harvard Law School, and I can't thank everyone there enough. The other fellows and the various Harvard professors I spent time with helped me think through these issues, as did the students in the reading group I led in Spring 2014. Also, since January 2014, I have been the Chief Technology Officer at Resilient Systems, and I must thank them as well. Even though the book isn't directly related to what we do at the company, I was given free rein to write it.

Finally, I would like to thank my friends, and especially my spouse, Karen Cooper, for putting up with me in "book writing" mode. This one was easier than the last, I know, but it was still hard.

Thank you all.

Notes

INTRODUCTION

1 **It tracks where:** David J. Crandall et al. (8 Dec 2010), "Inferring social ties from geographic coincidences," *Proceedings of the National Academy of Sciences of the United States of America* 107, http://www.pnas.org/content/107/52/22436.short.

2 **The accumulated data:** German politician Malte Spitz demonstrated the power of geolocation data by making six months of his daily whereabouts available to journalists. Zeit Online (Mar 2011), "Tell-all telephone," *Zeit Online*, http://www.zeit.de/datenschutz/malte-spitz-data-retention.

2 **researchers were able:** Manlio De Domenico, Antonio Lima, and Mirco Musolesi (18–19 Jun 2012), "Interdependence and predictability of human mobility and social interactions," Nokia Mobile Data Challenge Workshop, Newcastle, UK, http://www.cs.bham.ac.uk/research/projects/nsl/mobility-prediction.

2 **Cell phone location analysis:** Coordinating cell phone tower data with actual recorded wiretap audio is very strong evidence in court that a defendant is not credible, as he can be shown to be lying by his own words. This type of evidence was instrumental in convicting Scott Peterson of murdering his wife in 2002 after his mistress, Amber Frey, cooperated with police. Associated Press (27 Aug 2004), "Testimony in Peterson trial turns to evidence from computers," *USA Today*, http://usatoday30.usatoday.com/news/nation/2004-08-27-peterson_x.htm.

2 **The police can "ping":** Evan Perez and Siobhan Gorman (15 Jun 2013), "Phones leave a telltale trail," *Wall Street Journal*, http://online.wsj.com/news/articles/SB10001424127887324049504578545352803220058. Trevor Hughes (7 Dec 2013), "Cellphone data aided in solving two Larimer County murders," *Coloradoan*, http://archive.coloradoan.com/article/20131207/NEWS01/312070068/Cellphone-data-aided-solving-two-Larimer-County-murders.

2 **police are using this data:** They are overstating its accuracy, though, and convicting innocent people on the basis of the data. *Economist* (6 Sep 2014), "The two towers," *Economist*, http://www.economist.com/news/united-states/21615622-junk-science-

putting-innocent-people-jail-two-towers. Mike Masnick (9 Sep 2014), "Turns out cell phone location data is not even close to accurate, but everyone falls for it," *Tech Dirt*, https://www.techdirt.com/articles/20140908/04435128452/turns-out-cell-phone-lo cation-data-is-not-even-close-to-accurate-everyone-falls-it.shtml.

2 **the government of Ukraine:** Heather Murphy (22 Jan 2014), "Ominous text mes sage sent to protesters in Kiev sends chills around the Internet," *The Lede, New York Times*, http://thelede.blogs.nytimes.com/2014/01/22/ominous-text-message-sent- to-protesters-in-kiev-sends-chills-around-the-internet.

2 **Michigan police sought information:** Michael Isikoff (18 Feb 2010), "FBI tracks suspects' cell phones without a warrant," *Newsweek*, http://www.newsweek.com/ fbi-tracks-suspects-cell-phones-without-warrant-75099.

2 **Companies use your phone:** Steve Olenski (17 Jan 2013), "Is location based adver tising the future of mobile marketing and mobile advertising?" *Forbes*, http://www .forbes.com/sites/marketshare/2013/01/17/is-location-based-advertising-the-fu ture-of-mobile-marketing-and-mobile-advertising. John McDermott (20 Feb 2014), "Why the Web's biggest players are gobbling up location-based apps," *Digiday*, http:// digiday.com/platforms/apple-google-microsoft-yahoo-are-betting-on-mobile.

3 **location data is so valuable:** Anton Troianovski (21 May 2013), "Phone firms sell data on customers," *Wall Street Journal*, http://online.wsj.com/news/articles/SB100 01424127887323463704578497153556847658. Rachel King (13 Jul 2013), "ACLU: AT&T customer privacy at risk," *CIO Journal, Wall Street Journal Blogs*, http://blogs .wsj.com/cio/2013/07/13/aclu-att-customer-privacy-at-risk.

3 **Companies like Sense Networks:** Hiawatha Bray (8 Jul 2013), "Cellphone data mined to create personal profiles," *Boston Globe*, http://www.bostonglobe.com/ business/2013/07/07/your-cellphone-yourself/eSvTK1UCqNOE7D4qbAcWPL/ story.html.

3 **Verint sells cell phone tracking systems:** Craig Timberg (24 Aug 2014), "For sale: Systems that can secretly track where cellphone users go around the globe," *Washing ton Post*, http://www.washingtonpost.com/business/technology/for-sale-systems- that-can-secretly-track-where-cellphone-users-go-around-the-globe/2014/08/24/ f0700e8a-f003-11e3-bf76-447a5df6411f_story.html.

3 **The company's website:** Verint (2014), "About Verint," http://www.verint.com/about.

3 **"blind" call to a phone:** Privacy International (2012), "Cobham sells monitoring centres, phone monitoring, technical surveillance and location monitoring technol ogy. British export law doesn't specifically regulate these technologies, so they can easily end up in the wrong hands," https://www.privacyinternational.org/sii/cobham.

3 **The company boasts:** The full list as of 2011 is Algeria, Australia, Austria, Belgium, Brunei, the Czech Republic, Georgia, Ghana, Ireland, Kuwait, Libya, Norway, Paki stan, Saudi Arabia, Singapore, the Slovak Republic, Spain, Sweden, Taiwan, Turkey, the United Kingdom, and the United States. Cobham (2011), "Tactical C4I systems: Eagle–Close Combat Radio (CCR)," https://s3.amazonaws.com/s3.documentcloud .org/documents/409237/115-cobham-tactical-c4i.pdf.

3 **Defentek . . . sells a system:** Craig Timberg (24 Aug 2014), "For sale: Systems that can secretly track where cellphone users go around the globe," *Washington Post*, http://www.washingtonpost.com/business/technology/for-sale-systems-that- can-secretly-track-where-cellphone-users-go-around-the-globe/2014/08/24/ f0700e8a-f003-11e3-bf76-447a5df6411f_story.html.

3 **Tobias Engel demonstrated:** Tobias Engel (9 Jan 2009), "Locating mobile phones using Signalling System #7," Chaos Computer Club, http://berlin.ccc.de/~tobi as/25c3-locating-mobile-phones.pdf.

3 **collect and sell it:** Kevin J. O'Brien (28 Oct 2012), "Data-gathering via apps presents a gray legal area," *New York Times*, http://www.nytimes.com/2012/10/29/technol ogy/mobile-apps-have-a-ravenous-ability-to-collect-personal-data.html.

3 **HelloSpy is an app:** There are quite a few of these tracking apps out there. HelloSpy is particularly blatant. Although the disclaimer on the home page states that it is designed for "ethical spying for parents," or use on a "mobile device that you own or have proper consent to monitor," the literature also trumpets its ability to operate in "stealth mode," and has a page dedicated to marital infidelity. See http://hellospy.com.

4 **spy on his wife or girlfriend:** StealthGenie is another spyware app. In 2014, its CEO was indicted and arrested for selling it in the US. Craig Timberg and Matt Zapatosly (29 Sep 2014), "Maker of StealthGenie, an app used for spying, is indicted in Virginia," *Washington Post*, http://www.washingtonpost.com/business/technol ogy/make-of-app-used-for-spying-indicted-in-virginia/2014/09/29/816b45b8-4805-11e4-a046-120a8a855cca_story.html.

4 **spy on their employees:** Spencer E. Ange and Lauren Weber (22 Oct 2013), "Memo to workers: The boss is watching," *Wall Street Journal*, http://online.wsj.com/news/articles/SB10001424052702303672404579151440488919138.

4 **cell phone location data:** Barton Gellman and Ashkan Soltani (4 Dec 2013), "NSA tracking cellphone locations worldwide, Snowden documents show," *Washington Post*, http://www.washingtonpost.com/world/national-security/nsa-tracking-cell phone-locations-worldwide-snowden-documents-show/2013/12/04/5492873a-5cf2-11e3-bc56-c6ca94801fac_story.html. Ashkan Soltani and Barton Gellman (10 Dec 2013), "New documents show how the NSA infers relationships based on mobile location data," *Washington Post*, http://www.washingtonpost.com/blogs/the-switch/wp/2013/12/10/new-documents-show-how-the-nsa-infers-relationships-based-on-mobile-location-data. James Glanz, Jeff Larson, and Andrew W. Lehren (27 Jan 2014), "Spy agencies tap data streaming from phone apps," *New York Times*, http://www.nytimes.com/2014/01/28/world/spy-agencies-scour-phone-apps-for-personal-data.html.

4 **even when they are turned off:** We don't know definitively whether this is true or not. Dana Priest (21 Jul 2013), "NSA growth fueled by need to target terrorists," *Washington Post*, http://www.washingtonpost.com/world/national-security/nsa-growth-fueled-by-need-to-target-terrorists/2013/07/21/24c93cf4-f0b1-11e2-bed3-b9b6fe264871_story.html. Ryan Gallagher (22 Jul 2013), "NSA can reportedly track phones even when they're turned off," *Slate*, http://www.slate.com/blogs/future_tense/2013/07/22/nsa_can_reportedly_track_cellphones_even_when_they_re_turned_off.html.

4 **golden age of surveillance:** As far as I know, this is Peter Swire's term. Peter Swire and Kenesa Ahmad (28 Nov 2011), "'Going dark' versus a 'golden age for surveil-lance,'" Center for Democracy and Technology, http://www.futureofprivacy.org/wp-content/uploads/Going-Dark-Versus-a-Golden-Age-for-Surveillance-Peter-Swire-and-Kenesa-A.pdf.

4 **"You have zero privacy anyway.":** Polly Sprenger (26 Jan 1999), "Sun on privacy: 'Get over it,'" *Wired*, http://archive.wired.com/politics/law/news/1999/01/17538.

4 **US military defines surveillance:** US Joint Chiefs of Staff (11 Aug 2011), "Joint Operations," Joint Publication 3-0, http://fas.org/irp/doddir/dod/jp3_0.pdf.

5 **if you let us have all your data:** Eric Schmidt and Jared Cohen (2013), *The New Digital Age: Reshaping the Future of People, Nations and Business*, Knopf, http://www.newdigitalage.com.

5 **That's the NSA's justification:** No one ever explicitly refers to the bargain, but everyone argues that surveillance is necessary to keep us safe. Patricia Zengerle and Tabassum Zakaria (18 Jun 2013), "NSA head, lawmakers defend surveillance programs," Reuters, http://www.reuters.com/article/2013/06/18/us-usa-security-idUS BRE95H15O20130618. Al Jazeera (29 Oct 2013), "NSA chief defends spy program in face of protest from allies," Al Jazeera, http://america.aljazeera.com/articles/2013/10/29/nsa-chief-defendsspyprogramamidusriftwitheurope.html.

11 **We need to think:** Technology critic Evgeny Morozov makes this point. Evgeny Morozov (22 Oct 2013), "The real privacy problem," *MIT Technology Review*, http://www.technologyreview.com/featuredstory/520426/the-real-privacy-problem.

1: DATA AS A BY-PRODUCT OF COMPUTING

16 **uniquely identify your computer:** Peter Eckersley (Jul 2010), "How unique is your web browser?" *Proceedings of the 10th International Conference on Privacy Enhancing Technologies*, Berlin, https://panopticlick.eff.org/browser-uniqueness.pdf.

16 **your smartphone pinpoints you:** Paul A. Zandbergen (26 Jun 2009), "Accuracy of iPhone locations: A comparison of assisted GPS, WiFi and cellular positioning," *Transactions in GIS* 13, http://onlinelibrary.wiley.com/doi/10.1111/j.1467-9671.2009.01152.x/abstract. Paul A. Zandbergen and Sean J. Barbeau (Jul 2011), "Positional accuracy of assisted GPS data from high-sensitivity GPS-enabled mobile phones," *Journal of Navigation* 64, http://www.paulzandbergen.com/files/Zandbergen_Barbeau_JON_2011.pdf.

17 **Modern cars are loaded with computers:** Ben Wojdyla (21 Feb 2012), "How it works: The computer inside your car," *Popular Mechanics*, http://www.popularmechanics.com/cars/how-to/repair/how-it-works-the-computer-inside-your-car.

17 **Much of that is automatically recorded:** Nate Cardozo (11 Feb 2013), "Mandatory black boxes in cars raise privacy questions," Electronic Frontier Foundation, https://www.eff.org/press/releases/mandatory-black-boxes-cars-raise-privacy-questions.

17 **A self-driving car:** Lucas Mearian (23 Jul 2013), "Self-driving cars could create 1GB of data a second," *Computer World*, http://www.computerworld.com/s/article/924 0992/Self_driving_cars_could_create_1GB_of_data_a_second.

17 **Embedded in digital photos:** Benjamin Henne, Maximilian Koch, and Matthew Smith (3–7 Mar 2014), "On the awareness, control and privacy of shared photo metadata," Distributed Computing & Security Group, Leibniz University, presented at the Eighteenth International Conference for Financial Cryptography and Data Security, Barbados, http://ifca.ai/fc14/papers/fc14_submission_117.pdf.

17 **If you upload the photo:** This is a particularly creepy story about camera metadata. Mathew Honan (19 Jan 2009), "I am here: One man's experiment with the location-aware lifestyle," *Wired*, http://www.wired.com/gadgets/wireless/magazine/17-02/lp_guineapig.

17 **automatic payment systems, such as EZPass:** Increasingly, governments are removing the anonymous cash option. Adrianne Jeffries (27 Mar 2013), "Golden Gate Bridge's new cashless tollway promises convenience in exchange for privacy," *Verge*, http://www.theverge.com/2013/3/27/4150702/golden-gate-bridges-new-cash less-tollway-promises-convenience-for-privacy. Anh Do (20 Mar 2014), "Orange County's toll roads going cashless," *Los Angeles Times*, http://www.latimes.com/local/lanow/la-me-ln-cashless-toll-roads-20140320-story.html. Trevor Pettiford (13 Jun 2014), "Veterans Expressway tolls to start going cashless," *Bay News 9*, http://www.baynews9.com/content/news/baynews9/news/article.html/content/news/articles/bn9/2014/6/13/veterans_expressway_.html. Martine Powers (17 Jul 2014), "Starting Monday, no more cash at Tobin tolls," *Boston Globe*, http://www.boston globe.com/metro/2014/07/16/starting-monday-more-cash-tobin/WZKMDils fLULQtYiGZCrEK/story.html.

18 **The smart thermostat:** Nest (2012), "Nest Learning Thermostat," http://certified .nest.com/resources/NEST_POS_brochure_r7_300.pdf.

18 **a smart refrigerator:** Eliza Barclay (4 May 2012), "The 'smart fridge' finds the lost lettuce, for a price," *The Salt: What's On Your Plate*, NPR, http://www.npr.org/blogs/thesalt/2012/05/03/151968878/the-smart-fridge-finds-the-lost-lettuce-for-a-price.

18 **a smart air conditioner:** Ry Crist (8 Jan 2014), "Haier's new air conditioner is the first Apple-certified home appliance," *CNET*, http://ces.cnet.com/8301-35306_1-57616915/haiers-new-air-conditioner-is-the-first-apple-certified-home-appliance.

18 **smart smoke and carbon monoxide detector:** Heather Kelley (15 Jan 2014), "Google wants to run your home with Nest," CNN, http://www.cnn.com/2014/01/15/tech/innovation/google-connect-home-nest.

18 **the smart power grid:** US Department of Energy (2008), "The smart grid: An introduction," http://energy.gov/sites/prod/files/oeprod/DocumentsandMedia/DOE_SG_Book_Single_Pages(1).pdf. US Department of Energy (2014), "What is the smart grid?" https://www.smartgrid.gov/the_smart_grid.

18 **when you're having sex:** Gregory Ferenstein, "How health trackers could reduce sexual infidelity," *Tech Crunch*, http://techcrunch.com/2013/07/05/how-health-track ers-could-reduce-sexual-infidelity.

18 **Give the device more information:** Fitabase (3 Dec 2013), "Privacy policy," http://www.fitabase.com/Privacy.

19 **Many medical devices:** Sarah E. Needleman (14 Aug 2012), "New medical devices get smart," *Wall Street Journal*, http://online.wsj.com/news/articles/SB10000872396 3904443181045775871410333340190.

19 **It's not just specialized devices:** Sara M. Watson (10 Oct 2013), "The latest smart-phones could turn us all into activity trackers," *Wired*, http://www.wired .com/2013/10/the-trojan-horse-of-the-latest-iphone-with-the-m7-coprocessor-we-all-become-qs-activity-trackers.

19 **Companies like 23andMe:** Thomas Goetz (17 Nov 2007), "23AndMe will decode your DNA for $1,000. Welcome to the age of genomics," *Wired*, http://www.wired .com/medtech/genetics/magazine/15-12/ff_genomics. Elizabeth Murphy (14 Oct 2013), "Inside 23andMe founder Anne Wojcicki's $99 DNA revolution," *Fast Company*, http://www.fastcompany.com/3018598/for-99-this-ceo-can-tell-you-what-might-kill-you-inside-23andme-founder-anne-wojcickis-dna-r.

19 **personalized marketing:** Charles Seife (27 Nov 2013), "23andMe is terrifying, but

not for the reasons the FDA thinks," *Scientific American*, http://www.scientificamerican.com/article/23andme-is-terrifying-but-not-for-reasons-fda.

19 **insurance companies may someday buy:** Rebecca Greenfield (25 Nov 2013), "Why 23andMe terrifies health insurance companies," *Fast Company*, http://www.fastcompany.com/3022224/innovation-agents/why-23andme-terrifies-health-insurance-companies.

19 **lifelogging apps:** Leo Kelion (6 Jan 2014), "CES 2014: Sony shows off life logging app and kit," *BBC News*, http://www.bbc.com/news/technology-25633647.

19 **it will include a video record:** Alec Wilkinson (28 May 2007), "Remember this? A project to record everything we do in life," *New Yorker*, http://www.newyorker.com/reporting/2007/05/28/070528fa_fact_wilkinson.

19 **Google Glass is the first wearable device:** Jenna Wortham (8 Mar 2013), "Meet Memoto, the lifelogging camera," *New York Times Blogs*, http://bits.blogs.nytimes.com/2013/03/08/meet-memoto-the-lifelogging-camera.

19 **Internet of Things:** Ken Hess (10 Jan 2014), "The Internet of Things outlook for 2014: Everything connected and communicating," *ZDNet*, http://www.zdnet.com/the-internet-of-things-outlook-for-2014-everything-connected-and-communicating-7000024930.

19 **smart cities:** Georgina Stylianou (29 Apr 2013), "Idea to have sensors track everything in city," *Press* (Christchurch), http://www.stuff.co.nz/the-press/business/the-rebuild/8606956/Idea-to-have-sensors-track-everything-in-city. Victoria Turk (Jul 2013), "City sensors: the Internet of Things is taking over our cities," *Wired*, http://www.wired.co.uk/magazine/archive/2013/07/everything-is-connected/city-sensors.

19 **smart toothbrushes:** Sam Byford (5 Jan 2014), "Kolibree's smart toothbrush claims to track and improve your dental hygiene," *Verge*, http://www.theverge.com/2014/1/5/5277426/kolibree-smart-toothbrush.

19 **smart light bulbs:** Margaret Rhodes (23 Sep 2014), "Ex-Tesla and NASA engineers make a light bulb that's smarter than you," *Wired*, http://www.wired.com/2014/09/ex-tesla-nasa-engineers-make-light-bulb-thats-smarter.

19 **smart sidewalk squares:** Charles Stross has discussed the implications of these. Charles Stross (25 Jun 2014), "YAPC::NA 2014 keynote: Programming Perl in 2034," *Charlie's Diary*, http://www.antipope.org/charlie/blog-static/2014/06/yapcna-2014-keynote-programmin.html.

19 **smart pill bottles:** Valentina Palladino (8 Jan 2014), "AdhereTech's smart pill bottle knows when you take, and miss, your medication," *Verge*, http://www.theverge.com/2014/1/8/5289022/adheretech-smart-pill-bottle.

19 **smart clothing:** Econocom (19 Sep 2013), "When fashion meets the Internet of Things," *emedia*, http://blog.econocom.com/en/blog/when-fashion-meets-the-internet-of-things. Michael Knigge (28 Aug 2014), "Tagging along: Is Adidas tracking soccer fans?" *Deutsche Welle*, http://www.dw.de/tagging-along-is-adidas-tracking-soccer-fans/a-1788463.

19 **because why not?:** We've seen this trend before. Digital clocks first became popular in the 1970s. Initially they were largely stand-alone devices—alarm clocks and watches—but as their price declined, they became embedded into other things: first your microwave, then your coffeepot, oven, thermostat, VCR, and television. Internet-enabled sensors are heading in that direction.

19 **Estimates put the current number:** Natasha Lomas (9 May 2013), "10BN+

wirelessly connected devices today, 30BN+ in 2020's 'Internet Of Everything,' says ABI Research," *Tech Crunch*, http://techcrunch.com/2013/05/09/internet-of-everything.

19 **The hype level is pretty high:** Valentina Palladino (10 Jan 2014), "Invisible intelligence: How tiny sensors could connect everything we own," *Verge*, http://www .theverge.com/2014/1/10/5293778/invisible-intelligence-tiny-sensors-that-con nect-everything.

20 **eyes and ears of the Internet:** Ben Hammersley (Jul 2013), "When the world becomes the Web," *Wired*, http://www.wired.co.uk/magazine/archive/2013/07/ everything-is-connected/when-the-world-becomes-the-web.

20 **Smart streetlights will gather data:** Newark Airport has installed these. Diane Cardwell (17 Feb 2014), "At Newark Airport, the lights are on, and they're watching you," *New York Times*, http://www.nytimes.com/2014/02/18/business/at-newark-airport-the-lights-are-on-and-theyre-watching-you.html.

20 **Cameras will only get better:** Olga Kharif (31 Oct 2013), "As drones evolve from military to civilian uses, venture capitalists move in," *Washington Post*, http://www .washingtonpost.com/business/as-drones-evolve-from-military-to-civilian-uses-venture-capitalists-move-in/2013/10/31/592ca862-419e-11e3-8b74-d89d714ca4dd_ story.html.

20 **Raytheon is planning to fly a blimp:** Paul McLeary (29 Jun 2014), "Powerful radar blimp to surveil Washington, Baltimore, out to sea," *Defense News*, http://www .defensenews.com/article/20140629/DEFREG02/306290012/Powerful-Radar-Blimp-Surveil-Washington-Baltimore-Out-Sea.

20 **An e-mail system is similar:** Some of that argument is here. Electronic Frontier Foundation (2014), "The government's word games when talking about NSA domestic spying," https://www.eff.org/nsa-spying/wordgames.

21 **an exabyte of data:** This is based on the reasonable assumption that a page is 2 kilobytes. It's not really fair, though, because so much of this data is voice, images, and video.

21 **creating more data per day:** M. G. Siegler (4 Aug 2010), "Eric Schmidt: Every 2 days we create as much information as we did up to 2003," *Tech Crunch*, http://tech crunch.com/2010/08/04/schmidt-data.

21 **76 exabytes of data will travel:** Cisco (10 Jun 2014), "Cisco visual networking index: Forecast and methodology, 2013–2018," http://www.cisco.com/c/en/us/solu tions/collateral/service-provider/ip-ngn-ip-next-generation-network/white_ paper_c11-481360.html.

21 **a petabyte of cloud storage will cost:** Chris M. Evans (18 Apr 2014), "IAAS Series: Cloud storage pricing: How low can they go?" *Architecting IT*, http://blog.architect ing.it/2014/04/18/iaas-series-cloud-storage-pricing-how-low-can-they-go.

21 **store every tweet ever sent:** K. Young (6 Sep 2012), "How much would it cost to store the entire Twitter Firehose?" *Mortar: Data Science at Scale*, http://blog.mortardata .com/post/31027073689/how-much-would-it-cost-to-store-the-entire-twitter.

21 **every phone call ever made:** Brewster Kahle (2013), "Cost to store all US phonecalls made in a year so it could be datamined," https://docs.google.com/spreadsheet/ ccc?key=0AuqlWHQKlooOdGJrSzhBVnh0WGlzWHpCZFNVcURkX0E#gid=0.

22 **In 2013, the NSA completed:** James Bamford (15 Mar 2012), "The NSA is building the country's biggest spy center (watch what you say)," *Wired*, http://www.wired .com/threatlevel/2012/03/ff_nsadatacenter/all.

22 **third largest in the world:** Forbes (19 Oct 2012), "The 5 largest data centers in the world," *Forbes*, http://www.forbes.com/pictures/fhgl45ijg/range-international-infor mation-hub.

22 **The details are classified:** Kashmir Hill (24 Jul 2013), "Blueprints of NSA's ridicu- lously expensive data center in Utah suggest it holds less info than thought," *Forbes*, http://www.forbes.com/sites/kashmirhill/2013/07/24/blueprints-of-nsa-data-cen ter-in-utah-suggest-its-storage-capacity-is-less-impressive-than-thought.

22 **cost $1.4 billion so far:** Siobhan Gorman (21 Oct 2013), "Contractors fight over delays to NSA data center," *Wall Street Journal*, http://online.wsj.com/news/articles/ SB10001424052702303672404579149902978119902.

22 **Google has the capacity:** Randall Munro (2013), "Google's datacenters on punch cards," *What If? XKCD*, https://what-if.xkcd.com/63.

22 **In 2011, Schrems demanded:** Cyrus Farivar (15 Nov 2012), "How one law student is making Facebook get serious about privacy," *Ars Technica*, http://arstechnica .com/tech-policy/2012/11/how-one-law-student-is-making-facebook-get-serious- about-privacy. Olivia Solon (28 Dec 2012), "How much data did Facebook have on one man? 1,200 pages of data in 57 categories," *BBC News*, http://www.wired.co.uk/ magazine/archive/2012/12/start/privacy-versus-facebook.

22 **Facebook sent him a CD:** Schrems's discovery led him to file a class action lawsuit against Facebook. Liat Clark (1 Aug 2014), "Facebook hit with international class action lawsuit," *Wired UK*, http://www.wired.co.uk/news/archive/2014-08/01/face book-class-action-lawsuit.

2: DATA AS SURVEILLANCE

23 **what we know about the NSA's surveillance:** Previous leakers include Thomas Drake, Mark Klein, and Bill Binney. Subsequent leakers have not been identified yet. Bruce Schneier (7 Aug 2014), "The US intelligence community has a third leaker," *Schneier on Security*, https://www.schneier.com/blog/archives/2014/08/the_us_ intellig.html.

23 **NSA collects the cell phone call records:** Glenn Greenwald (5 Jun 2013), "NSA col- lecting phone records of millions of Verizon customers daily," *Guardian*, http://www .theguardian.com/world/2013/jun/06/nsa-phone-records-verizon-court-order.

23 **One government defense:** Barack Obama (7 Jun 2013), "Statement by the Presi- dent," US Executive Office of the President, http://www.whitehouse.gov/the-press-of fice/2013/06/07/statement-president. James R. Clapper (7 Jun 2013), "DNI statement on recent unauthorized disclosures of classified information," Office of the Director of National Intelligence, http://www.dni.gov/index.php/newsroom/press-releases/191- press-releases-2013/868-dni-statement-on-recent-unauthorized-disclosures-of-class ified-information. Ed O'Keefe (6 Jun 2013), "Transcript: Dianne Feinstein, Saxby Chambliss explain, defend NSA phone records program," *Washington Post*, http:// www.washingtonpost.com/blogs/post-politics/wp/2013/06/06/transcript-dianne- feinstein-saxby-chambliss-explain-defend-nsa-phone-records-program.

24 **The intended point:** Am I the only one who finds it suspicious that President Obama always uses very specific words? He says things like, "Nobody is listening to your tele- phone calls." This leaves open the possibility that the NSA is recording, transcribing,

and analyzing your phone calls—and, very occasionally, reading them. This is more likely to be true, and something a pedantically minded president could claim he wasn't lying about.

24 **Collecting metadata on people:** This is a good general article on the intimacy of metadata. Dahlia Lithwick and Steve Vladeck (22 Nov 2013), "Taking the 'meh' out of metadata," *Slate*, http://www.slate.com/articles/news_and_politics/jurispru dence/2013/11/nsa_and_metadata_how_the_government_can_spy_on_your_ health_political_beliefs.html.

24 **Phone metadata reveals:** Edward W. Felten (23 Aug 2013), "Declaration of Professor Edward W. Felten," *American Civil Liberties Union et al. v. James R. Clapper et al.*, United States District Court, Southern District of New York (Case 1:13-cv-03994-WHP), https:// www.aclu.org/files/pdfs/natsec/clapper/2013.08.26%20ACLU%20PI%20Brief%20-%20 Declaration%20-%20Felten.pdf.

24 **It provides a window:** Yves-Alexandre de Montjoye et al. (2–5 Apr 2013), "Predicting people personality using novel mobile phone-based metrics," 6th International Confer- ence on Social Computing, Behavioral-Cultural Modeling and Prediction, Washington, D.C., http://realitycommons.media.mit.edu/download.php?file=deMontjoye2013predict ing-citation.pdf.

24 **It yields a detailed summary:** IBM offers a class in analyzing phone call metadata. IBM Corporation (2014), "9T225G: Telephone analysis using i2 Analyst's Notebook," http://www-03.ibm.com/services/learning/content/ites.wss/zz/en?pageType= course_description&courseCode=9T225G&cc=.

24 **personal nature of what the researchers:** Jonathan Mayer and Patrick Mutchler (12 Mar 2014), "MetaPhone: The sensitivity of telephone metadata," *Web Policy*, http:// webpolicy.org/2014/03/12/metaphone-the-sensitivity-of-telephone-metadata.

25 **Web search data is another source:** While it seems obvious that this is data and not metadata, it seems to be treated as metadata by the NSA. I believe its justification is that the search terms are encoded in the URLs. The NSA's XKEYSCORE slides talked about collecting "web-based searches," which further indicates that the NSA consid- ers this metadata. Glenn Greenwald (31 Jul 2013), "XKeyscore: NSA tool collects 'nearly everything a user does on the internet,'" *Guardian*, http://www.theguardian.com/ world/2013/jul/31/nsa-top-secret-program-online-data.

25 **The NSA claims it's metadata:** This demonstrates that the difference is more legal hairsplitting than anything else.

26 **When I typed "should I tell my w":** It's the same with "should I tell my girlfriend."

26 **Google knows who clicked:** Arwa Mahdawi (22 Oct 2013), "Google's autocomplete spells out our darkest thoughts," *Guardian*, http://www.theguardian.com/comment isfree/2013/oct/22/google-autocomplete-un-women-ad-discrimination-algorithms.

26 **Google's CEO Eric Schmidt admitted:** Derek Thompson (1 Oct 2010), "Google's CEO: 'The laws are written by lobbyists,'" *Atlantic*, http://www.theatlantic.com/ technology/archive/2010/10/googles-ceo-the-laws-are-written-by-lobbyists/63908.

26 **Your tweets tell the world:** You can search for the sleep patterns of any Twitter user. Amit Agarwal (2013), "Sleeping Time," *Digital Inspiration*, http://sleepingtime.org.

26 **Your buddy lists and address books:** Two studies of Facebook social graphs show how easy it is to predict these and other personal traits. Carter Jernigan and Behram R. T. Mistree (5 Oct 2009), "Gaydar: Facebook friendships expose sexual orienta- tion," *First Monday* 14, http://firstmonday.org/article/view/2611/2302. Michal Kos-

inski, David Stillwell, and Thore Graepel (11 Mar 2013), "Private traits and attributes are predictable from digital records of human behavior," *Proceedings of the National Academy of Sciences of the United States of America (Early Edition)*, http://www.pnas .org/content/early/2013/03/06/1218772110.abstract.

26 **Your e-mail headers reveal:** The MIT Media Lab tool Immersion builds a social graph from your e-mail metadata. MIT Media Lab (2013), "Immersion: A people-centric view of your email life," https://immersion.media.mit.edu.

26 **Metadata can be much more revealing:** Brian Lam (19 Jun 2013), "Phew, NSA is just collecting metadata. (You should still worry)," *Wired*, http://www.wired .com/2013/06/phew-it-was-just-metadata-not-think-again.

27 **metadata is far more meaningful:** Edward W. Felten (23 Aug 2013), "Declaration of Professor Edward W. Felten," *American Civil Liberties Union et al. v. James R. Clapper et al.*, United States District Court, Southern District of New York (Case 1:13-cv-03994-WHP), https://www.aclu.org/files/pdfs/natsec/clapper/2013.08.26%20ACLU%20PI% 20Brief%20-%20Declaration%20-%20Felten.pdf.

27 **"If you have enough metadata":** Alan Rusbridger (21 Nov 2013), "The Snowden leaks and the public," *New York Review of Books*, http://www.nybooks.com/articles/ archives/2013/nov/21/snowden-leaks-and-public.

27 **"We kill people based on metadata":** David Cole (10 May 2014), "'We kill people based on metadata,'" *New York Review of Books*, http://www.nybooks.com/blogs/ nyrblog/2014/may/10/we-kill-people-based-metadata.

27 **one spy for every 166 citizens:** John O. Koehler (1999), *Stasi: The Untold Story of the East German Secret Police*, Westview Press, http://books.google.com/books?id=wax WwxYltt8C.

28 **Roving wiretaps meant:** Mary DeRosa (2005), "Section 206: Roving surveillance authority under FISA: A summary," *Patriot Debates*, http://apps.americanbar.org/ natsecurity/patriotdebates/section-206.

29 **The motivations are different:** David Lyon makes this point. David Lyon (2003), *Surveillance after September 11*, Polity, http://www.polity.co.uk/book.asp?ref=0745631819.

29 **Another device allows me to see all the data:** BrickHouse Security (2014), "iPhone / Android Spy Stick," *Skymall*, https://www.skymall.com/iphone-%2F-an droid-spy-stick/28033GRP.html.

29 **I can buy a keyboard logger:** Keyloggers.com (2014), "Top keyloggers of 2014 com-parison and reviews," http://www.keyloggers.com.

29 **I can buy call intercept software:** Stealth Genie (2014), "Live call intercept," http://www.stealthgenie.com/features/live-call-intercept.html.

29 **I can buy a remote-controlled drone helicopter:** Amazon.com (2014), "DJI Phantom 2 Ready to Fly Quadcopter - With Zenmuse H3-2D Camera Gimbal: $959.00 (list $999)," Amazon.com, http://www.amazon.com/Dji-Phantom-Ready-Fly-Quadcopter/dp/B00H7HPU54.

30 **Professional surveillance devices:** There are prototypes for flying sensors that resemble birds and insects, and even smaller sensors—no larger than dust parti-cles—that will float around in the wind. Elisabeth Bumiller and Thom Shanker (19 Jun 2011), "War evolves with drones, some tiny as bugs," *New York Times*, http:// www.nytimes.com/2011/06/20/world/20drones.html. John W. Whitehead (15 Apr 2013), "Roaches, mosquitoes, and birds: The coming micro-drone revolution," Ruth-erford Institute, https://www.rutherford.org/publications_resources/john_white

heads_commentary/roaches_mosquitoes_and_birds_the_coming_micro_
drone_revolution.

30 **Sprint charges law enforcement:** Ashkan Soltani (9 Jan 2014), "The cost of surveillance," http://ashkansoltani.org/2014/01/09/the-cost-of-surveillance. Kevin S. Bank-
ston and Ashkan Soltani (9 Jan 2014), "Tiny constables and the cost of surveillance:
Making cents out of *United States v. Jones*," *Yale Law Journal* 123, http://yalelawjournal
.org/forum/tiny-constables-and-the-cost-of-surveillance-making-cents-out-of-unit
ed-states-v-jones.

30 **FBI was required to:** Carrie Johnson (21 Mar 2012), "FBI still struggling with Supreme
Court's GPS ruling," *NPR Morning Edition*, http://www.npr.org/2012/03/21/149011887/
fbi-still-struggling-with-supreme-courts-gps-ruling.

31 **the repossession business:** Shawn Musgrave (5 Mar 2014), "A vast hidden surveillance network runs across America, powered by the repo industry," *BetaBoston/Boston
Globe*, http://betaboston.com/news/2014/03/05/a-vast-hidden-surveillance-network-
runs-across-america-powered-by-the-repo-industry. Shawn Musgrave (5 Mar 2014),
"Massive license plate location database just like Instagram, Digital Recognition Network insists," *BetaBoston/Boston Globe*, http://betaboston.com/news/2014/03/05/
massive-license-plate-location-database-just-like-instagram-digital-recogni
tion-network-insists.

31 **2.5 billion records:** Vigilant Video (23 Feb 2009), "Site specific preparation sheet
for LEARN V.4.0 server installation," https://www.aclu.org/files/FilesPDFs/ALPR/
texas/alprpra_portharthurPD_portarthurtx%20%287%29.pdf.

31 **In addition to repossession businesses:** Cyrus Farivar (27 Feb 2012), "Your car,
tracked: The rapid rise of license plate readers," *Ars Technica*, http://arstechnica
.com/tech-policy/2012/09/your-car-tracked-the-rapid-rise-of-license-plate-read
ers. Catherine Crump (18 Jul 2013), "You are being tracked: How license plate readers
are being used to record Americans' movements," American Civil Liberties Union,
https://www.aclu.org/files/assets/071613-aclu-alprreport-opt-v05.pdf.

31 **states' driver's license databases:** Craig Timberg and Ellen Nakashima (16 Jun
2013), "State photo-ID databases become troves for police," *Washington Post*, http://
www.washingtonpost.com/business/technology/state-photo-id-databases-be
come-troves-for-police/2013/06/16/6f014bd4-ced5-11e2-8845-d970ccb04497_story
.html.

31 **single national database:** Josh Hicks (18 Feb 2014), "Homeland Security wants to
build national database using license plate scanners," *Washington Post*, http://www
.washingtonpost.com/blogs/federal-eye/wp/2014/02/18/homeland-security-
wants-to-build-national-database-using-license-plate-scanners. Dan Froomkin (17
Mar 2014), "Reports of the death of a national license-plate tracking database have been
greatly exaggerated," *Intercept*, https://firstlook.org/theintercept/2014/03/17/1756li
cense-plate-tracking-database.

31 **In the UK, a similar government-run system:** James Bridle (18 Dec 2013), "How
Britain exported next-generation surveillance," *Medium*, https://medium.com/mat
ter-archive/how-britain-exported-next-generation-surveillance-d15b5801b79e. Jennifer Lynch and Peter Bibring (6 May 2013), "Automated license plate readers threaten
our privacy," Electronic Frontier Foundation, https://www.eff.org/deeplinks/2013/
05/alpr.

31 **It enforces London's:** The police also get access to the data. Hélène Mulholland (2

Apr 2012), "Boris Johnson plans to give police access to congestion charge cameras," *Guardian*, http://www.theguardian.com/politics/2012/apr/02/boris-johnson-police-congestion-charge.

31 **automatic face recognition:** Dan Froomkin (17 Mar 2014), "Reports of the death of a national license-plate tracking database have been greatly exaggerated," *Intercept*, https://firstlook.org/theintercept/2014/03/17/1756license-plate-tracking-database.

32 **the FBI has a database:** US Federal Bureau of Investigation (15 Sep 2014), "FBI announces full operational capability of the next generation identification system," http://www.fbi.gov/news/pressrel/press-releases/fbi-announces-full-operational-capability-of-the-next-generation-identification-system.

32 **Dubai police are integrating:** William Maclean (2 Oct 2014), "Dubai detectives to get Google Glass to fight crime," Reuters, http://www.reuters.com/article/2014/10/02/us-emirates-dubai-google-police-idUSKCN0HR0W320141002.

32 **the FBI can demand that data:** Glenn Greenwald (5 Jun 2013), "NSA collecting phone records of millions of Verizon customers daily," *Guardian*, http://www.theguardian.com/world/2013/jun/06/nsa-phone-records-verizon-court-order.

32 **tracking the movements of cars:** Brandon Griggs (20 Aug 2013), "New Google Maps can help you avoid traffic," CNN, http://www.cnn.com/2013/08/20/tech/mobile/google-waze-mobile-maps.

33 **If you're reading this book on a Kindle:** Alexandra Alter (19 Jul 2012), "Your e-Book is reading you," *Wall Street Journal*, http://online.wsj.com/news/articles/SB10001424052702304870304577490950051438304.

33 **It just happens:** The same thing happens when you watch videos on Netflix, Amazon, Hulu, or any other streaming video service.

33 **these actions generate surveillance records:** Jennifer 8. Lee (21 Mar 2002), "Welcome to the database lounge," *New York Times*, http://www.nytimes.com/2002/03/21/technology/welcome-to-the-database-lounge.html. Katie R. Holloman and D. Evan Ponder (2007), "Clubs, bars, and the driver's license scanning system," in *Privacy in a Transparent World*, ed. Amy Albert, Ethica Publishing, http://www.ethicapublishing.com/7CH5.htm.

33 **"How Privileged Are You?":** Buzzfeed (10 Apr 2014), "How privileged are you?" http://www.buzzfeed.com/regajha/how-privileged-are-you.

34 **Over two million people have taken that quiz:** Caitlin Dewey (26 Jun 2014), "The scary, eye-opening truth of Internet tracking—on Buzzfeed quizzes, and everywhere else," *Washington Post*, http://www.washingtonpost.com/news/the-intersect/wp/2014/06/26/the-scary-eye-opening-truth-of-internet-tracking-on-buzzfeed-quizzes-and-everywhere-else.

34 **sites like WebMD collect data:** Marco D. Heusch (28 Oct 2013), "Privacy threats when seeking online health information," *JAMA Internal Medicine*, http://archinte.jamanetwork.com/article.aspx?articleid=1710119.

34 **160 billion pieces annually:** Ron Nixon (3 Jul 2013), "U.S. Postal Service logging all mail for law enforcement," *New York Times*, http://www.nytimes.com/2013/07/04/us/monitoring-of-snail-mail.html.

34 **Drones are getting smaller:** Ms. Smith (18 Jun 2012), "The future of drone surveillance: Cyborg insect drones," *Network World*, http://www.networkworld.com/article/2222611/microsoft-subnet/the-future-of-drone-surveillance--swarms-of-cyborg-insect-drones.html.

34 **Face recognition is the easiest:** Ravi Subban and Dattatreya P. Mankame (2014), "Human face recognition biometric techniques: Analysis and review," *Recent Advances in Intelligent Informatics: Advances in Intelligent Systems and Computing* 235, http://link.springer.com/chapter/10.1007%2F978-3-319-01778-5_47.

34 **face recognition algorithms started:** Chaochao Lu and Xiaoou Tang (15 Apr 2014), "Surpassing human-level face verification performance on LFW with GaussianFace," arXiv:1404.3840 [cs.CV], http://arxiv.org/abs/1404.3840.

34 **iris scanners that work at a distance:** Barry Fox (5 Feb 2007), "Invention: Covert iris scanner," *New Scientist,* http://www.newscientist.com/article/dn11110-invention-covert-iris-scanner.html.

34 **gait recognition systems:** Zhaoxiang Zhang, Maodi Hu, and Yunhong Wang (2011), "A survey of advances in biometric gait recognition," *Biometric Recognition,* Lecture Notes in Computer Science 7098, Springer-Verlag, http://link.springer.com/chapter/10.1007%2F978-3-642-25449-9_19.

34 **contactless RFID chip cards:** Katherine Albrecht (2008), "RFID tag: You're it," *Scientific American* (Sep 2008): 72–77, http://www.scientificamerican.com/article/how-rfid-tags-could-be-used. University of Washington College of Engineering (22 Feb 2008), "University launches RFID people tracking experiment," *RFID Journal,* http://www.rfidjournal.com/articles/view?6924. Christopher Zara (8 Jan 2013), "Disney World's RFID tracking bracelets are a slippery slope, warns privacy advocate," *International Business Times,* http://www.ibtimes.com/disney-worlds-rfid-tracking-bracelets-are-slippery-slope-warns-privacy-advocate-1001790.

34 **Many retail stores are surreptitiously tracking:** Quentin Hardy (7 Mar 2013), "Technology turns to tracking people offline," *New York Times,* http://bits.blogs.nytimes.com/2013/03/07/technology-turns-to-tracking-people-offline.

34 **which aisles they walk down:** Stephanie Clifford and Quentin Hardy (15 Jul 2013), "Attention, shoppers: Store is tracking your cell," *New York Times,* http://www.nytimes.com/2013/07/15/business/attention-shopper-stores-are-tracking-your-cell.html. Brian Fung (19 Oct 2013), "How stores use your phone's WiFi to track your shopping habits," *Washington Post,* http://www.washingtonpost.com/blogs/the-switch/wp/2013/10/19/how-stores-use-your-phones-wifi-to-track-your-shopping-habits. Latanya Sweeney (12 Feb 2014), "My phone at your service," US Federal Trade Commission, http://www.ftc.gov/news-events/blogs/techftc/2014/02/my-phone-your-service.

35 **People can be tracked at public events:** Bram Bonne et al. (4–7 Jun 2013), "WiFiPi: Involuntary tracking of visitors at mass events," 14th International Symposium and Workshops on World of Wireless, Mobile and Multimedia Networks, Madrid, http://ieeexplore.ieee.org/xpl/articleDetails.jsp?arnumber=6583443.

35 **The company quickly retracted the remarks:** Jim Edwards (9 Jan 2014), "Ford exec retracts statements about tracking drivers with the GPS in their cars," *Business Insider,* http://www.businessinsider.com/ford-jim-farley-retracts-statements-tracking-drivers-gps-2014-1.

35 **a lot of wiggle room for Ford:** Curt Magleby (3 Feb 2014), Letter to the Honorable Al Franken, United States Senate, re: Collection of location information, http://www.franken.senate.gov/files/letter/140212FordResponse.pdf.

35 **Government Accountability Office report:** US Government Accountability Office (6 Dec 2013), "In-car location-based services: Companies are taking steps to protect privacy, but some risks may not be clear to consumers," Report to the Chair-

man, Subcommittee on Privacy, Technology and the Law, Committee on the Judiciary, US Senate, GAO-14-81, http://www.gao.gov/products/GAO-14-81.

35 **Radar in the terahertz range:** British Broadcasting Corporation (10 Mar 2008), "Camera 'looks' through clothing," *BBC News*, http://news.bbc.co.uk/2/hi/technology/7287135.stm. Rocco Parascandola (23 Jan 2013), "NYPD Commissioner says department will begin testing a new high-tech device that scans for concealed weapons," *New York Daily News*, http://www.nydailynews.com/new-york/nypd-readies-scan-and-frisk-article-1.1245663. Carter M. Armstrong (17 Aug 2012), "The truth about terahertz," *IEEE Spectrum*, http://spectrum.ieee.org/aerospace/military/the-truth-about-terahertz.

35 **Cameras can "listen" to phone conversations:** Larry Hardesty (4 Aug 2014), "Extracting audio from visual information," *MIT News*, http://newsoffice.mit.edu/2014/algorithm-recovers-speech-from-vibrations-0804. Abe Davis et al. (10–14 Aug 2014), "The visual microphone: Passive recovery of sound from video," 41st International Conference on Computer Graphics and Interactive Techniques (SIGGRAPH 2014), Vancouver, British Columbia, http://people.csail.mit.edu/mrub/papers/VisualMic_SIGGRAPH2014.pdf.

35 **turn your cell phone's microphone on remotely:** Erik Kain (30 Dec 2013), "The NSA reportedly has total access to the Apple iPhone," *Forbes*, http://www.forbes.com/sites/erikkain/2013/12/30/the-nsa-reportedly-has-total-access-to-your-iphone.

35 **body odor recognition systems:** Shaun Waterman (9 Mar 2009), "DHS wants to use human body odor as biometric identifier, clue to deception," UPI, http://www.upi.com/Top_News/Special/2009/03/09/DHS-wants-to-use-human-body-odor-as-biometric-identifier-clue-to-deception/UPI-20121236627329.

35 **identifying people by their typing style:** Pranav Dixit (19 Aug 2014), "Banks now know who you are from how you type," *Gizmodo*, http://gizmodo.com/your-phone-can-now-identify-you-based-on-how-you-type-1623733346.

35 **identifying people by their writing style:** It's called stylometry. Sadia Afroz et al. (18–21 May 2014), "Doppelgänger finder: Taking stylometry to the underground," IEEE Symposium on Security & Privacy, Oakland, California, http://www.cs.gmu.edu/~mccoy/papers/oakland2014-underground.pdf.

35 **tens of millions of voiceprints:** Raphael Satter (13 Oct 2014), "Voiceprints being harvested by the millions," Associated Press, http://www.washingtonpost.com/business/technology/millions-of-voiceprints-quietly-being-harvested/2014/10/13/b34e291a-52af-11e4-b86d-184ac281388d_story.html. Raphael Satter (13 Oct 2014), "Banks harvest callers' voiceprints to fight fraud," Associated Press, http://www.washingtonpost.com/world/europe/banks-harvest-callers-voiceprints-to-fight-fraud/2014/10/13/715c6e56-52ad-11e4-b86d-184ac281388d_story.html.

35 **Store clerks will know your name:** Nicola Clark (17 Mar 2014), "Airlines use digital technology to get even more personal," *New York Times*, http://www.nytimes.com/2014/03/18/business/airlines-use-digital-technology-to-get-even-more-personal.html.

35 **Billboards will know who you are:** Andrew Hough (10 Mar 2010), "'Minority Report' digital billboard 'watches consumers shop,'" *Telegraph*, http://www.telegraph.co.uk/technology/news/7411249/Minority-Report-digital-billboard-watches-consumers-shop.html.

35 **Grocery store shelves will know:** Clint Boulton (11 Oct 2013), "Snackmaker mod-

ernizes the impulse buy with sensors, analytics," *Wall Street Journal Blogs*, http://blogs.wsj.com/cio/2013/10/11/snackmaker-modernizes-the-impulse-buy-with-sensors-analytics.

35 **Your car will know who is in it:** This excellent science fiction short story explores some of these ideas. Ken Liu (Dec 2012), "The perfect match," *Lightspeed Magazine*, http://www.lightspeedmagazine.com/fiction/the-perfect-match.

36 **Facebook tracks me:** Bryan Acohido (15 Nov 2011), "Facebook tracking is under scrutiny," *USA Today*, http://usatoday30.usatoday.com/tech/news/story/2011-11-15/facebook-privacy-tracking-data/51225112/1.

36 **It can probably make good guesses:** Cotton Delo (22 Feb 2013), "Facebook to partner with Acxiom, Epsilon to match store purchases with user profiles," *Advertising Age*, http://adage.com/article/digital/facebook-partner-acxiom-epsilon-match-store-purchases-user-profiles/239967.

36 **I try not to use Google search:** I use DuckDuckGo, which does not collect personal information about its users. See https://duckduckgo.com.

37 **I use various blockers:** Jonathan Mayer (17 Feb 2012), "Safari trackers," *Web Policy*, http://webpolicy.org/2012/02/17/safari-trackers.

37 **Google has about a third:** Benjamin Mako Hill (11 May 2014), "Google has most of my email because it has all of yours," *Copyrighteous*, http://mako.cc/copyrighteous/google-has-most-of-my-email-because-it-has-all-of-yours.

37 **police forces have installed surveillance cameras:** Mun Wong (4 May 2011), "Top 5 cities with the largest surveillance camera networks," *VinTech Journal*, http://www.vintechnology.com/journal/uncategorized/top-5-cities-with-the-largest-surveillance-camera-networks. David Barrett (10 Jul 2013), "One surveillance camera for every 11 people in Britain, says CCTV survey," *Telegraph*, http://www.telegraph.co.uk/technology/10172298/One-surveillance-camera-for-every-11-people-in-Britain-says-CCTV-survey.html. Thales Group (11 Apr 2014), "Mexico City, the world's most ambitious urban security programme," https://www.thalesgroup.com/en/worldwide/security/case-study/mexico-city-worlds-most-ambitious-urban-security-programme.

37 **That data is almost certainly digital:** Seagate Technology LLC (2012), "Video surveillance storage: How much is enough?" http://m.seagate.com/files/staticfiles/docs/pdf/whitepaper/video-surv-storage-tp571-3-1202-us.pdf.

38 **Jeremy Bentham conceived of his "panopticon":** Jeremy Bentham (1791), *The Panopticon, or the Inspection-House*, T. Payne, http://cartome.org/panopticon2.htm.

38 **idea has been used as a metaphor:** Oscar H. Gandy Jr. (1993), *The Panoptic Sort: A Political Economy of Personal Information*, Westview Press, http://books.google.com/books?id=wreFAAAAMAAJ.

38 **on the Internet and off:** Tom Brignall III (2002), "The new panopticon: The Internet viewed as a structure of social control," Tennessee Tech University, http://unpan1.un.org/intradoc/groups/public/documents/apcity/unpan003570.pdf.

38 **All of us are being watched:** Ellen Nakashima (16 Jan 2007), "Enjoying technology's conveniences but not escaping its watchful eyes," *Washington Post*, http://www.washingtonpost.com/wp-dyn/content/article/2007/01/15/AR2007011501304.html.

3: ANALYZING OUR DATA

39 **Target was right:** Charles Duhigg (16 Feb 2012), "How companies learn your secrets," *New York Times*, http://www.nytimes.com/2012/02/19/magazine/shopping-habits.html.

39 **amassing and saving all kinds of data:** Gregory Piatetsky (8 Dec 2013), "3 stages of Big Data," *KD Nuggets*, http://www.kdnuggets.com/2013/12/3-stages-big-data.html.

39 **Barack Obama mined data extensively:** Michael Scherer (7 Nov 2012), "Inside the secret world of the data crunchers who helped Obama win," *Time*, http://swampland.time.com/2012/11/07/inside-the-secret-world-of-quants-and-data-crunchers-who-helped-obama-win.

40 **allowed academics to mine their data:** Here are two examples. Lars Backstrom et al. (5 Jan 2012), "Four degrees of separation," arXiv:1111.4570 [cs.SI], http://arxiv.org/abs/1111.4570. Russell B. Clayton (Jul 2014), "The third wheel: The impact of Twitter use on relationship infidelity and divorce," *Cyberpsychology, Behavior, and Social Networking* 17, http://www.cs.vu.nl/~eliens/sg/local/cyber/twitter-infidelity.pdf.

40 **Facebook can predict:** The experiment correctly discriminates between homosexual and heterosexual men in 88% of cases, African Americans and Caucasian Americans in 95% of cases, and Democrats and Republicans in 85% of cases. Michal Kosinski, David Stillwell, and Thore Graepel (11 Mar 2013), "Private traits and attributes are predictable from digital records of human behavior," *Proceedings of the National Academy of Sciences of the United States of America, Early Edition*, http://www.pnas.org/content/early/2013/03/06/1218772110.

40 **The company knows you're engaged:** Sara M. Watson (14 Mar 2012), "I didn't tell Facebook I'm engaged, so why is it asking about my fiancé?" *Atlantic*, http://www.theatlantic.com/technology/archive/2012/03/i-didnt-tell-facebook-im-engaged-so-why-is-it-asking-about-my-fianc/254479.

40 **gay before you come out:** Katie Heaney (19 Mar 2013), "Facebook knew I was gay before my family did," *BuzzFeed*, http://www.buzzfeed.com/katieheaney/facebook-knew-i-was-gay-before-my-family-did.

40 **may reveal that to other people:** Geoffrey A. Fowler (13 Oct 2012), "When the most personal secrets get outed on Facebook," *Wall Street Journal*, http://online.wsj.com/news/articles/SB10000872396390444168504578008740578200224.

40 **it could get you killed:** For a while in 2014, there was a flaw in the gay hookup app Grindr that would reveal the location of gay men anywhere in the world, including countries like Uganda, Russia, and Iran. John Aravosis (26 Aug 2014), "Popular gay dating app Grindr faces creepy security breach allegations," *America Blog*, http://americablog.com/2014/08/grindr-users-unwittingly-giving-away-exact-location.html.

40 **when the ads are on track:** Sara M. Watson (16 Sep 2014), "Ask the decoder: Stalked by socks," *Al Jazeera*, http://america.aljazeera.com/articles/2014/9/16/the-decoder-stalkedbysocks.html.

41 **targeted at us specifically:** Sylvan Lane (13 Aug 2014), "16 creepiest targeted Facebook ads," *Mashable*, http://mashable.com/2014/08/13/facebook-ads-creepy.

41 **data mining is a hot technology:** Guy Gugliotta (19 Jun 2006), "Data mining still needs a clue to be effective," *Washington Post*, http://www.washingtonpost.com/wp-dyn/content/article/2006/06/18/AR2006061800524.html. Phillip Segal (28 Mar

2011), "Data mining is dumbed down intelligence," *Ethical Investigator*, http://www.ethicalinvestigator.com/internet/data-mining-is-dumbed-down-intelligence. Ogi Ogas (8 Feb 2013), "Beware the big errors of 'Big Data,'" *Wired*, http://www.wired.com/2013/02/big-data-means-big-errors-people.

41 **go backwards in time:** Barton Gellman and Ashkan Soltani (18 Mar 2014), "NSA surveillance program reaches 'into the past' to retrieve, replay phone calls," *Washington Post*, http://www.washingtonpost.com/world/national-security/nsa-surveillance-program-reaches-into-the-past-to-retrieve-replay-phone-calls/2014/03/18/226d2646-ade9-11e3-a49e-76adc9210f19_story.html.

42 **Untangling this sort of wrongdoing:** US Department of Justice (16 Dec 2009), "Credit Suisse agrees to forfeit $536 million in connection with violations of the International Emergency Economic Powers Act and New York State law," http://www.justice.gov/opa/pr/2009/December/09-ag-1358.html. Office of the District Attorney, New York County (10 Dec 2012), "Standard Chartered Bank reaches $327 million settlement for illegal transactions," http://manhattanda.org/node/3440/print. Office of the District Attorney, New York County (30 Jun 2014), "BNP Paribas Bank pleads guilty, pays $8.83 billion in penalties for illegal transactions," http://manhattanda.org/node/4884/print.

42 **blood taken from riders years earlier:** Scott Rosenfield (23 Jul 2013), "Top 3 finishers in 1998 Tour test positive," *Outside Online*, http://www.outsideonline.com/news-from-the-field/Top-3-Finishers-in-1998-Tour-Test-Positive.html.

42 **a database called XKEYSCORE:** Glenn Greenwald (21 Jul 2013), "XKeyscore: NSA tool collects 'nearly everything a user does on the internet,'" *Guardian*, http://www.theguardian.com/world/2013/jul/31/nsa-top-secret-program-online-data. US National Security Agency (8 Jan 2007), "XKEYSCORE (training slides)," https://www.eff.org/document/2013-07-31-guard-xkeyscore-training-slides (page 2).

42 **One called MARINA:** James Ball (30 Sep 2013), "NSA stores metadata of millions of web users for up to a year, secret files show," *Guardian*, http://www.theguardian.com/world/2013/sep/30/nsa-americans-metadata-year-documents.

42 **Another NSA database, MYSTIC:** Ryan Devereaux, Glenn Greenwald, and Laura Poitras (19 May 2014), "Data pirates of the Caribbean: The NSA is recording every cell phone call in the Bahamas," *Intercept*, https://firstlook.org/theintercept/article/2014/05/19/data-pirates-caribbean-nsa-recording-every-cell-phone-call-bahamas. Julian Assange (23 May 2014), "WikiLeaks statement on the mass recording of Afghan telephone calls by the NSA," *WikiLeaks*, https://wikileaks.org/WikiLeaks-statement-on-the-mass.html.

43 **The NSA stores telephone metadata:** David Kravets (17 Jan 2014), "Obama revamps NSA phone metadata spying program," *Wired*, http://www.wired.com/2014/01/obama-nsa.

43 **If you use encryption:** I do not know whether this includes all encrypted SSL sessions. My guess is that the NSA is able to decrypt a lot of SSL in real time. Matthew Green (2 Dec 2013), "How does the NSA break SSL?" *A Few Thoughts on Cryptographic Engineering*, http://blog.cryptographyengineering.com/2013/12/how-does-nsa-break-ssl.html.

43 **NSA needed to increase its storage capacity:** Barton Gellman and Ashkan Soltani (4 Dec 2013), "NSA tracking cellphone locations worldwide, Snowden documents show," *Washington Post*, http://www.washingtonpost.com/world/national-security/

nsa-tracking-cellphone-locations-worldwide-snowden-documents-show/
2013/12/04/5492873a-5cf2-11e3-bc56-c6ca94801fac_story.html.

43 **This is the point of:** James Bamford (15 Mar 2012), "The NSA is building the country's biggest spy center (watch what you say)," *Wired*, http://www.wired.com/
threatlevel/2012/03/ff_nsadatacenter/all.

43 **The FBI stores our data, too:** Kevin Poulsen (27 Jan 2014), "If you used this secure
webmail site, the FBI has your inbox," *Wired*, http://www.wired.com/2014/01/tormail.

43 **The state of New York retains:** Cyrus Farivar (27 Feb 2012), "Your car, tracked: The
rapid rise of license plate readers," *Ars Technica*, http://arstechnica.com/tech-pol
icy/2012/09/your-car-tracked-the-rapid-rise-of-license-plate-readers. Steve Orr (26
Jul 2014), "New York knows where your license plate goes," *Democrat and Chronicle*,
http://www.democratandchronicle.com/story/news/2014/07/26/new-york-license-
plate-readers/13179727.

43 **AT&T beat them all:** Declan McCullagh (19 Mar 2013), "Cops: U.S. law should
require logs of your text messages," *CNET*, http://news.cnet.com/8301-13578_3-
57575039-38/cops-u.s-law-should-require-logs-of-your-text-messages.

44 **three hops away from Alice:** Philip Bump (17 Jul 2013), "The NSA admits it analyzes more people's data than previously revealed," *Atlantic Wire*, http://www
.thewire.com/politics/2013/07/nsa-admits-it-analyzes-more-peoples-data-previ
ously-revealed/67287.

44 **Making sense of the data:** Jonathan Mayer writes about the difficulty of analyzing
this data. Jonathan Mayer and Patrick Muchler (9 Dec 2013), "MetaPhone: The NSA
three-hop," *Web Policy*, http://webpolicy.org/2013/12/09/metaphone-the-nsa-three-
hop.

44 **phone numbers common to unrelated people:** Amy Davidson (16 Dec 2013),
"The domino's hypothetical: Judge Leon vs. the N.S.A.," *New Yorker*, http://www
.newyorker.com/news/amy-davidson/the-dominos-hypothetical-judge-leon-vs-
the-n-s-a.

44 **NSA documents note:** Barton Gellman and Laura Poitras (10 Jul 2013), "NSA slides
explain the PRISM data-collection program," *Washington Post*, http://www.wash
ingtonpost.com/wp-srv/special/politics/prism-collection-documents.

44 **total number of people being surveilled:** Shane Harris (17 Jul 2013), "Three
degrees of separation is enough to have you watched by the NSA," *Foreign Policy*,
http://complex.foreignpolicy.com/posts/2013/07/17/3_degrees_of_separation_is_
enough_to_have_you_watched_by_the_nsa.

44 **President Obama directed the NSA:** Tony Bradley (17 Jan 2014), "NSA reform:
What President Obama said, and what he didn't," *Forbes*, http://www.forbes.com/
sites/tonybradley/2014/01/17/nsa-reform-what-president-obama-said-and-what-
he-didnt.

44 **This is what both the NSA:** James Risen and Laura Poitras (20 Sep 2013), "NSA
gathers data on social connections of U.S. citizens," *New York Times*, http://www
.nytimes.com/2013/09/29/us/nsa-examines-social-networks-of-us-citizens.html.

44 **One of Facebook's most successful:** Vauhini Vara (23 Aug 2007), "Facebook gets
personal with ad targeting plan," *Wall Street Journal*, http://online.wsj.com/news/
articles/SB118783296519606151.

45 **Google . . . searches all of your Gmail:** If either Google or Microsoft finds evidence of child pornography, it will report you to the police. Matthew Sparkes (4 Aug

2014), "Why Google scans your emails for child porn," *Telegraph*, http://www.tele graph.co.uk/technology/google/11010182/Why-Google-scans-your-emails-for-child-porn.html. Leo Kelion (6 Aug 2014), "Microsoft tip leads to child porn arrest in Pennsylvania," *BBC News*, www.bbc.co.uk/go/em/fr/-/news/technology-28682686.

45 **The NSA does something similar:** The PCLOB has stated that NSA collection under Section 702 of the FISA Amendments Act does not collect on the basis of key-words, although that's just one authority. And there's a lot of room for weaseling. Pri-vacy and Civil Liberties Oversight Board (2 Jul 2014), "Report on the surveillance program operated pursuant to Section 702 of the Foreign Intelligence Surveillance Act," http://www.pclob.gov/All%20Documents/Report%20on%20the%20Section%20 702%20Program/PCLOB-Section-702-Report.pdf. Jennifer Granick (11 Feb 2014), "Eight questions PCLOB should ask about Section 702," *Just Security*, https://justsecu rity.org/7001/questions-pclob-section-702.

45 **the NSA targets people:** Jacob Appelbaum et al. (3 Jul 2014), "NSA targets the pri vacy-conscious," *Panorama*, http://daserste.ndr.de/panorama/aktuell/nsa230_page-1 .html.

45 **the NSA chains together hops:** Marcy Wheeler (15 Oct 2013), "About that May 2007 FISC opinion," *Empty Wheel*, http://www.emptywheel.net/2013/10/15/about-that-may-2007-fisc-opinion.

45 **the same location as a target:** Marcy Wheeler (16 May 2014), "The 'automated query' at the telecoms will include 'correlations,'" *Empty Wheel*, http://www.empty wheel.net/2014/05/16/the-automated-query-at-the-telecoms-will-include-correla tions. Marcy Wheeler (28 Jun 2014), "NSA's new-and-improved call chaining process, now with no calls required," *Empty Wheel*, http://www.emptywheel.net/2014/06/28/ nsas-new-and-improved-call-chaining-process-now-with-no-calls-required.

46 **The NSA uses cell phone location:** The program is code-named CO-TRAVELLER. Barton Gellman and Ashkan Soltani (4 Dec 2013), "NSA tracking cellphone locations worldwide, Snowden documents show," *Washington Post*, http://www.washingtonpost .com/world/national-security/nsa-tracking-cellphone-locations-worldwide-snowden-documents-show/2013/12/04/5492873a-5cf2-11e3-bc56-c6ca94801fac_story.html.

46 **The NSA tracks the locations of phones:** US National Security Administration (2012), "Summary of DNR and DNI Co-Travel analytics," https://www.eff.org/ files/2013/12/11/20131210-wapo-cotraveler_overview.pdf.

46 **The NSA has a program where it trawls:** Julian Sanchez (11 Oct 2013), "Other uses of the NSA call records database: Fingerprinting burners?" *Just Security*, http://just security.org/2013/10/11/nsa-call-records-database-fingerprinting-burners.

46 **The NSA collects data on people:** Barton Gellman and Ashkan Soltani (4 Dec 2013), "NSA tracking cellphone locations worldwide, Snowden documents show," *Washing-ton Post*, http://www.washingtonpost.com/world/national-security/nsa-tracking-cellphone-locations-worldwide-snowden-documents-show/2013/12/04/5492873a-5cf2-11e3-bc56-c6ca94801fac_story.html.

47 **phones that were used by a particular target:** The technique is basically CO-TRAVELLER. If there's a phone that is always in the same network as your pri-mary phone, it's likely to be found in your pocket. US Department of Justice (13 Feb 2012), "Criminal complaint," *United States of America v. Jose Aguijo, et al.*, (Case num-ber under seal), United States District Court, Northern District of Illinois, Eastern Division, http://www.justice.gov/usao/iln/pr/chicago/2013/pr0222_01d.pdf.

47 **A single geofencing company:** Hiawatha Bray (30 Apr 2014), "How location-based apps will shape the future of shopping," *Discover*, http://blogs.discovermagazine.com/crux/2014/04/30/how-location-based-apps-will-shape-the-future-of-shopping.

47 **Microsoft does the same thing:** Lauren Johnson (9 Jun 2014), "Why Microsoft is wrapping location-based ads around retail stores: Tests significantly lifted foot traffic," *Advertising Week*, http://www.adweek.com/news/technology/why-microsoft-wrapping-location-based-ads-around-retail-stores-158189.

47 **Sense Networks uses location data:** Hiawatha Bray (8 Jul 2013), "Cellphone data mined to create personal profiles," *Boston Globe*, http://www.bostonglobe.com/business/2013/07/07/your-cellphone-yourself/eSvTK1UCqNOE7D4qbAcWPL/story.html.

47 **Vigilant Solutions . . . collect license plate data:** Ali Winston (17 Jun 2014), "Plans to expand scope of license-plate readers alarm privacy advocates," Center for Investigative Reporting, http://cironline.org/reports/plans-expand-scope-license-plate-readers-alarm-privacy-advocates-6451.

47 **the linking of identities:** This article discusses the FBI's plans to do just that. Electronic Privacy Information Center (Dec 2013), "The FBI's Next Generation Identification program: Big Brother's ID system?" *Spotlight on Surveillance*, https://epic.org/privacy/surveillance/spotlight/ngi.html.

48 **I have an Oyster card:** There were concerns about tracking people by their Oyster cards when the technology was introduced in London in 2003. Aaron Scullion (25 Sep 2003), "Smart cards track commuters," *BBC News*, http://news.bbc.co.uk/2/hi/technology/3121652.stm.

48 **the value of correlating different streams:** Greg Weston, Glenn Greenwald, and Ryan Gallagher (30 Jan 2014), "CSEC used airport Wi-Fi to track Canadian travellers: Edward Snowden documents," *CBC News*, http://www.cbc.ca/news/politics/csec-used-airport-wi-fi-to-track-canadian-travellers-edward-snowden-documents-1.2517881.

49 **display personal information:** Alessandro Acquisti, Ralph Gross, and Fred Stutzman (4 Aug 2011), "Faces of Facebook: Privacy in the age of augmented reality," Black Hat 2011, Las Vegas, Nevada, http://www.heinz.cmu.edu/~acquisti/face-recognition-study-FAQ/acquisti-faces-BLACKHAT-draft.pdf.

49 **software that correlates data:** Scott Ellart (7 Dec 1999), "System and method for converting data between data sets (US 5999937 A)," US Patent and Trademark Office, http://www.google.com/patents/US5999937.

49 **match your online profile:** Cotton Delo (22 Feb 2013), "Facebook to partner with Acxiom, Epsilon to match store purchases with user profiles," *Advertising Age*, http://adage.com/article/digital/facebook-partner-acxiom-epsilon-match-store-purchases-user-profiles/239967.

49 **ExactData can sell lists of people:** Caroline Cooper and Claire Gordon (2 Apr 2014), "The people making money off your drinking habits and STDs," Al Jazeera, http://america.aljazeera.com/watch/shows/america-tonight/articles/2014/4/2/the-people-makingmoneyoffyourdrinkinghabitsandstds.html.

50 **Chinese military hackers:** Max Fisher (19 Feb 2013), "Chinese hackers outed themselves by logging into their personal Facebook accounts," *Washington Post*, http://www.washingtonpost.com/blogs/worldviews/wp/2013/02/19/chinese-hackers-outed-themselves-by-logging-into-their-personal-facebook-accounts.

50 **Hector Monsegur:** Paul Roberts (7 Mar 2012), "Chats, car crushes and cut 'n paste sowed seeds of LulzSec's demise," *Threatpost*, http://threatpost.com/chats-car-crushes-and-cut-n-paste-sowed-seeds-lulzsecs-demise-030712/76298.

50 **Paula Broadwell:** Chris Soghoian (13 Nov 2012), "Surveillance and security lessons from the Petraeus scandal," American Civil Liberties Union, https://www.aclu.org/blog/technology-and-liberty-national-security/surveillance-and-security-lessons-petraeus-scandal.

50 **A member of the hacker group Anonymous:** Dan Oakes (12 Apr 2012), "Hacking case's body of evidence," *Sydney Morning Herald*, http://www.smh.com.au/technology/technology-news/hacking-cases-body-of-evidence-20120412-1wsbh.html.

51 **Israeli assassins were quickly identified:** Ronen Bergman et al. (17 Jan 2011), "An eye for an eye: The anatomy of Mossad's Dubai operation," *Der Spiegel*, http://www.spiegel.de/international/world/an-eye-for-an-eye-the-anatomy-of-mossad-s-dubai-operation-a-739908.html.

51 **techniques for anonymizing data:** Paul Ohm (13 Aug 2009), "Broken promises of privacy: Responding to the surprising failure of anonymization," *UCLA Law Review* 57, http://papers.ssrn.com/sol3/papers.cfm?abstract_id=1450006.

51 **researchers were able to attach names:** Michael Barbaro and Tom Zeller Jr. (9 Aug 2006), "A face is exposed for AOL Search No. 4417749," *New York Times*, http://www.nytimes.com/2006/08/09/technology/09aol.html.

51 **Researchers were able to de-anonymize people:** Arvind Narayanan and Vitaly Shmatikov (18–20 May 2008), "Robust de-anonymization of large sparse datasets," 2008 IEEE Symposium on Security and Privacy, Oakland, California, http://dl.acm.org/citation.cfm?id=1398064 and http://www.cs.utexas.edu/~shmat/shmat_oak08netflix.pdf.

52 **correlation opportunities pop up:** Also for research purposes, in the mid-1990s the Massachusetts Group Insurance Commission released hospital records from state employees with the names, addresses, and Social Security numbers removed. Computer scientist Latanya Sweeney—then an MIT graduate student—demonstrated that she could de-anonymize records by correlating birth dates and ZIP codes with the voter registration database. Latanya Sweeney (Jun 1997), "Weaving technology and policy together to maintain confidentiality," *Journal of Law, Medicine and Ethics* 25, http://onlinelibrary.wiley.com/doi/10.1111/j.1748-720X.1997.tb01885.x/abstract.

52 **just a city, town, or municipality:** Latanya Sweeney (2000), "Simple demographics often identify people uniquely," Carnegie Mellon University, Data Privacy Working Paper 3, http://dataprivacylab.org/projects/identifiability/paper1.pdf.

52 **Other researchers reported similar results:** Philippe Golle (30 Oct 2006), "Revisiting the uniqueness of simple demographics in the US population," 5th ACM Workshop on Privacy in the Electronic Society (WPES'06), Alexandria, Virginia, http://crypto.stanford.edu/~pgolle/papers/census.pdf.

52 **identify people from their anonymous DNA:** Melissa Gymrek et al. (18 Jan 2013), "Identifying personal genomes by surname inference," *Science* 339, http://www.sciencemag.org/content/339/6117/321.abstract. John Bohannon et al. (18 Jan 2013), "Genealogy databases enable naming of anonymous DNA donors," *Science* 339, http://www.sciencemag.org/content/339/6117/262.

52 **Alfred Kinsey's sex research data:** Adam Tanner (11 Oct 2013), "Anonymous sex

survey takers get identified in data dive," *Forbes*, http://www.forbes.com/sites/adamtanner/2013/10/11/decoding-the-secrets-of-sex-data.

52 **It's counterintuitive:** Arvind Narayanan and Vitaly Shmatikov (Jun 2010), "Myths and fallacies of 'personally identifiable information,'" *Communications of the ACM* 53, http://dl.acm.org/citation.cfm?id=1743558.

53 **We can be uniquely identified:** Ryan Gallagher (25 Aug 2014), "The surveillance engine: How the NSA built its own secret Google," *Intercept*, https://firstlook.org/theintercept/2014/08/25/icreach-nsa-cia-secret-google-crisscross-proton.

53 **four time/date/location points:** Yves-Alexandre de Montjoye et al. (4 Feb 2013), "Unique in the crowd: The privacy bounds of human mobility," *Scientific Reports* 3, Article 1376, http://www.nature.com/srep/2013/130325/srep01376/full/srep01376.html.

53 **these sorts of tweaks:** I don't mean to imply that it's impossible to anonymize a data set, only that it's very difficult to do correctly and easy to get wrong. So many people think that replacing sensitive data with random numbers is enough, but it's not. Often, it doesn't help at all.

53 **This is why regulation:** Here's an example of the DHS regulations. Mary Ellen Callahan (Mar 2012), "Handbook for safeguarding sensitive personally identifiable information," US Department of Homeland Security, http://www.dhs.gov/sites/default/files/publications/privacy/Guidance/handbookforsafeguardingsensitivePII_march_2012_webversion.pdf.

4: THE BUSINESS OF SURVEILLANCE

54 **Brightest Flashlight Free:** Casey Houser (16 Oct 2013), "Use your flashlight app for trick-or-treating," *Gazelle*, https://www.gazelle.com/thehorn/2013/10/16/use-your-flashlight-app-for-trick-or-treating.

54 **the app collected location information:** Cecilia Kang (5 Dec 2013), "Flashlight app kept users in the dark about sharing location data," *Washington Post*, http://www.washingtonpost.com/business/technology/flashlight-app-kept-users-in-the-dark-about-sharing-location-data-ftc/2013/12/05/1be26fa6-5dc7-11e3-be07-006c776266ed_story.html.

55 **researchers discovered it in 2012:** Jason Hong (30 Nov 2012), "Analysis of Brightest Flashlight Free for Android," *Jason Hong's Confabulations*, http://confabulator.blogspot.com/2012/11/analysis-of-brightest-flashlight-free.html.

55 **The US Federal Trade Commission got involved:** US Federal Trade Commission (5 Dec 2013), "Android Flashlight app developer settles FTC charges it deceived consumers: 'Brightest Flashlight' app shared users' location, device ID without consumers' knowledge," http://www.ftc.gov/news-events/press-releases/2013/12/android-flashlight-app-developer-settles-ftc-charges-it-deceived.

55 **we are offered a package deal:** Sometimes surveillance is coerced. In order for me to get my warranty for a product, I often have to give up personal information to the company that built the product.

56 **Enterprises like DoubleClick:** Within days of searching Google for a particular vacation location, I started receiving Travelocity ads for that location. I don't even have a Travelocity account.

56 **Most of the companies tracking you:** Peter Eckersley (21 Sep 2009), "How online tracking companies know most of what you do online (and what social networks are doing to help them)," Electronic Frontier Foundation, https://www.eff.org/deep links/2009/09/online-trackers-and-social-networks.

56 **If you want to see who's tracking you:** Samuel Gibbs (28 Oct 2013), "Mozilla's Lightbeam Firefox tool shows who's tracking your online movements," *Guardian*, http://www.theguardian.com/technology/2013/oct/28/mozilla-lightbeam-track ing-privacy-cookies.

57 **One reporter discovered that 105:** Alexis Madrigal (29 Feb 2012), "I'm being followed: How Google—and 104 other companies—are tracking me on the web," *Atlantic*, http://www.theatlantic.com/technology/archive/2012/02/im-being-followed-how-google-151-and-104-other-companies-151-are-tracking-me-on-the-web/253758.

57 **Dictionary.com installed over 200:** Julia Angwin (30 Jul 2010), "The Web's new gold mine: Your secrets," *Wall Street Journal*, http://online.wsj.com/news/articles/SB10001424052748703940904575395073512989404.

57 **The apps there track you:** Scott Thurm and Yukari Iwatani Kane (18 Dec 2010), "Your apps are watching you," *Wall Street Journal*, http://online.wsj.com/news/arti cles/SB10001424052748704368004576027751867039730.

57 **The app required the ability:** Andrew Cunningham (5 Jul 2013), "Samsung and Jay-Z give the Internet a master's class in how not to make an app," *Ars Technica*, http://arstechnica.com/gadgets/2013/07/samsung-and-jay-z-give-the-internet-a-masters-class-in-how-not-to-make-an-app.

57 **the Angry Birds game even collects:** Frances Zhang, Fuming Shih, and Daniel Weitzner (4–8 Nov 2013), "No surprises: measuring intrusiveness of smartphone applications by detecting objective context deviations," 12th ACM Workshop on Privacy in the Electronic Society (WPES'13), Berlin, Germany, http://dl.acm.org/citation.cfm?id=2517864.

57 **Broadband companies like Comcast:** Douglas Rushkoff (6 Jul 2012), "Will your Internet provider be spying on you?" CNN, http://www.cnn.com/2012/07/06/opinion/rushkoff-online-monitoring. David Kravets (25 Feb 2013), "ISPs now monitoring for copyright infringement," *Wired*, http://www.wired.com/2013/02/copyright-scoff laws-beware.

57 **Verizon, Microsoft, and others:** Casey Johnston (3 Dec 2012), "How to get targeted ads on your TV? Try a camera in your set-top box," *Ars Technica*, http://arstechnica .com/tech-policy/2012/12/how-to-get-targeted-ads-on-your-tv-a-camera-in-your-set-top-box. Christopher Zara (26 Jul 2013), "Is your cable box spying on you? Behavior-de tecting devices from Verizon, Microsoft and others worry privacy advocates," *International Business Times*, http://www.ibtimes.com/your-cable-box-spying-you-behavior-detecting-devices-verizon-microsoft-others-worry-privacy-1361587.

57 **It's less Big Brother:** It's interesting that we commonly use ideas from fiction to talk about surveillance and privacy: something is Orwellian or Kafkaesque, or akin to Tolkien's "Eye of Sauron." Bruce Schneier (18 Apr 2014), "Metaphors of surveillance," *Schneier on Security*, https://www.schneier.com/blog/archives/2014/04/metaphors_of_su.html.

57 **other ways to uniquely track you:** Peter Eckersley (Jul 2010), "How unique is your web browser?" *Proceedings of the 10th International Conference on Privacy Enhancing*

Technologies, https://panopticlick.eff.org/browser-uniqueness.pdf. Keaton Mowery and Hovav Shacham (24 May 2012), "Pixel perfect: Fingerprinting canvas in HTML5," Web 2.0 Security and Privacy, San Francisco, California, http://cseweb.ucsd .edu/~hovav/papers/ms12.html. Julia Angwin (21 Jul 2014), "Meet the online tracking device that is virtually impossible to block," *Pro Publica*, http://www.propublica.org/ article/meet-the-online-tracking-device-that-is-virtually-impossible-to-block. Gunes Acar et al. (10 Aug 2014), "The web never forgets: persistent tracking mechanisms in the wild," ACM Conference on Computer and Communications Security (CCS 2014), Scottsdale, Arizona, https://securehomes.esat.kuleuven.be/~gacar/per sistent/index.html.

58 **Google tried to compel this:** Google (5 Jul 2014), Post re: Removal of Google+ username restrictions, https://plus.google.com/+googleplus/posts/V5XkYQYYJqy.

58 **Facebook pretty much demands real names:** Facebook has been reconsidering the policy after being confronted by users who are potentially endangered by it. Facebook (2014), "What names are allowed on Facebook?" https://www.facebook .com/help/112146705538576. Reed Albergotti (2 Oct 2014), "Facebook changes realname policy after uproar from drag queens," *Wall Street Journal*, http://online.wsj. com/articles/facebook-changes-real-name-policy-after-uproar-from-drag-queens-1412223040.

58 **It quickly became clear:** People's willingness to pay has changed somewhat. Lots of us are now used to paying small amounts, or even large amounts over time, for smartphone apps, but the surveillance aspect of Internet business has remained. Even apps you pay for spy on you.

59 **"Free" is a special price:** Kristina Shampanier, Nina Mazar, and Dan Ariely (Dec 2007), "Zero as a special price: The true value of free products," *Marketing Science* 26, http://web.mit.edu/ariely/www/MIT/Papers/zero.pdf.

59 **Free warps our normal sense:** Scott Bradner (3 Aug 2010), "The price of free Internet: A piece of your soul," *Network World*, http://www.networkworld.com/colum nists/2010/080310bradner.html.

59 **Facebook has done it systematically:** Kurt Opsahl (28 Apr 2010), "Facebook's eroding privacy policy: A timeline," Electronic Frontier Foundation, https://www .eff.org/deeplinks/2010/04/facebook-timeline.

59 **Facebook has also changed:** This is an excellent interactive graphic. Matt McKeon (15 May 2010), "The evolution of privacy on Facebook," http://mattmckeon.com/ facebook-privacy.

59 **Google has done much the same:** Associated Press (2 Apr 2013), "Timeline: A look at developments linked to Google privacy concerns," *CTV News*, http://www .ctvnews.ca/sci-tech/timeline-a-look-at-developments-linked-to-google-privacy-concerns-1.1220927.

59 **Apple is somewhat of an exception:** Rich Mogull (25 Jun 2014), "Why Apple really cares about your privacy," *Macworld*, http://www.macworld.com/article/2366921/ why-apple-really-cares-about-your-privacy.html.

59 **It uses iTunes purchase information:** Charles Arthur (18 Sep 2014), "Apple's Tim Cook attacks Google and Facebook over privacy flaws," *Guardian*, http://www .theguardian.com/technology/2014/sep/18/apple-tim-cook-google-facebook-priva cy-surveillance.

60 **It's very big business for Amazon:** Jay Greene (18 Mar 2014), "Amazon easing into $1 billion sideline business: ad sales," *Union Bulletin*, http://union-bulletin.com/news/2014/mar/18/amazon-easing-1b-sideline-business-ad-sales. Nadia Tuma and Laura Simpson (23 Jan 2014), "Why Amazon's data store doesn't scare people—but Facebook's does," *Advertising Age*, http://adage.com/article/guest-columnists/americans-scared-amazon-s-data-store/290953.

61 **Companies have increasingly:** Amy Harmon (24 Aug 2001), "As public records go online, some say they're too public," *New York Times*, http://www.nytimes.com/2001/08/24/nyregion/as-public-records-go-online-some-say-they-re-too-public.html. Mark Ackerman (26 Aug 2013), "Sales of public data to marketers can mean big $$ for governments," *CBS Denver*, http://denver.cbslocal.com/2013/08/26/sales-of-public-data-to-marketers-can-mean-big-for-governments.

61 **data brokers like Acxiom:** This is a good article on Acxiom. Natasha Singer (16 Jun 2012), "Mapping, and sharing, the consumer genome," *New York Times*, http://www.nytimes.com/2012/06/17/technology/acxiom-the-quiet-giant-of-consumer-database-marketing.html.

61 **These companies buy:** The World Privacy Forum estimates that there are about 4,000 data brokers. Pam Dixon (18 Dec 2013), "Testimony of Pam Dixon, Executive Director, World Privacy Forum, before the U.S. Senate Committee on Commerce, Science, and Transportation: What information do data brokers have on consumers, and how do they use it?" *World Privacy Forum*, http://www.worldprivacyforum.org/2013/12/testimony-what-information-do-data-brokers-have-on-consumers.

62 **The more data you produce:** Craig Timberg (27 May 2014), "Brokers use 'billions' of data points to profile Americans," *Washington Post*, http://www.washingtonpost.com/business/technology/brokers-use-billions-of-data-points-to-profile-americans/2014/05/27/b4207b96-e5b2-11e3-a86b-362fd5443d19_story.html.

62 **The breadth and depth:** *Wall Street Journal* ran an excellent series that discussed the enormous amount of surveillance data different companies collect. *Wall Street Journal*, "What They Know" series index, http://online.wsj.com/public/page/what-they-know-digital-privacy.html.

62 **They collect everything:** US Senate Committee on Commerce, Science, and Transportation, Office of Oversight and Investigations, Majority Staff (18 Dec 2013), "A review of the data broker industry: Collection, use, and sale of consumer data for marketing purposes," Staff report for Chairman Rockefeller, http://consumercal.org/wp-content/uploads/2013/12/senate_2013_data_broker_report.pdf.

62 **Data brokers use your data:** Lois Beckett (13 Sep 2013), "Everything we know about what data brokers know about you," *Pro Publica*, https://www.propublica.org/article/everything-we-know-about-what-data-brokers-know-about-you.

62 **Acxiom can provide you with that:** Natasha Singer (5 Sep 2013), "Acxiom lets consumers see data it collects," *New York Times*, http://www.nytimes.com/2013/09/05/technology/acxiom-lets-consumers-see-data-it-collects.html.

62 **InfoUSA has sold lists:** Charles Duhigg (20 May 2007), "Bilking the elderly, with a corporate assist," *New York Times*, http://www.nytimes.com/2007/05/20/business/20tele.html.

62 **both brokers were fined by the FTC:** US Senate Committee on Commerce, Science, and Transportation, Office of Oversight and Investigations, Majority Staff (18

Dec 2013), "A review of the data broker industry: Collection, use, and sale of consumer data for marketing purposes," Staff report for Chairman Rockefeller, http://consumer cal.org/wp-content/uploads/2013/12/senate_2013_data_broker_report.pdf.

62 **We use systems that spy on us:** Joseph Turow (7 Feb 2012), "A guide to the digital advertising industry that's watching your every click," *Atlantic*, http://www.theat lantic.com/technology/archive/2012/02/a-guide-to-the-digital-advertising-industry-thats-watching-your-every-click/252667.

62 **If something is free:** It's not known who first said this. Jonathan Zittrain (21 Mar 2012), "Meme patrol: 'When something online is free, you're not the customer, you're the product,'" *The Future of the Internet and How to Stop It*, http://blogs.law.harvard .edu/futureoftheinternet/2012/03/21/meme-patrol-when-something-online-is-free-youre-not-the-customer-youre-the-product.

62 **as Al Gore said:** Nelson Wyatt (7 Nov 2013), "Former U.S. vice-president Al Gore predicts lawmakers will rein in surveillance," *Vancouver Sun*, http://www.vancouversun .com/news/Former+vicepresident+Gore+predicts+lawmakers+will+rein/9129866/ story.html.

63 **There's a famous quote:** Laurence Green (5 Jul 2010), "Why creativity will buy you more success than money," *Telegraph*, http://www.telegraph.co.uk/finance/ businessclub/7872084/Why-creativity-will-buy-you-more-success-than-money .html.

63 **If you know exactly who:** At least, that's the theory. There are people who argue that this isn't as effective as one might think. Douglas Rushkoff (2013), *Present Shock: When Everything Happens Now*, Current, http://www.rushkoff.com/present-shock.

63 **a national lawn care company:** Real Green Systems (2014), "Measurement Assistant: An online measuring software application combining aerial photography and measuring tools," https://www.realgreen.com/measurement_assistant.html.

63 **This also works in political advertising:** Nathan Abse (Oct 2012), "Big data delivers on campaign promise: Microtargeted political advertising in Election 2012," Interactive Advertising Bureau, http://www.iab.net/media/file/Innovations_In_ Web_Marketing_and_Advertising_delivery.pdf.

63 **Obama used big data:** Michael Scherer (7 Nov 2012), "Inside the secret world of the data crunchers who helped Obama win," *Time*, http://swampland.time.com/ 2012/11/07/inside-the-secret-world-of-quants-and-data-crunchers-who-helped-obama-win. Sasha Issenberg (19 Dec 2012), "How President Obama's campaign used big data to rally individual voters," *MIT Technology Review*, http://www.technologyreview .com/featuredstory/509026/how-obamas-team-used-big-data-to-rally-voters.

63 **This data is used to target:** Ed Pilkington and Amanda Michel (17 Feb 2012), "Obama, Facebook and the power of friendship: The 2012 data election," *Guardian*, http://www.theguardian.com/world/2012/feb/17/obama-digital-data-machine-facebook-election. Tanzina Vega (20 Feb 2012), "Online data helping campaigns customize ads," *New York Times*, http://www.nytimes.com/2012/02/21/us/politics/ campaigns-use-microtargeting-to-attract-supporters.html.

63 **A lot of commercial surveillance:** Many data brokers now allow you to correct errors. Any corrections you make improve the quality of the data they sell to others. Your corrections help them, yet they depict it as some sort of right you now have.

63 **this information can be valuable:** In 2014, Shutterfly sent e-mail congratulations to people who had just had a baby, and made some mistakes. The mistakes were

what made the press. Kashmir Hill (14 May 2014), "Shutterfly congratulates a bunch of people without babies on their 'new arrivals,'" *Forbes*, http://www.forbes.com/sites/kashmirhill/2014/05/14/shutterfly-congratulates-a-bunch-of-people-without-babies-on-their-new-arrivals.

64 **the data is enormously better:** There's a lot of anecdotal evidence about how wrong targeted advertising gets things, but much of that comes from the fact that we notice the mistakes more than we notice the bull's-eyes.

64 **physical locations of people on Twitter:** Jalal Mahmud, Jeffrey Nichols, and Clemens Drews (7 Mar 2014), "Home location identification of Twitter users," arXiv:1403.2345 [cs.SI], http://arxiv.org/abs/1403.2345.

64 **surveillance-based advertising is oversold:** This essay, for example, questions the effectiveness of Internet advertising. Derek Thompson (13 Jun 2014), "A dangerous question: Does Internet advertising work at all?" *Atlantic*, http://www.theatlantic.com/business/archive/2014/06/a-dangerous-question-does-internet-advertising-work-at-all/372704.

64 **one of the kids died in a car crash:** In 2014, OfficeMax sent a promotional mailing addressed to "Mike Seay/Daughter Killed in Car Crash/Or Current Business." That was a database error, but it illustrates the personal nature of data these data brokers collect. Amy Merrick (23 Jan 2014), "A death in the database," *New Yorker*, http://www.newyorker.com/online/blogs/currency/2014/01/ashley-seay-officemax-car-crash-death-in-the-database.html.

64 **advertising that's too targeted feels creepy:** Blase Ur et al. (2 Apr 2012), "Smart, useful, scary, creepy: Perceptions of online behavioral advertising," CyLab, Carnegie Mellon University, Pittsburgh, Pennsylvania, https://www.cylab.cmu.edu/research/techreports/2012/tr_cylab12007.html.

64 **the "uncanny valley":** Farhad Manjoo (23 Aug 2012), "The uncanny valley of Internet advertising," *Slate*, http://www.slate.com/articles/technology/technology/2012/08/the_uncanny_valley_of_internet_advertising_why_do_creepy_targeted_ads_follow_me_everywhere_i_go_on_the_web_.html. Sara M. Watson (16 Jun 2014), "Data doppelgängers and the uncanny valley of personalization," *Atlantic*, http://www.theatlantic.com/technology/archive/2014/06/data-doppelgangers-and-the-uncanny-valley-of-personalization/372780.

65 **People are okay with sloppily:** Mike Masnick (11 Mar 2008), "Where's the line between personalized advertising and creeping people out?" *Tech Dirt*, http://www.techdirt.com/articles/20080311/121305499.shtml.

65 **"creepy" is relative:** Blase Ur et al. (2 Apr 2012), "Smart, useful, scary, creepy: Perceptions of online behavioral advertising," CyLab, Carnegie Mellon University, Pittsburgh, Pennsylvania, https://www.cylab.cmu.edu/research/techreports/2012/tr_cylab12007.html.

65 **depends a lot on our familiarity:** Evan Selinger (22 Aug 2012), "Why do we love to call new technologies 'creepy'?" *Slate*, http://www.slate.com/articles/technology/future_tense/2012/08/facial_recognition_software_targeted_advertising_we_love_to_call_new_technologies_creepy_.html. Omer Tene and Jules Polonetsky (16 Sep 2013), "A theory of creepy: Technology, privacy, and shifting social norms," *Yale Journal of Law & Technology*, http://yjolt.org/theory-creepy-technology-privacy-and-shifting-social-norms.

65 **ads that follow us around:** Sara M. Watson (16 Sep 2014), "Ask the decoder: Stalked

by socks," Al Jazeera, http://america.aljazeera.com/articles/2014/9/16/the-decod er-stalkedbysocks.html.

65 **click on a link to find out why:** Mike Isaac (2 Nov 2011), "New Google 'transparency' feature aims to reduce ad-targeting creepiness," *Wired*, http://www.wired .com/2011/11/google-ad-transparency-target. Todd Essig (27 Feb 2012), "'Big Data' got you creeped out? Transparency can help," *Forbes*, http://www.forbes.com/sites/ toddessig/2012/02/27/big-data-got-you-creeped-out-transparency-can-help.

65 **Recipients of these mailings:** Charles Duhigg (19 Feb 2012), "How companies learn your secrets," *New York Times*, http://www.nytimes.com/2012/02/19/maga zine/shopping-habits.html.

66 **50 million people have installed AdBlock Plus:** Kashmir Hill (21 Aug 2013), "Use of ad blocking is on the rise," *Forbes*, http://www.forbes.com/sites/kashmirhill/ 2013/08/21/use-of-ad-blocking-is-on-the-rise.

66 **the value of a single:** Victor Luckerson (7 Mar 2014), "Twitter's ad prices are in free fall," *Time*, http://time.com/16032/twitter-ad-prices-decline. Brian Womack (16 Apr 2014), "Google revenue falls short of estimates, ad prices drop," *Bloomberg Business Week*, http://www.businessweek.com/news/2014-04-16/google-revenue-falls-short-of-estimates-as-ad-prices-decline-1.

66 **a common commodity:** Emily Steel (12 Jun 2013), "Companies scramble for consumer data," *Financial Times*, http://link.ft.com/r/S4XZQQ/Z8K8I2/9ZND5E/972 MV7/VTD3N8/SN/h. Ken Figueredo (19 Jun 2013), "Prices and value of consumer data," *More with Mobile*, http://www.more-with-mobile.com/2013/06/prices-and-value-of-consumer-data.html.

66 **the value of each user:** Tristan Louis (31 Aug 2013), "How much is a user worth?" *Forbes*, http://www.forbes.com/sites/tristanlouis/2013/08/31/how-much-is-a-user-worth.

66 **already reached the peak:** Tim Hwang and Adi Kamdar (9 Oct 2013), "The theory of peak advertising and the future of the web," Peakads.org, http://peakads.org/ images/Peak_Ads.pdf. Tim Hwang (19 Mar 2014), "The Peak Advertising Institute," *Knight News Challenge*, https://www.newschallenge.org/challenge/2014/feedback-review/the-peak-advertising-institute.

66 **I don't think anyone knows:** Doc Searls (23 Mar 2009), "After the advertising bubble bursts," *Doc Searls Weblog*, http://blogs.law.harvard.edu/doc/2009/03/23/ after-the-advertising-bubble-bursts.

66 **early tropes of the Internet:** Moshe Yudkowsky (2005), *The Pebble and the Avalanche: How Taking Things Apart Creates Revolutions*, Berrett-Koehler Publishers, http://www.pebbleandavalanche.com.

67 **eBay connected buyers and sellers:** Mark Graham (2008), "Warped geographies of development: The Internet and theories of economic development," *Geography Compass* 2/3, http://www.geospace.co.uk/files/compass.pdf.

67 **music promotion and distribution:** Mike Masnick (19 Jun 2013), "Hollywood's new talking point: Gatekeepers are awesome," *Tech Dirt*, https://www.techdirt .com/articles/20130613/18243923466/hollywoods-new-talking-point-gatekeepers-are-awesome.shtml.

67 **airline tickets:** Alina M. Chircu and Robert J. Kauffman (1998), "Analyzing market transformation in the presence of Internet-driven disintermediation: The case of online travel reservation providers," Management Information Systems Research Center, http:// citeseerx.ist.psu.edu/viewdoc/download?doi=10.1.1.196.4820&rep=rep1&type=pdf.

67 **in some cases—advertising:** Tim Williams (3 Jun 2013), "The disintermediation of the advertising agency business," *LinkedIn*, http://www.linkedin.com/today/post/article/20130603205503-2042198-the-disintermediation-of-the-agency-business.

67 **Google CEO Eric Schmidt said:** Eric Schmidt and Jared Cohen (2013), *The New Digital Age: Reshaping the Future of People, Nations and Business*, Knopf, http://www.newdigitalage.com.

68 **A variety of economic effects:** Carl Shapiro and Hal Varian (1998), *Information Rules: A Strategic Guide to the Network Economy*, Harvard Business Review Press, http://www.inforules.com.

68 **Google controls two-thirds:** comScore (21 Jun 2014), "comScore releases June 2014 U.S. search engine rankings," https://www.comscore.com/Insights/Market-Rankings/comScore-Releases-June-2014-US-Search-Engine-Rankings.

68 **have Facebook accounts:** Maeve Duggan and Aaron Smith (30 Dec 2013), "Social media update 2013," Pew Research Internet Project, http://www.pewinternet.org/2013/12/30/social-media-update-2013.

68 **Amazon controls about:** Troy (12 May 2013), "Highlights from the U.S. Book Consumer Annual Review," *AALBC.com's Discussion Forum*, http://aalbc.com/tc/index.php/topic/2051-highlights-from-the-us-book-consumer-annual-review.

68 **Comcast owns about:** Trefis Team (24 Jul 2014), "Comcast earnings grow 15% on good broadband growth," *Forbes*, http://www.forbes.com/sites/greatspeculations/2014/07/24/comcast-earnings-grow-15-on-good-broadband-growth.

68 **In 2001, eBay started hiding:** Matthew Fordahl (2 Feb 2001), "eBay to hide members' e-mail addresses," *ABC News*, http://abcnews.go.com/Technology/story?id=98958.

68 **in 2011, it banned e-mail addresses:** eBay (1 Oct 2011), "E-mail addresses and some links no longer permitted in listings," http://pages.ebay.com/sellerinformation/news/links2011.html.

68 **in 2012, it banned them from user-to-user:** eBay (2 Oct 2012), "Sellers: E-mail addresses and some URLs no longer allowed in member-to-member messages," http://announcements.ebay.com/2012/10/sellers-e-mail-addresses-and-some-urls-no-longer-allowed-in-member-to-member-messages.

68 **Websites that profit from advertising:** Steven Levy (22 Apr 2014), "Inside the science that delivers your scary-smart Facebook and Twitter feeds," *Wired*, http://www.wired.com/2014/04/perfect-facebook-feed.

68 **sites that allow you to opt out:** Nate Anderson (24 Jul 2008), ".06% opt out: NebuAd hides link in 5,000-word privacy policy," *Ars Technica*, http://arstechnica.com/uncategorized/2008/07/06-opt-out-nebuad-hides-link-in-5000-word-privacy-policy.

68 **The relationship is more feudal:** Bruce Schneier (26 Nov 2012), "When it comes to security, we're back to feudalism," *Wired*, http://www.wired.com/2012/11/feudal-security.

69 **We like having someone else:** Rachel King (15 Oct 2012), "Consumers actually really like cloud storage, report says," *ZDNet*, http://www.zdnet.com/consumers-actually-really-like-cloud-storage-report-says-7000005784.

70 **the rise of cloud computing:** This is a good introduction to cloud computing. Michael Armbrust et al. (10 Feb 2009), "Above the clouds: A Berkeley view of cloud computing," Technical Report No. UCB/EECS-2009-28, Electrical Engineering and Computer Sciences, University of California at Berkeley, http://www.eecs.berkeley.edu/Pubs/TechRpts/2009/EECS-2009-28.pdf.

70 **they turn our data over:** Both Google and Microsoft have turned child porn suspects over to the FBI on their own initiative. Robert Macpherson (4 Aug 2014), "Google defends child porn tip-offs to police," *Yahoo! News*, http://news.yahoo.com/google-defends-child-porn-tip-offs-police-025343404.html. Leo Kelion (6 Aug 2014), "Microsoft tip leads to child porn arrest in Pennsylvania," *BBC News*, http://www.bbc.com/news/technology-28682686.

70 **the rise of user devices:** Jonathan Zittrain (2009), "Tethered appliances, software as service, and perfect enforcement," in *The Future of the Internet and How to Stop It*, Yale University Press, http://dash.harvard.edu/bitstream/handle/1/4455262/Zittrain_Future%20of%20the%20Internet.pdf.

70 **Apple has rules about what software:** Meg Albus (5 Sep 2013), "Don't get rejected by Apple!" *PBS Producer Exchange*, https://projects.pbs.org/confluence/pages/viewpage.action?pageId=34046325.

70 **In 2009, Amazon automatically deleted:** Brad Stone (18 Jul 2009), "Amazon erases Orwell books from Kindle," *New York Times*, http://www.nytimes.com/2009/07/18/technology/companies/18amazon.html.

71 **vendors are moving to a subscription model:** Sam Grobart (14 Nov 2013), "Software makers' subscription drive," *Business Week*, http://www.businessweek.com/articles/2013-11-14/2014-outlook-software-makers-subscription-drive.

71 **Adobe did that with Creative Cloud:** David Pogue (17 Sep 2013), "Adobe's software subscription model means you can't own your software," *Scientific American*, http://www.scientificamerican.com/article/adobe-software-subscription-model-means-you-cant-own-your-software.

71 **if I decide to abandon those services:** Google is much better at letting users leave with their data than many other companies are.

71 **Political scientist Henry Farrell:** Henry Farrell (Fall 2013), "The tech intellectuals," *Democracy* 30, http://www.democracyjournal.org/30/the-tech-intellectuals.php.

71 **It's not reasonable to tell people:** This isn't to say that these things are essential and that it's impossible to get along without them. I don't have a Facebook account. I know people who don't have cell phones, and one person who doesn't shop online at all. We do have a choice, but living without any of these things can be very difficult, both personally and professionally.

72 **Opting out just isn't a viable choice:** Jessica Goldstein (29 Apr 2014), "Meet the woman who did everything in her power to hide her pregnancy from Big Data," *Think Progress*, http://thinkprogress.org/culture/2014/04/29/3432050/can-you-hide-from-big-data.

5: GOVERNMENT SURVEILLANCE AND CONTROL

73 **The documents from Snowden:** Barton Gellman and Ashkan Soltani (14 Oct 2013), "NSA collects millions of e-mail address books globally," *Washington Post*, http://www.washingtonpost.com/world/national-security/nsa-collects-millions-of-e-mail-address-books-globally/2013/10/14/8e58b5be-34f9-11e3-80c6-7e6dd8d22d8f_story.html. Barton Gellman and Ashkan Soltani (30 Oct 2013), "NSA infiltrates links to Yahoo, Google data centers worldwide, Snowden documents say," *Washington Post*, http://www.washingtonpost.com/world/national-security/nsa-infiltrates-links-to-

yahoo-google-data-centers-worldwide-snowden-documents-say/2013/10/30/
e51d661e-4166-11e3-8b74-d89d714ca4dd_story.html. Barton Gellman and Laura
Poitras (7 Jun 2013), "U.S., British intelligence mining data from nine U.S. Internet
companies in broad secret program," *Washington Post*, http://www.washingtonpost
.com/investigations/us-intelligence-mining-data-from-nine-us-internet-companies-
in-broad-secret-program/2013/06/06/3a0c0da8-cebf-11e2-8845-d970ccb04497_
story.html.

74 **The NSA was formed in 1952:** US Executive Office of the President (24 Oct 1952),
Memorandum to Secretary of State and Secretary of Defense re: Communications
Intelligence Agency, US National Security Agency, http://www.nsa.gov/public_
info/_files/truman/truman_memo.pdf.

74 **US signals intelligence and codebreaking:** Thomas L. Burns (1990), "The origins
of the National Security Agency 1940–1952 (U)," Center for Cryptologic History, US
National Security Agency, http://www.nsa.gov/public_info/_files/cryptologic_his
tories/origins_of_nsa.pdf.

74 **Secrets of fact:** Several political scientists have written about the difference
between secrets and mysteries, or puzzles and mysteries. Joseph S. Nye Jr. (Jul/Aug
1994), "Peering into the future," *Foreign Affairs*, http://www.foreignaffairs.com/arti
cles/50102/joseph-s-nye-jr/peering-into-the-future. Gregory F. Treverton (Sep 2001),
"Reshaping national intelligence for an age of information," Research Brief 5, European Union Center for California, http://eucenter.scrippscollege.edu/files/2011/06/
Treverton-05.pdf.

74 **"Never again" was an impossible mandate:** Dan Geer (9 Oct 2013), "Tradeoffs in
cyber security," http://geer.tinho.net/geer.uncc.9x13.txt.

74 **Modern government surveillance monitors:** Under the 1978 FISA law that regulated NSA surveillance, targets inside the US had to be "agents of a foreign power."
When the law was amended in 2008 under the FAA—FISA Amendments Act—a
target could be any foreigner.

75 **This latest mission rose in importance:** Dana Priest (21 Jul 2013), "NSA growth
fueled by need to target terrorists," *Washington Post*, http://www.washingtonpost
.com/world/national-security/nsa-growth-fueled-by-need-to-target-terrorists/
2013/07/21/24c93cf4-f0b1-11e2-bed3-b9b6fe264871_story.html.

75 **If the NSA tapped:** The NSA did that in 1984. William J. Broad (8 Nov 1998), "A tale
of daring American submarine espionage," *New York Times*, http://www.nytimes
.com/1998/11/08/us/a-tale-of-daring-american-submarine-espionage.html.

75 **Google doesn't store:** Google (2014), "Data center locations," https://www.google
.com/about/datacenters/inside/locations/index.html.

76 **It has a larger intelligence budget:** Barton Gellman and Greg Miller (29 Aug 2013),
"U.S. spy network's successes, failures and objectives detailed in 'black budget' summary," *Washington Post*, http://www.washingtonpost.com/world/national-security/
black-budget-summary-details-us-spy-networks-successes-failures-and-objec
tives/2013/08/29/7e57bb78-10ab-11e3-8cdd-bcdc09410972_story.html. Ewan MacAskill and Jonathan Watts (29 Aug 2013), "US intelligence spending has doubled since
9/11, top secret budget reveals," *Guardian*, http://www.theguardian.com/world/2013/
aug/29/us-intelligence-spending-double-9-11-secret-budget.

76 **The Internet's physical wiring:** Ryan Singel (10 Oct 2007), "NSA's lucky break:
How the U.S. became switchboard to the world," *Wired*, https://web.archive.org/

web/20071019223411/http://www.wired.com/politics/security/news/2007/10/
domestic_taps. Christopher Mims (8 Jun 2013), "Why the NSA has access to 80% of
online communication even if Google doesn't have a 'backdoor,'" *Quartz*, http://qz
.com/92369/why-nsa-has-access-to-80-of-online-communication-even-if-google-
doesnt-have-a-back-door.

76 **The goal of the NSA's surveillance:** Ewen MacAskill and James Ball (2 Nov 2013),
"Portrait of the NSA: no detail too small in quest for total surveillance," *Guardian*,
http://www.theguardian.com/world/2013/nov/02/nsa-portrait-total-surveillance.
Glenn Greenwald (2014), *No Place to Hide: Edward Snowden, the NSA and the US Surveillance State*, Macmillan, chap. 3, http://leaksource.info/2014/07/31/glenn-green
walds-no-place-to-hide-nsa-documents-excerpts.

76 **no evidence to suggest:** Of course, I don't know for sure. Bill Binney, another NSA
whistleblower, has said otherwise, but he has provided no evidence. Antony Loewenstein (10 Jul 2014), "The ultimate goal of the NSA is total population control," *Guardian*,
http://www.theguardian.com/commentisfree/2014/jul/11/the-ultimate-goal-of-the-
nsa-is-total-population-control.

76 **we know it is doing so:** Ryan Devereaux, Glenn Greenwald, and Laura Poitras (19
May 2014), "Data pirates of the Caribbean: The NSA is recording every cell phone call
in the Bahamas," *Intercept*, https://firstlook.org/theintercept/article/2014/05/19/data-
pirates-caribbean-nsa-recording-every-cell-phone-call-bahamas. Julian Assange (23
May 2014), "WikiLeaks statement on the mass recording of Afghan telephone calls
by the NSA," *WikiLeaks*, https://wikileaks.org/WikiLeaks-statement-on-the-mass
.html.

76 **The agency's 2013 budget:** Barton Gellman and Greg Miller (29 Aug 2013), "'Black
budget' summary details U.S. spy network's successes, failures and objectives," *Washington Post*, http://www.washingtonpost.com/world/national-security/black-bud
get-summary-details-us-spy-networks-successes-failures-and-objectives/2013/
08/29/7e57bb78-10ab-11e3-8cdd-bcdc09410972_story.html.

76 **it directly employs:** Dana Priest (21 Jul 2013), "NSA growth fueled by need to target
terrorists," *Washington Post*, http://www.washingtonpost.com/world/national-
security/nsa-growth-fueled-by-need-to-target-terrorists/2013/07/21/24c93cf4-
f0b1-11e2-bed3-b9b6fe264871_story.html.

76 **many more as contractors:** 70% of the intelligence budget goes to private firms;
483,000 contractors have top-secret clearance, representing 34% of the 1.4 million people cleared at that level. Robert O'Harrow Jr., Dana Priest, and Marjorie Censer (10 Jun
2013), "NSA leaks put focus on intelligence apparatus's reliance on outside contractors,"
Washington Post, http://www.washingtonpost.com/business/nsa-leaks-put-focus-on-
intelligence-apparatuss-reliance-on-outside-contractors/2013/06/10/e940c4ba-d20e-
11e2-9f1a-1a7cdee20287_story.html. Jonathan Fahey and Adam Goldman (10 Jun 2013),
"Leak highlights key role of private contractors," Associated Press, http://bigstory.ap
.org/article/leak-highlights-key-role-private-contractors.

76 **the total for 2013 was $53 billion:** Barton Gellman and Greg Miller (29 Aug 2013),
"'Black budget' summary details U.S. spy network's successes, failures and objectives,"
Washington Post, http://www.washingtonpost.com/world/national-security/black-
budget-summary-details-us-spy-networks-successes-failures-and-objectives/2013/
08/29/7e57bb78-10ab-11e3-8cdd-bcdc09410972_story.html.

76 **the US spends $72 billion annually:** Steven Aftergood (Mar 2014), "Intelligence

budget data," Federation of American Scientists Intelligence Resource Program, http://fas.org/irp/budget/index.html.

77 **the capabilities were developed:** "We believe that the military missions in Iraq and Afghanistan have also had a large but difficult-to-measure impact on decisions about technical collection and communications technologies." Richard A. Clarke et al. (12 Dec 2013), "Liberty and security in a changing world: Report and recommendations of The President's Review Group on Intelligence and Communications Technologies," US Executive Office of the President, p. 187, http://www.whitehouse.gov/sites/default/files/docs/2013-12-12_rg_final_report.pdf.

77 **Executive Order 12333:** The feds call it "twelve triple-three." US Executive Office of the President (4 Dec 1981), "Executive Order 12333—United States intelligence activities," *Federal Register*, http://www.archives.gov/federal-register/codification/executive-order/12333.html. Alex Abdo (29 Sep 2014), "New documents shed light on one of the NSA's most powerful tools," *Free Future*, https://www.aclu.org/blog/national-security/new-documents-shed-light-one-nsas-most-powerful-tools.

77 **some protection for US citizens:** Mark Jaycox (5 Nov 2013), "Three leaks, three weeks, and what we've learned about the US government's other spying authority: Executive Order 12333," Electronic Frontier Foundation, https://www.eff.org/deeplinks/2013/10/three-leaks-three-weeks-and-what-weve-learned-about-governments-other-spying.

77 **Section 215 of the USA PATRIOT Act:** US Congress (2001), "USA Patriot Act Section 215," http://www.gpo.gov/fdsys/pkg/BILLS-107hr3162enr/pdf/BILLS-107hr3162enr.pdf.

77 **a secret court interpreted this:** Marcy Wheeler (14 Aug 2014), "George W. Bush's false heroes: The real story of a secret Washington sham," *Salon*, http://www.salon.com/2014/08/14/george_w_bushs_false_heroes_the_real_story_of_a_secret_washington_sham.

77 **Section 702 of the FISA:** There's also the Protect America Act (PAA) of 2007. It was overturned and replaced by the FAA, but any existing authorizations under PAA were grandfathered. We don't know how many there are, so we don't know how important this is. James Risen (6 Aug 2007), "Bush signs law to widen reach for wiretapping," *New York Times*, http://www.nytimes.com/2007/08/06/washington/06nsa.html. Ryan Singel (6 Aug 2007), "Analysis: New law gives government six months to turn Internet and phone systems into permanent spying architecture," *Wired*, http://www.wired.com/2007/08/analysis-new-la.

78 **The NSA has minimization rules:** One Snowden document discusses the NSA minimization procedures. US National Security Agency (8 Jan 2007), "Minimization procedures used by the National Security Agency in connection with acquisitions of foreign intelligence information pursuant to Section 702 of the Foreign Intelligence Surveillance Act, as amended," http://www.theguardian.com/world/interactive/2013/jun/20/exhibit-b-nsa-procedures-document.

78 **The NSA does a lot of playing around:** Jennifer Granick (25 Aug 2014), "Intercept reporting raises broader metadata minimization question," *Just Security*, http://justsecurity.org/14327/intercept-reporting-raises-broader-metadata-minimization-question. Marcy Wheeler (26 Aug 2014), "SPCMA and ICREACH," *Empty Wheel*, http://www.emptywheel.net/2014/08/26/spcma-and-icreach.

78 **A 2014 analysis:** Barton Gellman, Julie Tate, and Ashkan Soltani (5 Jul 2014), "In

NSA-intercepted data, those not targeted far outnumber the foreigners who are," *Washington Post*, http://www.washingtonpost.com/world/national-security/in-nsa-intercepted-data-those-not-targeted-far-outnumber-the-foreigners-who-are/2014/07/05/8139adf8-045a-11e4-8572-4b1b969b6322_story.html.

79 **tightly connected with the NSA:** Nadia Kayyali (21 May 2014), "How the NSA is transforming law enforcement," *Gizmodo*, http://gizmodo.com/how-the-nsa-is-transforming-law-enforcement-1579438984.

79 **We know there is considerable sharing:** Ryan Gallagher (25 Aug 2014), "The surveillance engine: How the NSA built its own secret Google," *Intercept*, https://firstlook.org/theintercept/2014/08/25/icreach-nsa-cia-secret-google-crisscross-proton.

80 **initial legal basis:** The most significant expansion of the NSA's authority occurred in 2005, under the USA PATRIOT Improvement and Reauthorization Act. Some of the provisions have been struck down as unconstitutional.

80 **because Smith shared those phone numbers:** John Villasenor (30 Dec 2013), "What you need to know about the third-party doctrine," *Atlantic*, http://www.theatlantic.com/technology/archive/2013/12/what-you-need-to-know-about-the-third-party-doctrine/282721.

80 **a tool called an IMSI-catcher:** IMSI is International Mobile Subscriber Identity, which is the unique serial number your cell phone broadcasts so that the cellular system knows where you are.

80 **the code name StingRay:** AmberJack is another. "Stingray" is now used as a generic term for IMSI-catchers.

80 **collect identification and location:** Joel Hruska (17 Jun 2014), "Stingray, the fake cell phone tower cops and carriers use to track your every move," *Extreme Tech*, http://www.extremetech.com/mobile/184597-stingray-the-fake-cell-phone-tower-cops-and-providers-use-to-track-your-every-move.

81 **The FBI is so scared?** Lauren Walker (23 Sep 2014), "New documents reveal information about police cellphone tracking devices," *Newsweek*, http://www.newsweek.com/new-documents-reveal-information-about-police-cell-phone-tracking-devices-272746.

81 **instructs them to lie:** Kim Zetter (19 Jun 2014), "Emails show feds asking Florida cops to deceive judges," *Wired*, http://www.wired.com/2014/06/feds-told-cops-to-deceive-courts-about-stingray.

81 **federal marshals seized the documents:** Nathan Freed Wessler (3 Jun 2014), "U.S. Marshals seize local cops' cell phone tracking files in extraordinary attempt to keep information from public," *Free Future*, https://www.aclu.org/blog/national-security-technology-and-liberty/us-marshals-seize-local-cops-cell-phone-tracking-files. Kim Zetter (3 Jun 2014), "U.S. Marshals seize cops' spying records to keep them from the ACLU," *Wired*, http://www.wired.com/2014/06/feds-seize-stingray-documents.

81 **The National Counterterrorism Center:** National Counterterrorism Center (2007), "Terrorist Identities Datamart Environment (TIDE)," https://web.archive.org/web/20140712154829/http://www.nctc.gov/docs/Tide_Fact_Sheet.pdf. Richard A. Best Jr. (19 Dec 2011), "The National Counterterrorism Center (NCTC): Responsibilities and potential congressional concerns," Congressional Research Service, http://fas.org/sgp/crs/intel/R41022.pdf. Matt Sledge (16 Feb 2013), "National Counterterrorism Center's 'terrorist information' rules outlined in document," *Huff-*

ington Post, http://www.huffingtonpost.com/2013/02/15/national-counterterror ism-center-nctc-terrorist-information_n_2697190.html.

81 **a huge database of US citizens:** Karen DeYoung (25 Mar 2007), "Terror database has quadrupled in four years," *Washington Post*, http://www.washingtonpost.com/ wp-dyn/content/article/2007/03/24/AR2007032400944.html.

81 **where the various watch lists:** Julia Angwin (13 Dec 2013), "U.S. terrorism agency to tap a vast database of citizens," *Wall Street Journal*, http://online.wsj.com/news/ articles/SB10001424127887324478304578171623040640006.

81 **procedures for getting on these lists:** Jeremy Scahill and Ryan Devereaux (5 Aug 2014), "Watch commander: Barack Obama's secret terrorist-tracking system, by the numbers," *Intercept*, https://firstlook.org/theintercept/article/2014/08/05/watch-com mander.

81 **Tamerlan Tsarnaev was on this list:** Eric Schmitt and Michael S. Schmidt (24 Apr 2013), "2 U.S. agencies added Boston bomb suspect to watch lists," *New York Times*, http://www.nytimes.com/2013/04/25/us/tamerlan-tsarnaev-bomb-suspect-was-on-watch-lists.html.

81 **Organized Crime Drug Enforcement Task Forces:** US Department of Justice (2014), "Organized Crime Drug Enforcement Task Forces," http://www.justice.gov/ criminal/taskforces/ocdetf.html.

81 **Comprehensive National Cybersecurity Initiative:** US Executive Office of the President (2009), "The Comprehensive National Cybersecurity Initiative," http:// www.whitehouse.gov/issues/foreign-policy/cybersecurity/national-initiative.

81 **Bureau of Alcohol, Tobacco, and Firearms:** Robert Beckhusen (5 Apr 2013), "The ATF wants 'massive' online database to find out who your friends are," *Wired*, http:// www.wired.com/2013/04/atf-database.

81 **Even the Pentagon has spied:** Lisa Myers, Douglas Pasternak, and Rich Gardella (14 Dec 2005), "Is the Pentagon spying on Americans?" *NBC News*, http://www.nbcnews .com/id/10454316/ns/nbc_nightly_news_with_brian_williams-nbc_news_investi gates/t/pentagon-spying-americans. Marcy Wheeler (24 Jul 2007), "Cunningham, CIFA, and Cheney, a new chronology," *Empty Wheel*, http://www.emptywheel .net/2007/07/24/cunningham-cifa-and-cheney-a-new-chronology.

81 **Naval Criminal Investigative Service:** In 2014, a federal court ruled this practice illegal, and threw out a child pornography conviction based on it. Victoria Cavaliere (18 Sep 2014), "U.S. court rules Navy wrongfully monitored computers in child porn probe," Reuters, http://www.reuters.com/article/idUSKBN0HD2EU20140918.

81 **the US has set up "fusion centers":** Robert Mueller (15 Nov 2004), "The FBI: Improving intelligence for a safer America," address delivered to the Town Hall Los Angeles, Los Angeles, California, http://www.fbi.gov/news/speeches/the-fbi-im proving-intelligence-for-a-safer-america. US Department of Homeland Security (4 Sep 2012), "Fusion centers handout," http://www.dhs.gov/sites/default/files/publi cations/Fusion%20Centers%20Handout.pdf. US House of Representatives (Jul 2013), "Majority staff report on the national network of fusion centers," Committee on Homeland Security, http://homeland.house.gov/sites/homeland.house.gov/ files/documents/CHS%20SLFC%20Report%202013%20FINAL.pdf.

82 **local police access to:** Torin Monahan (2010), "The future of security? Surveillance operations at Homeland Security fusion centers," *Social Justice* 37, http://www .socialjusticejournal.org/archive/120_37_2-3/120_07Monahan.pdf.

82 **supposed to focus on terrorism:** Priscilla M. Regan, Torin Monahan, and Krista Craven (3 Dec 2013), "Constructing the suspicious: Data production, circulation, and interpretation by DHS Fusion Centers," *Administration and Society*, http://aas .sagepub.com/content/early/2013/11/29/0095399713513141.abstract.

82 **There's minimal oversight:** Michael German and Jay Stanley (Dec 2007), "What's wrong with fusion centers?" American Civil Liberties Union, https://www.aclu.org/ files/pdfs/privacy/fusioncenter_20071212.pdf. Sharon Bradford Franklin et al. (6 Sep 2012), "Recommendations for fusion centers: Preserving privacy and civil liberties while protecting against crime and terrorism," Constitution Project, http:// www.constitutionproject.org/pdf/fusioncenterreport.pdf.

82 **spied on political protesters:** Colin Moynihan (22 May 2014), "Officials cast wide net in monitoring Occupy protests," *New York Times*, http://www.nytimes.com/ 2014/05/23/us/officials-cast-wide-net-in-monitoring-occupy-protests.html. Mara Verheyden-Hilliard and Carl Messineo (5 May 2014), "Out of the shadows: The hidden role of the Fusion Centers in the nationwide spying operation against the Occupy movement and peaceful protest in America," Partnership for Civil Justice, http://www.justiceonline.org/one-nation-under-surveillance/out-of-the-shadows-pcjf-report.pdf.

82 **Joint Terrorism Task Forces:** US Federal Bureau of Investigation (2010), "Protecting America from terrorist attack: Our Joint Terrorism Task Forces," http://www .fbi.gov/about-us/investigate/terrorism/terrorism_jttfs. US Department of Homeland Security (19 Dec 2013), "Fusion Centers and Joint Terrorist Task Forces," http:// www.dhs.gov/fusion-centers-and-joint-terrorism-task-forces.

82 **shrouded in extreme secrecy:** American Civil Liberties Union (Sep 2013), "Unleashed and unaccountable: The FBI's unchecked abuse of authority," https:// www.aclu.org/sites/default/files/assets/unleashed-and-unaccountable-fbi-report .pdf. Roberto Scalese (10 Apr 2014), "ACLU sues FBI, US attorney for Todashev, Task Force records," *Boston Globe*, http://www.boston.com/news/local/massachusetts/ 2014/04/10/aclu-sues-fbi-attorney-for-todashev-task-force-records/MYWzetg 75Zy3DIpLB1nyrO/story.html.

82 **investigating political activists:** American Civil Liberties Union of Colorado (24 Aug 2010), "New documents confirm: FBI's Joint Terrorism Task Force targets peaceful activists for harassment, political surveillance," http://aclu-co.org/new-documents-confirm-fbis-joint-terrorism-task-force-targets-peaceful-activ ists-for-harassment-political-surveillance. Kevin Gosztola (4 Jul 2014), "FBI, JTTF and US Marshals are reportedly visiting political activists about thirty year-old case," *Dissenter*, http://dissenter.firedoglake.com/2014/07/04/fbi-jttf-us-marshals-service-are-reportedly-visiting-political-activists-about-thirty-year-old-case.

82 **spreading anti-Islamic propaganda:** Spencer Ackerman (23 Sep 2011), "New evidence of anti-Islam bias underscores deep challenges for FBI's reform pledge," *Wired*, http://www.wired.com/2011/09/fbi-islam-domination/all.

82 **harassing innocent civilians:** Adam Gabbatt (1 Aug 2013), "New York woman visited by police after researching pressure cookers online," *Guardian*, http://www .theguardian.com/world/2013/aug/01/new-york-police-terrorism-pressure-cooker. Carlos Miller (23 May 2014), "Terrorist Task Force cop visits man at home for photographing police buildings," *Photography Is Not a Crime*, http://photographyisnotac rime.com/2014/05/23/terrorist-task-force-cop-visits-man-home-photographing-

police-buildings. Steve Annear (11 Jul 2014), "ACLU files lawsuit after feds eye photographer's 'suspicious' behavior," *Boston Magazine*, http://www.bostonmagazine.com/news/blog/2014/07/11/aclu-james-prigoff-terrorism-task-force-lawsuit.

82 **listening posts in Oman:** Duncan Campbell (3 Jun 2014), "Revealed: GCHQ's beyond top secret Middle Eastern Internet spy base," *Register,* http://www.theregister.co.uk/2014/06/03/revealed_beyond_top_secret_british_intelligence_middleeast_internet_spy_base.

82 **Cyprus:** Nicky Hager and Stefania Maurizi (5 Nov 2013), "Cyprus: The home of British/American Internet surveillance in the Middle East," *L'Espresso*, http://espresso.repubblica.it/inchieste/2013/11/04/news/the-history-of-british-intelligence-operations-in-cyprus-1.139978. Richard Norton-Taylor (28 Nov 2013), "Secret memos show efforts of MI5, MI6 and GCHQ to maintain Cyprus base," *Guardian*, http://www.theguardian.com/uk-news/2013/nov/29/intelligence-mi5-mi6-gchq-cyprus-national-archives.

82 **Germany:** Sven Becker et al. (18 Jun 2014), "New NSA revelations: Inside Snowden's Germany file," *Der Spiegel,* http://www.spiegel.de/international/germany/new-snowden-revelations-on-nsa-spying-in-germany-a-975441.html. Hubert Gude et al. (18 Jun 2014), "Spying together: Germany's deep cooperation with the NSA," *Der Spiegel,* http://www.spiegel.de/international/germany/the-german-bnd-and-american-nsa-cooperate-more-closely-than-thought-a-975445.html.

82 **France:** Jacques Follorou and Glenn Greenwald (21 Oct 2013), "France in the NSA's crosshair: Phone networks under surveillance," *Le Monde*, http://www.lemonde.fr/technologies/article/2013/10/21/france-in-the-nsa-s-crosshair-phone-networks-under-surveillance_3499741_651865.html. Jacques Follorou and Franck Johannes (4 Jul 2013), "Revelations on the French Big Brother," *Société,* http://www.lemonde.fr/societe/article/2013/07/04/revelations-on-the-french-big-brother_3442665_3224.html.

82 **Denmark:** Ryan Gallagher (18 Jun 2014), "How secret partners expand NSA's surveillance dragnet," *Intercept,* https://firstlook.org/theintercept/article/2014/06/18/nsa-surveillance-secret-cable-partners-revealed-rampart-a.

82 **Australia:** Jason Om (30 Oct 2013), "Spy expert says Australia operating as 'listening post' for US agencies including the NSA," *ABC News Australia*, http://www.abc.net.au/news/2013-10-30/australia-acting-as-listening-post-for-us-spy-agencies/5056534.

82 **New Zealand:** Glenn Greenwald and Ryan Gallagher (15 Sep 2014), "New Zealand launched mass surveillance project while publicly denying it," *Intercept,* https://firstlook.org/theintercept/2014/09/15/new-zealand-gcsb-speargun-mass-surveillance.

82 **probably every other country:** Craig Timberg (6 Jun 2014), "Vodafone reveals that governments are collecting personal data without limits," *Washington Post,* http://www.washingtonpost.com/business/technology/governments-collecting-personal-data-without-limit-says-vodafone/2014/06/06/ff0cfc1a-edb4-11e3-9b2d-114aded544be_story.html.

82 **surveillance of Indonesia:** Michael R. Gordon (7 Feb 2014), "Indonesia takes aim at Australia over spying on talks," *New York Times*, http://www.nytimes.com/2014/02/18/world/asia/indonesia-takes-aim-at-australia-over-spying-but-not-the-us.html.

83 **Russia collects, stores, and analyzes:** Andrei Soldatov and Irina Borogan (Fall 2013), "Russia's surveillance state," *World Policy Journal*, http://www.worldpolicy

.org/journal/fall2013/Russia-surveillance. James A. Lewis (18 Apr 2014), "Reference note on Russian communications surveillance," Center for Strategic and International Studies, http://csis.org/publication/reference-note-russian-communications-surveillance.

83 **built right into its Internet:** The latest version, SORM 3, collects bulk surveillance data from all communications systems, providing both real-time and historical access. Andrei Soldatov and Irina Borogan (21 Dec 2012), "In ex-Soviet states, Russian spy tech still watches you," *Wired,* http://www.wired.com/2012/12/russias-hand/all.

83 **the 2014 Sochi Olympics:** Owen Matthews (12 Feb 2014), "Russia tests 'total surveillance' at the Sochi Olympics," *Newsweek,* http://www.newsweek.com/2014/02/14/russia-tests-total-surveillance-sochi-olympics-245494.html. Joshua Kopstein (13 Feb 2014), "Sochi's other legacy," *New Yorker,* http://www.newyorker.com/tech/elements/sochis-other-legacy.

83 **this data is also used against:** Gus Hosein (2010), "Privacy as a political right," *Index on Censorship* 39, https://www.privacyinternational.org/reports/privacy-as-a-political-right/surveillance-of-political-movements#footnote5_5pc3hb7.

83 **China, too, attempts to monitor:** James A. Lewis (2006), "The architecture of control: Internet surveillance in China," Center for Strategic and International Studies, http://csis.org/files/media/csis/pubs/0706_cn_surveillance_and_information_technology.pdf.

83 **China also uses location information:** Australian (4 Mar 2011), "China mobile phone tracking system attacked as 'Big Brother' surveillance," *Australian,* http://www.theaustralian.com.au/news/world/china-mobile-phone-tracking-system-attacked-as-big-brother-surveillance/story-e6frg6so-1226015917086.

83 **turns mobile phones on remotely:** Frank Langfitt (29 Jan 2013), "In China, beware: A camera may be watching you," *NPR Morning Edition,* http://www.npr.org/2013/01/29/170469038/in-china-beware-a-camera-may-be-watching-you.

83 **monitors physical spaces:** Calum MacLeod (3 Jan 2013), "China surveillance targets crime—and dissent," *USA Today,* http://www.usatoday.com/story/news/world/2013/01/03/china-security/1802177.

83 **Messages containing words:** Vernon Silver (8 Mar 2013), "Cracking China's Skype surveillance software," *Bloomberg Business Week,* http://www.businessweek.com/articles/2013-03-08/skypes-been-hijacked-in-china-and-microsoft-is-o-dot-k-dot-with-it.

83 **30,000 Internet police:** John Markoff (1 Oct 2008), "Surveillance of Skype messages found in China," *New York Times,* http://www.nytimes.com/2008/10/02/technology/internet/02skype.html.

83 **India:** John Ribeiro (13 Jan 2011), "RIM allows India access to consumer BlackBerry messaging," *CIO,* http://www.cio.com/article/654438/RIM_Allows_India_Access_to_Consumer_BlackBerry_Messaging. Amol Sharma (28 Oct 2011), "RIM facility helps India in surveillance efforts," *Wall Street Journal,* http://online.wsj.com/news/articles/SB10001424052970204505304577001592335138870. First Post (31 Dec 2012), "Telecos agree to real-time intercept for Blackberry messages," *First Post,* http://tech.firstpost.com/news-analysis/telecos-agree-to-real-time-intercept-for-blackberry-messages-212476.html.

83 **Russia:** Alexei Anishchuk (25 Apr 2011), "BlackBerry firm seeks security 'balance' in Russia," Reuters, http://www.reuters.com/article/2011/04/25/us-blackberry-russia-idUSTRE73O1ZL20110425.

83 **Saudi Arabia:** Al Jazeera (4 Aug 2010), "Saudi ban on BlackBerry from Friday," Al Jazeera, http://www.aljazeera.com/news/middleeast/2010/08/2010844243386999 .html.

83 **the UAE:** Josh Halliday (18 Apr 2011), "UAE to tighten BlackBerry restrictions," *Guardian*, http://www.theguardian.com/technology/2011/apr/18/uae-blackberry-e-mails-secure.

83 **Indonesia:** Jakarta Post (15 Sep 2011), "Government asks RIM to open access to wiretap Blackberry users," *Jakarta Post*, http://www.thejakartapost.com/news/2011/09/15/government-asks-rim-open-access-wiretap-blackberry-users.html.

83 **BlackBerry cut a deal with India:** R. Jai Krishna (8 Aug 2012), "India sees resolution to BlackBerry dispute," *Wall Street Journal*, http://online.wsj.com/news/articles/SB10000872396390443404004577576614174157698. British Broadcasting Corporation (11 Jul 2013), "India is 'ready to use' Blackberry message intercept system," *BBC News*, http://www.bbc.com/news/technology-23265091.

84 **China helped Iran build surveillance:** James Ball and Benjamin Gottlieb (25 Sep 2012), "Iran tightens online control by creating own network," *Guardian*, http://www.theguardian.com/world/2012/sep/25/iran-state-run-internet.

84 **far more oppressive and totalitarian:** H. J. Albrecht (2003), "Albrecht 2003—Rechtswirklichkeit und Effizienz der Überwachung der Telekommunikation nach den §§ 100a, 100b StPO und anderer verdeckter Ermittlungsmaßnahmen: Abschlussbericht," Max Planck Institute for Foreign and International Criminal Law, http://www.gesmat .bundesgerichtshof.de/gesetzesmaterialien/16_wp/telekueberw/rechtswirklich keit_%20abschlussbericht.pdf.

84 **the US has far more legal controls:** Winston Maxwell and Christopher Wolf (23 May 2012), "A global reality: Governmental access to data in the cloud: A comparative analysis of ten international jurisdictions," Hogan Lovells, http://www.cil.cnrs .fr/CIL/IMG/pdf/Hogan_Lovells_White_Paper_Government_Access_to_Cloud_ Data_Paper_1_.pdf.

84 **countries like Thailand:** David Stout (9 Jul 2014), "Thailand's junta arrests an editor over a Facebook comment," *Time*, http://time.com/2968680/thailand-junta-editor-facebook-thanapol-eawsakul-fah-diew-khan.

84 **India:** British Broadcasting Corporation (20 Nov 2012), "India woman arrested over Facebook post in 'shock,'" *BBC News*, http://www.bbc.com/news/world-asia-india-20405457. Agence France-Presse (19 Nov 2012), "Indians arrested for Facebook post on Mumbai shutdown," *South China Morning Post*, http://www.scmp .com/news/asia/article/1086094/indians-arrested-facebook-post-mumbai-shut down.

84 **Malaysia:** Asia News Network (4 Jun 2013), "Woman detained for allegedly insulting Malaysian king on Facebook," *Straits Times*, http://news.asiaone.com/News/ Latest+News/Science+and+Tech/Story/A1Story20130604-427357.html.

84 **Iranian hacker broke into:** It's also possible that another government was behind the original attack, and the Iranians just piggybacked on that success. Hans Hoogstraaten et al. (13 Aug 2012), "Black Tulip: Report of the investigation into the DigiNotar Certificate Authority breach," Project PR-110202, Fox-IT BV, http://www .rijksoverheid.nl/bestanden/documenten-en-publicaties/rapporten/2012/08/13/ black-tulip-update/black-tulip-update.pdf.

85 **He passed this ability on to others:** Somini Sengupta (11 Sep 2011), "Hacker rat-

tles security circles," *New York Times*, http://www.nytimes.com/2011/09/12/tech
nology/hacker-rattles-internet-security-circles.html.

85 **300,000 Iranian Gmail accounts:** Gregg Keizer (6 Sep 2011), "Hackers spied on
300,000 Iranians using fake Google certificate," *Computer World*, http://www.com
puterworld.com/s/article/9219731/Hackers_spied_on_300_000_Iranians_using_
fake_Google_certificate.

85 **a piece of malware called GhostNet:** Information Warfare Monitor (29 Mar 2009),
"Tracking GhostNet: Investigating a cyber espionage network," Citizen Lab, Munk
Centre for International Studies, University of Toronto, http://www.infowar-monitor
.net/ghostnet.

85 **Flame is a surveillance tool:** Ellen Nakashima (28 May 2012), "Newly identified
computer virus, used for spying, is 20 times size of Stuxnet," *Washington Post*, http://
www.washingtonpost.com/world/national-security/newly-identified-computer-vi
rus-used-for-spying-is-20-times-size-of-stuxnet/2012/05/28/gJQAWa3VxU_story
.html.

85 **Red October:** Dan Goodin (14 Jan 2013), "Massive espionage malware targeting
governments undetected for 5 years," *Ars Technica*, http://arstechnica.com/secu
rity/2013/01/red-Oct-computer-espionage-network-may-have-stolen-terabytes-of-
data.

85 **Turla, which targeted:** Peter Apps and Jim Finkle (7 Mar 2014), "Suspected Russian
spyware Turla targets Europe, United States," Reuters, http://www.reuters.com/arti
cle/2014/03/07/us-russia-cyberespionage-insight-idUSBREA260YI20140307.

85 **The Mask:** Kaspersky Lab (10 Feb 2014), "Unveiling 'Careto': The masked APT," *Securelist*, http://www.securelist.com/en/downloads/vlpdfs/unveilingthemask_v1.0.pdf.

85 **Iranian hackers have:** Ellen Nakashima (29 May 2014), "Iranian hackers target
U.S. officials," *Washington Post*, http://www.washingtonpost.com/world/nation
al-security/iranian-hackers-are-targeting-us-officials-through-social-networks-
report-says/2014/05/28/7cb86672-e6ad-11e3-8f90-73e071f3d637_story.html.

85 **Tailored Access Operations group:** Matthew M. Aid (10 Jun 2013), "Inside the
NSA's ultra-secret China hacking group," *Foreign Policy*, http://www.foreignpolicy
.com/articles/2013/06/10/inside_the_nsa_s_ultra_secret_china_hacking_group.

86 **TAO infiltrates computers remotely:** Bruce Schneier (4 Oct 2013), "Attacking Tor:
How the NSA targets users' online anonymity," *Guardian*, http://www.theguardian
.com/world/2013/oct/04/tor-attacks-nsa-users-online-anonymity.

86 **TAO has developed specialized software:** The code names for these programs
are even cooler. And, most interestingly, this top-secret NSA document seems not
to have come from Edward Snowden. Leaksource (30 Dec 2013), "NSA's ANT Division catalog of exploits for nearly every major software/hardware/firmware," http://
leaksource.info/2013/12/30/nsas-ant-division-catalog-of-exploits-for-nearly-ev
ery-major-software-hardware-firmware. Der Spiegel (29 Dec 2013), "Inside TAO:
Documents reveal top NSA hacking unit," *Der Spiegel*, http://www.spiegel.de/inter
national/world/the-nsa-uses-powerful-toolbox-in-effort-to-spy-on-global-net
works-a-940969.html. Jacob Appelbaum, Judith Horchert, and Christian Stöcker (29
Dec 2013), "Shopping for spy gear: Catalog advertises NSA toolbox," *Der Spiegel*,
http://www.spiegel.de/international/world/catalog-reveals-nsa-has-back-doors-
for-numerous-devices-a-940994.html.

86 **80,000 computers worldwide:** Matthew M. Aid (15 Oct 2013), "The NSA's new

code breakers," *Foreign Policy*, http://www.foreignpolicy.com/articles/2013/10/15/the_nsa_s_new_codebreakers.

86 **know a lot about China:** This describes one of the Chinese military hacking units. Mandiant (18 Feb 2013), "APT1: Exposing one of China's cyber espionage units," http://intelreport.mandiant.com/Mandiant_APT1_Report.pdf.

86 **against Google:** Kim Zetter (13 Jan 2010), "Google hackers targeted source code of more than 30 companies," *Wired*, http://www.wired.com/2010/01/google-hack-attack.

86 **against the Canadian government:** Greg Weston (16 Feb 2011), "Foreign hackers attack Canadian government," *CBC News*, http://www.cbc.ca/news/politics/foreign-hackers-attack-canadian-government-1.982618.

86 **against the *New York Times*:** Nicole Perlroth (31 Jan 2013), "Hackers in China attacked the Times for last 4 months," *New York Times*, http://www.nytimes.com/2013/01/31/technology/chinese-hackers-infiltrate-new-york-times-computers.html.

86 **against the security company RSA:** Riva Richmond (2 Apr 2011), "The RSA hack: How they did it," *New York Times*, http://bits.blogs.nytimes.com/2011/04/02/the-rsa-hack-how-they-did-it. Kelly Jackson Higgins (29 Mar 2012), "China hacked RSA, U.S. official says," *Information Week*, http://www.darkreading.com/attacks-breaches/china-hacked-rsa-us-official-says/d/d-id/1137409.

86 **other US corporations:** Ellen Nakashima (19 May 2014), "U.S. announces first charges against foreign country in connection with cyberspying," *Washington Post*, http://www.washingtonpost.com/world/national-security/us-to-announce-first-criminal-charges-against-foreign-country-for-cyberspying/2014/05/19/586c9992-df45-11e3-810f-764fe508b82d_story.html.

86 **against the US military:** Julian E. Barnes (4 Mar 2008), "Chinese hacking worries Pentagon," *Los Angeles Times*, http://articles.latimes.com/2008/mar/04/world/fg-uschina4. Ellen Nakashima (27 May 2013), "Confidential report lists U.S. weapons system designs compromised by Chinese cyberspies," *Washington Post*, http://www.washingtonpost.com/world/national-security/confidential-report-lists-us-weapons-system-designs-compromised-by-chinese-cyberspies/2013/05/27/a42c3e1c-c2dd-11e2-8c3b-0b5e9247e8ca_story.html.

86 **Chinese government malware:** We don't know that the Chinese government was behind this, but the circumstantial evidence is pretty damning. Andy Greenberg (1 Apr 2013), "Evidence mounts that Chinese government hackers spread Android malware," *Forbes*, http://www.forbes.com/sites/andygreenberg/2013/04/01/evidence-mounts-that-chinese-government-hackers-spread-android-malware.

86 **Chinese hackers breached:** Ellen Nakashima and Lisa Rein (11 Jul 2014), "Chinese hack aims at federal workers' data," *Washington Post*, http://www.washingtonpost.com/world/national-security/chinese-hackers-go-after-us-workers-personal-data/2014/07/10/92db92e8-0846-11e4-8a6a-19355c7e870a_story.html.

86 **a long history of spying:** Peter Schweizer (Jan/Feb 1996), "The growth of economic espionage: America is target number one," *Foreign Affairs*, http://www.foreignaffairs.com/articles/51617/peter-schweizer/the-growth-of-economic-espionage-america-is-target-number-one.

86 **it does engage in economic espionage:** David E. Sanger (20 May 2014), "With spy charges, U.S. treads fine line in fighting Chinese espionage," *New York Times*, http://www.nytimes.com/2014/05/20/us/us-treads-fine-line-in-fighting-chinese-espionage.html. Jack Goldsmith (25 Mar 2013), "Why the USG complaints against Chinese eco-

nomic cyber-snooping are so weak," *Lawfare*, http://www.lawfareblog.com/2013/03/why-the-usg-complaints-against-chinese-economic-cyber-snooping-are-so-weak.

86 **Brazilian oil company Petrobras:** O Globo (8 Sep 2013), "NSA documents show United States spied Brazilian oil giant," *O Globo*, http://g1.globo.com/fantastico/noticia/2013/09/nsa-documents-show-united-states-spied-brazilian-oil-giant.html.

87 **SWIFT international bank payment system:** Der Spiegel (15 Sep 2013), "'Follow the money': NSA spies on international payments," *Der Spiegel*, http://www.spiegel.de/international/world/spiegel-exclusive-nsa-spies-on-international-bank-transactions-a-922276.html.

87 **NSA claimed that the economic benefits:** Kenneth W. Dam and Herbert S. Lin, eds. (1996), *Cryptography's Role in Securing the Information Society*, National Academies Press, http://www.nap.edu/catalog.php?record_id=5131.

87 **an Italian cyberweapons manufacturer called Hacking Team:** Morgan Marquis-Boire et al. (24 Jun 2014), "Police story: Hacking Team's government surveillance malware," Citizen Lab, Munk School of Global Affairs, University of Toronto, https://citizenlab.org/2014/06/backdoor-hacking-teams-tradecraft-android-implant. William Anderson (24 Jun 2014), "Hacking Team 2.0: The story goes mobile," *Securelist*, http://securelist.com/blog/research/63693/hackingteam-2-0-the-story-goes-mobile.

87 **Ethiopia used this software:** Bill Marczak et al. (12 Feb 2014), "Hacking Team and the targeting of Ethiopian journalists," Citizen Lab, Munk School of Global Affairs, University of Toronto, https://citizenlab.org/2014/02/hacking-team-targeting-ethiopian-journalists. Craig Timberg (12 Feb 2014), "Foreign regimes use spyware against journalists, even in U.S.," *Washington Post*, http://www.washingtonpost.com/business/technology/foreign-regimes-use-spyware-against-journalists-even-in-us/2014/02/12/9501a20e-9043-11e3-84e1-27626c5ef5fb_story.html.

87 **We labeled the Chinese actions:** Andrew Jacobs, Miguel Helft, and John Markoff (13 Jan 2010), "Google, citing attack, threatens to exit China," *New York Times*, http://www.nytimes.com/2010/01/13/world/asia/13beijing.html. David E. Sanger (6 May 2013), "U.S. blames China's military directly for cyberattacks," *New York Times*, http://www.nytimes.com/2013/05/07/world/asia/us-accuses-chinas-military-in-cyberattacks.html.

87 **sometimes invoking:** New York Times (7 May 2013), "China and cyberwar (editorial)," *New York Times*, http://www.nytimes.com/2013/05/08/opinion/china-and-cyberwar.html. David E. Sanger and Elisabeth Bumiller (31 May 2011), "Pentagon to consider cyberattacks acts of war," *New York Times*. http://www.nytimes.com/2011/06/01/us/politics/01cyber.html.

87 **more moderate language:** Barack Obama (17 Jan 2014), "Obama's speech on N.S.A. phone surveillance," *New York Times*, http://www.nytimes.com/2014/01/18/us/politics/obamas-speech-on-nsa-phone-surveillance.html.

88 **the Chinese company Huawei:** Michael S. Schmidt, Keith Bradsher, and Christine Hauser (8 Oct 2012), "U.S. panel cites risks in Chinese equipment," *New York Times*, http://www.nytimes.com/2012/10/09/us/us-panel-calls-huawei-and-zte-national-security-threat.html.

88 **NSA has been doing exactly the same:** US National Security Agency (24 Jun 2008), "SOUFFLETROUGH: ANT product data," http://leaksource.files.wordpress.com/2013/12/nsa-ant-souffletrough.jpg. US National Security Agency (24 Jun 2008), "FEEDTROUGH: ANT product data," http://leaksource.files.wordpress.com/2013/12/nsa-ant-

feedthrough.jpg. US National Security Agency (24 Jun 2008), "JETPLOW: ANT product data," http://leaksource.files.wordpress.com/2013/12/nsa-ant-jetplow.jpg. US National Security Agency (24 Jun 2008), "HEADWATER: ANT product data," http://leaksource .files.wordpress.com/2013/12/nsa-ant-headwater.jpg. US National Security Agency (24 Jun 2008), "HALLUXWATER: ANT product data," http://leaksource.files.wordpress .com/2013/12/nsa-ant-halluxwater.jpg.

88 **American-made equipment sold in China:** Jeremy Hsu (26 Mar 2014), "U.S. suspicions of China's Huawei based partly on NSA's own spy tricks," *IEEE Spectrum*, http://spectrum.ieee.org/tech-talk/computing/hardware/us-suspicions-of-chi nas-huawei-based-partly-on-nsas-own-spy-tricks.

88 **international espionage and attack:** In military terms, hacking for espionage is Computer Network Exfiltration—CNE—and hacking to cause damage is Computer Network Attack—CNA. Alexander Klimburg and Heli Tirmaa-Klaar (15 Apr 2011), "Cybersecurity and cyberpower: Concepts, conditions and capabilities for cooperation for action within the EU," Directorate-General for External Policies of the Union, http://www.europarl.europa.eu/RegData/etudes/etudes/join/2011/433828/ EXPO-SEDE_ET(2011)433828_EN.pdf. Alexander Klimburg (2 Sep 2014), "Shades of cyber grey: Espionage and attack in cyberspace," *Fletcher Forum of World Affairs*, http://www.fletcherforum.org/2014/09/02/klimburg.

88 **Modern cyberespionage is a form of cyberattack:** It is not, however, "cyberwar." That term has been way overused in political discourse. For a good antidote, try this book. Thomas Rid (2013), *Cyber War Will Not Take Place*, Oxford University Press, http://thomasrid.org/no-cyber-war.

88 **nationwide Internet blackout:** James Bamford (13 Aug 2014), "Edward Snowden: The untold story," *Wired*, http://www.wired.com/2014/08/edward-snowden.

88 **30 countries have cyberwar divisions:** Even more have cyberwar capabilities. George Mason University School of Public Policy (Feb 2014), "Cyber security export markets 2014," Virginia Economic Development Partnership, http://exportvirginia .org/wp-content/uploads/2014/02/Report-on-Cyber-Security-Preface.pdf

88 **Estonia was the victim:** Joshua Davis (21 Aug 2007), "Hackers take down the most wired country in Europe," *Wired*, https://web.archive.org/web/20071019223411/ http://www.wired.com/politics/security/magazine/15-09/ff_estonia.

89 **ex-Soviet republic of Georgia:** John Markoff (13 Aug 2008), "Before the gunfire, cyberattacks," *New York Times* http://www.nytimes.com/2008/08/13/technology/ 13cyber.html.

89 **South Korea was the victim:** Matthew Weaver (8 Jul 2009), "Cyberattackers target South Korea and US," *Guardian*, http://www.theguardian.com/world/2009/jul/08/ south-korea-cyber-attack.

89 **a pro-Kremlin youth group:** Charles Clover (11 Mar 2009), "Kremlin-backed group behind Estonia cyber blitz," *Financial Times*, http://www.ft.com/cms/s/0/ 57536d5a-0ddc-11de-8ea3-0000779fd2ac.html.

89 **the only person convicted:** Computer Weekly (13 Mar 2009), "Kids responsible for Estonia attack," *Computer Weekly*, http://www.computerweekly.com/news/22400 88733/Kids-responsible-for-Estonia-attack.

89 **Stuxnet is the first military-grade:** David Kushner (26 Feb 2013), "The real story of Stuxnet," *IEEE Spectrum*, http://spectrum.ieee.org/telecom/security/the-real- story-of-stuxnet. Kim Zetter (2014), *Countdown to Zero Day: Stuxnet and the Launch*

of the World's First Digital Weapon, Crown Publishers, http://books.google.com/
books/?id=iBTpnQEACAAJ.

89 **It was launched in 2009:** William J. Broad, John Markoff, and David E. Sanger (15
Jan 2011), "Israeli test on worm called crucial in Iran nuclear delay," *New York Times,*
http://www.nytimes.com/2011/01/16/world/middleeast/16stuxnet.html.

89 **2012 attack against Saudi Aramco:** Nicole Perlroth (23 Oct 2012), "In cyberattack
on Saudi firm, U.S. sees Iran firing back," *New York Times,* http://www.nytimes
.com/2012/10/24/business/global/cyberattack-on-saudi-oil-firm-disquiets-us
.html. Reuters (9 Dec 2012), "Aramco says cyberattack was aimed at production,"
New York Times, http://www.nytimes.com/2012/12/10/business/global/saudi-ar
amco-says-hackers-took-aim-at-its-production.html.

90 **it makes sense to share data:** Derek S. Reveron (Summer 2008), "Counterterrorism and intelligence cooperation," *Journal of Global Change and Governance* 1,
http://www.globalaffairsjournal.com/archive/Summer08/REVERON.pdf.

90 **It makes the best sense to join:** Ross Anderson (23–24 Jun 2014), "Privacy versus
government surveillance: Where network effects meet public choice," 13th Annual
Workshop on the Economics of Information Security, Pennsylvania State University, http://weis2014.econinfosec.org/papers/Anderson-WEIS2014.pdf.

90 **the Five Eyes:** Nick Perry and Paisley Dodds (16 Jul 2013), "5-nation spy alliance too
vital for leaks to harm," Associated Press, http://bigstory.ap.org/article/experts-
say-us-spy-alliance-will-survive-snowden.

90 **the Nine Eyes:** Henrik Moltke and Sebastian Gjerding (4 Nov 2013), "Denmark part
of NSA inner circle," *Information,* http://www.information.dk/477405.

90 **the Fourteen Eyes:** Der Spiegel (22 Jul 2013), "'Key partners': Secret links between
Germany and the NSA," *Der Spiegel,* http://www.spiegel.de/international/world/
german-intelligence-worked-closely-with-nsa-on-data-surveillance-a-912355
html. Hubert Gude et al. (18 Jun 2014), "Spying together: Germany's deep cooperation with the NSA," *Der Spiegel,* http://www.spiegel.de/international/germany/the-
german-bnd-and-american-nsa-cooperate-more-closely-than-thought-a-975445
.html.

90 **Belgium, Italy, Spain, and Sweden:** Ewen MacAskill and James Ball (2 Nov 2013),
"Portrait of the NSA: No detail too small in quest for total surveillance," *Guardian,*
http://www.theguardian.com/world/2013/nov/02/nsa-portrait-total-surveillance.

90 **the US partners with countries:** Jay Solomon and Siobhan Gorman (21 May 2009),
"Pakistan, India and U.S. begin sharing intelligence," *Wall Street Journal,* http://
online.wsj.com/news/articles/SB124287405244442187.

90 **regimes like Saudi Arabia's:** Ellen Knickmeyer and Siobhan Gorman (9 May
2012), "Behind foiled jet plot, stronger Saudi ties," *Wall Street Journal,* http://online
.wsj.com/news/articles/SB10001424052702304543904577394373945627482. Glenn
Greenwald and Murtaza Hussain (25 Jul 2014), "The NSA's new partner in spying:
Saudi Arabia's brutal state police," *Intercept,* https://firstlook.org/theintercept/
2014/07/25/nsas-new-partner-spying-saudi-arabias-brutal-state-police.

90 **this gives the NSA access:** Edward Snowden (7 Mar 2014), "Statement to the European Parliament," European Parliament, http://www.europarl.europa.eu/docu
ment/activities/cont/201403/20140307ATT80674/20140307ATT80674EN.pdf.

90 **the NSA spies on the Turkish government:** Andy Müller-Maguhn et al. (31 Aug
2014), "A two-faced friendship: Turkey is 'partner and target' for the NSA," *Der Spiegel,*

http://www.spiegel.de/international/documents-show-nsa-and-gchq-spied-on-part
ner-turkey-a-989011.html. Laura Poitras et al. (31 Aug 2014), "How the NSA helped
Turkey kill Kurdish rebels," *Intercept*, https://firstlook.org/theintercept/2014/08/31/
nsaturkeyspiegel.

91 **NSA spies on the government of . . . Germany:** David E. Sanger (1 May 2014), "U.S.
and Germany fail to reach a deal on spying," *New York Times*, http://www.nytimes
.com/2014/05/02/world/europe/us-and-germany-fail-to-reach-a-deal-on-spying
.html. Mark Landler (2 May 2014), "Merkel signals that tension persists over U.S. spying," *New York Times*, http://www.nytimes.com/2014/05/03/world/europe/merkel-
says-gaps-with-us-over-surveillance-remain.html. Andy Müller-Maguhn et al. (14
Sep 2014), "Treasure map: The NSA breach of Telekom and other German firms," *Der
Spiegel*, http://www.spiegel.de/international/world/snowden-documents-indicate-
nsa-has-breached-deutsche-telekom-a-991503.html.

91 **we spy on all of our partners:** Many people believe that the US and the UK spy on
each other's citizens as a way of getting around their own domestic laws. It's legal as
long as they can convince themselves that it's "inadvertent."

91 **when the NSA touts its:** Justin Elliott and Theodoric Meyer (23 Oct 2013), "Claim
on 'attacks thwarted' by NSA spreads despite lack of evidence," *Pro Publica*, http://
www.propublica.org/article/claim-on-attacks-thwarted-by-nsa-spreads-despite-
lack-of-evidence.

91 **The NSA gives Israel's:** Glenn Greenwald, Laura Poitras, and Ewen MacAskill (11
Sep 2013), "NSA shares raw intelligence including Americans' data with Israel," *Guardian*, http://www.theguardian.com/world/2013/sep/11/nsa-americans-personal-data-
israel-documents.

91 **Even historical enemies:** Political considerations still matter. China has a serious
problem with Uighur terrorists, and would certainly welcome US help in dealing with
the threat. The US won't help, of course, because continuing Uighur terrorism will help
weaken China. Chien-peng Chung (2002), "China's 'war on terror': September 11 and
Uighur separatism," *Foreign Affairs*, http://www.foreignaffairs.com/articles/58030/
chien-peng-chung/chinas-war-on-terror-september-11-and-uighur-separatism. Elizabeth van Wie Davis (Jan 2008), "Uyghur Muslim ethnic separatism in Xinjiang,
China," Asia-Pacific Center for Security Studies, http://www.apcss.org/college/publi
cations/uyghur-muslim-ethnic-separatism-in-xinjiang-china.

91 **After 9/11, Russia rebranded:** John Laughland (8 Sep 2004), "The Chechens'
American friends," *Guardian*, http://www.theguardian.com/world/2004/sep/08/
usa.russia. Simon Shuster (19 Sep 2011), "How the war on terrorism did Russia a
favor," *Time*, http://content.time.com/time/world/article/0,8599,2093529,00.html.
James Gordon Meek (19 Feb 2014), "The secret battles between US forces and
Chechen terrorists," *ABC News*, http://abcnews.go.com/Blotter/secret-battles-us-
forces-chechen-terrorists/story?id=22580688.

91 **In 2011, Russia warned the US:** Tom Winter (25 Mar 2014), "Russia warned U.S.
about Tsarnaev, but spelling issue let him escape," *NBC News*, http://www.nbcnews
.com/storyline/boston-bombing-anniversary/russia-warned-u-s-about-tsarnaev-
spelling-issue-let-him-n60836.

91 **We returned the favor:** Laura Smith-Spart and Nick Paton Walsh (4 Feb 2014),
"United States reveals 'specific' threats to Olympic Games," CNN, http://www.cnn
.com/2014/02/04/world/europe/russia-sochi-winter-olympics.

6: CONSOLIDATION OF INSTITUTIONAL CONTROL

92 **more an alliance of interests:** Communications professor Robert M. McChesney called the symbiotic relationship between big data and big government "a marriage made in heaven, with dire implications for liberty and democracy." Robert M. McChesney (2013), *Digital Disconnect: How Capitalism Is Turning the Internet against Democracy*, New Press, p. 21, http://books.google.com/books/?id=j_7EkTI8kVQC.

92 **the NSA gets direct access:** We knew this even before Edward Snowden, from the previous NSA whistleblower Mark Klein. Mark Klein (8 Jun 2006), "Declaration of Mark Klein," *Hepting, et al., v. AT&T, et al.*, United States District Court, Northern District of California (No. C-06-0672-VRW), https://www.eff.org/files/filenode/att/Mark%20Klein%20Unredacted%20Decl-Including%20Exhibits.pdf. Ellen Nakashima (7 Nov 2007), "A story of surveillance," *Washington Post*, http://www.washingtonpost.com/wp-dyn/content/article/2007/11/07/AR2007110700006.html.

93 **GCHQ pays telcos:** James Ball, Luke Harding, and Juliette Garside (2 Aug 2013), "BT and Vodafone among telecoms companies passing details to GCHQ," *Guardian*, http://www.theguardian.com/business/2013/aug/02/telecoms-bt-vodafone-cables-gchq.

93 **Vodafone gives:** Vodafone (2014), "Law enforcement disclosure report," http://www.vodafone.com/content/sustainabilityreport/2014/index/operating_responsibly/privacy_and_security/law_enforcement.html. Peter Svensson (9 Jun 2014), "Vodafone report sparks global surveillance debate," Associated Press, http://bigstory.ap.org/article/cellphone-operator-wades-surveillance-debate. Juliette Garside (5 Jun 2014), "Vodafone reveals existence of secret wires that allow state surveillance," *Guardian*, http://www.theguardian.com/business/2014/jun/06/vodafone-reveals-secret-wires-allowing-state-surveillance.

93 **French government eavesdrops:** Jacques Follorou and Glenn Greenwald (25 Oct 2013), "France in the NSA's crosshair: Wanadoo and Alcatel targeted," *Le Monde*, http://www.lemonde.fr/technologies/article/2013/10/21/france-in-the-nsa-s-crosshair-wanadoo-and-alcatel-targeted_3499739_651865.html. Jacques Follorou (21 Mar 2014), "Espionnage: Comment Orange et les services secrets coopèrent," *Le Monde*, http://www.lemonde.fr/international/article/2014/03/20/dgse-orange-des-liaisons-incestueuses_4386264_3210.html.

93 **About a dozen countries:** British Broadcasting Corporation (8 Apr 2014), "Top EU court rejects EU-wide data retention law," *BBC News*, http://www.bbc.com/news/world-europe-26935096.

93 **Internet cafes in Iran:** Iran Media Program (8 Apr 2013), "Digital media: FATA polices Internet cafés with 20 new regulations," Annenberg School for Communication, http://www.iranmediaresearch.org/en/blog/218/13/04/08/1322.

93 **Vietnam:** Reporters Without Borders (2013), "Vietnam," in *Enemies of the Internet*, http://surveillance.rsf.org/en/vietnam.

93 **India:** Rama Lakshmi (1 Aug 2011), "India's new Internet rules criticized," *Washington Post*, http://www.washingtonpost.com/world/indias-new-internet-rules-criticized/2011/07/27/gIQA1zS2mI_story.html.

93 **US government bought data:** Chris Jay Hoofnagle (1 Aug 2003), "Big Brother's little helpers: How Choicepoint and other commercial data brokers collect, process, and package your data for law enforcement," *North Carolina Journal of International*

Law and Commercial Regulations 29, http://papers.ssrn.com/sol3/papers.cfm?abstract_id=582302. Jon D. Michaels (6 Oct 2008), "All the president's spies: Private-public intelligence partnerships in the war on terror," *California Law Review* 96, http://papers.ssrn.com/sol3/papers.cfm?abstract_id=1279867.

93 **data from Torch Concepts:** Matthew L. Wald (21 Feb 2004), "U.S. calls release of JetBlue data improper," *New York Times*, http://www.nytimes.com/2004/02/21/business/21blue.html.

93 **a database of Mexican voters:** CR Staff (1 May 2003), "U.S. government purchase data on Mexico's 65 million registered voters," Information Clearinghouse, http://www.informationclearinghouse.info/article3186.htm.

93 **US law requires financial institutions:** US Financial Crimes Enforcement Network (11 May 2014), "Bank Secrecy Act requirements: A quick reference guide for money services business," http://www.fincen.gov/financial_institutions/msb/materials/en/bank_reference.html.

94 **States like Illinois:** Kenneth Lowe (29 Jun 2008), "Illinois made $64.3 million selling driver's license information," *Herald-Review*, http://herald-review.com/business/local/illinois-made-million-selling-driver-s-license-information/article_43c51a15-c885-575e-ac5d-0c01cc9acb6b.html.

94 **Ohio:** Joe Guillen (11 Jul 2010), "Ohio collects millions selling driving records with your personal information," *Plain Dealer*, http://www.cleveland.com/open/index.ssf/2010/07/ohio_collects_millions_selling.html.

94 **Texas:** Tim Cushing (13 Feb 2013), "Texas DMV sells personal information to hundreds of companies; Drivers not allowed to opt-out," *Tech Dirt*, http://www.techdirt.com/articles/20130212/21285321958/texas-dmv-sells-personal-information-to-hundreds-companies-drivers-not-allowed-to-opt-out.shtml.

94 **Florida:** Jeff Weinsier (12 Oct 2011), "Florida makes $63M selling drivers' info," *Local 10*, http://www.local10.com/news/Florida-Makes-63M-Selling-Drivers-Info/3078462.

94 **voter registration data:** Kim Zetter (11 Dec 2003), "For sale: The American voter," *Wired*, http://archive.wired.com/politics/security/news/2003/12/61543.

94 **The UK government proposed:** Rowena Maxon (18 Apr 2014), "HMRC to sell taxpayers' financial data," *Guardian*, http://www.theguardian.com/politics/2014/apr/18/hmrc-to-sell-taxpayers-data.

94 **UK National Health Service:** Randeep Ramesh (19 Jan 2014), "NHS patient data to be made available for sale to drug and insurance firms," *Guardian*, http://www.theguardian.com/society/2014/jan/19/nhs-patient-data-available-companies-buy.

94 **There's a feedback loop:** This has been called "data laundering." Chris Jay Hoofnagle (2 Sep 2014), "The Potemkinism of privacy pragmatism," *Slate*, http://www.slate.com/articles/technology/future_tense/2014/09/data_use_regulation_the_libertarian_push_behind_a_new_take_on_privacy.single.html.

94 **you can configure your browser:** Geoff Duncan (9 Jun 2012), "Why Do Not Track may not protect anybody's privacy," *Digital Trends*, http://www.digitaltrends.com/mobile/why-do-not-track-may-not-protect-anybodys-privacy.

94 **It's a bit different in Europe:** European Parliament and Council of Europe (24 Oct 1995), "Directive 95/46/EC of the European Parliament and of the Council of 24 October 1995 on the protection of individuals with regard to the processing of personal data and on the free movement of such data," http://eur-lex.europa.eu/LexUriServ/LexUriServ.do?uri=CELEX:31995L0046:en:HTML. Council of Europe (Apr

2014), "Handbook on European data protection law," http://www.echr.coe.int/Doc uments/Handbook_data_protection_ENG.pdf.

94 **data can flow from the EU:** Zack Whittaker (25 Apr 2011), "Safe harbor: Why EU data needs 'protecting' from US law," *ZDNet*, http://www.zdnet.com/blog/igenera tion/safe-harbor-why-eu-data-needs-protecting-from-us-law/8801.

95 **public-private surveillance partnership:** Jay Stanley (Aug 2004), "The surveil-lance-industrial complex," American Civil Liberties Union, https://www.aclu.org/sites/default/files/FilesPDFs/surveillance_report.pdf.

95 **1,931 different corporations:** Dana Priest and William M. Arkin (19 Jul 2010), "A hidden world, growing beyond control," *Washington Post*, http://projects.washing tonpost.com/top-secret-america/articles/a-hidden-world-growing-beyond-control.

95 **70% of the US intelligence budget:** Robert O'Harrow Jr., Dana Priest, and Marjo-rie Censer (10 Jun 2013), "NSA leaks put focus on intelligence apparatus's reliance on outside contractors," *Washington Post*, http://www.washingtonpost.com/business/nsa-leaks-put-focus-on-intelligence-apparatuss-reliance-on-outside-contrac tors/2013/06/10/e940c4ba-d20e-11e2-9f1a-1a7cdee20287_story.html.

95 **Keith Alexander started:** It seems unlikely that he would have had the spare time necessary to invent things directly applicable to his job. Shane Harris (29 Jun 2014), "The NSA's cyber-king goes corporate," *Foreign Policy*, http://www.foreignpolicy.com/arti cles/2014/07/29/the_crypto_king_of_the_NSA_goes_corporate_keith_alexander_patents. Conor Friedersdorf (31 Jul 2014), "Keith Alexander's unethical get-rich-quick plan," *Atlantic*, http://www.theatlantic.com/politics/archive/2014/07/keith-alexanders-unethical-get-rich-quick-plan/375367.

95 **He's hired the NSA's:** Spencer Ackerman (17 Oct 2014), "Senior NSA official moon-lighting for private security firm," *Guardian*, http://www.theguardian.com/us-news/2014/oct/17/senior-nsa-official-moonlighting-private-cybersecurity-firm.

95 **FinFisher:** Elaman-Gamma Group (2011), "German security solutions," *Wikileaks*, https://s3.amazonaws.com/s3.documentcloud.org/documents/810435/313-ela man-product-list-finfisher.pdf.

95 **the FinFisher toolkit:** Morgan Marquis-Boire and Bill Marczak (29 Aug 2012), "The smartphone who loved me: FinFisher goes mobile?" Citizen Lab, Munk School of Global Affairs, University of Toronto, http://citizenlab.org/2012/08/the-smart phone-who-loved-me-finfisher-goes-mobile. Nicole Perlroth (30 Aug 2012), "Soft-ware meant to fight crime is used to spy on dissidents," *New York Times*, http://www.nytimes.com/2012/08/31/technology/finspy-software-is-tracking-political-dissi dents.html.

96 **The Moroccan government:** Bill Marczak et al. (17 Feb 2014), "Mapping Hacking Team's 'untraceable' spyware," Citizen Lab, Munk School of Global Affairs, Univers-ity of Toronto, https://citizenlab.org/2014/02/mapping-hacking-teams-untraceable-spyware.

96 **arrested dissidents in Bahrain:** Vernon Silver and Ben Elgin (22 Aug 2011), "Tor-ture in Bahrain becomes routine with help from Nokia Siemens," *Bloomberg News*, http://www.bloomberg.com/news/2011-08-22/torture-in-bahrain-becomes-rou tine-with-help-from-nokia-siemens-networking.html.

96 **The conference ISS World:** Ms. Smith (10 Nov 2011), "Secret snoop conference for gov't spying: Go stealth, hit a hundred thousand targets," *Network World*, http://www.networkworld.com/article/2221080/microsoft-subnet/secret-snoop-conference-

for-gov-t-spying---go-stealth--hit-a-hundred-thousand-targe.html. Jennifer Valentino-DeVries, Julia Angwin, and Steve Stecklow (19 Nov 2011), "Document trove exposes surveillance methods," *Wall Street Journal*, http://online.wsj.com/news/articles/SB10 001424052970203611404577044192607407780. Vernon Silver (21 Dec 2011), "Spies fail to escape spyware in $5 billion bazaar for cyber arms," *Bloomberg News*, http://www.bloomberg.com/news/2011-12-22/spies-fail-to-escape-spyware-in-5-billion-bazaar-for-cyber-arms.html.

96 **The 2014 brochure:** ISS World Training (3–4 Mar 2014), "ISS World Middle East," J. W. Marriott, Dubai, UAE, http://www.issworldtraining.com/iss_mea/Brochure01.pdf.

96 **Many countries send representatives:** Privacy International has a list of who attended between 2006 and 2009. Privacy International (2012), "Surveillance Who's Who," https://www.privacyinternational.org/sww.

96 **There are similar conferences:** Uwe Buse and Marcel Rosenbach (8 Dec 2011), "The transparent state enemy: Western surveillance technology in the hands of despots," *Der Spiegel*, http://www.spiegel.de/international/world/the-transparent-state-enemy-western-surveillance-technology-in-the-hands-of-despots-a-802317.html.

96 **big US defense contractors:** Visiongain (8 Jan 2013), "'Global cyberwarfare market to be worth $16.96bn in 2013' says Visiongain Report," Reuters, http://www.reuters.com/article/2013/01/08/idUSnPre7f3zna+100+PRN20130108. James Bamford (12 Jun 2013), "The secret war," *Wired*, http://www.wired.com/2013/06/general-keith-alexander-cyberwar/all.

96 **The French company Bull SA:** Paul Sonne and Margaret Coker (30 Aug 2011), "Firms aided Libyan spies," *Wall Street Journal*, http://online.wsj.com/news/articles/SB10001424053111904199404576538721260166388.

96 **Nigeria used the Israeli firm:** Elbit Systems (24 Apr 2013), "Elbit Systems awarded a $40 million contract to supply a country in Africa with the Wise Intelligence Technology (WiT[TM]) System," http://ir.elbitsystems.com/phoenix.zhtml?c=61849&p=irol-newsArticle&ID=1810121.

96 **Syria used the German company:** Der Spiegel (11 Apr 2012), "Monitoring the opposition: Siemens allegedly sold surveillance gear to Syria," *Der Spiegel*, http://www.spiegel.de/international/business/ard-reports-siemens-sold-surveillance-technology-to-syria-a-826860.html.

96 **the Italian company Area SpA:** Ben Elgin and Vernon Silver (3 Nov 2011), "Syria crackdown gets Italy firm's aid with U.S.-Europe spy gear," *Bloomberg News*, http://www.bloomberg.com/news/2011-11-03/syria-crackdown-gets-italy-firm-s-aid-with-u-s-europe-spy-gear.html.

96 **The Gadhafi regime in Libya:** Paul Sonne and Margaret Coker (30 Aug 2011), "Firms aided Libyan spies," *Wall Street Journal*, http://online.wsj.com/news/articles/SB10001424053111904199404576538721260166388.

96 **systems used in Azerbaijan:** Sarah Kendzior and Katy Pearce (11 May 2012), "How Azerbaijan demonizes the Internet to keep citizens offline," *Slate*, http://www.slate.com/blogs/future_tense/2012/05/11/azerbaijan_eurovision_song_contest_and_keeping_activists_and_citizens_off_the_internet_.html.

96 **and Uzbekistan:** Sarah Kendzior (Jul 2012), "Digital freedom of expression in Uzbekistan: An example of social control and censorship," New America Foundation, http://newamerica.net/sites/newamerica.net/files/policydocs/KendziorFINAL7172012.pdf.

96 **There are few laws:** Open Technology Institute (9 Dec 2013), "International agreement reached controlling export of mass and intrusive surveillance technology," New America Foundation, http://oti.newamerica.net/blogposts/2013/international_agreement_reached_controlling_export_of_mass_and_intrusive_surveillance.

97 **built for corporate use:** Uwe Buse and Marcel Rosenbach (8 Dec 2011), "The transparent state enemy: Western surveillance technology in the hands of despots," *Der Spiegel*, http://www.spiegel.de/international/world/the-transparent-state-enemy-western-surveillance-technology-in-the-hands-of-despots-a-802317.html.

97 **US-based Blue Coat sells:** The complete list is Afghanistan, Bahrain, Burma, China, Egypt, India, Indonesia, Iraq, Kenya, Kuwait, Lebanon, Malaysia, Nigeria, Qatar, Russia, Saudi Arabia, Singapore, South Korea, Syria, Thailand, Turkey, and Venezuela. Irene Poetranto et al. (9 Nov 2011), "Behind Blue Coat: Investigations of commercial filtering in Syria and Burma," Citizen Lab, Munk School of Global Affairs, University of Toronto, https://citizenlab.org/2011/11/behind-blue-coat. Irene Poetranto et al. (29 Nov 2011), "Behind Blue Coat: An update from Burma," Citizen Lab, Munk School of Global Affairs, University of Toronto, https://citizenlab.org/2011/11/behind-blue-coat-an-update-from-burma. Morgan Marquis-Boire et al. (15 Jan 2013), "Planet Blue Coat: Mapping global censorship and surveillance tools," Citizen Lab, Munk School of Global Affairs, University of Toronto, https://citizenlab.org/2013/01/planet-blue-coat-mapping-global-censorship-and-surveillance-tools.

97 **Netsweeper is a . . . filtering product:** Adam Senft et al. (20 Feb 2014), "Internet filtering in a failed state: The case of Netsweeper in Somalia," Citizen Lab, Munk School of Global Affairs, University of Toronto, https://citizenlab.org/2014/02/internet-filtering-failed-state-case-netsweeper-somalia. Helmi Noman et al. (20 Jun 2013), "O Pakistan, we stand on guard for thee: An analysis of Canada-based Netsweeper's role in Pakistan's censorship regime," Citizen Lab, Munk School of Global Affairs, University of Toronto, https://citizenlab.org/2013/06/o-pakistan.

97 **Fortinet is used to censor:** Open Net Initiative (12 Oct 2005), "Internet filtering in Burma 2005," https://opennet.net/sites/opennet.net/files/ONI_Burma_Country_Study.pdf. New Light of Myanmar (16 May 2004), "Prime minister attends ceremony to introduce Fortinet Antivirus Firewall," *New Light of Myanmar*, http://www.myanmar.gov.mm/NLM-2004/May04/enlm/May16_h1.html.

97 **governments of Tunisia and Iran:** Ben Arnoldy (10 Oct 2007), "When US-made 'censorware' ends up in iron fists," *Christian Science Monitor*, http://www.csmonitor.com/2007/1010/p01s01-ussc.html.

97 **also allows the bad guys:** United Nations Office on Drugs and Crime (Sep 2012), "The use of the Internet for terrorist purposes," http://www.unodc.org/documents/frontpage/Use_of_Internet_for_Terrorist_Purposes.pdf.

97 **facial recognition technology that Disney uses:** Planet Biometrics (2 Mar 2011), "Biometrics cruise into the Disney Dream," http://www.planetbiometrics.com/article-details/i/504.

98 **Communications Assistance for Law Enforcement Act:** US Congress (2012), "Department of State Rewards Program Update and Technical Corrections Act of 2012," Public Law 283, http://www.gpo.gov/fdsys/pkg/PLAW-112publ283/html/PLAW-112publ283.htm.

98 **The FBI is currently lobbying:** Charlie Savage (7 May 2013), "U.S. weighs wide

overhaul of wiretap laws," *New York Times*, http://www.nytimes.com/2013/05/08/us/politics/obama-may-back-fbi-plan-to-wiretap-web-users.html.

98 **The FBI's ultimate goal:** Charlie Savage (27 Sep 2010), "U.S. tries to make it easier to wiretap the Internet," *New York Times*, http://www.nytimes.com/2010/09/27/us/27wiretap.html.

99 **Lavabit was an e-mail service:** Tim Rogers (Nov 2013), "The real story of Lavabit's founder," *D Magazine*, http://www.dmagazine.com/publications/d-magazine/2013/november/real-story-of-lavabit-founder-ladar-levison.

99 **Levison received a National Security Letter:** Spencer Ackerman (9 Aug 2013), "Lavabit e-mail service abruptly shut down citing government interference," *Guardian*, http://www.theguardian.com/technology/2013/aug/08/lavabit-e-mail-shut-down-edward-snowden. Ladar Levison (20 May 2014), "Secrets, lies and Snowden's email: Why I was forced to shut down Lavabit," *Guardian*, http://www.theguardian.com/commentisfree/2014/may/20/why-did-lavabit-shut-down-snowden-email.

99 **The agency can force you to modify:** Declan McCullagh (24 Jul 2013), "Feds put heat on Web firms for master encryption keys," *CNET*, http://www.cnet.com/news/feds-put-heat-on-web-firms-for-master-encryption-keys.

100 **Your business has been commandeered:** Levison was threatened with arrest for shutting down Lavabit rather than letting the FBI have unfettered access to all of its users. Michael Isikoff (13 Aug 2013), "Lavabit.com owner: 'I could be arrested' for resisting surveillance order," *NBC News*, http://www.nbcnews.com/news/other/lavabit-com-owner-i-could-be-arrested-resisting-surveillance-order-f6C10908072.

100 **US government convinced Skype:** Serge Malenkovich (21 Mar 2013), "Does Big Brother watch your Skype?" *Kaspersky Lab Daily*, http://blog.kaspersky.com/skype-government-surveillance. James Risen and Nick Wingfield (20 Jun 2013), "Silicon Valley and spy agency bound by strengthening web," *New York Times*, http://www.nytimes.com/2013/06/20/technology/silicon-valley-and-spy-agency-bound-by-strengthening-web.html.

100 **We don't know what the changes were:** Microsoft Corporation (13 Oct 2011), "Microsoft officially welcomes Skype," *Microsoft News Center*, http://www.microsoft.com/en-us/news/press/2011/oct11/10-13skypepr.aspx.

100 **we know they happened:** Glenn Greenwald (11 Jul 2013), "Microsoft handed the NSA access to encrypted messages," *Guardian*, http://www.theguardian.com/world/2013/jul/11/microsoft-nsa-collaboration-user-data.

100 **US government secretly threatened Yahoo:** Craig Timberg (11 Sep 2014), "U.S. threatened massive fine to force Yahoo to release data," *Washington Post*, http://www.washingtonpost.com/business/technology/us-threatened-massive-fine-to-force-yahoo-to-release-data/2014/09/11/38a7f69e-39e8-11e4-9c9f-ebb47272e40e_story.html.

100 **the NSA paid RSA Security:** Joseph Menn (20 Dec 2013), "Secret contract tied NSA and security industry pioneer," Reuters, http://www.reuters.com/article/2013/12/20/us-usa-security-rsa-idUSBRE9BJ1C220131220.

100 **the NSA hacked into the trunk:** Level 3 Communications has the NSA code name of "LITTLE." As a general rule, if your service provider has an NSA code name, you're probably screwed. Nicole Perlroth (25 Nov 2013), "N.S.A. may have hit Internet companies at a weak spot," *New York Times*, http://www.nytimes.com/2013/11/26/technology/a-peephole-for-the-nsa.html.

100 **The angry response:** Brandon Downey (30 Oct 2013), "This is the big story in tech today," *Google Plus*, https://plus.google.com/+BrandonDowney/posts/SfYy8xbDWGG.

101 **The agency creates fake Facebook pages:** Ryan Gallagher and Glenn Greenwald (12 Mar 2014), "How the NSA plans to infect 'millions' of computers with malware," *Intercept*, https://firstlook.org/theintercept/article/2014/03/12/nsa-plans-infect-millions-computers-malware.

101 **intercepts Cisco equipment:** Sean Gallagher (14 May 2014), "Photos of an NSA 'upgrade' factory show Cisco router getting implant," *Ars Technica*, http://arstechnica.com/tech-policy/2014/05/photos-of-an-nsa-upgrade-factory-show-cisco-router-getting-implant. Sarah Silbert (16 May 2014), "Latest Snowden leak reveals the NSA intercepted and bugged Cisco routers," *Engadget*, http://www.engadget.com/2014/05/16/nsa-bugged-cisco-routers.

101 **NSA's BULLRUN program:** James Ball, Julian Borger, and Glenn Greenwald (5 Sep 2013), "Revealed: How US and UK spy agencies defeat internet privacy and security," *Guardian*, http://www.theguardian.com/world/2013/sep/05/nsa-gchq-encryption-codes-security. Nicole Perlroth, Jeff Larson, and Scott Shane (5 Sep 2013), "N.S.A. able to foil basic safeguards of privacy on Web," *New York Times*, http://www.nytimes.com/2013/09/06/us/nsa-foils-much-internet-encryption.html.

102 **British, Russian, Israeli:** Brian Krebs (28 May 2014), "Backdoor in call monitoring, surveillance gear," *Krebs on Security*, http://krebsonsecurity.com/2014/05/backdoor-in-call-monitoring-surveillance-gear.

102 **they have employees secretly:** Peter Maass and Laura Poitras (10 Oct 2014), "Core secrets: NSA saboteurs in China and Germany," *Intercept*, https://firstlook.org/theintercept/2014/10/10/core-secrets.

102 **Eric Schmidt tried to reassure:** Martin Bryant (7 Mar 2014), "Google is 'pretty sure' its data is now protected against government spying, Eric Schmidt says," *Next Web*, http://thenextweb.com/google/2014/03/07/google-pretty-sure-protected-government-spying-eric-schmidt-says.

7: POLITICAL LIBERTY AND JUSTICE

107 **the First Unitarian Church of Los Angeles sued:** David Greene (27 Jan 2014), "Deep dive into *First Unitarian Church v. NSA*: Why freedom of association matters," Electronic Frontier Foundation, https://www.eff.org/deeplinks/2014/01/deep-dive-first-unitarian-church-v-nsa-why-freedom-association-matters.

107 **Today, the church is worried:** Joshua Eaton (15 Aug 2014), "Challenging the surveillance state," *UU World*, http://www.uuworld.org/ideas/articles/297088.shtml.

107 **Yochai Benkler likens NSA surveillance:** Yochai Benkler (13 Sep 2013), "Time to tame the NSA behemoth trampling our rights," *Guardian*, http://www.theguardian.com/commentisfree/2013/sep/13/nsa-behemoth-trampling-rights.

107 **Even the politically conservative:** Economist (16 Nov 2013), "The recorded world: Every step you take," *Economist*, http://www.economist.com/news/leaders/21589862-cameras-become-ubiquitous-and-able-identify-people-more-safeguards-privacy-will-be.

108 **which give prosecutors discretion:** Harvey Silverglate and Tim Lynch (Jan/Feb 2010), "The criminalization of almost everything," *Cato Policy Report*, http://www

.cato.org/policy-report/januaryfebruary-2010/criminalization-almost-everything.
Harvey Silverglate (2011), *Three Felonies a Day: How the Feds Target the Innocent*,
Encounter Books, http://www.threefeloniesaday.com. G. H. Reynolds (8 Jul 2013),
"Ham sandwich nation: Due process when everything is a crime," *Columbia Law
Review* 113, http://columbialawreview.org/ham-sandwich-nation_reynolds.

108 **overly broad material witness laws:** Rose Ciotta (4 May 2003), "Critics see abuse
of material-witness law," *Philadelphia Inquirer*, http://articles.philly.com/2003-05-
04/news/25460033_1_material-witness-law-material-witnesses-material-wit
ness-statute. Anjana Malhotra (27 Jun 2005), "Witness to abuse: Human rights
abuses under the Material Witness Law since September 11," Human Rights Watch,
http://www.hrw.org/sites/default/files/reports/us0605_0.pdf. Naureen Shah et al.
(21 Jul 2014), "Illusion of justice: Human rights abuses in US terrorism prosecutions,"
Human Rights Watch, http://www.hrw.org/node/126101.

108 **expansion of the legally loaded terms:** In North Carolina, a sawed-off shotgun is
defined as a weapon of mass destruction. Jonathan Lemire (30 Aug 2011), "North Carolina student charged with having weapon of mass destruction for toting sawed-off
shotgun," *New York Daily News*, http://www.nydailynews.com/news/national/north-
carolina-student-charged-weapon-mass-destruction-toting-sawed-off-shotgun-
article-1.950971. Chris Berendt (29 Oct 2013), "Meth lab seized in Newton Grove, three
arrested," *Sampson Independent*, http://www.clintonnc.com/news/home_top-news/
2746038/Meth-lab-seized-in-Newton-Grove%3B-three-arrested.

109 **someone who donates $10:** Louis Jacobson (9 Jul 2013), "What's the definition of
'terrorism'?" *Politifact*, http://www.politifact.com/truth-o-meter/article/2013/jul/09/
whats-definition-terrorism.

109 **Daniel Solove calls the situation Kafkaesque:** Daniel J. Solove (2004), *The Digital
Person: Technology and Privacy in the Information Age*, New York University Press,
http://docs.law.gwu.edu/facweb/dsolove/Digital-Person/text/Digital-Person-CH3
.pdf.

109 **Surveillance data has been used:** The DHS was—and might still be—monitoring
social networking sites, watching for how people react to news that "reflects
adversely" on the US government. Ellen Nakashima (13 Jan 2012), "DHS monitoring
of social media worries civil liberties advocates," *Washington Post*, http://www
.washingtonpost.com/world/national-security/dhs-monitoring-of-social-media-
worries-civil-liberties-advocates/2012/01/13/gIQANPO7wP_story.html.

109 **Irishman Leigh Van Bryan tweeted:** British Broadcasting Corporation (31 Jan
2012), "Caution on Twitter urged as tourists barred from US," *BBC News*, http://
www.bbc.co.uk/news/technology-16810312.

110 **The US government had been surveilling:** Gerry Smith (25 Jun 2014), "How police
are scanning all of Twitter to detect terrorist threats," *Huffington Post*, http://www
.huffingtonpost.com/2014/06/25/dataminr-mines-twitter-to_n_5507616.html.

110 **he was questioned for five hours:** Philip Messing (13 Apr 2013), "JFK passenger
detained after talking about 'bomb' sandwich," *New York Post*, http://nypost
.com/2013/04/13/jfk-passenger-detained-after-talking-about-bomb-sandwich.

110 **vague promises of international:** This excellent essay makes that point. Praxis
(17 Jan 2014), "The world is now an airport: Surveillance and social control," *Medium*,
https://medium.com/i-m-h-o/9a1e5268ff39.

110 **Police arrested him for the crime:** Lauren Russell (24 Apr 2013), "When overshar-

ing online can get you arrested," CNN, http://www.cnn.com/2013/04/18/tech/
social-media/online-oversharing-arrests.

110 **jailed because of a racist tweet:** British Broadcasting Corporation (27 Mar 2012),
"Fabrice Muamba: Racist Twitter user jailed for 56 days," *BBC News*, http://www
.bbc.co.uk/news/uk-wales-17515992.

110 **tasteless Facebook post:** British Broadcasting Corporation (4 Jun 2014), "Man
jailed for offensive Ann Maguire Facebook post," *BBC News*, http://www.bbc.co.uk/
news/uk-england-27696446.

110 **US military targets drone strikes:** Jeremy Scahill and Glenn Greenwald (10 Feb
2014), "The NSA's secret role in the U.S. assassination program," *Intercept*, https://
firstlook.org/theintercept/article/2014/02/10/the-nsas-secret-role. Cori Crider (4
Mar 2014), "Killing in the name of algorithms," Al Jazeera, http://america.aljazeera
.com/opinions/2014/3/drones-big-data-waronterrorobama.html.

110 **The second is "signature strikes":** John Kaag and Sarah Kreps (2014), *Drone Warfare*, Wiley, chap. 12, http://books.google.com/books?id=I8oOBAAAQBAJ.

110 **half of all kills were signature strikes:** Richard Engel and Robert Windrem (5 Jun
2013), "CIA didn't always know who it was killing in drone strikes, classified documents
show," *NBC News*, http://investigations.nbcnews.com/_news/2013/06/05/18781930-cia-
didnt-always-know-who-it-was-killing-in-drone-strikes-classified-documents-show.

111 **surveillance that is essentially indefinite:** Karen McVeigh (27 Aug 2013), "NSA surveillance program violates the constitution, ACLU says," *Guardian*, http://www
.theguardian.com/world/2013/aug/27/nsa-surveillance-program-illegal-aclu-lawsuit.

111 **the Great Firewall of China:** Oliver August (23 Oct 2007), "The Great Firewall:
China's misguided—and futile—attempt to control what happens online," *Wired*,
http://www.oliveraugust.com/journalism_chinas-internet-heroes.htm.

111 **The goal is less to banish:** Gary King, Jennifer Pan, and Margaret E Roberts (May
2013), "How censorship in China allows government criticism but silences collective
expression," *American Political Science Review* 107, http://gking.harvard.edu/publi
cations/how-censorship-china-allows-government-criticism-silences-collective-
expression.

111 **The firewall works pretty well:** Caitlin Dewey (12 Aug 2013), "Wikipedia largely
alone in defying Chinese self-censorship demands," *Washington Post*, http://www
.washingtonpost.com/blogs/worldviews/wp/2013/08/12/wikipedia-largely-
alone-in-defying-chinese-self-censorship-demands.

111 **more government censorship on the Internet:** Ronald Deibert et al., eds. (2010),
Access Controlled: The Shaping of Power, Rights, and Rule in Cyberspace, MIT Press,
http://mitpress.mit.edu/books/access-controlled. John D. Sutter (19 Jun 2012),
"Google reports 'alarming' rise in government censorship requests," CNN, http://
www.cnn.com/2012/06/18/tech/web/google-transparency-report.

111 **France, Germany, and Austria censor:** Forbes (25 Dec 2000), "Swastika.com,"
Forbes, http://www.forbes.com/forbes/2000/1225/6616164s1.html.

111 **Vietnam's "Decree 72":** British Broadcasting Corporation (1 Sep 2013), "Vietnam
internet restrictions come into effect," *BBC News*, http://www.bbc.com/news/
world-asia-23920541.

111 **Many countries censor content:** Ronald Deibert et al., eds, (2008), *Access Denied:
The Practice and Policy of Global Internet Filtering*, MIT Press, http://mitpress.mit
.edu/books/access-denied.

111 **The UK censors pornography:** Ben Quinn (10 Oct 2011), "Biggest four UK ISPs switching to 'opt-in' system for pornography," *Guardian*, http://www.theguardian.com/society/2011/oct/11/pornography-internet-service-providers. Anthony Faiola (28 Sep 2013), "Britain's harsh crackdown on Internet porn prompts free-speech debate," *Washington Post*, http://www.washingtonpost.com/world/europe/britains-harsh-crackdown-on-internet-porn-prompts-free-speech-debate/2013/09/28/d1f5caf8-2781-11e3-9372-92606241ae9c_story.html.

111 **the US censored WikiLeaks:** Ewen MacAskill (1 Dec 2010), "WikiLeaks website pulled by Amazon after U.S. political pressure," *Guardian*, http://www.theguardian.com/media/2010/dec/01/wikileaks-website-cables-servers-amazon.

112 **Russian law requiring bloggers:** Neil MacFarquhar (6 May 2014), "Russia quietly tightens reins on web with 'Bloggers Law,'" *New York Times*, http://www.nytimes.com/2014/05/07/world/europe/russia-quietly-tightens-reins-on-web-with-bloggers-law.html.

112 **Those who do the reporting:** The deputizing of citizens to report on each other is toxic to society. It creates a pervasive fear that unravels the social bonds that hold society together. Bruce Schneier (26 Apr 2007), "Recognizing 'hinky' vs. citizen informants," *Schneier on Security*, https://www.schneier.com/blog/archives/2007/04/recognizing_hin_1.html.

112 **Internet companies in China:** Jason Q. Ng (12 Mar 2012), "How China gets the Internet to censor itself," *Waging Nonviolence*, http://wagingnonviolence.org/feature/how-china-gets-the-internet-to-censor-itself.

112 **the more severe the consequences:** Cuiming Pang (2008), "Self-censorship and the rise of cyber collectives: An anthropological study of a Chinese online community," *Intercultural Communication Studies* 18, http://www.uri.edu/iaics/content/2008v17n3/05%20Cuiming%20Pang.pdf.

112 **Surveillance has a:** Gregory L. White and Philip G. Zimbardo (May 1975), "The chilling effects of surveillance: Deindividuation and reactance," Office of Naval Research/National Technical Information Service, http://www.dtic.mil/dtic/tr/fulltext/u2/a013230.pdf.

112 **The net result is that GPS:** US Supreme Court (23 Jan 2012), "Decision," *United States v. Jones* (No. 10-1259), http://caselaw.lp.findlaw.com/scripts/getcase.pl?court=US&navby=case&vol=000&invol=10-1259#opinion1.

112 **Eben Moglen wrote:** Eben Moglen (27 May 2014), "Privacy under attack: The NSA files revealed new threats to democracy," *Guardian*, http://www.theguardian.com/technology/2014/may/27/-sp-privacy-under-attack-nsa-files-revealed-new-threats-democracy.

113 **Sources are less likely to contact:** G. Alex Sinha (28 Jul 2014), "With liberty to monitor all," Human Rights Watch, http://www.hrw.org/reports/2014/07/28/liberty-monitor-all.

113 **Lawyers working on cases:** In 2014, we learned that the Australian Signals Directorate (ASD), Australia's NSA counterpart, eavesdropped on communications between the US law firm Mayer Brown and its client the government of Indonesia. The ASD passed those communications to the NSA. James Risen and Laura Poitras (15 Feb 2014), "Spying by NSA ally entangled US law firm," *New York Times*, http://www.nytimes.com/2014/02/16/us/eavesdropping-ensnared-american-law-firm.html.

113 **they worry that their conversations:** G. Alex Sinha (28 Jul 2014), "With liberty to

monitor all," Human Rights Watch, http://www.hrw.org/reports/2014/07/28/liberty-monitor-all-0.

113 **Post-9/11 surveillance has caused:** PEN America (2013), "Chilling effects: NSA surveillance drives U.S. writers to self-censor," http://www.pen.org/sites/default/files/Chilling%20Effects_PEN%20American.pdf.

113 **A Pew Research Center study:** The survey was taken just after the stories broke that the NSA was collecting telephone metadata from Verizon, and presumably from everyone else, and collecting Internet data from companies like Google, Yahoo, Facebook, Microsoft, and Twitter. Elizabeth Dwoskin (26 Aug 2014), "Survey: People don't want to talk online about the NSA," *Wall Street Journal*, http://blogs.wsj.com/digits/2014/08/26/survey-people-dont-want-to-talk-online-about-the-nsa.

113 **nearly half of Americans have changed:** Amrita Jayakumar (2 Apr 2014), "Americans say they're shopping less online. Blame the NSA," *Washington Post*, http://www.washingtonpost.com/blogs/the-switch/wp/2014/04/02/americans-say-theyre-shopping-less-online-blame-the-nsa.

113 **Surveillance has chilled Internet use:** Dawinder S. Sidhu (2007), "The chilling effect of government surveillance programs on the use of the Internet by Muslim-Americans," *University of Maryland Law Journal of Race, Religion, Gender and Class* 7, http://papers.ssrn.com/sol3/papers.cfm?abstract_id=1002145.

113 **groups like environmentalists:** David Greene (6 Nov 2013), "EFF files 22 firsthand accounts of how NSA surveillance chilled the right to association," Electronic Frontier Foundation, https://www.eff.org/press/releases/eff-files-22-firsthand-accounts-how-nsa-surveillance-chilled-right-association.

113 **After the Snowden revelations:** Alex Marthews and Catherine Tucker (24 Mar 2014), "Government surveillance and Internet search behavior," Social Science Research Network, http://papers.ssrn.com/sol3/papers.cfm?abstract_id=2412564.

113 **UN High Commissioner on Human Rights:** United Nations High Commissioner for Human Rights (30 Jun 2014), "The right to privacy in the digital age," http://www.ohchr.org/EN/HRBodies/HRC/RegularSessions/Session27/Documents/A.HRC.27.37_en.pdf.

114 **French president Nicolas Sarkozy:** Liz Klimas (22 Mar 2012), "Simply visiting terrorist websites could mean jail time in France," *Blaze*, http://www.theblaze.com/stories/2012/03/22/simply-visiting-terrorist-websites-could-mean-jail-time-in-france.

114 **Think of how you act:** Rachel Clark (11 Jul 2013), "'Everything about everyone': the depth of Stasi surveillance in the GDR," *View East*, http://thevieweast.wordpress.com/2013/07/11/everything-about-everyone-the-depth-of-stasi-surveillance-in-the-gdr. Oka Efagene (20 Aug 2014), "Your calls may soon be monitored: NCC," *Pulse*, http://pulse.ng/lifestyle/tech/security-vs-privacy-your-calls-may-soon-be-monitored-ncc-id3066105.html.

115 **There is value in dissent:** Carl Joachim Friedrich (Oct 1939), "Democracy and dissent," *Political Quarterly* 10, http://onlinelibrary.wiley.com/doi/10.1111/j.1467-923X.1939.tb00987.x/abstract.

115 **Defending this assertion:** Bruce Schneier (2012), *Liars and Outliers: Enabling the Trust That Society Needs to Thrive*, Wiley, chap. 16, http://www.wiley.com/WileyCDA/WileyTitle/productCd-1118143302.html.

115 **Frank Zappa said something similar:** Frank Zappa and Peter Occhiogrosso

(1989), *The Real Frank Zappa Book*, Poseidon Press, p. 185, http://books.google.com/books?id=FB0O_HCpBy0C.

115 **We need imperfect security:** Washington University law professor Neil Richards makes the point that "new ideas often develop best away from the intense scrutiny of public exposure." Neil M. Richards (May 2013), "The dangers of surveillance," *Harvard Law Review* 126, http://papers.ssrn.com/sol3/papers.cfm?abstract_id=2239412.

116 **township can use aerial surveillance:** The city of Baltimore uses aerial photography to look for building permit violations by comparing photographs over time with its database of issued permits. Doug Donovan (7 Sep 2004), "A bird's-eye view of every part of the city," *Baltimore Sun*, http://articles.baltimoresun.com/2004-09-07/news/0409070310_1_images-deck-aerial.

116 **replacing that judgment:** Gregory Conti (4 Apr 2014), "A conservation theory of governance for automated law enforcement," We Robot 2014, Coral Gables, Florida, http://robots.law.miami.edu/2014/wp-content/uploads/2013/06/Shay-etal-TheoryofConservation_final.pdf.

116 **Ubiquitous surveillance could lead:** The "Cannibal Cop," who chatted online with pals about raping and eating his wife and other women, but never acted on it, serves as an example. Daniel Beekman and Dareh Gregorian (1 Jul 2014), "'Cannibal cop' released into custody of his mother after conviction overturned in stunning reversal," *New York Daily News*, http://www.nydailynews.com/new-york/nyc-crime/conviction-cannibal-nypd-overturned-article-1.1850334. Daniel Engber (2 Jul 2014), "The cannibal cop goes free, but what about the murderous mechanic?" *Slate*, http://www.slate.com/articles/news_and_politics/crime/2014/07/the_cannibal_cop_gilberto_valle_goes_free_what_about_michael_van_hise_and.html.

116 **Already law enforcement agencies:** Walter L. Perry et al. (2013), "Predictive policing: The role of crime forecasting in law enforcement operations," RAND Corporation, https://www.ncjrs.gov/pdffiles1/nij/grants/243830.pdf. US National Institute of Justice (13 Jan 2014), "Predictive policing research," http://www.nij.gov/topics/law-enforcement/strategies/predictive-policing/Pages/research.aspx.

116 **This notion of making certain crimes:** Michael L. Rich (Mar 2013), "Should we make crime impossible?" *Harvard Journal of Law and Public Policy* 36, http://www.harvard-jlpp.com/wp-content/uploads/2013/04/36_2_795_Rich.pdf.

116 **Yochai Benkler said:** Yochai Benkler (4 Dec 2013), "System and conscience: NSA bulk surveillance and the problem of freedom," Center for Research on Computation and Society, Harvard University, http://crcs.seas.harvard.edu/event/yochai-benkler-crcs-lunch-seminar and https://www.youtube.com/watch?v=6EUueRpCzpw.

117 **secrecy is necessary:** William E. Colby (1976), "Intelligence secrecy and security in a free society," *International Security* 1, http://people.exeter.ac.uk/mm394/Intelligence%20Secrecy%20and%20Security.pdf. James E. Knott (Summer 1975), "Secrecy and intelligence in a free society," *Studies in Intelligence* 19, https://www.cia.gov/library/center-for-the-study-of-intelligence/kent-csi/vol19no2/html/v19i2a01p_0001.htm.

117 **This notion of military secrecy:** Pamela O. Long and Alex Roland (1994), "Military secrecy in antiquity and early medieval Europe: A critical reassessment," *History and Technology* 11, http://www.tandfonline.com/doi/abs/10.1080/07341519408581866?journalCode=ghat20.

117 **recently has changed:** Lewis A. Coser (Summer 1963), "The dysfunctions of military secrecy," *Social Problems* 11, http://www.jstor.org/discover/10.2307/798801.

117 **In World War II, we extended:** The secrecy and deception around D-Day is an excellent example. Jon S. Wendell (1997), "Strategic deception behind the Normandy invasion," US Air Force, http://www.globalsecurity.org/military/library/report/1997/Wendell.htm. Dan Lamothe (6 Jun 2014), "Remembering the military secrecy and lies that made D-Day successful," *Washington Post*, http://www.washingtonpost.com/news/checkpoint/wp/2014/06/06/remembering-the-military-secrecy-and-lies-that-made-d-day-successful.

117 **entire areas of knowledge:** Steven Aftergood (Oct 1999), "Government secrecy and knowledge production: A survey of some general issues," in *Secrecy and Knowledge Production*, ed. Judith Reppy, Cornell University Peace Studies Program Occasional Paper #23, http://large.stanford.edu/publications/crime/references/dennis/occasional-paper23.pdf. Francis B. Kapper (Oct 1999), "The role of government in the production and control of scientific and technical knowledge," ibid. Koen Vermeir and Daniel Margocsy (Jun 2012), "States of secrecy: An introduction," *British Journal of the History of Science* 45, http://journals.cambridge.org/action/displayAbstract?fromPage=online&aid=8608487&fileId=S0007087412000052.

117 **After 9/11, we generalized:** Peter Galison (Autumn 2004), "Removing knowledge," *Critical Inquiry* 31, http://www.fas.harvard.edu/~hsdept/bios/docs/Removing%20Knowledge.pdf.

117 **No one knows the exact number:** Ibid.

117 **almost 5 million people:** US Office of Management and Budget (Feb 2014), "Suitability and security processes review," http://www.fas.org/sgp/othergov/omb/suitsec-2014.pdf.

117 **all the details of NSA surveillance:** Director of National Intelligence Clapper: "Disclosure of this still-classified information regarding the scope and operational details of N.S.A. intelligence activities implicated by plaintiffs' allegations could be expected to cause extremely grave damage to the national security of the United States." James R. Clapper (20 Dec 2013), "Public declaration of James R. Clapper, Director of National Intelligence," *Jewel et al. v. National Security Agency et al.* (08-cv-4873-JSW; *Shubert, et al., v. Obama, et al.* (07-cv-693-JSW), United States District Court for the Northern District of California, http://www.dni.gov/files/documents/1220/DNI%20Clapper%202013%20Jewel%20Shubert%20SSP%20Unclassified%20Signed%20Declaration.pdf.

117 **You weren't even allowed:** Post-Snowden, the secret FISA Court has declassified many of its more general rulings. Another thing that would never have happened had Snowden not done what he did.

118 **police requests for cell phone:** Jennifer Valentino-DeVries (2 Jun 2014), "Sealed court files obscure rise in electronic surveillance," *Wall Street Journal*, http://online.wsj.com/news/article_email/sealed-court-files-obscure-rise-in-electronic-surveillance-1401761770-lMyQjAxMTA0MDAwMzEwNDMyWj.

118 **The UK police won't even admit:** Joseph Cox (7 Aug 2014), "UK police won't admit they're tracking people's phone calls," *Vice*, http://motherboard.vice.com/read/uk-police-wont-admit-theyre-tracking-peoples-phone-calls.

118 **Those who receive such a letter:** This is a fascinating first-person account of what it's like to receive a National Security Letter. It was published anonymously, but was later revealed to be the work of Internet Archive founder Brewster Kahle. Anonymous (23 Mar 2007), "My National Security Letter gag order," *Washington Post*,

http://www.washingtonpost.com/wp-dyn/content/article/2007/03/22/AR200
7032201882.html.

118 **the reason the FBI:** Kim Zetter (3 Mar 2014), "Florida cops' secret weapon: Warrantless cellphone tracking," *Wired*, http://www.wired.com/2014/03/stingray. Kim
Zetter (4 Mar 2014), "Police contract with spy tool maker prohibits talking about
device's use," *Wired*, http://www.wired.com/2014/03/harris-stingray-nda.

118 **local police departments refuse:** Darwin Bond-Graham and Ali Winston (30 Oct
2013), "All tomorrow's crimes: The future of policing looks a lot like good branding," *SF
Weekly*, http://www.sfweekly.com/2013-10-30/news/predpol-sfpd-predictive-policing-
compstat-lapd/full.

118 **The US has a complex:** Jennifer K. Elsea (10 Jan 2013), "The protection of classified
information: The legal framework," Congressional Research Service, http://fas.org/
sgp/crs/secrecy/RS21900.pdf.

118 **The executive branch abuses:** Carrie Newton Lyons (2007), "The state secrets
privilege: Expanding its scope through government misuse," *Lewis and Clark Law
Review* 99, http://www.fas.org/sgp/jud/statesec/lyons.pdf. Sudha Setty (Jul 2012),
"The rise of national security secrets," *Connecticut Law Review* 44, http://connecti
cutlawreview.org/files/2012/09/5.Setty-FINAL.pdf. D. A. Jeremy Telman (Mar 2012),
"Intolerable abuses: Rendition for torture and the state secrets privilege," *Alabama
Law Review* 63, http://scholar.valpo.edu/cgi/viewcontent.cgi?article=1136&contex
t=law_fac_pubs.

118 **The executive branch keeps secrets:** Eric Lichtblau and Scott Shane (9 Jul 2006),
"Ally warned Bush on keeping spying from Congress," *New York Times*, http://www
.nytimes.com/2006/07/09/washington/09hoekstra.html. Scott Shane (11 Jul 2009),
"Cheney is linked to concealment of C.I.A. project," *New York Times*, http://www
.nytimes.com/2009/07/12/us/politics/12intel.html. Paul Lewis (31 Jul 2013), "White
House unable to confirm if Congress briefed on NSA spy program," *Guardian*, http://
www.theguardian.com/world/2013/jul/31/white-house-congress-nsa-xkeyscore.

118 **The NSA keeps secrets:** Barton Gellman (15 Aug 2013), "What to say, and not to say,
to 'our overseers,'" *Washington Post*, http://apps.washingtonpost.com/g/page/
national/what-to-say-and-not-to-say-to-our-overseers/390.

118 **including Congress:** Glenn Greenwald (4 Aug 2013), "Members of Congress denied
access to basic information about NSA," *Guardian*, http://www.theguardian.com/
commentisfree/2013/aug/04/congress-nsa-denied-access.

118 **keep secrets from the rest of Congress:** Spencer Ackerman (14 Aug 2013), "Intelligence committee urged to explain if they withheld crucial NSA document," *Guardian*,
http://www.theguardian.com/world/2013/aug/14/nsa-intelligence-committee-
under-pressure-document.

118 **Secret courts keep their own secrets:** Charlie Savage and Laura Poitras (11 Mar
2014), "How a court secretly evolved, extending U.S. spies' reach," *New York Times*,
http://www.nytimes.com/2014/03/12/us/how-a-courts-secret-evolution-extended-
spies-reach.html.

119 **even the Supreme Court:** Emily Peterson (30 Sep 2011), "Under seal: Secrets at the
Supreme Court," Reporters Committee for Freedom of the Press, http://www.rcfp
.org/browse-media-law-resources/news-media-law/news-media-law-summer-
2011/under-seal-secrets-supreme-cour.

119 **President Obama has been:** Cora Currier (30 Jul 2013), "Charting Obama's crack-

down on national security leaks," *Pro Publica*, http://www.propublica.org/special/
sealing-loose-lips-charting-obamas-crackdown-on-national-security-leaks.

119 **only three previous prosecutions:** Leonard Downie Jr. and Sara Rafsky (Oct 2013),
"Leak investigations and surveillance in post-9/11 America," Committee to Protect
Journalists, https://www.cpj.org/reports/2013/10/obama-and-the-press-us-leaks-sur
veillance-post-911.php. David Pozen (20 Dec 2013), "The leaky leviathan: Why the government condemns and condones unlawful disclosures of information," *Harvard Law
Review* 127, http://harvardlawreview.org/2013/12/the-leaky-leviathan-why-the-govern
ment-condemns-and-condones-unlawful-disclosures-of-information.

119 **Thomas Drake, an NSA whistleblower:** Daniel Ellsberg (30 May 2014), "Snowden
would not get a fair trial—and Kerry is wrong," *Guardian*, http://www.theguardian
.com/commentisfree/2014/may/30/daniel-ellsberg-snowden-fair-trial-kerry-espion
age-act.

119 **Chelsea Manning was prohibited:** David Dishneau (20 Jul 2012), "Manning
largely barred from discussing WikiLeaks harm," Associated Press, http://seattle-
times.com/html/nationworld/2018724246_apusmanningwikileaks.html.

119 **Edward Snowden claims:** The country is fairly evenly divided on this point. Seth
Motel (15 Apr 2014), "NSA coverage wins Pulitzer, but Americans remain divided on
Snowden leaks," Pew Research Center, http://www.pewresearch.org/fact-tank/
2014/04/15/nsa-coverage-wins-pulitzer-but-americans-remain-divided-on-
snowden-leaks.

119 **John Kerry insisted that:** Jonathan Topaz (28 May 2014), "John Kerry: Edward
Snowden a 'coward . . . traitor,'" *Politico*, http://www.politico.com/story/2014/05/
edward-snowden-coward-john-kerry-msnbc-interview-nsa-107157.html.

119 **Hillary Clinton proclaimed:** Phoebe Greenwood (4 Jul 2014), "Edward Snowden
should have right to legal defense in US, says Hillary Clinton," *Guardian*, http://
www.theguardian.com/world/2014/jul/04/edward-snowden-legal-defence-hil
lary-clinton-interview.

119 **Both comments are examples:** Daniel Ellsberg (30 May 2014), "Snowden would
not get a fair trial—and Kerry is wrong," *Guardian*, http://www.theguardian.com/
commentisfree/2014/may/30/daniel-ellsberg-snowden-fair-trial-kerry-espionage-
act. Trevor Timm (23 Dec 2013), "If Snowden returned to US for trial, could court
admit any NSA leak evidence?" *Boing Boing*, http://boingboing.net/2013/12/23/
snowden.html.

120 **His anger set off a series:** Nate Anderson (13 May 2014), "How a mayor's quest to
unmask a foul-mouthed Twitter user blew up in his face," *Ars Technica*, http://ars
technica.com/tech-policy/2014/05/how-a-mayors-quest-to-unmask-a-foul-
mouthed-twitter-user-blew-up-in-his-face. Kim Zetter (12 Jun 2014), "ACLU sues
after Illinois mayor has cops raid guy parodying him on Twitter," *Wired*, http://
www.wired.com/2014/06/peoria-mayor-twitter-parody.

120 **police in New Jersey routinely:** Jenna Portnoy (19 Mar 2014), "Attorney General
to State Police: Stop photographing protesters at Chris Christie town halls,"
Star-Ledger, http://www.nj.com/politics/index.ssf/2014/03/attorney_general_to_state
_police_stop_photographing_protesters_at_chris_christie_town_halls.html.

120 **the CIA illegally hacked:** Mark Mazzetti and Carl Hulse (31 Jul 2014), "Inquiry by CIA
affirms it spied on Senate panel," *New York Times*, http://www.nytimes.com/2014/08/01/
world/senate-intelligence-commitee-cia-interrogation-report.html.

120 **the NSA had been spying:** Laura Poitras, Marcel Rosenbach, and Holger Stark (26 Aug 2013), "Codename 'Apalachee': How America spies on Europe and the UN," *Der Spiegel*, http://www.spiegel.de/international/world/secret-nsa-documents-show-how-the-us-spies-on-europe-and-the-un-a-918625.html.

120 **two intercept operators in 2008:** Brian Ross, Vic Walter, and Anna Schecter (9 Oct 2008), "Inside account of U.S. eavesdropping on Americans," *ABC News Nightline*, http://abcnews.go.com/Blotter/exclusive-inside-account-us-eavesdropping-ameri cans/story?id=5987804.

120 **again from Snowden in 2014:** Cyrus Farivar (17 Jul 2014), "Snowden: NSA employees routinely pass around intercepted nude photos," *Ars Technica*, http://arstechnica .com/tech-policy/2014/07/snowden-nsa-employees-routinely-pass-around-inter cepted-nude-photos.

120 **agents sometimes spy on people:** Siobhan Gorman (23 Aug 2013), "NSA officers spy on love interests," *Wall Street Journal Washington Wire*, http://blogs.wsj.com/ washwire/2013/08/23/nsa-officers-sometimes-spy-on-love-interests.

121 **the agency broke its own privacy rules:** US National Security Agency (3 May 2012), "NSAW SID intelligence oversight quarterly report: First quarter calendar year 2012 (1 Jan–31 Mar 2012)," http://www2.gwu.edu/~nsarchiv/NSAEBB/NSAEBB436/ docs/EBB-044.pdf.

121 **the real number is probably:** The NSA is deliberately not automating its auditing system, which means it finds only as many violations as it decides to put people on the task. Marcy Wheeler (20 Aug 2013), "If NSA commits database query violations, but nobody audits them, do they really happen?" *Empty Wheel*, http://www.empty wheel.net/2013/08/20/if-nsa-commits-database-query-violations-but-nobody-audits-them-do-they-really-happen.

121 **tried to induce him:** Shaun Usher (5 Jan 2012), "Like all frauds your end is approach-ing," *Letters of Note*, http://www.lettersofnote.com/2012/01/king-like-all-frauds-your-end-is.html.

121 **the FBI's COINTELPRO:** US Senate (26 Apr 1976), "Final report of the Select Commit-tee to Study Governmental Operations with Respect to Intelligence Activities, United States Senate, Book II: Intelligence activities and the rights of Americans," US Govern-ment Printing Office, p. 213, https://archive.org/details/finalreportofsel02unit.

122 **US has spied on the Occupy:** Michael S. Schmidt and Colin Moynihan (24 Dec 2012), "FBI counterterrorism agents monitored Occupy movement, records show," *New York Times*, http://www.nytimes.com/2012/12/25/nyregion/occupy-movement-was-inves tigated-by-fbi-counterterrorism-agents-records-show.html. Beau Hodai (9 Jun 2013), "Government surveillance of Occupy movement," *Sourcewatch*, http://www.source watch.org/index.php/Government_Surveillance_of_Occupy_Movement.

122 **pro- and anti-abortion activists:** Charlie Savage and Scott Shane (16 Dec 2009), "Intelligence improperly collected on U.S. citizens," *New York Times*, http://www .nytimes.com/2009/12/17/us/17disclose.html.

122 **peace activists:** American Civil Liberties Union (25 Oct 2006), "ACLU uncovers FBI surveillance of Maine peace activists," https://www.aclu.org/national-security/ aclu-uncovers-fbi-surveillance-maine-peace-activists.

122 **other political protesters:** American Civil Liberties Union (29 Jun 2010), "Policing free speech: Police surveillance and obstruction of First Amendment-protected activity," https://www.aclu.org/files/assets/Spyfiles_2_0.pdf. Linda E. Fisher (2004),

"Guilt by expressive association: Political profiling, surveillance and the privacy of groups," *Arizona Law Review* 46, http://www.arizonalawreview.org/pdf/46-4/46ari zlrev621.pdf. US Department of Justice (Sep 2010), "A review of the FBI's investigations of certain domestic advocacy groups," http://www.justice.gov/oig/special/s1009r.pdf.

122 **The NSA and FBI spied:** Glenn Greenwald and Murtaza Hussain (9 Jul 2014), "Under surveillance: Meet the Muslim-American leaders the FBI and NSA have been spying on," *Intercept*, https://firstlook.org/theintercept/article/2014/07/09/under-surveillance.

122 **The New York Police Department:** Associated Press (2012), "Highlights of AP's Pulitzer Prize-winning probe into NYPD intelligence operations," Associated Press, http://www.ap.org/media-center/nypd/investigation, and http://www.ap.org/Index/AP-In-The-News/NYPD.

123 **Boston's fusion center spied:** Kade Crockford (25 May 2014), "Documents show Boston's 'antiterrorism' fusion center obsessively documented Occupy Boston," Privacy SOS, http://privacysos.org/node/1417. Carol Rose and Kade Crockford (30 May 2014), "When police spy on free speech, democracy suffers," *Cognoscenti*, http://cognoscenti.wbur.org/2014/05/30/boston-regional-intelligence-center-carol-rose-kade-crockford.

123 **the city teamed with IBM:** Luke O'Neil (13 Aug 2014), "Beantown's Big Brother: How Boston police used facial recognition technology to spy on thousands of music festival attendees," *Noisey*, http://noisey.vice.com/blog/beantowns-big-brother.

123 **Pentagon's Counterintelligence Field Activity:** Lisa Myers, Douglas Pasternak, and Rich Gardella (14 Dec 2005), "Is the Pentagon spying on Americans?" *NBC News*, http://www.nbcnews.com/id/10454316/ns/nbc_nightly_news_with_brian_wil liams-nbc_news_investigates/t/pentagon-spying-americans. Marcy Wheeler (24 Jul 2007), "Cunningham, CIFA, and Cheney, a new chronology," *Empty Wheel*, http://www.emptywheel.net/2007/07/24/cunningham-cifa-and-cheney-a-new-chronology.

123 **collecting data on the porn-viewing habits:** Glenn Greenwald, Ryan Grim, and Ryan Gallagher (26 Nov 2013), "Top-secret document reveals NSA spied on porn habits as part of plan to discredit 'radicalizers,'" *Huffington Post*, http://www.huff ingtonpost.com/2013/11/26/nsa-porn-muslims_n_4346128.html.

123 **fake Facebook page:** Chris Hamby (6 Oct 2014), "Government set up a fake Facebook page in a woman's name," *Buzzfeed*, http://www.buzzfeed.com/chrishamby/government-says-federal-agents-can-impersonate-woman-online.

123 **School administrators installed spyware:** William Bender (23 Feb 2010), "Lawyer: L. Merion is mum on number of webcam pictures," *Philadelphia Inquirer*, http://arti cles.philly.com/2010-02-23/news/24957453_1_webcam-laptops-students.

124 **This turned out to be a dead end:** Eric Lichtblau and James Risen (23 Jun 2006), "Bank data is sifted by U.S. in secret to block terror," *New York Times*, http://www .nytimes.com/2006/06/23/washington/23intel.html. Loek Essers (3 Jul 2014), "EU court orders more transparency over US-EU terrorist finance tracking program," *PC World*, http://www.pcworld.com/article/2450760/eu-court-orders-more-transparen cy-over-useu-terrorist-finance-tracking-program.html. Monika Ermert (23 Oct 2013), "European Parliament: No more bank data transfers to US for anti-terror investiga tions," *Intellectual Property Watch*, http://www.ip-watch.org/2013/10/23/europe an-parliament-no-more-bank-data-transfers-to-us-for-anti-terror-investigations.

124 **far more commonly used:** ACLU (7 Mar 2002), "How the USA-Patriot Act expands

law enforcement "sneak and peek" warrants," https://www.aclu.org/technology-and-liberty/how-usa-patriot-act-expands-law-enforcement-sneak-and-peek-warrants. Trevor Timm (26 Oct 2011), "Ten years after the Patriot Act, a look at the three most dangerous provisions affecting ordinary Americans," *Electronic Frontier Foundation*, https://www.eff.org/deeplinks/2011/10/ten-years-later-look-three-scariest-provisions-usa-patriot-act.

124 **surveillance against drug smugglers:** The NSA has been sharing information with the DEA since the 1970s. James Bamford (2008), *The Shadow Factory: The Ultra-Secret NSA from 9/11 to Eavesdropping on America*, Doubleday, http://books.google.com/books?id=8zJmxWNTxrwC.

124 **DEA staff were instructed:** John Shiffman and Kristina Cooke (5 Aug 2013), "U.S. directs agents to cover up program used to investigate Americans," Reuters, http://www.reuters.com/article/2013/08/05/us-dea-sod-idUSBRE97409R20130805. Hanni Fakhoury (6 Aug 2013), "DEA and NSA team up to share intelligence, leading to secret use of surveillance in ordinary investigations," Electronic Frontier Foundation, https://www.eff.org/deeplinks/2013/08/dea-and-nsa-team-intelligence-laundering. John Shiffman and David Ingram (7 Aug 2013), "IRS manual detailed DEA's use of hidden intel evidence," Reuters, http://www.reuters.com/article/2013/08/07/us-dea-irs-idUSBRE9761AZ20130807.

124 **NSA's term is:** NSA whistleblower Bill Binney described it thus: ". . . when you can't use the data, you have to go out and do a parallel construction, [which] means you use what you would normally consider to be investigative techniques, [and] go find the data. You have a little hint, though. NSA is telling you where the data is . . . ." Alexa O'Brien (30 Sep 2014), "Retired NSA technical director explains Snowden docs," *Second Sight*, http://www.alexaobrien.com/secondsight/wb/binney.html.

124 **Dread Pirate Roberts:** Brian Krebs (14 Oct 2014), "Silk Road lawyers poke holes in FBI's story," *Krebs on Security*, http://krebsonsecurity.com/2014/10/silk-road-lawyers-poke-holes-in-fbis-story.

124 **surveillance intended to nab terrorists:** Rob Evans and Paul Lewis (26 Oct 2009), "Police forces challenged over files held on law-abiding protesters," *Guardian*, http://www.theguardian.com/uk/2009/oct/26/police-challenged-protest-files.

124 **all sorts of minor criminal cases:** Gordon Rayner and Richard Alleyne (12 Apr 2008), "Council spy cases hit 1,000 a month," *Telegraph*, http://www.telegraph.co.uk/news/uknews/1584808/Council-spy-cases-hit-1000-a-month.html. Sarah Lyall (24 Oct 2009), "Britons weary of surveillance in minor cases," *New York Times*, http://www.nytimes.com/2009/10/25/world/europe/25surveillance.html.

124 **Israel, for instance:** James Bamford (16 Sep 2014), "Israel's NSA scandal," *New York Times*, http://www.nytimes.com/2014/09/17/opinion/israels-nsa-scandal.html.

125 **A system that is overwhelmingly powerful:** This essay makes that point. Daniel Davies (23 Sep 2014), "Every single IT guy, every single manager . . . ," *Crooked Timber*, http://crookedtimber.org/2014/09/23/every-single-it-guy-every-single-manager.

125 **Hillary Clinton gave a speech:** Hillary Rodham Clinton (21 Jan 2010), "Internet freedom," *Foreign Policy*, http://www.foreignpolicy.com/articles/2010/01/21/internet_freedom.

125 **US State Department funds:** US Department of State (2014), "Internet freedom," http://www.state.gov/e/eb/cip/netfreedom/index.htm.

126 **one of the defenses:** British Broadcasting Corporation (2 Jun 2014), "'We are being

watched' say Egyptians on social media," *BBC News*, http://www.bbc.com/news/blogs-trending-27665568.

126 **Indians are worried:** Jayshree Bajoria (5 Jun 2014), "India's snooping and Snowden," *India Real Time*, http://blogs.wsj.com/indiarealtime/2014/06/05/indias-snooping-and-snowden.

126 **Both China and Russia:** Shannon Tiezzi (28 Mar 2014), "China decries US 'hypocrisy' on cyber-espionage," *Diplomat*, http://thediplomat.com/2014/03/china-decries-us-hypocrisy-on-cyber-espionage. Xinhua News Agency (11 Jul 2014), "Putin calls US surveillance practice 'utter hypocrisy,'" *China Daily*, http://www.chinadaily.com.cn/world/2014-07/11/content_17735783.htm.

126 **Facebook's Mark Zuckerberg:** Mark Zuckerberg (13 Mar 2014), "As the world becomes more complex . . . ," *Facebook*, https://www.facebook.com/zuck/posts/10101301165605491.

8: COMMERCIAL FAIRNESS AND EQUALITY

127 **Accretive Health is:** Office of the Minnesota Attorney General (19 Jan 2012), "Attorney General Swanson sues Accretive Health for patient privacy violations," Office of the Minnesota Attorney General, http://www.ag.state.mn.us/Consumer/Press Release/120119AccretiveHealth.asp.

127 **settled a Minnesota lawsuit:** Tony Kennedy and Maura Lerner (31 Jul 2012), "Accretive is banned from Minnesota," *Star-Tribune*, http://www.startribune.com/lifestyle/health/164313776.html.

128 **companies use surveillance data:** Kate Crawford and Jason Schultz (2014), "Big data and due process: Toward a framework to redress predictive privacy harms," *Boston College Law Review* 55, http://papers.ssrn.com/sol3/papers.cfm?abstract_id=2325784.

128 **"Redlining" is a term:** Marc Hochstein (26 Jun 2000), "Wells kills web link after Acorn sues," *American Banker*, http://www.americanbanker.com/issues/165_119/-128168-1.html. Gary A. Hernandez, Katherine J. Eddy, and Joel Muchmore (Fall 2001), "Insurance weblining and unfair discrimination in cyberspace," *Southern Methodist University Law Review* 54, http://heinonline.org/HOL/LandingPage?collection=journals&handle=hein.journals/smulr54&div=91.

128 **easier to do on the Internet:** Bill Davidow (5 Mar 2014), "Redlining for the 21st century," *Atlantic*, http://www.theatlantic.com/business/archive/2014/03/redlining-for-the-21st-century/284235.

128 **Wells Fargo bank created:** Michael Liedtke (22 Jun 2000), "Lawsuit alleges Wells Fargo uses Internet to promote discrimination," *Los Angeles Times*, http://articles.latimes.com/2000/jun/22/business/fi-43532. Ronna Abramson (23 Jun 2000), "Wells Fargo accused of 'redlining' on the Net," *Computer World*, http://www.computerworld.com/article/2596352/financial-it/wells-fargo-accused-of--redlining--on-the-net.html.

128 **This practice is called weblining:** Marcia Stepanek (3 Apr 2000), "Weblining," *Bloomberg Businessweek*, http://www.businessweek.com/2000/00_14/b3675027.htm. Casey Johnston (10 Oct 2013), "Denied for that loan? Soon you may thank online data collection," *Ars Technica*, http://arstechnica.com/business/2013/10/denied-for-that-loan-soon-you-may-thank-online-data-collection.

128 **report on big data concluded:** US Executive Office of the President (1 May 2014), "Big data: Seizing opportunities, preserving values," http://www.whitehouse.gov/sites/default/files/docs/big_data_privacy_report_may_1_2014.pdf.

129 **Uber's surge pricing:** Uber had to modify its pricing so as not to run afoul of New York State's prohibitions against price-gouging during emergencies. Mike Isaac (8 Jul 2014), "Uber reaches deal with New York on surge pricing in emergencies," *New York Times*, http://bits.blogs.nytimes.com/2014/07/08/uber-reaches-agreement-with-n-y-on-surge-pricing-during-emergencies. Peter Himler (12 Aug 2014), "UBER: So cool, yet so uncool," *Forbes*, http://www.forbes.com/sites/peterhimler/2014/08/12/uber-so-cool-but-so-uncool.

129 **different prices and options:** Jennifer Valentino-DeVries, Jeremy Singer-Vine, and Ashkan Soltani (24 Dec 2012), "Websites vary prices, deals based on users' information," *Wall Street Journal*, http://online.wsj.com/news/articles/SB10001424127887323777204578189391813881534. Michael Schrage (29 Jan 2014), "Big data's dangerous new era of discrimination," *Harvard Business Review*, http://blogs.hbr.org/2014/01/big-datas-dangerous-new-era-of-discrimination.

129 **Depending on who you are:** Emily Steele and Julia Angwin (4 Aug 2010), "On the Web's cutting edge, anonymity in name only," *Wall Street Journal*, http://online.wsj.com/news/articles/SB10001424052748703294904575385532109190198.

130 **other companies . . . are also adjusting prices:** Jennifer Valentino-DeVries, Jeremy Singer-Vine, and Ashkan Soltani (24 Dec 2012), "Websites vary prices, deals based on users' information," *Wall Street Journal*, http://online.wsj.com/news/articles/SB10001424127887323777204578189391813881534.

130 **we all have a customer score:** Pam Dixon and Robert Gellman (2 Apr 2014), "The scoring of America: How secret consumer scores threaten your privacy and your future," World Privacy Forum, http://www.worldprivacyforum.org/wp-content/uploads/2014/04/WPF_Scoring_of_America_April2014_fs.pdf.

130 **a series of recruiting ads:** Jessica E. Vascellaro (7 Mar 2011), "TV's next wave: Tuning in to you," *Wall Street Journal*, http://online.wsj.com/articles/SB10001424052748704288304576171251689944350.

130 **Orbitz highlighted different prices:** Dana Mattioli (23 Aug 2012), "On Orbitz, Mac users steered to pricier hotels," *Wall Street Journal*, http://online.wsj.com/news/articles/SB10001424052702304458604577488822667325882.

130 **different offers based on:** Bill McGee (3 Apr 2013), "Do travel deals change based on your browsing history?" *USA Today*, http://www.usatoday.com/story/travel/columnist/mcgee/2013/04/03/do-travel-deals-change-based-on-your-browsing-history/2021993.

130 **Many sites estimate:** Michael Fertik (15 Jan 2013), "The rich see a different Internet than the poor," *Scientific American*, http://www.scientificamerican.com/article/rich-see-different-internet-than-the-poor.

131 **women feel less attractive on Mondays:** Lucia Moses (2 Oct 2013), "Marketers should take note of when women feel least attractive: What messages to convey and when to send them," *Adweek*, http://www.adweek.com/news/advertising-branding/marketers-should-take-note-when-women-feel-least-attractive-152753. Kim Bates (4 Oct 2013), "Beauty vulnerability: What got lost in translation," *Adweek*, http://www.adweek.com/news/advertising-branding/beauty-vulnerability-what-got-lost-translation-152909.

131 **different ages and genders respond:** Frank N. Magid Associates (2011), "How America shops and spends 2011," Newspaper Association of America, http://www .naa.org/docs/newspapermedia/data/howamericashopsandspends_2011.pdf. Nielsen (8 Mar 2013), "Does gender matter?" http://www.nielsen.com/us/en/ insights/news/2013/does-gender-matter-.html.

131 **Lenddo is a Philippine company:** Katie Lobosco (27 Aug 2013), "Facebook friends could change your credit score," CNN, http://money.cnn.com/2013/08/26/technol ogy/social/facebook-credit-score.

131 **American Express has reduced:** Carrie Teegardin (21 Dec 2008), "Card companies adjusting credit limits: For some, lowering based on where they shop," *Atlanta Journal-Constitution*, https://web.archive.org/web/20110728060844/http://www.ajc.com/news/ content/business/stories/2008/12/21/creditcards_1221.html.

131 **the "panoptic sort":** Oscar H. Gandy Jr. (1993), *The Panoptic Sort: A Political Economy of Personal Information*, Westview Press, http://books.google.com/books?id=wre FAAAAMAAJ.

131 **power to use discriminatory criteria:** This paper discusses all the different ways companies can discriminate with big data. Solon Barocas and Andrew D. Selbst (14 Sep 2014), "Big data's disparate impact," Social Science Research Network, http:// papers.ssrn.com/sol3/papers.cfm?abstract_id=2477899.

131 **High-end restaurants:** Casey Johnston (13 Apr 2014), "When the restaurant you Googled Googles you back," *Ars Technica*, http://arstechnica.com/staff/2014/04/ when-the-restaurant-you-googled-googles-you-back.

132 **If you allow your insurance company:** Hilary Osborne (13 Aug 2012), "Aviva to trial smartphone car insurance technology," *Guardian*, http://www.theguardian.com/ money/2012/aug/13/aviva-trial-smartphone-car-insurance-technology. Randall Stross (25 Nov 2012), "So you're a good driver? Let's go to the monitor," *New York Times*, http:// www.nytimes.com/2012/11/25/business/seeking-cheaper-insurance-drivers- accept-monitoring-devices.html. Brad Tuttle (6 Aug 2013), "Big data is my copilot: Auto insurers push devices that track driving habits," *Time*, http://business.time.com/ 2013/08/06/big-data-is-my-copilot-auto-insurers-push-devices-that-track-driv ing-habits.

132 **distributing Fitbits to its employees:** Nancy Gohring (7 Jul 2014), "This company saved $300k on insurance by giving employees Fitbits," *CiteWorld*, http://www.cite world.com/article/2450823/internet-of-things/appirio-fitbit-experiment.html.

132 **several schools are requiring:** Lee Crane (5 Sep 2013), "Gym class is about to get even worse for the athletically dis-inclined," *Digital Trends*, http://www.digitaltrends .com/sports/gym-class-is-about-to-get-even-worse-for-the-athletically-dis-in clined. Emily Miels (28 May 2014), "Heart rate monitors allow Memorial High School students to get the most out of their workouts," *Leader-Telegram*, http://www.leader- telegram.com/news/front_page/article_ec2f0b72-e627-11e3-ac95-0019bb2963f4 .html. Katie Wiedemann (14 Aug 2014), "Heart rate monitors now required in Dubuque P.E. classes," KCRG, http://www.kcrg.com/subject/news/heart-rate-monitors-now- required-in-dubuque-physical-education-classes-20140814.

132 **Hewlett-Packard analyzed:** Joel Schechtman (14 Mar 2013), "Book: HP piloted pro- gram to predict which workers would quit," *Wall Street Journal*, http://blogs.wsj.com/ cio/2013/03/14/book-hp-piloted-program-to-predict-which-workers-would-quit.

132 **Workplace surveillance is:** This paper gives an excellent overview of workplace

surveillance. Alex Roxenblat, Tamara Kneese, and danah boyd (8 Oct 2014), "Workplace surveillance," *Data and Society Research Institute*, http://www.datasociety.net/pubs/fow/WorkplaceSurveillance.pdf.

132 **our employer is the most dangerous:** Ellen Messmer (31 Mar 2010), "Feel like you're being watched at work? You may be right," *Network World*, http://www.networkworld.com/article/2205938/data-center/feel-like-you-re-being-watched-at-work--you-may-be-right.html. Ann Bednarz (24 Feb 2011), "Pay no attention to that widget recording your every move," *Network World*, http://www.networkworld.com/article/2200315/data-breach/pay-no-attention-to-that-widget-recording-your-every-move.html. Josh Bersin (25 Jun 2014), "Quantified self: Meet the quantified employee," *Forbes*, http://www.forbes.com/sites/joshbersin/2014/06/25/quantified-self-meet-the-quantified-employee.

132 **corporate electronic communications:** This is an excellent review of workplace monitoring techniques and their effects on privacy. Corey A. Ciocchetti (2010), "The eavesdropping employer: A twenty-first century framework for employee monitoring," Daniels College of Business, University of Denver, http://www.futureofprivacy.org/wp-content/uploads/2010/07/The_Eavesdropping_Employer_%20A_Twenty-First_Century_Framework.pdf.

132 **new field called "workplace analytics":** Don Peck (20 Nov 2013), "They're watching you at work," *Atlantic*, http://www.theatlantic.com/magazine/archive/2013/12/theyre-watching-you-at-work/354681. Hannah Kuchler (17 Feb 2014), "Data pioneers watching us work," *Financial Times*, http://www.ft.com/intl/cms/s/2/d56004b0-9581-11e3-9fd6-00144feab7de.html.

132 **For some people, that's okay:** A friend told me about her feelings regarding personalized advertising. She said that, as an older woman, she keeps getting ads for cosmetic medical procedures, drugs for "old" diseases, and other things that serve as a constant reminder of her age. She finds it unpleasant. Lynn Sudbury and Peter Simcock (2008), "The senior taboo? Age based sales promotions, self-perceived age and the older consumer," *European Advances in Consumer Research* 8, http://www.acrwebsite.org/volumes/eacr/vol8/eacr_vol8_28.pdf.

133 **people are refraining from looking up:** Deborah C. Peel (7 Feb 2014), "Declaration of Deborah C. Peel, M.D., for Patient Privacy Rights Foundation in support of Plaintiffs' Motion for Partial Summary Judgment," *First Unitarian Church et al. v. National Security Agency et al.* (3:13-cv-03287 JSW), United States District Court for the Northern District of California, https://www.eff.org/files/2013/11/06/all plaintiffsdeclarations.pdf.

133 **surveillance data is being used:** Andrew Odlyzko (5–6 Jun 2014), "The end of privacy and the seeds of capitalism's destruction," Privacy Law Scholars Conference, Washington, D.C., http://www.law.berkeley.edu/plsc.htm.

134 **In their early days:** Paddy Kamen (5 Jul 2001), "So you thought search engines offer up neutral results? Think again," *Toronto Star*, http://www.commercialalert.org/issues/culture/search-engines/so-you-thought-search-engines-offer-up-neutral-results-think-again.

134 **search engines visually differentiated:** Gary Ruskin (16 Jul 2001), Letter to Donald Clark, US Federal Trade Commission, re: Deceptive advertising complaint against AltaVista Co., AOL Time Warner Inc., Direct Hit Technologies, iWon Inc., LookSmart Ltd., Microsoft Corp. and Terra Lycos S.A., Commercial Alert, http://

www.commercialalert.org/PDFs/SearchEngines.pdf. Heather Hippsley (27 Jun 2002), Letter to Gary Ruskin re: Complaint requesting investigation of various Internet search engine companies for paid placement and paid inclusion programs, US Federal Trade Commission, http://www.ftc.gov/sites/default/files/documents/closing_letters/commercial-alert-response-letter/commercialalertletter.pdf.

134 **Google is now accepting money:** Danny Sullivan (30 May 2012), "Once deemed evil, Google now embraces 'paid inclusion,'" *Marketing Land*, http://marketingland.com/once-deemed-evil-google-now-embraces-paid-inclusion-13138.

134 **FTC is again taking an interest:** Michael Cooney (25 Jun 2013), "FTC tells Google, Yahoo, Bing, others to better differentiate ads in web content searches," *Network World*, http://www.networkworld.com/community/blog/ftc-tells-google-yahoo-bing-others-better-differentiate-ads-web-content-searches. Mary K. Engle (24 Jun 2013), "Letter re: Search engine advertising practices," US Federal Trade Commission, http://www.ftc.gov/sites/default/files/attachments/press-releases/ftc-consumer-protection-staff-updates-agencys-guidance-search-engine-industryon-need-distinguish/130625searchenginegeneralletter.pdf.

134 **Payments for placement:** Josh Constine (3 Oct 2012), "Facebook now lets U.S. users pay $7 to promote posts to the news feeds of more friends," *Tech Crunch*, http://techcrunch.com/2012/10/03/us-promoted-posts.

134 **increasing voter turnout:** Robert M. Bond et al. (13 Sep 2012), "A 61-million-person experiment in social influence and political mobilization," *Nature* 489, http://www.nature.com/nature/journal/v489/n7415/full/nature11421.html.

134 **It would be hard to detect:** Jonathan Zittrain explores this possibility. Jonathan Zittrain (1 Jun 2014), "Facebook could decide an election without anyone ever finding out," *New Republic*, http://www.newrepublic.com/article/117878/information-fiduciary-solution-facebook-digital-gerrymandering.

135 **Facebook could easily tilt:** Many US elections are very close. A 0.01% change would have elected Al Gore in 2000. In 2008, Al Franken beat Norm Coleman in the Minnesota Senate race by only 312 votes.

135 **Google might do something similar:** Robert Epstein (23-26 May 2013), "Democracy at risk: Manipulating search rankings can shift voters' preferences substantially without their awareness," 25th Annual Meeting of the Association for Psychological Science, Washington, D.C., http://aibrt.org/downloads/EPSTEIN_and_Robertson_2013-Democracy_at_Risk-APS-summary-5-13.pdf.

135 **sinister social networking platform:** "When the amount of information is so great, so transparent, so pervasive, you can use absolutely nothing but proven facts and still engage in pure propaganda, pure herding." Dan Geer, quoted in Jonathan Zittrain (20 Jun 2014), "Engineering an election," *Harvard Law Review Forum* 127, http://harvardlawreview.org/2014/06/engineering-an-election.

135 **China does this:** Ai Weiwei (17 Oct 2012), "China's paid trolls: Meet the 50-Cent Party," *New Statesman*, http://www.newstatesman.com/politics/politics/2012/10/china%E2%80%99s-paid-trolls-meet-50-cent-party. Mara Hvistendahl (22 Aug 2014), "Study exposes Chinese censors' deepest fears," *Science* 345, http://www.sciencemag.org/content/345/6199/859.full. Gary King, Jennifer Pan, and Margaret E. Roberts (22 Aug 2014), "Reverse-engineering censorship in China: Randomized experimentation and participant observation," *Science* 345, http://www.sciencemag.org/content/345/6199/1251722.

135 **Samsung has done much:** Philip Elmer-DeWitt (16 Apr 2013), "Say it ain't so, Samsung," *Fortune*, http://fortune.com/2013/04/16/say-it-aint-so-samsung.

135 **Many companies manipulate:** Bryan Horling and Matthew Kulick, (4 Dec 2009), "Personalized search for everyone," *Google Official Blog*, http://googleblog.blogspot.com/2009/12/personalized-search-for-everyone.html. Tim Adams (19 Jan 2013), "Google and the future of search: Amit Singhal and the Knowledge Graph," *Guardian*, http://www.theguardian.com/technology/2013/jan/19/google-search-knowledge-graph-singhal-interview.

135 **The first listing in a Google search:** Chitika Online Advertising Network (7 Jun 2013), "The value of Google result positioning," https://cdn2.hubspot.net/hub/239330/file-61331237-pdf/ChitikaInsights-ValueofGoogleResultsPositioning.pdf.

135 **the Internet you see:** Joseph Turow (2013), *The Daily You: How the New Advertising Industry Is Defining Your Identity and Your Worth*, Yale University Press, http://yalepress.yale.edu/yupbooks/book.asp?isbn=9780300165012.

135 **the "filter bubble":** Eli Pariser (2011), *The Filter Bubble: What the Internet Is Hiding from You*, Penguin Books, http://www.thefilterbubble.com.

135 **on a large scale it's harmful:** Cass Sunstein (2009), *Republic.com 2.0*, Princeton University Press, http://press.princeton.edu/titles/8468.html.

135 **We don't want to live:** To be fair, this trend is older and more general than the Internet. Robert D. Putnam (2000), *Bowling Alone: The Collapse and Revival of American Community*, Simon and Schuster, http://bowlingalone.com.

135 **Facebook ran an experiment:** Adam D. I. Kramer, Jamie E. Guillory, and Jeffrey T. Hancock (17 Jun 2014), "Experimental evidence of massive-scale emotional contagion through social networks," *Proceedings of the National Academy of Sciences of the United States of America* 111, http://www.pnas.org/content/111/24/8788.full.

136 **women feel less attractive:** Lucia Moses (2 Oct 2013), "Marketers should take note of when women feel least attractive: What messages to convey and when to send them," *Adweek*, http://www.adweek.com/news/advertising-branding/marketers-should-take-note-when-women-feel-least-attractive-152753.

136 **companies want to better determine:** Mark Buchanan (17 Aug 2007), "The science of subtle signals," *strategy+business magazine*, http://web.media.mit.edu/~sandy/Honest-Signals-sb48_07307.pdf.

136 **That gives them enormous power:** All of this manipulation has the potential to be much more damaging on the Internet, because the very architecture of our social systems is controlled by corporations. Harvard law professor Lawrence Lessig has written about computing architecture as a mechanism of control. Lawrence Lessig (2006), *Code: And Other Laws of Cyberspace, Version 2.0*, Basic Books, http://codev2.cc.

136 **Candidates and advocacy groups:** Ed Pilkington and Amanda Michel (17 Feb 2012), "Obama, Facebook and the power of friendship: The 2012 data election," *Guardian*, http://www.theguardian.com/world/2012/feb/17/obama-digital-data-machine-facebook-election. Tanzina Vega (20 Feb 2012), "Online data helping campaigns customize ads," *New York Times*, http://www.nytimes.com/2012/02/21/us/politics/campaigns-use-microtargeting-to-attract-supporters.html. Nathan Abse (Oct 2012), "Big data delivers on campaign promise: Microtargeted political advertising in Election 2012," Interactive Advertising Bureau, http://www.iab.net/media/file/Innovations_In_Web_Marketing_and_Advertising_delivery.pdf.

136 **They can also fine-tune:** Sasha Issenberg (19 Dec 2012), "How President Obama's campaign used big data to rally individual voters," *MIT Technology Review*, http://www.technologyreview.com/featuredstory/509026/how-obamas-team-used-big-data-to-rally-voters.

136 **more efficiently gerrymander:** Micah Altman, Karin MacDonald, and Michael MacDonald (2005), "Pushbutton gerrymanders: How computing has changed redistricting," in *Party Lines: Competition, Partisanship, and Congressional Redistricting*, ed. Thomas E. Mann and Bruce E. Cain, Brookings Institution Press, http://openscholar .mit.edu/sites/default/files/dept/files/pushbutton.pdf. Robert Draper (19 Sep 2012), "The league of dangerous mapmakers," *Atlantic*, http://www.theatlantic.com/maga zine/archive/2012/10/the-league-of/309084. Tracy Jan (23 Jun 2013), "Turning the political map into a partisan weapon," *Boston Globe*, http://www.bostonglobe.com/news/nation/2013/06/22/new-district-maps-reaped-rewards-for-gop-congress-but-cost-fewer-moderates-more-gridlock/B6jCugm94tpBvVu77ay0wJ/story.html.

136 **fundamental effects on democracy:** Arch Puddington (9 Oct 2013), "To renew American democracy, eliminate gerrymandering," Freedom House, http://www .freedomhouse.org/blog/renew-american-democracy-eliminate-gerrymandering. Press Millen (20 Jul 2014), "With NC gerrymandering, democracy is the loser," *News Observer*, http://www.newsobserver.com/2014/07/20/4014754/with-nc-gerryman dering-democracy.html.

137 **Kevin Mitnick broke into:** John Markoff (16 Feb 1995), "A most-wanted cyberthief is caught in his own web," *New York Times*, http://www.nytimes.com/1995/02/16/us/a-most-wanted-cyberthief-is-caught-in-his-own-web.html.

137 **hackers broke into:** Robert O'Harrow Jr. (17 Feb 2005), "ID data conned from firm," *Washington Post*, http://www.washingtonpost.com/wp-dyn/articles/A30897-2005 Feb16.html.

137 **hackers broke into Home Depot's:** Brian Krebs (2 Sep 2014), "Banks: Credit card breach at Home Depot," *Krebs on Security*, http://krebsonsecurity.com/2014/09/banks-credit-card-breach-at-home-depot. Robin Sidel (18 Sep 2014), "Home Depot's 56 million card breach bigger than Target's," *Wall Street Journal*, http://online.wsj .com/articles/home-depot-breach-bigger-than-targets-1411073571.

137 **from JPMorgan Chase:** Dominic Rushe (3 Oct 2014), "JP Morgan Chase reveals massive data breach affecting 76m households," *Guardian*, http://www.theguard ian.com/business/2014/oct/02/jp-morgan-76m-households-affected-data-breach.

137 **criminals have legally purchased:** Brian Krebs (20 Oct 2013), "Experian sold consumer data to ID theft service," *Krebs on Security*, http://krebsonsecurity.com/2013/10/experian-sold-consumer-data-to-id-theft-service.

137 **Cybercrime is older than the Internet:** M. E. Kabay (2008), "A brief history of computer crime: An introduction for students," Norwich University, http://www .mekabay.com/overviews/history.pdf.

137 **Or he files a fake tax return:** This is becoming a huge problem in the US. Michael Kranish (16 Feb 2014), "IRS is overwhelmed by identity theft fraud," *Boston Globe*, http://www.bostonglobe.com/news/nation/2014/02/16/identity-theft-taxpayer-in formation-major-problem-for-irs/7SC0BarZMDvy07bbhDXwvN/story.html. Steve Kroft (21 Sep 2014), "Biggest IRS scam around: Identity tax refund fraud," *CBS News*, http://www.cbsnews.com/news/irs-scam-identity-tax-refund-fraud-60-minutes.

138 **Government databases:** In 2014, we learned that Chinese hackers broke into a

database containing personal information about US security-clearance holders. We don't know whether these were criminals looking for information to help them commit fraud, or government intelligence personnel looking for information to help them coerce people in positions of access. Michael S. Schmidt, David E. Sanger, and Nicole Perlroth (9 Jul 2014), "Chinese hackers pursue key data on U.S. workers," *New York Times*, http://www.nytimes.com/2014/07/10/world/asia/chinese-hackers-pursue-key-data-on-us-workers.html.

138 **many more data vulnerabilities:** This is just an example. A piece of malware infected over 1,000 companies in 2014, stealing credit card details. Many of the companies infected did not know they were victims. Nicole Perlroth (8 Sep 2014), "Home Depot data breach could be the largest yet," *New York Times*, http://bits.blogs .nytimes.com/2014/09/08/home-depot-confirms-that-it-was-hacked.

138 **arrested in 2010 for "sextortion":** Richard Winton (1 Sep 2011), "'Sextortion': 6 years for O.C. hacker who victimized women, girls," *Los Angeles Times*, http:// latimesblogs.latimes.com/lanow/2011/09/sextortion-six-years-for-oc-hacker-who-forced-women-to-give-up-naked-pics-.html.

138 **The most insidious RATs:** Nate Anderson (10 Mar 2013), "Meet the men who spy on women through their webcams," *Ars Technica*, http://arstechnica.com/tech-pol icy/2013/03/rat-breeders-meet-the-men-who-spy-on-women-through-their-web cams.

139 **computer companies that spied:** Kashmir Hill (25 Sep 2012), "FTC says rent-to-own computers captured couples having sex," *Forbes*, http://www.forbes.com/sites/ kashmirhill/2012/09/25/ftc-its-not-cool-to-put-spyware-on-rent-to-own-comput ers-without-customer-consent. Dara Kerr (22 Oct 2013), "Aaron's computer rental chain settles FTC spying charges," *CNET*, http://www.cnet.com/news/aarons-com puter-rental-chain-settles-ftc-spying-charges.

9: BUSINESS COMPETITIVENESS

140 **I wrote my first book:** The book had a 1994 copyright date, but was published in October 1993. Bruce Schneier (1994), *Applied Cryptography: Protocols, Algorithms, and Source Code in C*, Wiley, https://www.schneier.com/book-applied.html.

140 **It was a big deal:** Wired (Apr 1996), "On newsstands now: Crypto catalog," *Wired*, http://archive.wired.com/wired/archive/4.04/updata.html.

141 **over 250 cryptography products:** Stephen T. Walker (12 Oct 1993), "Oral testimony by Stephen T. Walker, President, Trusted Information Systems, Inc., for Subcommittee on Economic Policy, Trade and Environment, Committee on Foreign Affairs, US House of Representatives," http://fas.org/irp/congress/1993_hr/931012_ walker_oral.htm.

141 **It was a scare story:** Here are some references for the current scare story in action. Ellen Nakashima (26 Jul 2014), "Proliferation of new online communications services poses hurdles for law enforcement," *Washington Post*, http://www.washingtonpost .com/world/national-security/proliferation-of-new-online-communications-ser vices-poses-hurdles-for-law-enforcement/2014/07/25/645b13aa-0d21-11e4-b8e5-d0de80767fc2_story.html. Orin Kerr (19 Sep 2014), "Apple's dangerous game," *Washington Post*, http://www.washingtonpost.com/news/volokh-conspiracy/wp/2014/

09/19/apples-dangerous-game. Brent Kendall (25 Sep 2014), "FBI director raises concerns about smartphones," *Wall Street Journal*, http://online.wsj.com/articles/fbi-di rector-raises-concerns-about-smartphone-security-plans-1411671434.

141 **They passed the CALEA law:** FBI director Louis Freeh put it this way: "We're in favor of strong encryption, robust encryption. The country needs it, industry needs it. We just want to make sure we have a trap door and key under some judge's authority where we can get there if somebody is planning a crime." A similar quote from the FBI's general counsel from 2010 was in Chapter 6. Brock N. Meeks (12 May 1995), "Jacking in from the narco-terrorist encryption port," *CyberWire Dispatch*, http://www.cyberwire.com/cwd/cwd.95.05.12a.html.

141 **This was marketed as "key escrow":** Wayne Madsen (Nov 1994), "The Clipper controversy," *Information Systems Security* 3, http://www.sciencedirect.com/science/arti cle/pii/1353485894900973. Matt Blaze (5–9 Dec 2011), "Key escrow from a safe distance: Looking back at the Clipper Chip," 27th Annual Computer Security Applications Conference, Orlando, Florida, http://www.crypto.com/papers/escrow-acsac11.pdf.

141 **device with the Clipper Chip:** The US military had something similar from the NSA since 1987: the STU-III. Department of Defense Security Institute (Feb 1997), "STU-III handbook for industry," http://www.tscm.com/STUIIIhandbook.html.

142 **Nobody wanted encryption:** Hal Abelson et al. (Jun 1999), "The risks of key recovery, key escrow, and trusted third-party encryption," *World Wide Web Journal* 2, https://www.schneier.com/paper-key-escrow.html.

142 **The US government was the only:** Crypto Museum (2014), "AT&T TSD-3600-E Telephone Encryptor," http://www.cryptomuseum.com/crypto/att/tsd3600.

142 **other key escrow initiatives:** Dorothy E. Denning and Dennis K. Branstad (Mar 1996), "A taxonomy for key escrow encryption systems," *Communications of the ACM* 39, http://faculty.nps.edu/dedennin/publications/Taxonomy-CACM.pdf.

142 **over 800 encryption products:** Lance J. Hoffman et al. (10 Jun 1999), "Growing development of foreign encryption products in the face of U.S. export regulations," Report GWU-CPI-1999-02, Cyberspace Policy Institute, George Washington University School of Engineering and Applied Science, http://cryptome.org/cpi-survey.htm.

142 **the crypto wars:** This is a good account of those times. Steven Levy (May 1993), "Crypto rebels," *Wired*, http://archive.wired.com/wired/archive/1.02/crypto.reb els_pr.html.

143 **NSA surveillance is costing:** These three aspects were discussed in this document. Danielle Kehl et al. (29 Jul 2014), "Surveillance costs: The NSA's impact on the economy, Internet freedom and cyberspace," Open Technology Institute, New America Foundation, http://www.newamerica.net/publications/policy/surveillance_costs_the_nsas_ impact_on_the_economy_internet_freedom_cybersecurity.

143 **the PRISM program:** Barton Gellman and Laura Poitras (7 Jun 2013), "U.S., British intelligence mining data from nine U.S. Internet companies in broad secret program," *Washington Post*, http://www.washingtonpost.com/investigations/us-intel ligence-mining-data-from-nine-us-internet-companies-in-broad-secret-pro gram/2013/06/06/3a0c0da8-cebf-11e2-8845-d970ccb04497_story.html.

143 **US cloud companies were losing:** David Gilbert (4 Jul 2013), "Companies turn to Switzerland for cloud storage following NSA spying revelations," *International Business Times*, http://www.ibtimes.co.uk/business-turns-away-dropbox-towards-swit zerland-nsa-486613.

143 **moving their data outside the US:** Ellen Messmer (8 Jan 2014), "NSA scandal spooking IT pros in UK, Canada," *Network World*, http://www.networkworld.com/ article/2173190/security/nsa-scandal-spooking-it-pros-in-uk--canada.html.

143 **NSA revelations made executives:** NTT Communications (28 Mar 2014), "NSA after-shocks: How Snowden has changed ICT decision-makers' approach to the cloud," http://nsaaftershocks.com/wp-content/themes/nsa/images/NTTC_Report_ WEB.pdf.

143 **Estimates of how much business:** Daniel Castro (5 Aug 2013), "How much will PRISM cost the U.S. cloud computing industry?" Information Technology and Inno- vation Foundation, http://www.itif.org/publications/how-much-will-prism-cost- us-cloud-computing-industry. Andrea Peterson (7 Aug 2013), "NSA snooping could cost U.S. tech companies $35 billion over three years," *Washington Post*, http://www .washingtonpost.com/blogs/the-switch/wp/2013/08/07/nsa-snooping-could-cost- u-s-tech-companies-35-billion-over-three-years.

143 **Forrester Research believes:** James Staten (14 Aug 2013), "The cost of PRISM will be larger than ITIF projects," *James Staten's Blog*, http://blogs.forrester.com/james_ staten/13-08-14-the_cost_of_prism_will_be_larger_than_itif_projects.

143 **Cisco reported:** Christopher Mims (14 Nov 2013), "Cisco's disastrous quarter shows how NSA spying could freeze US companies out of a trillion-dollar opportunity," *Quartz*, http://qz.com/147313/ciscos-disastrous-quarter-shows-how-nsa-spying-could-freeze- us-companies-out-of-a-trillion-dollar-opportunity.

143 **AT&T also reported:** Anton Troianovski, Thomas Gryta, and Sam Schechner (30 Oct 2013), "NSA fallout thwarts AT&T," *Wall Street Journal*, http://online.wsj.com/ news/articles/SB10001424052702304073204579167873091999730.

143 **IBM lost sales in China:** Wolf Richter (17 Oct 2013), "NSA revelations kill IBM hardware sales in China," *Testosterone Pit*, http://www.testosteronepit.com/ home/2013/10/17/nsa-revelations-kill-ibm-hardware-sales-in-china.html.

143 **So did Qualcomm:** Spencer E. Ante (22 Nov 2013), "Qualcomm CEO says NSA fall- out impacting China business," *Wall Street Journal*, http://online.wsj.com/news/ articles/SB10001424052702304337404579214353783842062.

143 **Verizon lost a large German:** Mark Scott (26 Jun 2014), "Irked by NSA, Germany cancels deal with Verizon," *New York Times*, http://www.nytimes.com/2014/06/27/ business/angered-by-nsa-activities-germany-cancels-verizon-contract.html.

143 **There's more:** Stephen L. Carter (13 Feb 2014), "U.S. tech's costly trust gap," *Bloomberg BusinessWeek*, http://www.businessweek.com/articles/2014-02-13/nsa- snooping-backlash-could-cost-u-dot-s-dot-tech-companies-billions. Claire Cain Miller (22 Mar 2014), "N.S.A. spying imposing cost on tech firms," *New York Times*, http://www.nytimes.com/2014/03/22/business/fallout-from-snowden-hurting- bottom-line-of-tech-companies.html.

144 **wrote to the Obama administration:** Ashley Lau (18 May 2014), "Cisco chief urges Obama to curb NSA surveillance activity," Reuters, http://www.reuters.com/ article/2014/05/18/cisco-systems-nsa-idUSL1N0O40F420140518.

144 **the NSA intercepts:** Sean Gallagher (14 May 2014), "Photos of an NSA 'upgrade' factory show Cisco router getting implant," *Ars Technica*, http://arstechnica.com/ tech-policy/2014/05/photos-of-an-nsa-upgrade-factory-show-cisco-router-get- ting-implant.

144 **Mark Zuckerberg said it best:** Dominic Rushe (11 Sep 2013), "Zuckerberg: US gov-

ernment 'blew it' on NSA surveillance," *Guardian*, http://www.theguardian.com/technology/2013/sep/11/yahoo-ceo-mayer-jail-nsa-surveillance.

144 **trying to build a domestic cloud:** Cornelius Rahn (13 Sep 2011), "Deutsche Telekom wants 'German cloud' to shield data from U.S.," *Bloomberg News*, http://www.bloomberg.com/news/2011-09-13/deutsche-telekom-wants-german-cloud-to-shield-data-from-u-s-.html.

144 **German courts have recently ruled:** Allison Grande (20 Nov 2013), "Google's policies violate German privacy law, court says," *Law 360*, http://www.law360.com/articles/490316/google-s-policies-violate-german-privacy-law-court-says.

144 **Facebook:** Loek Essers (18 Feb 2014), "Facebook must comply with German data protection law, court rules," *PC World*, http://www.pcworld.com/article/2098720/facebook-must-comply-with-german-data-protection-law-court-rules.html.

144 **Apple:** Loek Essers (7 May 2013), "Berlin court: Apple's privacy policy violates German protection law," *Macworld*, http://www.macworld.com/article/2038070/apples-privacy-policy-violates-german-data-protection-law-berlin-court-rules.html.

144 **banning all US companies:** Der Spiegel (5 Aug 2013), "NSA blowback: German minister floats US company ban," *Der Spiegel*, http://www.spiegel.de/international/business/german-minister-on-eu-company-ban-for-privacy-violation-a-914824.html.

145 **Data privacy is shaping up:** Krista Hughes (27 Mar 2014), "Data privacy shapes up as a next-generation trade barrier," Reuters, http://www.reuters.com/article/2014/03/27/us-usa-trade-tech-analysis-idUSBREA2Q1K120140327.

145 **We also don't know:** Many US tech executives are worried about protectionism against their companies. Stephen Lawson (8 Oct 2014), "Jitters over US surveillance could break the Internet, tech executives warn," *IT World*, http://www.itworld.com/security/440886/jitters-over-us-surveillance-could-break-internet-tech-leaders-warn.

145 **stepping in to take advantage:** Georg Mascolo and Ben Scott (Oct 2013), "Lessons from the summer of Snowden: The hard road back to trust," Open Technology Institute, New America Foundation, http://www.newamerica.net/sites/newamerica.net/files/policydocs/NAF-OTI-WC-SummerOfSnowdenPaper.pdf. Mark Scott (11 Jun 2014), "European firms turn privacy into sales pitch," *New York Times*, http://bits.blogs.nytimes.com/2014/06/11/european-firms-turn-privacy-into-sales-pitch.

145 **hundreds of non-US companies:** ProtonMail is a Swiss company that is offering e-mail services that are beyond the reach of the NSA. John Biggs (23 Jun 2014), "ProtonMail is a Swiss secure mail provider that won't give you up to the NSA," *Tech Crunch*, http://techcrunch.com/2014/06/23/protonmail-is-a-swiss-secure-mail-provider-that-wont-give-you-up-to-the-nsa.

145 **A 2000 study found:** Jonathan W. Palmer, Joseph P. Bailey, and Samer Faraj (Mar 2000), "The role of intermediaries in the development of trust on the WWW: The use and prominence of trusted third parties and privacy statements," *Journal of Computer-Mediated Communication* 5, http://onlinelibrary.wiley.com/doi/10.1111/j.1083-6101.2000.tb00342.x/full.

146 **customers were willing to pay more:** Janice Y. Tsai et al. (Jun 2007), "The effect of online privacy information on purchasing behavior: An experimental study," 6th Workshop on the Economics of Information Security (WEIS), Pittsburgh, Pennsylvania, http://weis2007.econinfosec.org/papers/57.pdf.

146 **there are exceptions:** Cadie Thompson (7 Mar 2014), "Want privacy online? Start-ups bet users are ready to pay," *NBC News*, http://www.nbcnews.com/tech/security/want-privacy-online-start-ups-bet-users-are-ready-pay-n47186.

146 *not* **tracking its users:** DuckDuckGo, http://www.duckduckgo.com.

146 **Ello is a social network:** Sharon Profis (26 Sep 2014), "10 things to know about Ello, the ad-free social network," CNET, http://www.cnet.com/how-to/what-is-ello-the-ad-free-social-network.

10: PRIVACY

147 **The most common misconception:** This article from 1979, for example, looks at privacy as a way to conceal facts about oneself in order to inflate one's reputation. Richard A. Posner (1979), "Privacy, secrecy and reputation," *Buffalo Law Review* 28, http://chicagounbound.uchicago.edu/cgi/viewcontent.cgi?article=2832&context=journal_articles.

147 **this makes no sense:** Daniel Solove regularly demolishes the "nothing to hide" argument. Daniel J. Solove (Nov/Dec 2007), "'I've got nothing to hide' and other mis-understandings of privacy," *San Diego Law Review* 44, http://papers.ssrn.com/sol3/papers.cfm?abstract_id=998565. Daniel J. Solove (15 May 2011), "Why privacy matters even if you have 'nothing to hide,'" *Chronicle of Higher Education*, https://chronicle.com/article/Why-Privacy-Matters-Even-if/127461.

147 **Google CEO Eric Schmidt:** Huffington Post (25 May 2011), "Google CEO on privacy (VIDEO): 'If you have something you don't want anyone to know, maybe you shouldn't be doing it,'" *Huffington Post*, http://www.huffingtonpost.com/2009/12/07/google-ceo-on-privacy-if_n_383105.html.

147 **Schmidt banned employees:** Elinor Mills (14 Jul 2005), "Google balances privacy, reach," *CNET*, http://news.cnet.com/Google-balances-privacy,-reach/2100-1032_3-5787483.html. Randall Stross (28 Aug 2005), "Google anything, so long as it's not Google," *New York Times*, http://www.nytimes.com/2005/08/28/technology/28digi.html.

147 **Facebook's Mark Zuckerberg:** Bobbie Johnson (10 Jan 2010), "Privacy no longer a social norm, says Facebook founder," *Guardian*, http://www.theguardian.com/technology/2010/jan/11/facebook-privacy.

148 **bought the four houses:** Brian Bailey (11 Oct 2013), "Mark Zuckerberg buys four houses near his Palo Alto home," *San Jose Mercury News*, http://www.mercurynews.com/business/ci_24285169/mark-zuckerberg-buys-four-houses-near-his-palo-alto-home.

148 **few secrets we don't tell** *someone***:** Peter E. Sand (Spring/Summer 2006), "The privacy value," *I/S: A Journal of Law and Policy* 2, http://moritzlaw.osu.edu/students/groups/is/files/2012/02/5-Sand.pdf.

148 **We use pseudonyms:** Judith Donath (2014), *The Social Machine: Designs for Living Online*, MIT Press, https://encrypted.google.com?id=XcgmnwEACAAJ.

148 **a remarkable naïveté:** David Kirkpatrick (2010), *The Facebook Effect: The Inside Story of the Company That Is Connecting the World*, Simon and Schuster, https://www.facebook.com/thefacebookeffect.

148 **Privacy is an inherent human right:** Eben Moglen defines privacy in three parts: "First is secrecy, or our ability to keep the content of our messages known

only to those we intend to receive them. Second is anonymity, or secrecy about who is sending and receiving messages, where the content of the messages may not be secret at all. It is very important that anonymity is an interest we can have both in our publishing and in our reading. Third is autonomy, or our ability to make our own life decisions free from any force that has violated our secrecy or our anonymity." Eben Moglen (27 May 2014), "Privacy under attack: The NSA files revealed new threats to democracy," *Guardian*, http://www.theguardian.com/technology/2014/may/27/-sp-privacy-under-attack-nsa-files-revealed-new-threats-democracy. George Washington University Law School professor Daniel J. Solove divides privacy into six parts: "(1) the right to be let alone; (2) limited access to the self; (3) secrecy; (4) control of personal information; (5) personhood; and (6) intimacy." Daniel J. Solove (Jul 2002), "Conceptualizing privacy," *California Law Review* 90, http://scholarship.law.berkeley.edu/cgi/viewcontent.cgi?article=1408&context=californialawreview.

148 **Internet ethnographer danah boyd:** danah boyd (2014), *It's Complicated: The Social Lives of Networked Teens*, Yale University Press, p. 76, http://www.danah.org/books/ItsComplicated.pdf.

148 **When we lose privacy:** This dystopia has been explored in fiction. Dave Eggers (2013), *The Circle*, Knopf, http://www.mcsweeneys.net/articles/a-brief-q-a-with-dave-eggers-about-his-new-novel-the-circle.

149 **You may know this feeling:** Helen Nissenbaum (Fall 2011), "A contextual approach to privacy online," *Daedalus* 11, http://www.amacad.org/publications/daedalus/11_fall_nissenbaum.pdf. Alexis C. Madrigal (29 Mar 2012), "The philosopher whose fingerprints are all over the FTC's new approach to privacy," *Atlantic*, http://www.theatlantic.com/technology/print/2012/03/the-philosopher-whose-fingerprints-are-all-over-the-ftcs-new-approach-to-privacy/254365.

149 **Privacy violations are intrusions:** George E. Panichas (May 2014), "An intrusion theory of privacy," *Res Publica* 20, http://link.springer.com/article/10.1007%2Fs11158-014-9240-3.

149 **strong physiological basis for privacy:** Peter H. Klopfer and Daniel I. Rubenstein (Summer 1977), "The concept *privacy* and its biological basis," *Journal of Social Issues* 33, https://www.princeton.edu/~dir/pdf_dir/1977_Klopfer_Rubenstein_JSocIssues.pdf.

149 **Surveillance makes us feel like prey:** Peter Watts (9 May 2014), "The scorched earth society: A suicide bomber's guide to online privacy," Symposium of the International Association of Privacy Professionals, Toronto, Ontario, http://www.rifters.com/real/shorts/TheScorchedEarthSociety-transcript.pdf.

149 **Studies show that we are:** Sidney M. Jourard (Spring 1966), "Some psychological aspects of privacy," *Law and Contemporary Problems* 31, http://scholarship.law.duke.edu/cgi/viewcontent.cgi?article=3110&context=lcp. Stephen T. Margulis (Jul 2003), "Privacy as a social issue and behavioral concept," *Journal of Social Issues* 59, http://onlinelibrary.wiley.com/doi/10.1111/1540-4560.00063/abstract.

149 **Surveillance strips us of our dignity:** James Q. Whitman (Apr 2004), "The two western cultures of privacy: Dignity versus liberty," *Yale Law Journal* 113, http://www.yalelawjournal.org/article/the-two-western-cultures-of-privacy-dignity-versus-liberty.

149 **It threatens our very selves:** Michael P. Lynch (22 Jun 2013), "Privacy and the threat

to the self," *New York Times*, http://opinionator.blogs.nytimes.com/2013/06/22/priva
cy-and-the-threat-to-the-self.

150 **Oliver North learned this:** They were subpoenaed in the Iran-Contra affair.
Michael Tackett (14 Feb 1987), "Computer log tells Iran tale: Printouts give probers
memos by key officials," *Chicago Tribune*, http://articles.chicagotribune.com/1987-
02-14/news/8701120148_1_nsc-staff-professional-office-system-profs.

150 **Bill Gates learned this:** Elizabeth Wasserman (17 Nov 1998), "Gates deposition
makes judge laugh in court," CNN, http://edition.cnn.com/TECH/computing/9811/17/
judgelaugh.ms.idg.

150 **100 female celebrities learned it:** Bill Hutchinson (31 Aug 2014), "Jennifer Lawrence, other celebrities have nude photos leaked on Internet after massive hacking
scandal," *New York Daily News*, http://www.nydailynews.com/entertainment/gos
sip/jennifer-lawrence-celebrities-nude-photos-leaked-internet-article-1.192
3369.

150 **Some bars record the IDs:** The company Servall Biometrics markets driver's license
scanners for this purpose. Servall Biometrics (2014), "ClubSecurity: ID scanners for
bars and nightclubs," http://www.servallbiometrics.com/index.php/products.

151 **Charles Stross described this:** Charles Stross (14 May 2007), "Shaping the future,"
Charlie's Diary, http://www.antipope.org/charlie/blog-static/2007/05/shaping_
the_future.html.

151 **We won't forget anything:** A Ted Chiang short story explores this idea. Ted Chiang
(Fall 2013), "The truth of fact, the truth of feeling," *Subterranean Press Magazine*, http://
subterraneanpress.com/magazine/fall_2013/the_truth_of_fact_the_truth_of_feel
ing_by_ted_chiang.

151 **Having everything recorded:** Communication scholar Harold Innis first described
the bias inherent in different forms of communication. He noted that some mediums
preserved communication in time, while others worked across space. These proper-
ties led to different forms of control and social engagement. Harold Innis (1951), *The
Bias of Communication*, University of Toronto Press, http://books.google.com?
id=egwZyS26booC.

151 **We misremember:** The research here is fascinating. We even forget details of important events. Several researchers studied people's memories of where they were when
the space shuttle exploded, the O. J. Simpson verdict was announced, and the terrorist
attacks of 9/11 occurred. John Neil Bohannon III (Jul 1988), "Flashbulb memories for
the space shuttle disaster: A tale of two theories," *Cognition* 29, http://www.sciencedi
rect.com/science/article/pii/0010027788900364. Heike Schmolck, Elizabeth A. Buffalo, and Larry R. Squire (Jan 2000), "Memory distortions develop over time: Recollec-
tions of the O. J. Simpson trial verdict after 15 and 32 months," *Psychological Science* 11,
http://psycnet.apa.org/psycinfo/2000-15144-007. Jennifer M. Talarico and David C.
Rubin (Sep 2003), "Confidence, not consistency, characterizes flashbulb memories,"
Psychological Science 14, http://911memory.nyu.edu/abstracts/talarico_rubin.pdf.
Andrew R. A. Conway et al. (Jul 2008), "Flashbulb memory for 11 September 2001,"
Applied Cognitive Psychology 23, http://onlinelibrary.wiley.com/doi/10.1002/acp.1497/
abstract.

151 **Even minor infractions:** Michelle Natividad Rodriguez and Maurice Emsellem
(Mar 2011), "65 million need not apply: The case for reforming criminal background

checks for employment," National Employment Law Project, http://www.nelp.org/page/-/65_Million_Need_Not_Apply.pdf.

151 **Losing the ephemeral:** Wendy Hui Kyong Chun (Autumn 2008), "The enduring ephemeral, or the future is a memory," *Critical Inquiry* 35, http://www.ucl.ac.uk/art-history/events/past-imperfect/chun-reading.

152 **That's just plain wrong:** Bruce Schneier (27 Feb 2014), "NSA robots are 'collecting' your data, too, and they're getting away with it," *Guardian*, http://www.theguardian.com/commentisfree/2014/feb/27/nsa-robots-algorithm-surveillance-bruce-schneier.

152 **all sorts of NSA word games:** Electronic Frontier Foundation (2013), "The government's word games when talking about NSA domestic spying," https://www.eff.org/nsa-spying/wordgames. Trevor Timm (14 Aug 2013), "A guide to the deceptions, misinformation, and word games officials use to mislead the public about NSA surveillance," Electronic Frontier Foundation, https://www.eff.org/deeplinks/2013/08/guide-deceptions-word-games-obfuscations-officials-use-mislead-public-about-nsa.

152 **The word "collect":** A 1982 procedures manual says, ". . . information shall be considered as 'collected' only when it has been received for use by an employee of a DoD intelligence component in the course of his official duties." And ". . . data acquired by electronic means is 'collected' only when it has been processed into intelligible form." US Department of Defense, Office of the Under Secretary of Defense for Policy (Dec 1982), "Procedures governing the activities of DoD intelligence components that affect United States persons," DoD 5240-1R, p. 15, http://www.fas.org/irp/doddir/dod/d5240_1_r.pdf.

152 **It doesn't mean collect:** The DoD even cautions against thinking about and using words accurately. "Procedure 2 introduces the reader of DoD 5240.1-R to his or her first entry into the 'maze' of the regulation. To begin the journey, it is necessary to stop first and adjust your vocabulary. The terms and words used in DoD 5240.1-R have very specific meanings, and it is often the case that one can be led astray by relying on the generic or commonly understood definition of a particular word." US Defense Intelligence Agency, Defense HUMINT Service (Aug 2004), *Intelligence Law Handbook*, Defense Intelligence Management Document CC-0000-181-95, https://www.aclu.org/files/assets/eo12333/DIA/Intelligence%20Law%20Handbook%20Defense%20HUMINT%20Service.pdf.

152 **All those books are stored:** Andrea Mitchell (9 Jun 2013), "Transcript of Andrea Mitchell's interview with Director of National Intelligence James Clapper," *NBC News*, http://www.nbcumv.com/mediavillage/networks/nbcnews/pressreleases?pr=contents/press-releases/2013/06/09/nbcnewsexclusiv1370799482417.xml.

152 **Clapper asserts he didn't lie:** Ron Wyden (12 Mar 2013), "Wyden in intelligence hearing on GPS surveillance & Nat'l Security Agency collection," *YouTube*, https://www.youtube.com/watch?v=QwiUVUJmGjs.

152 **no human reads those Gmail messages:** Google (2014), "Ads in Gmail," https://support.google.com/mail/answer/6603?hl=en.

153 **You might be told:** In 2010, the TSA assured us that its full-body scanners were not saving data. Documents released to the Electronic Privacy Information Center showed that the scanners were shipped with hard drives and USB ports. Ginger McCall (3 Aug 2010), "Documents reveal that body scanners routinely store and record images," Electronic Privacy Information Center, http://epic.org/press/EPIC_Body_Scanner_Press_Release_08_03_10.pdf. Declan McCullagh (4 Aug 2010), "Feds admit

storing checkpoint body scan images," *CNET*, http://www.cnet.com/news/feds-admit-storing-checkpoint-body-scan-images. US Transportation Security Administration (6 Aug 2010), "TSA response to 'Feds admit storing checkpoint body scan images,'" *TSA Blog*, http://blog.tsa.gov/2010/08/tsa-response-to-feds-admit-storing.html.

153 **The primary difference:** This is why we're not worried about Furbies, but would be if they contained recording devices. Although for a while, the NSA was worried. British Broadcasting Corporation (13 Jan 1999), "Furby toy or Furby spy?" *BBC News*, http://news.bbc.co.uk/2/hi/americas/254094.stm.

154 **If you do object:** Bruce Schneier (21 Oct 2013), "Why the NSA's defense of mass data collection makes no sense," *Atlantic*, http://www.theatlantic.com/politics/archive/2013/10/why-the-nsas-defense-of-mass-data-collection-makes-no-sense/280715.

154 **The means to perform identification:** Bruce Schneier (2000), *Secrets and Lies: Digital Security in a Networked World*, Wiley, chap. 9, http://www.wiley.com/Wiley CDA/WileyTitle/productCd-0471453803.html.

155 **We can't even be sure:** Charles Glaser (1 Jun 2011), "Deterrence of cyber attacks and U.S. national security," Report GW-CSPRI-2011-5, George Washington University Cyber Security Policy and Research Institute, http://www.cspri.seas.gwu.edu/uploads/2/1/3/2/21324690/2011-5_cyber_deterrence_and_security_glaser.pdf. Joseph S. Nye Jr. (May 2010), "Cyber power," Harvard Kennedy School, Belfer Center for Science and International Affairs, http://belfercenter.ksg.harvard.edu/files/cyber-power.pdf.

155 **The 2007 cyberattack against Estonia:** Charles Clover (11 Mar 2009), "Kremlin-backed group behind Estonia cyber blitz," *Financial Times*, http://www.ft.com/cms/s/0/57536d5a-0ddc-11de-8ea3-0000779fd2ac.html. Christian Love (12 Mar 2009), "Kremlin loyalist says launched Estonia cyber-attack," Reuters, http://www.reuters.com/article/2009/03/12/us-russia-estonia-cyberspace-idUSTRE52B4D820090312.

156 **It took analysts months:** Nicole Perlroth (31 Jan 2013), "Hackers in China attacked the Times for last 4 months," *New York Times*, http://www.nytimes.com/2013/01/31/technology/chinese-hackers-infiltrate-new-york-times-computers.html.

156 **who was behind Stuxnet:** William J. Broad, John Markoff, and David E. Sanger (15 Jan 2011), "Israeli test on worm called crucial in Iran nuclear delay," *New York Times*, http://www.nytimes.com/2011/01/16/world/middleeast/16stuxnet.html. David E. Sanger (1 Jun 2012), "Obama order sped up wave of cyberattacks against Iran," *New York Times*, http://www.nytimes.com/2012/06/01/world/middleeast/obama-ordered-wave-of-cyberattacks-against-iran.html.

156 **proposals to eliminate anonymity:** Limiting anonymity doesn't eliminate trolls. People's behavior online is complicated, and more a function of the loosening of social restrictions than of anonymity. John Suler (Jun 2004), "The online disinhibition effect," *Cyber Psychology and Behavior* 7, http://online.liebertpub.com/doi/abs/10.1089/1094931041291295.

156 **annoys countries like China:** Philipp Winter and Stefan Lindskog (6 Aug 2012), "How the Great Firewall of China is blocking Tor," Second USENIX Workshop on Free and Open Communications on the Internet, Bellevue, Washington, https://www.usenix.org/system/files/conference/foci12/foci12-final2.pdf.

157 **Leon Panetta said publicly:** Leon Panetta (11 Oct 2012), "Remarks by Secretary Panetta on cybersecurity to the Business Executives for National Security, New York

City," US Department of Defense, http://www.defense.gov/transcripts/transcript
.aspx?transcriptid=5136.

11: SECURITY

158 **we tend to focus on rare:** Bruce Schneier (17 May 2007), "Virginia Tech lesson:
Rare risks breed irrational responses," *Wired*, http://archive.wired.com/politics/
security/commentary/securitymatters/2007/05/securitymatters_0517.

158 **we fear terrorists more:** Washington's Blog (15 Aug 2014), "You're nine times more
likely to be killed by a police officer than a terrorist," *Washington's Blog*, http://www
.washingtonsblog.com/2014/08/youre-nine-times-likely-killed-police-officer-ter
rorist.html.

159 **connect-the-dots metaphor:** Spencer Ackerman (13 Dec 2013), "NSA review to
leave spying programs largely unchanged, reports say," *Guardian*, http://www
.theguardian.com/world/2013/dec/13/nsa-review-to-leave-spying-programs-large
ly-unchanged-reports-say.

159 **That doesn't stop us:** When we look back at an event and see all the evidence, we
often believe we should have connected the dots. There's a name for that: hindsight
bias. The useful bits of data are obvious after the fact, but were only a few items in a
sea of millions of irrelevant data bits beforehand. And those data bits could have
been assembled to point in a million different directions.

159 **the "narrative fallacy":** Nassim Nicholas Taleb (2007), "The narrative fallacy," in
The Black Swan: The Impact of the Highly Improbable, Random House, chap. 6, http://
www.fooledbyrandomness.com.

159 **The TSA's no-fly list:** Associated Press (2 Feb 2012), "U.S. no-fly list doubles in one
year," *USA Today*, http://usatoday30.usatoday.com/news/washington/story/2012-
02-02/no-fly-list/52926968/1.

159 **the watch list:** Eric Schmitt and Michael S. Schmidt (24 Apr 2013), "2 U.S. agencies
added Boston bomb suspect to watch list," *New York Times*, https://www.nytimes
.com/2013/04/25/us/tamerlan-tsarnaev-bomb-suspect-was-on-watch-lists.html.

160 **Detecting credit card fraud:** E. W. T. Ngai et al. (Feb 2011), "The application of
data mining techniques in financial fraud detection: A classification framework
and an academic review of literature," *Decision Support Systems* 50, https://www
.sciencedirect.com/science/article/pii/S0167923610001302. Siddhartha Bhattacha-
ryya et al. (Feb 2011), "Data mining for credit card fraud: A comparative study," *Decision Support Systems* 50, https://www.sciencedirect.com/science/article/pii/
S0167923610001326.

160 **a billion active credit cards:** Erika Harrell and Lynn Langton (12 Dec 2013), "Victims of identity theft 2012," US Bureau of Justice Statistics, http://www.bjs.gov/
index.cfm?ty=pbdetail&iid=4821.

160 **the IRS uses data mining:** US Government Accountability Office (2013), "Offshore
tax evasion: IRS has collected billions of dollars, but may be missing continued evasion," Report GAO-13-318, http://www.gao.gov/assets/660/653369.pdf. IBM Corporation (2011), "New York State Tax: How predictive modeling improves tax revenues and
citizen equity," https://www.ibm.com/smarterplanet/us/en/leadership/nystax/assets/
pdf/0623-NYS-Tax_Paper.pdf.

160 **the police use it:** Walter L. Perry et al. (2013), "Predictive policing: The role of crime forecasting in law enforcement operations," RAND Corporation, https://www.ncjrs .gov/pdffiles1/nij/grants/243830.pdf.

160 **Terrorist plots are different:** John Mueller and Mark G. Stewart (2011), *Terror, Security, and Money: Balancing the Risks, Benefits, and Costs of Homeland Security*, Oxford University Press, chap. 2, http://books.google.com/books?id=jyYGL2jZBC4C.

160 **even highly accurate . . . systems:** Jeff Jonas and Jim Harper (11 Dec 2006), "Effective counterterrorism and the limited role of predictive data mining," Cato Institute, http://www.cato.org/publications/policy-analysis/effective-counterterrorism-limited-role-predictive-data-mining. Fred H. Cate (Summer 2008), "Government data mining: The need for a legal framework," *Harvard Civil Rights-Civil Liberties Law Review* 43, http://www.law.harvard.edu/students/orgs/crcl/vol43_2/435-490_Cate.pdf.

161 **false positives completely overwhelm:** G. Stuart Mendenhall and Mark Schmidhofer (Winter 2012-13), "Screening tests for terrorism," *Regulation*, http://object .cato.org/sites/cato.org/files/serials/files/regulation/2013/1/v35n4-4.pdf. Corey Chivers (6 Jun 2013), "How likely is the NSA PRISM program to catch a terrorist?" *Bayesian Biologist*, http://bayesianbiologist.com/2013/06/06/how-likely-is-the-nsa-prism-program-to-catch-a-terrorist. Marcy Wheeler (15 Jun 2013), "The inefficacy of Big Brother: Associations and the terror factory," *Empty Wheel*, http://www.empty wheel.net/2013/06/15/the-inefficacy-of-big-brother-associations-and-the-terror-factory.

161 **millions of people will be falsely accused:** In statistics, this is called the base rate fallacy, and it applies in other domains as well. For example, even highly accurate medical tests are problematic as screening tools if the incidence of the disease is sufficiently rare in the general population. I am deliberately not walking you through the math. Those who are interested can read the details. Jeff Jonas and Jim Harper (11 Dec 2006), "Effective counterterrorism and the limited role of predictive data mining," Cato Institute, http://object.cato.org/sites/cato.org/files/pubs/pdf/ pa584.pdf.

161 **"you need the haystack":** J. D. Tuccille (19 Jul 2013), "Why spy on everybody? Because 'you need the haystack to find the needle,' says NSA chief," *Reason*, http:// reason.com/blog/2013/07/19/why-spy-on-everybody-because-you-need-th.

161 **adding much more noise:** Mike Masnick (15 Oct 2013), "Latest revelations show how collecting all the haystacks to find the needle makes the NSA's job harder," *Tech Dirt*, https://www.techdirt.com/articles/20131014/17303424880/latest-revelations-show-how-collecting-all-haystacks-to-find-data-makes-nsas-job-harder.shtml.

161 **so much irrelevant data:** Chris Young (12 Mar 2012), "Military intelligence redefined: Big Data in the battlefield," *Forbes*, http://www.forbes.com/sites/techon omy/2012/03/12/military-intelligence-redefined-big-data-in-the-battlefield.

161 **NSA's eavesdropping program:** Matt Briggs (7 Jun 2013), "Data mining: PRISM, NSA and false positives: Update," *William M. Briggs*, http://wmbriggs.com/blog/ ?p=8239.

162 **thousands of tips:** Lowell Bergman et al. (17 Jan 2006), "Spy agency data after Sept. 11 led F.B.I. to dead ends," *New York Times*, http://www.nytimes.com/2006/01/17/ politics/17spy.html.

162 **Suspicious Activity Reports:** US Government Accountability Office (26 Mar 2013), "Information sharing: Additional actions could help ensure that efforts to

share terrorism-related suspicious activity reports are effective," Report GAO-13-233, http://www.gao.gov/assets/660/652995.pdf.

162 **led to just one success:** Yochai Benkler (8 Oct 2013), "Fact: The NSA gets negligible intel from Americans' metadata. So end collection," *Guardian*, http://www.theguardian.com/commentisfree/2013/oct/08/nsa-bulk-metadata-surveillance-intelligence. Peter Bergen (Jan 2014), "Do NSA's bulk surveillance programs stop terrorists?" New America Foundation, http://newamerica.net/publications/policy/do_nsas_bulk_surveillance_programs_stop_terrorists.

162 **that was probably trumped up:** Marcy Wheeler (12 Dec 2013), "Did DOJ prosecute Basaaly Moalin just to have a Section 215 'success'?" *Empty Wheel*, http://www.emptywheel.net/2013/12/12/did-doj-prosecute-basaaly-moalin-just-to-have-a-section-215-success.

162 **Each rare individual:** Airplane security provides many examples. In 2001, Richard Reid put a bomb in his shoe, and the primary effect is that we've all had to take our shoes off at airports since then.

163 **Several analyses:** Francis Gouillart (10 Jun 2013), "Big data NSA spying is not even an effective strategy," *Fortune*, http://management.fortune.cnn.com/2013/06/10/big-data-nsa-spying-is-not-even-an-effective-strategy. Ed Pilkington and Nicholas Watt (12 Jun 2013), "NSA surveillance played little role in foiling terror plots, experts say," *Guardian*, http://www.theguardian.com/world/2013/jun/12/nsa-surveillance-data-terror-attack. Washington's Blog (13 Jun 2013), "The dirty little secret about mass surveillance: It doesn't keep us safe," *Washington's Blog*, http://www.washingtonsblog.com/2013/06/the-dirty-little-secret-about-nsa-spying-it-doesnt-work.html.

163 **Data mining is simply the wrong tool:** Jeffrey W. Seifert (3 Apr 2008), "Data mining and homeland security: An overview," Congressional Research Service, http://www.fas.org/sgp/crs/homesec/RL31798.pdf.

163 **enabled the NSA to prevent 9/11:** Peter Bergen (30 Dec 2013), "Would NSA surveillance have stopped 9/11 plot?" CNN, http://www.cnn.com/2013/12/30/opinion/bergen-nsa-surveillance-september-11.

163 **wasn't able to prevent:** Simon Shuster (19 Apr 2013), "The brothers Tsarnaev: Clues to the motives of the alleged Boston bombers," *Time*, http://world.time.com/2013/04/19/the-brothers-tsarnaevs-motives.

163 **The NSA collected data:** Marcy Wheeler (12 Apr 2014), "The day after government catalogs data NSA collected on Tsarnaevs, DOJ refuses to give Dzhokhar notice," *Empty Wheel*, http://www.emptywheel.net/2014/04/12/the-day-after-government-catalogs-data-nsa-collected-on-tsarnaevs-doj-refuses-to-give-dzhokhar-notice.

163 **failures were the result:** National Commission on Terrorist Attacks (2004), *The 9/11 Commission Report: Final Report of the National Commission on Terrorist Activities upon the United States*, http://www.gpo.gov/fdsys/pkg/GPO-911REPORT/pdf/GPO-911REPORT.pdf.

163 **Mass surveillance didn't catch:** Dan Eggen, Karen DeYoung, and Spencer S. Hsu (27 Dec 2009), "Plane suspect was listed in terror database after father alerted U.S. officials," *Washington Post*, http://www.washingtonpost.com/wp-dyn/content/article/2009/12/25/AR2009122501355.html.

163 **the liquid bombers ... were captured:** Dominic Casciani (7 Sep 2009), "Liquid bomb plot: What happened," *BBC News*, http://news.bbc.co.uk/2/hi/uk_news/8242479.stm.

163 **comes from targeted surveillance:** The NSA has touted 54 terrorist successes,

but this number doesn't pass scrutiny. Most weren't actually terrorist plots, and they were mostly outside the US. Justin Elliott and Theodoric Meyer (23 Oct 2013), "Claim on 'attacks thwarted' by NSA spreads despite lack of evidence," *Pro Publica*, http://www.propublica.org/article/claim-on-attacks-thwarted-by-nsa-spreads-despite-lack-of-evidence.

163 **FBI identifies potential terrorist plots:** Kevin Strom and John Hollywood (2010), "Building on clues: Examining successes and failures in detecting U.S. terrorist plots," Institute for Homeland Security Solutions, http://sites.duke.edu/ihss/files/2011/12/Building_on_Clues_Strom.pdf.

164 **the money we're wasting:** Bruce Schneier (8 Sep 2005), "Terrorists don't do movie plots," *Wired*, http://archive.wired.com/politics/security/commentary/securitymatters/2005/09/68789.

165 **the attacker has the advantage:** Bruce Schneier (2012), *Liars and Outliers: Enabling the Trust That Society Needs to Thrive*, Wiley, chap. 16, http://www.wiley.com/WileyCDA/WileyTitle/productCd-1118143302.html.

165 **It's easier to break things:** Ross Anderson (2 Oct 2001), "Why information security is hard: An economic perspective," University of Cambridge Computer Laboratory, http://www.acsac.org/2001/papers/110.pdf. Matthew Miller, Jon Brickey, and Gregory Conti (29 Nov 2012), "Why your intuition about cyber warfare is probably wrong," *Small Wars Journal*, http://smallwarsjournal.com/jrnl/art/why-your-intuition-about-cyber-warfare-is-probably-wrong.

165 **Complexity is the worst enemy:** Bruce Schneier (19 Nov 1999), "A plea for simplicity: You can't secure what you don't understand," *Information Security*, https://www.schneier.com/essay-018.html.

165 **Software security is generally poor:** Edward Tufte (2003), "Why producing good software is difficult," *Edward Tufte Forum*, http://www.edwardtufte.com/bboard/q-and-a-fetch-msg?msg_id=0000D8. James Kwak (8 Aug 2012), "Software runs the world: How scared should we be that so much of it is so bad?" *Atlantic*, http://www.theatlantic.com/business/archive/2012/08/software-runs-the-world-how-scared-should-we-be-that-so-much-of-it-is-so-bad/260846.

166 **retailer Target Corporation:** Michael Riley et al. (13 Mar 2014), "Missed alarms and 40 million stolen credit card numbers: How Target blew it," *Bloomberg Businessweek*, http://www.businessweek.com/articles/2014-03-13/target-missed-alarms-in-epic-hack-of-credit-card-data.

166 **a catastrophe for the company:** Elizabeth A. Harris et al. (17 Jan 2014), "A sneaky path into Target customers' wallets," *New York Times*, http://www.nytimes.com/2014/01/18/business/a-sneaky-path-into-target-customers-wallets.html.

166 **its CEO, Gregg Steinhafel, resigned:** Elizabeth A. Harris (6 May 2014), "Faltering Target parts ways with chief," *New York Times*, http://www.nytimes.com/2014/05/06/business/target-chief-executive-resigns.html.

167 **Compare this with the:** Nicole Perlroth (31 Jan 2013), "Hackers in China attacked the Times for last 4 months," *New York Times*, http://www.nytimes.com/2013/01/31/technology/chinese-hackers-infiltrate-new-york-times-computers.html.

169 **Multiprogram Research Facility:** Its current goal is exaflop computation speeds, or one quintillion operations per second. James Bamford (15 Mar 2012), "The NSA is building the country's biggest spy center (watch what you say)," *Wired*, http://www.wired.com/threatlevel/2012/03/ff_nsadatacenter/all.

169 **It secretly inserts weaknesses:** Bruce Schneier (4 Oct 2013), "Attacking Tor: How the NSA targets users' online anonymity," *Guardian*, http://www.theguardian.com/world/2013/oct/04/tor-attacks-nsa-users-online-anonymity.

169 **"endpoint security is so terrifically weak":** Glenn Greenwald and Edward Snowden (17 Jun 2013), "Edward Snowden: NSA whistleblower answers reader questions," *Guardian*, http://www.theguardian.com/world/2013/jun/17/edward-snowden-nsa-files-whistleblower.

171 **Discoverers can sell vulnerabilities:** The ethics of this is discussed here. Serge Egelman, Cormac Herley, and Paul C. van Oorschot (9-12 Sep 2013), "Markets for zero-day exploits: Ethics and implications," New Security Paradigms Workshop, Banff, Alberta, Canada, http://www.nspw.org/papers/2013/nspw2013-egelman.pdf.

171 **a robust market in zero-days:** Stefan Frei (5 Dec 2013), "The known unknowns: Empirical analysis of publicly-unknown security vulnerabilities," NSS Labs, https://www.nsslabs.com/system/files/public-report/files/The%20Known%20Unknowns_1.pdf.

171 **both governments and:** Andy Greenberg (21 Mar 2012), "Meet the hackers who sell spies the tools to crack your PC (and get paid six-figure fees)," *Forbes*, http://www.forbes.com/sites/andygreenberg/2012/03/21/meet-the-hackers-who-sell-spies-the-tools-to-crack-your-pc-and-get-paid-six-figure-fees. Both Russia and North Korea are big spenders when it comes to zero-days. Nicole Perlroth and David E. Sanger (13 Jul 2013), "Nations buying as hackers sell flaws in computer code," *New York Times*, http://www.nytimes.com/2013/07/14/world/europe/nations-buying-as-hackers-sell-computer-flaws.html. Office of the Secretary of Defense (4 Feb 2014), "Military and security developments involving the Democratic People's Republic of North Korea 2013," http://www.defense.gov/pubs/North_Korea_Military_Power_Report_2013-2014.pdf.

171 **discoverers can sell to criminals:** Dancho Danchev (2 Nov 2008), "Black market for zero day vulnerabilities still thriving," *ZDNet*, http://www.zdnet.com/blog/security/black-market-for-zero-day-vulnerabilities-still-thriving/2108.

171 **Undiscovered zero-day vulnerabilities:** Here is the most important research into that question. Eric Rescorla (7 Feb 2005), "Is finding security holes a good idea?" RTFM, Inc., http://www.rtfm.com/bugrate.pdf. Sandy Clark et al. (6–10 Dec 2010), "Familiarity breeds contempt: The honeymoon effect and the role of legacy code in zero-day vulnerabilities," 26th Annual Computer Security Applications Conference, Austin, Texas, http://dl.acm.org/citation.cfm?id=1920299. Andy Ozment and Stuart E. Schechter (11 May 2006), "Milk or wine: Does software security improve with age?" MIT Lincoln Laboratory, https://research.microsoft.com/pubs/79177/milkorwine.pdf.

171 **economics of software development:** This is even worse with embedded devices and the Internet of Things. Bruce Schneier (6 Jan 2014), "The Internet of Things is wildly insecure—and often unpatchable," *Wired*, http://www.wired.com/2014/01/theres-no-good-way-to-patch-the-internet-of-things-and-thats-a-huge-problem.

171 **how the NSA and GCHQ think:** James Ball, Julian Borger, and Glenn Greenwald (5 Sep 2013), "Revealed: How US and UK spy agencies defeat internet privacy and security," *Guardian*, http://www.theguardian.com/world/2013/sep/05/nsa-gchq-encryption-codes-security.

171 **We know the NSA:** These four points were made in this document. Danielle Kehl et al. (29 Jul 2014), "Surveillance costs: The NSA's impact on the economy, Internet free-

dom and cyberspace," Open Technology Institute, New America Foundation, http://www.newamerica.net/publications/policy/surveillance_costs_the_nsas_impact_on_the_economy_internet_freedom_cybersecurity.

172 **the White House tried to clarify:** Michael Daniel (28 Apr 2014), "Heartbleed: Understanding when we disclose cyber vulnerabilities," *White House Blog*, http://www.whitehouse.gov/blog/2014/04/28/heartbleed-understanding-when-we-disclose-cyber-vulnerabilities.

172 **Stuxnet, used four zero-days:** Ryan Naraine (14 Sep 2010), "Stuxnet attackers used 4 Windows zero-day exploits," *ZDNet*, http://www.zdnet.com/blog/security/stuxnet-attackers-used-4-windows-zero-day-exploits/7347.

172 **agency jargon NOBUS:** Andrea Peterson (4 Oct 2013), "Why everyone is left less secure when the NSA doesn't help fix security flaws," *Washington Post*, http://www.washingtonpost.com/blogs/the-switch/wp/2013/10/04/why-everyone-is-left-less-secure-when-the-nsa-doesnt-help-fix-security-flaws.

172 **it discloses and closes:** David E. Sanger (12 Apr 2014), "Obama lets N.S.A. exploit some Internet flaws, officials say," *New York Times*, http://www.nytimes.com/2014/04/13/us/politics/obama-lets-nsa-exploit-some-internet-flaws-officials-say.html. Kim Zetter (15 Apr 2014), "Obama: NSA must reveal bugs like Heartbleed, unless they help the NSA," *Wired*, http://www.wired.com/2014/04/obama-zero-day.

172 **how to make NOBUS decisions:** There have been some attempts. Andy Ozment (2–3 Jun 2005), "The likelihood of vulnerability rediscovery and the social utility of vulnerability hunting," Workshop on Economics and Information Security, Cambridge, Massachusetts, http://infosecon.net/workshop/pdf/10.pdf.

172 **They're inherently destabilizing:** Robert Axelrod and Rumen Iliev (28 Jan 2014), "Timing of cyber conflict," *Proceedings of the National Academy of Sciences of the United States of America* 111, http://www.pnas.org/content/early/2014/01/08/1322638111.full.pdf.

173 **Backdoors aren't new:** This is a nice nontechnical description of backdoors. Serdar Yegulalp (13 Jun 2014), "Biggest, baddest, boldest software backdoors of all time," *Tech World*, http://www.techworld.com.au/slideshow/547475/pictures_biggest_baddest_boldest_software_backdoors_all_time.

173 **the US government is deliberately:** James Ball, Julian Borger, and Glenn Greenwald (5 Sept 2013), "Revealed: How US and UK spy agencies defeat Internet privacy and security," *Guardian*, http://www.theguardian.com/world/2013/sep/05/nsa-gchq-encryption-codes-security. Guardian (5 Sep 2013), "Project Bullrun—classification guide to the NSA's decryption program," *Guardian*, http://www.theguardian.com/world/interactive/2013/sep/05/nsa-project-bullrun-classification-guide, http://cryptome.org/2013/09/nsa-bullrun-2-16-guardian-13-0905.pdf.

173 **One of the NSA documents:** US National Security Agency (2012), "SIGINT Enabling Project," http://www.propublica.org/documents/item/784285-sigint-enabling-project.html.

173 **The NSA also pressured Microsoft:** Lorenzo Franceschi-Bicchierai (11 Sep 2013), "Did the FBI lean on Microsoft for access to its encryption software?" *Mashable*, http://mashable.com/2013/09/11/fbi-microsoft-bitlocker-backdoor.

174 **Deliberately created vulnerabilities:** Jesse Emspak (16 Aug 2012), "FBI surveillance backdoor might open door to hackers," *NBC News*, http://www.nbcnews.com/id/48695618/ns/technology_and_science-security/t/fbi-surveillance-backdoor-

might-open-door-hackers. Ben Adida et al. (17 May 2013), "CALEA II: Risks of wiretap modifications to endpoints," Center for Democracy and Technology, https://www.cdt.org/files/pdfs/CALEAII-techreport.pdf. Bruce Schneier (29 May 2013), "The FBI's new wiretap plan is great news for criminals," *Foreign Policy*, http://www.foreignpolicy.com/articles/2013/05/29/the_fbi_s_new_wiretapping_plan_is_great_news_for_criminals.

174 **Government-mandated access:** Susan Landau (2011), *Surveillance or Security? The Risks Posed by New Wiretapping Technologies*, MIT Press, http://mitpress.mit.edu/books/surveillance-or-security. New York Times (21 Sep 2013), "Close the NSA's backdoors," *New York Times*, http://www.nytimes.com/2013/09/22/opinion/sunday/close-the-nsas-back-doors.html.

174 **Ericsson built this:** Vassilis Prevelakis and Diomidis Spinellis (29 Jun 2007), "The Athens affair," *IEEE Spectrum*, http://spectrum.ieee.org/telecom/security/the-athens-affair.

174 **Something similar occurred in Italy:** Alexander Smoltczyk (5 Oct 2006), "Eavesdropping on La Bella Vita: Listening quietly in Italy," *Der Spiegel*, http://www.spiegel.de/international/spiegel/eavesdropping-on-la-bella-vita-listening-quietly-in-italy-a-440880.html. John Leyden (14 Apr 2008), "Preatoni breaks silence over Telecom Italia spying probe," *Register*, http://www.theregister.co.uk/2008/04/14/telecom_italia_spying_probe_update.

174 **Chinese hackers exploited:** Bruce Schneier (23 Jan 2010), "U.S. enables Chinese hacking of Google," CNN, http://www.cnn.com/2010/OPINION/01/23/schneier.google.hacking/index.html.

174 **every phone switch sold:** Susan Landau (23 Mar 2012), "The large immortal machine and the ticking time bomb," Social Sciences Resarch Network (republished Nov 2013 in *Journal of Telecommunications and High Tech Law* 11), http://papers.ssrn.com/sol3/papers.cfm?abstract_id=2028152.

174 **NSA regularly exploits:** Lawrence Lessig (20 Oct 2014), "Institutional corruption and the NSA: Lawrence Lessig interviews Edward Snowden at Harvard Law," *LeakSourceInfo/YouTube*, http://www.youtube.com/watch?v=DksIFG3Skb4.

174 **Bermuda phone system:** Ryan Devereaux, Glenn Greenwald, and Laura Poitras (19 May 2014), "Data pirates of the Caribbean: The NSA is recording every cell phone call in the Bahamas," *Intercept*, https://firstlook.org/theintercept/article/2014/05/19/data-pirates-caribbean-nsa-recording-every-cell-phone-call-bahamas.

174 **Another objective of the SIGINT:** US National Security Agency (2012), "SIGINT Enabling Project," http://www.propublica.org/documents/item/784285-sigint-enabling-project.html.

175 **NSA influenced the adoption:** Craig Timberg and Ashkan Soltani (14 Dec 2013), "NSA cracked popular cellphone encryption," *Washington Post*, http://www.washingtonpost.com/business/technology/by-cracking-cellphone-code-nsa-has-capacity-for-decoding-private-conversations/2013/12/13/e119b598-612f-11e3-bf45-61f69f54fc5f_story.html.

175 **a backdoored random number generator:** Dan Shumow and Niels Ferguson (21 Aug 2007), "On the possibility of a backdoor in the NIST SP800-90 Dual_EC_PRNG," Microsoft Corporation, http://rump2007.cr.yp.to/15-shumow.pdf. Matthew Green (18 Sep 2013), "The many flaws of Dual_EC_DRBG," *Cryptography Engineering*, http://blog.cryptographyengineering.com/2013/09/the-many-flaws-of-dualec

drbg.html. D.W. (18 Sep 2013), "Explaining weakness of Dual_EC_PRNG to wider audience?" *Cryptography Stack Exchange*, https://crypto.stackexchange.com/questions/10417/explaining-weakness-of-dual-ec-drbg-to-wider-audience.

175 **the NSA masquerades:** Ryan Gallagher and Glenn Greenwald (12 Mar 2014), "How the NSA plans to infect 'millions' of computers with malware," *Intercept*, https://firstlook.org/theintercept/article/2014/03/12/nsa-plans-infect-millions-computers-malware.

175 **The UK's GCHQ can find:** Glenn Greenwald (14 Jul 2014), "Hacking online polls and other ways British spies seek to control the Internet," *Intercept*, https://firstlook.org/theintercept/2014/07/14/manipulating-online-polls-ways-british-spies-seek-control-internet.

175 **just better-funded hacker tools:** Bruce Schneier (21 May 2014), "The NSA is not made of magic," *Schneier on Security*, https://www.schneier.com/blog/archives/2014/05/the_nsa_is_not_.html.

175 **Academics have discussed ways:** Nicholas Weaver (13 Mar 2014), "A close look at the NSA's most powerful Internet attack tool," *Wired*, http://www.wired.com/2014/03/quantum. Matt Brian (20 Jun 2014), "Hackers use Snowden leaks to reverse-engineer NSA surveillance devices," *Engadget*, http://www.engadget.com/2014/06/20/nsa-bugs-reverse-engineered.

176 **one top-secret program:** Bruce Schneier (4 Oct 2013), "Attacking Tor: How the NSA targets users' online anonymity," *Guardian*, http://www.theguardian.com/world/2013/oct/04/tor-attacks-nsa-users-online-anonymity.

176 **technology that allows:** We have learned a lot about QUANTUM since my initial story. Nicholas Weaver (13 Mar 2014), "A close look at the NSA's most powerful attack tool," *Wired*, http://www.wired.com/2014/03/quantum. Claudio Guarnieri (24 Jan 2014), "The Internet is compromised," *Medium*, https://medium.com/@botherder/the-internet-is-compromised-4c66984abd7d. Der Spiegel (30 Dec 2013), "NSA-Dokumente: So bernimmt der Geheimdienst fremde Rechner," *Der Spiegel*, http://www.spiegel.de/fotostrecke/nsa-dokumente-so-uebernimmt-der-geheimdienst-fremde-rechner-fotostrecke-105329.html. Der Spiegel (30 Dec 2013), "NSA-Dokumente: So knackt der Geheimdienst Internetkonten," *Der Spiegel*, http://www.spiegel.de/fotostrecke/nsa-dokumente-so-knackt-der-geheimdienst-internetkonten-fotostrecke-105326.html.

176 **Chinese government uses:** Nicholas Weaver, Robin Sommer, and Vern Paxson (8–11 Feb 2009), "Detecting forged TCP reset packets," Network and Distributed System Security Symposium (NDSS 2009), San Diego, California, http://www.icir.org/vern/papers/reset-injection.ndss09.pdf.

176 **Hacking Team sells:** Morgan Marquis-Boire (15 Aug 2014), "Schrodinger's cat video and the death of clear-text," Citizen Lab, Munk School of Global Affairs, University of Toronto, https://citizenlab.org/2014/08/cat-video-and-the-death-of-clear-text. Morgan Marquis-Boire (15 Aug 2014), "You can get hacked just by watching this cat video on YouTube," *Intercept*, https://firstlook.org/theintercept/2014/08/15/cat-video-hack. Cora Currier and Morgan Marquis-Boire (30 Oct 2014), "Secret manuals show the spyware sold to despots and cops worldwide," *Intercept*, https://firstlook.org/theintercept/2014/10/30/hacking-team.

176 **there are hacker tools:** Airpwn (27 May 2009), "Airpwn 1.4," *Sourceforge*, http://airpwn.sourceforge.net/Airpwn.html.

176 **Techniques first developed:** Tom Simonite (19 Sep 2012), "Stuxnet tricks copied by computer criminals," *MIT Technology Review*, http://www.technologyreview .com/news/429173/stuxnet-tricks-copied-by-computer-criminals.

176 **software that Elcomsoft sells:** Andy Greenberg (2 Sep 2014), "The police tool that pervs use to steal nude pics from Apple's iCloud," *Wired*, http://www.wired.com/ 2014/09/eppb-icloud.

176 **once-secret techniques:** Mobistealth (2014), "Ultimate cell phone monitoring software," http://www.mobistealth.com.

177 **Stuxnet's target was Iran:** Jarrad Shearer (26 Feb 2013), "W32.Stuxnet," Symantec Corporation, http://www.symantec.com/security_response/writeup.jsp?docid=2010-071400-3123-99.

177 **computers owned by Chevron:** Matthew J. Schwartz (12 Nov 2012), "Cyber weapon friendly fire: Chevron Stuxnet fallout," *Information Week*, http://www.dark reading.com/attacks-and-breaches/cyber-weapon-friendly-fire-chevron-stuxnet-fallout/d/d-id/1107339.

177 **industrial plants in Germany:** Robert McMillan (14 Sep 2010), "Siemens: Stuxnet worm hit industrial systems," *Computer World*, http://www.computerworld.com/s/ article/9185419/Siemens_Stuxnet_worm_hit_industrial_systems.

177 **failure of an Indian satellite:** Jeffrey Carr (29 Sep 2010), "Did the Stuxnet worm kill India's Insat-4B satellite?" *Forbes*, http://www.forbes.com/sites/firewall/2010/09/29/ did-the-stuxnet-worm-kill-indias-insat-4b-satellite.

177 **Internet blackout in Syria:** James Bamford (13 Aug 2014), "Edward Snowden: The untold story," *Wired*, http://www.wired.com/2014/08/edward-snowden.

177 **a technique called DNS injection:** Anonymous (Jul 2012), "The collateral damage of internet censorship by DNS injection," *ACM SIGCOMM Computer Communication Review* 42, http://www.sigcomm.org/sites/default/files/ccr/papers/2012/July/231 7307-2317311.pdf.

177 **public revelations of the NSA's activities:** Ian Bremmer (18 Nov 2013), "Lost legitimacy: Why governing is harder than ever," *Foreign Affairs*, http://www.foreignaf fairs.com/articles/140274/ian-bremmer/lost-legitimacy.

177 **US interests have been significantly harmed:** Vivienne Walt (30 Jun 2013), "European officials infuriated by alleged NSA spying on friendly diplomats," *Time*, http:// world.time.com/2013/06/30/european-officials-infuriated-by-alleged-nsa-spy ing-on-friendly-diplomats. Anne Gearan (21 Oct 2013), "Report that NSA collected French phone records causing diplomatic headache for U.S.," *Washington Post*, http:// www.washingtonpost.com/world/national-security/report-that-nsa-collected-french-phone-records-causing-diplomatic-headache-for-us/2013/10/21/bfa74f22-3a76-11e3-a94f-b58017bfee6c_story.html. Zachary Keck (31 Oct 2013), "Outrage over NSA spying spreads to Asia," *Diplomat*, http://thediplomat.com/2013/10/outrage-over-nsa-spying-spreads-to-asia. Matthew Karnitschnig (9 Feb 2014), "NSA flap strains ties with Europe," *Wall Street Journal*, http://online.wsj.com/news/articles/SB1 0001424052702303874504579372832399168684.

177 **Relations between the US:** David E. Sanger (1 May 2014), "U.S. and Germany fail to reach a deal on spying," *New York Times*, http://www.nytimes.com/2014/05/02/ world/europe/us-and-germany-fail-to-reach-a-deal-on-spying.html. Mark Landler (2 May 2014), "Merkel signals that tension persists over U.S. spying," *New York Times*,

http://www.nytimes.com/2014/05/03/world/europe/merkel-says-gaps-with-us-over-surveillance-remain.html.

178 **Brazil's president:** Juan Forero (17 Sep 2013), "NSA spying scandal spoils dinner at the White House for Brazil's president," *Washington Post*, http://www.washington post.com/world/nsa-spying-scandal-spoils-dinner-at-the-white-house-for-bra zils-president/2013/09/17/24f5acf6-1fc5-11e3-9ad0-96244100e647_story.html.

12: PRINCIPLES

182 **if our personal spaces and records:** These issues are explored in these books. Daniel Solove (2011), *Nothing to Hide: The False Tradeoff between Privacy and Security*, Yale University Press, http://papers.ssrn.com/sol3/papers.cfm?abstract_id=1827982. Susan Landau (2011), *Surveillance or Security? The Risks Posed by New Wiretapping Technologies*, MIT Press, http://mitpress.mit.edu/books/surveillance-or-security.

182 **When the security versus privacy:** The psychology of security explains a lot of our behavior. Bruce Schneier (11–14 Jun 2008), "The psychology of security," in Serge Vaudenay, ed., *Progress in Cryptology: AFRICACRYPT 2008: First International Conference on Cryptology in Africa, Casablanca, Morocco, Proceedings*, Springer, https://www.schneier.com/paper-psychology-of-security.pdf. Daniel Gardner (2008), *The Science of Fear: Why We Fear Things We Shouldn't—And Put Ourselves in Greater Danger*, Penguin, http://books.google.com/books?id=bmyboRubog4C.

183 **The government basically said:** Of course, costs can affect different people in different ways. Politicians fear that they'll get blamed for future attacks, so they have an incentive to push for lots of visible security measures. Citizens, especially members of unpopular political and religious groups, become the obvious targets for surveillance, but lack a strong, coherent voice to fight back. And large security programs are expensive, benefiting government contractors and the politicians they support.

183 **find an acceptable trade-off:** This paper tries to model that with game theory. Tiberiu Dragu (Feb 2011), "Is there a trade-off between security and liberty? Executive bias, privacy protections, and terrorism prevention," *American Political Science Review* 105, http://journals.cambridge.org/download.php?file=%2FPSR%2FS0003055410000614a .pdf&code=193cd836312527364579326df0a7aa58.

183 **We need to recognize:** Susan Landau (2011), *Surveillance or Security? The Risks Posed by New Wiretapping Technologies*, MIT Press, http://mitpress.mit.edu/books/surveillance-or-security.

184 **Tor is an excellent example:** Electronic Frontier Foundation (28 Nov 2012), "How to help protect your online anonymity using Tor," https://www.eff.org/sites/default/files/filenode/Basic_Tor_Intro_Guide_FNL.pdf.

184 **the NSA is continually trying:** Everyone else is too, of course. Roger Dingledine (30 Jul 2014), "Tor security advisory: 'Relay early' traffic confirmation attack," *Tor Project Blog*, https://blog.torproject.org/blog/tor-security-advisory-relay-early-traffic-con firmation-attack.

184 **has been unsuccessful:** US National Security Agency (8 Jan 2007), "Tor Stinks," http://cryptome.org/2013/10/nsa-tor-stinks.pdf.

184 **the FBI was hacking into:** Kevin Poulsen (5 Aug 2014), "Visit the wrong website and the FBI could end up in your computer," *Wired*, http://www.wired.com/2014/08/operation_torpedo.

184 **both the NSA and the GCHQ:** Leo Kelion (22 Aug 2014), "NSA and GCHQ agents 'leak Tor bugs,' alleges developer," *BBC News*, http://www.bbc.com/news/technology-28886462.

185 **Governments have always spied:** Anthony Zurcher (31 Oct 2013), "Roman Empire to the NSA: A world history of government spying," *BBC News*, http://www.bbc.com/news/magazine-24749166.

185 **spy stories in the Old Testament:** John M. Cardwell (Winter 1978), "A Bible lesson on spying," *Studies in Intelligence*, http://southerncrossreview.org/44/cia-bible.htm.

185 **We don't (yet) design:** There is an important and complicated discussion that needs to happen about the relative risks of terrorism, and how much damage terrorists can do with the technologies available to them, but it is beyond the scope of this book. Bruce Schneier (14 Mar 2013), "Our security models will never work—no matter what we do," *Wired*, http://www.wired.com/2013/03/security-when-the-bad-guys-have-technology-too-how-do-we-survive.

186 **both corporations and governments:** Of course, the process of trusting is far less rational than that. Bruce Schneier (2012), *Liars and Outliers: Enabling the Trust That Society Needs to Thrive*, Wiley, http://www.wiley.com/WileyCDA/WileyTitle/productCd-1118143302.html.

186 **too much information is exempted:** Isolated bubbles of secrecy are always required in any organization, so that people within the organization can do their job properly: votes in a tenure committee, or deliberations preceding a controversial decision. Making things like this transparent can suppress some of the independence of the decision-making process. Deciders will be more concerned about how their decision processes will look to outsiders than they will be with making a good decision.

186 **we cannot judge the fairness:** Adrian J. Lee and Sheldon H. Jacobson (May 2012), "Addressing passenger risk uncertainty for aviation security screening," *Transportation Science* 46, http://pubsonline.informs.org/doi/abs/10.1287/trsc.1110.0384. Susan Stellin (21 Oct 2013), "Security check now starts long before you fly," *New York Times*, http://www.nytimes.com/2013/10/22/business/security-check-now-starts-long-before-you-fly.html. Alissa Wickham (7 Mar 2014), "TSA halts program to screen passengers' online data," *Law 360*, http://www.law360.com/articles/516452/tsa-halts-program-to-screen-passengers-online-data.

186 **the IRS's algorithms:** Amber Torrey (Apr 2008), "The discriminant analysis used by the IRS to predict profitable individual tax return audits," Bryant University, http://digitalcommons.bryant.edu/cgi/viewcontent.cgi?article=1000&context=honors_mathematics.

187 **the existing power imbalance:** This is the problem with David Brin's transparent society: transparency is not value-free. When a police officer demands to see your ID, your being able to see his ID doesn't balance things out. David Brin (1998), *The Transparent Society: Will Technology Force Us to Choose between Privacy and Freedom?* Basic Books, http://www.davidbrin.com/transparentsociety1.html.

187 **the same with transparency and surveillance:** Iceland's Pirate Party (yes, it's a real political party) put it extremely well in 2014: "The individual's right to privacy means protecting the powerless from the abuse of the more powerful, and transpar-

ency means opening the powerful to the supervision of the powerless." Paul Fontaine (19 Aug 2014), "Prime Minister learns what 'transparency' means," *Grapevine*, http://grapevine.is/news/2014/08/19/prime-minister-learns-what-transparency-means.

187 **Institutional transparency reduces:** There are, of course, exceptions to this rule. There is value in ankle monitors for people convicted of crimes, even though that reduces the power of the criminals being monitored.

187 **Transparency doesn't come easily:** Peter Watts (9 May 2014), "The scorched earth society: A suicide bomber's guide to online privacy," Symposium of the International Association of Privacy Professionals, Toronto, Ontario, http://www.rifters.com/real/shorts/TheScorchedEarthSociety-transcript.pdf.

187 **police harass and prosecute:** Ray Sanchez (19 Jul 2010), "Growing number of prosecutions for videotaping the police," *ABC News*, http://abcnews.go.com/US/TheLaw/videotaping-cops-arrest/story?id=11179076.

187 **some jurisdictions have:** Those laws are unconstitutional. Kathryn Marchocki (25 May 2014), "Court rules Free State project president had right to film Weare police during a traffic stop," *New Hampshire Union Leader*, http://www.unionleader.com/apps/pbcs.dll/article?AID=/20140525/NEWS07/140529379.

187 **Cops in Chicago have:** David Lepeska (27 Dec 2011), "When police abuse surveillance cameras," *CityLab*, http://www.citylab.com/politics/2011/12/surveillance-cameras-threat-police-privacy/806.

187 **San Diego Police Department:** Sara Libby (18 Aug 2014), "Even when police do wear cameras, don't count on seeing the footage," *CityLab*, http://www.citylab.com/crime/2014/08/even-when-police-do-wear-cameras-you-cant-count-on-ever-seeing-the-footage/378690.

187 **police routinely prevented protesters:** Chris Matyszczyk (14 Aug 2014), "Ferguson, Mo., unrest tests legal right to film police," *CNET*, http://www.cnet.com/news/ferguson-unrest-tests-legal-right-to-film-police. Hillel Italie (19 Aug 2014), "Ferguson arrests include at least 10 journalists," Associated Press, http://abcnews.go.com/Entertainment/wireStory/ferguson-arrests-include-10-journalists-25044845.

187 **Los Angeles police even:** Cyrus Farivar (8 Apr 2014), "LAPD officers monkey-wrenched cop-monitoring gear in patrol cars," *Ars Technica*, http://arstechnica.com/tech-policy/2014/04/lapd-officers-monkey-wrenched-cop-monitoring-gear-in-patrol-cars.

187 **declining half-life of secrets:** Peter Swire (5–6 Jun 2014), "The declining half-life of secrets and the future of signals intelligence," 7th Privacy Law Scholars Conference, Washington, D.C., http://www.law.berkeley.edu/plsc.htm.

188 **the NSA spied on the cell phone:** Jacob Appelbaum et al. (23 Oct 2013), "Berlin complains: Did US tap Chancellor Merkel's mobile phone?" *Der Spiegel*, http://www.spiegel.de/international/world/merkel-calls-obama-over-suspicions-us-tapped-her-mobile-phone-a-929642.html. Ian Traynor, Philip Oltermann, and Paul Lewis (23 Oct 2013), "Angela Merkel's call to Obama: Are you bugging my mobile phone?" *Guardian*, http://www.theguardian.com/world/2013/oct/23/us-monitored-angela-merkel-german.

188 **It was a private men's club:** This excellent book on Soviet spy Kim Philby talks about the clubbiness in spy agencies. Ben Macintyre (2014), *A Spy among Friends: Kim Philby and the Great Betrayal*, Crown, http://books.google.com/books?id=wIzIAgAAQBAJ.

188 **Moving from employer to employer:** Charles Stross (18 Aug 2013), "Spy kids," *Foreign Policy*, http://www.foreignpolicy.com/articles/2013/08/28/spy_kids_nsa_surveillance_next_generation.

188 **Recall that five million:** US Office of Management and Budget (Feb 2014), "Suitability and security processes review," http://www.fas.org/sgp/othergov/omb/suitsec-2014.pdf.

188 **Younger people are much more comfortable:** USC Annenberg School for Communication and Journalism (22 Apr 2013), "Is online privacy over? Findings from the USC Annenberg Center for the Digital Future show millennials embrace a new online reality," *USC Annenberg News*, http://annenberg.usc.edu/News%20and%20Events/News/130422CDF_Millennials.aspx. Mary Madden et al. (21 May 2013), "Teens, social media, and privacy," Pew Research Internet Project, http://www.pewinternet.org/files/2013/05/PIP_TeensSocialMediaandPrivacy_PDF.pdf.

188 **tougher sell convincing this crowd:** To be fair, we don't know whether this is a substantive difference between this generation and older generations, or whether this is a simple age-cohort effect that will change as they get older and have more secrets that matter.

189 **we should strive for transparency:** I think of institutional secrecy rather like chemotherapy. Yes, the cancer treatment would kill the patient slowly, but it kills the cancer cells faster, and is therefore a net benefit. If we could find an effective cancer treatment that wasn't so toxic, we would dump chemo in a minute. Anytime we can find a less harmful substitute for institutional secrecy, we should use it.

189 **This was nicely explained:** Charlie Rose, Inc. (29 Jul 2013), "General Michael Hayden, former director of the NSA and the CIA and principal with the Chertoff Group," *The Charlie Rose Show*, http://www.charlierose.com/watch/60247615.

191 **organizations are less likely:** Nassim Nicholas Taleb and Constantine Sandis (1 Oct 2013), "The skin in the game heuristic for protection against tail events," *Review of Behavioral Economics* 1, http://papers.ssrn.com/sol3/papers.cfm?abstract_id=2298292.

191 **Advancing technology adds:** Any complex system that is both nonlinear and tightly coupled will have catastrophic failures. Charles Perrow (1984), *Normal Accidents: Living with High-Risk Technologies*, Princeton University Press, https://encrypted.google.com/books?id=VC5hYoMw4N0C.

191 **If systemic imperfections:** Supposedly it's therapeutic to think this way. Kevin Griffin (23 Sep 2011), "Step 9 of Buddhist addiction recovery: The freedom of imperfection," *Huffington Post*, http://www.huffingtonpost.com/kevin-griffin/buddhist-addiction-recovery-step-9_b_958708.html.

192 **If something is going to fail:** Yacov Y. Haimes (Apr 2009), "On the definition of resilience in systems," *Risk Analysis: An International Journal* 29, http://onlinelibrary.wiley.com/doi/10.1111/j.1539-6924.2009.01216.x/abstract.

192 **resilience comes from:** Jesse Robbins et al. (Nov 2012), "Resilience engineering: Learning to embrace failure," *Communications of the ACM* 55, http://queue.acm.org/detail.cfm?id=2371297.

192 **I am advocating for:** Some ideas are here. Warigia Bowman and L. Jean Camp (Apr 2013), "Protecting the Internet from dictators: Technical and policy solutions to ensure online freedoms," *Innovation Journal* 18, http://www.innovation.cc/scholarly-style/warigia_camp_bowman5edits18vi1a3.pdf.

192 **the NSA has been entrusted:** James Bamford (2002), *Body of Secrets: Anatomy of the Ultra-Secret National Security Agency*, Anchor, http://www.randomhouse.com/features/bamford/author.html.

193 **Jack Goldsmith, a Harvard law:** Jack Goldsmith (12 Apr 2014), "Cyber paradox: Every offensive weapon is a (potential) chink in our defense—and vice versa," *Lawfare*, http://www.lawfareblog.com/2014/04/cyber-paradox-every-offensive-weapon-is-a-potential-chink-in-our-defense-and-vice-versa.

194 **StingRay might have been:** Stephanie K. Pell and Christopher Soghoian (15 May 2014), "Your secret Stingray's no secret anymore: The vanishing government monopoly over cell phone surveillance and its impact on national security and consumer privacy," *Harvard Journal of Law and Technology* (forthcoming), http://papers.ssrn.com/sol3/papers.cfm?abstract_id=2437678.

194 **dozens of these devices:** Kim Zetter (3 Sep 2014), "Phone firewall identifies rogue cell towers trying to intercept your calls," *Wired*, http://www.wired.com/2014/09/cryptophone-firewall-identifies-rogue-cell-towers. Ashkan Soltani and Craig Timberg (17 Sep 2014), "Tech firm tries to pull back curtain on surveillance efforts in Washington," *Washington Post*, http://www.washingtonpost.com/world/national-security/researchers-try-to-pull-back-curtain-on-surveillance-efforts-in-washington/2014/09/17/f8c1f590-3e81-11e4-b03f-de718edeb92f_story.html.

13: SOLUTIONS FOR GOVERNMENT

195 **President Obama set up:** Richard A. Clarke et al. (12 Dec 2013), "Liberty and security in a changing world: Report and recommendations of the President's Review Group on Intelligence and Communications Technologies," US Executive Office of the President, http://www.whitehouse.gov/sites/default/files/docs/2013-12-12_rg_final_report.pdf.

195 **"Necessary and Proportionate" principles:** Electronic Frontier Foundation (May 2014), "Necessary and proportionate: International principles on the applications of human rights law to communications surveillance: Background and supporting legal analysis," https://en.necessaryandproportionate.org.

196 **International Principles:** Electronic Frontier Foundation (5 Jan 2014), "13 international principles on the application of human rights to communication surveillance," https://necessaryandproportionate.org/files/2014/01/05/13p-onepagerfinal.pdf.

198 **Since 9/11, the Bush and Obama:** To take one example, Director of National Intelligence James Clapper said, "Disclosing information about the specific methods the government uses to collect communications can obviously give our enemies a 'playbook' of how to avoid detection." Associated Press (9 Jun 2013), "Intelligence chief James Clapper defends Internet spying program," *New York Daily News*, http://www.nydailynews.com/news/politics/intelligence-chief-james-clapper-defends-internet-spying-program-article-1.1367423.

198 **And sometimes we need:** In 2014, we learned that Israel intercepted diplomatic communications between US Secretary of State John Kerry and various countries in the Middle East. Der Spiegel (3 Aug 2014), "Wiretapped: Israel eavesdropped on John Kerry in Mideast talks," *Der Spiegel*, http://www.spiegel.de/international/

world/israel-intelligence-eavesdropped-on-phone-calls-by-john-kerry-a-984246
.html.

198 **Criminals can read up:** Conor Friedersdorf (18 Mar 2014), "Why isn't the Fourth
Amendment classified as top secret?" *Atlantic*, http://www.theatlantic.com/poli
tics/archive/2014/03/why-isnt-the-fourth-amendment-classified-as-top-secret/
284439.

199 **Yet the police regularly manage:** Remember that much of this came as a reaction
to police abuse. It isn't that the police are less likely to abuse the rules; it's that we've
had longer to develop rules to control them.

199 **Terrorists don't cause:** Bruce Schneier (31 Jul 2012), "Drawing the wrong lesson
from horrific events," CNN, http://www.cnn.com/2012/07/31/opinion/schneier-au
rora-aftermath/index.html.

199 **We have to design systems:** IT security people call nontransparent security systems "security by obscurity." Good security design is the opposite of that: it works
even if all the details are made public. Bruce Schneier (15 May 2002), "Secrecy, security, and obscurity," *Crypto-Gram*, https://www.schneier.com/crypto-gram-0205
.html#1.

199 **the US gave up trying:** Michael J. Selgelid (Sep 2009), "Governance of dual-use
research: An ethical dilemma," *Bulletin of the World Health Organization* 87, http://
www.who.int/bulletin/volumes/87/9/08-051383/en. Carl Zimmer (5 Mar 2012),
"Amateurs are new fear in creating mutant virus," *New York Times*, http://www
.nytimes.com/2012/03/06/health/amateur-biologists-are-new-fear-in-making-
a-mutant-flu-virus.html. Michael Specter (12 Mar 2012), "The deadliest virus,"
New Yorker, http://www.newyorker.com/magazine/2012/03/12/the-deadliest-virus.
Arturo Casadevall (Jan/Feb 2014), "Redaction of sensitive data in the publication of
dual use research of concern," *mBio* 5, http://www.ncbi.nlm.nih.gov/pmc/articles/
PMC3884058.

199 **Military thinkers now realize:** Beth M. Kaspar (Aug 2001), "The end of secrecy?
Military competitiveness in the age of transparency," Occasional Paper No. 23, Cen-
ter for Strategy and Technology, Air War College, Air University, Maxwell Air Force
Base, Alabama, http://www.fas.org/sgp/eprint/kaspar.pdf.

200 **The NSA has justified:** US National Security Agency (31 Oct 2013), "NSA's activities:
Valid foreign intelligence targets are the focus," http://www.nsa.gov/public_info/
press_room/2013/NSA_Activities_Valid_FI_Targets.pdf.

201 **We know from recently declassified:** In one opinion, Judge Bates held that the
"NSA exceeded the scope of authorized acquisition continuously." Spencer Ackerman (19 Nov 2013), "FISA court order that allowed NSA surveillance is revealed for
first time," *Guardian*, http://www.theguardian.com/world/2013/nov/19/court-or
der-that-allowed-nsa-surveillance-is-revealed-for-first-time. Yochai Benkler (16
Oct 2013), "How the NSA and FBI foil weak oversight," *Guardian*, http://www
.theguardian.com/commentisfree/2013/oct/16/nsa-fbi-endrun-weak-oversight.
John D. Bates (3 Oct 2011), "Memorandum opinion," (case title and number redacted),
US Foreign Intelligence Surveillance Court, https://www.aclu.org/files/assets/fisc_
opinion_10.3.2011.pdf. Marcy Wheeler (22 Aug 2014), "This is why you can't trust the
NSA. Ever," *Week*, http://theweek.com/article/index/266785/this-is-why-you-cant-
trust-the-nsa-ever.

201 **The NSA has gamed the rules:** Peter Wallsten (10 Aug 2013), "Lawmakers say

obstacles limited oversight of NSA's telephone surveillance program," *Washington Post*, http://www.washingtonpost.com/politics/2013/08/10/bee87394-004d-11e3-9a3e-916de805f65d_story.html.

201 **Members of Congress can't:** Glenn Greenwald (4 Aug 2013), "Members of Congress denied access to basic information about NSA," *Guardian*, http://www.theguardian.com/commentisfree/2013/aug/04/congress-nsa-denied-access.

201 **They can only bring along:** Ailsa Chang (11 Jun 2013), "What did Congress really know about NSA tracking?" *All Things Considered*, NPR, http://www.npr.org/blogs/itsallpolitics/2013/06/11/190742087/what-did-congress-really-know-about-nsa-tracking.

201 **they're lobbied heavily:** Ron Wyden (29 Jan 2014), "Wyden statement at Senate Intelligence Committee's open hearing," http://www.wyden.senate.gov/news/press-releases/wyden-statement-at-senate-intelligence-committees-open-hearing.

201 **Senator Dianne Feinstein:** Dianne Feinstein (28 Oct 2013), "Feinstein statement on intelligence collection of foreign leaders," http://www.feinstein.senate.gov/public/index.cfm/2013/10/feinstein-statement-on-intelligence-collection-of-foreign-leaders.

201 **Congressman Alan Grayson:** Alan Grayson (25 Oct 2013), "Congressional oversight of the NSA is a joke. I should know, I'm in Congress," *Guardian*, http://www.theguardian.com/commentisfree/2013/oct/25/nsa-no-congress-oversight.

201 **In 2014, I was invited:** Bruce Schneier (16 Jan 2014), "Today I briefed Congress on the NSA," *Schneier on Security*, https://www.schneier.com/blog/archives/2014/01/today_i_briefed.html.

202 **There's also political risk:** Peter Wallsten (10 Aug 2013), "Lawmakers say obstacles limited oversight of NSA's telephone surveillance program," *Washington Post*, http://www.washingtonpost.com/politics/2013/08/10/bee87394-004d-11e3-9a3e-916de805f65d_story.html. Glenn Greenwald (4 Aug 2013), "Members of Congress denied access to basic information about NSA," *Guardian*, http://www.theguardian.com/commentisfree/2013/aug/04/congress-nsa-denied-access.

202 **Executive Order 12333:** John Napier Tye (18 Jul 2014), "Meet Executive Order 12333: The Reagan rule that lets the NSA spy on Americans," *Washington Post*, http://www.washingtonpost.com/opinions/meet-executive-order-12333-the-reagan-rule-that-lets-the-nsa-spy-on-americans/2014/07/18/93d2ac22-0b93-11e4-b8e5-d0de80767fc2_story.html. Charlie Savage and Alicia Parlapiano (13 Aug 2014), "Two sets of rules for surveillance, within U.S. and on foreign soil," *New York Times*, http://www.nytimes.com/interactive/2014/08/13/us/two-sets-of-rules-for-surveillance.html. Ellen Nakashima and Ashkan Soltani (23 Jul 2014), "Privacy watchdog's next target: The least-known but biggest aspect of NSA surveillance," *Washington Post*, http://www.washingtonpost.com/blogs/the-switch/wp/2014/07/23/privacy-watchdogs-next-target-the-least-known-but-biggest-aspect-of-nsa-surveillance. Charlie Savage (13 Aug 2014), "Reagan-era order on surveillance violates rights, says departing aide," *New York Times*, http://www.nytimes.com/2014/08/14/us/politics/reagan-era-order-on-surveillance-violates-rights-says-departing-aide.html.

202 **It is supposed to:** Alex Abdo (29 Sep 2014), "New documents shed light on one of the NSA's most powerful tools," *Free Future*, https://www.aclu.org/blog/national-security/new-documents-shed-light-one-nsas-most-powerful-tools.

202 **the president believed:** Marcy Wheeler (7 Dec 2007), "Whitehouse reveals smok-

ing gun of White House claiming not to be bound by any law," *Empty Wheel*, https://www.emptywheel.net/2007/12/07/whitehouse-rips-the-white-house.

202 **The example the administration:** Justin Elliott (17 Jun 2013), "Remember when the Patriot Act debate was all about library records?" *Pro Publica*, http://www.propublica.org/article/remember-when-the-patriot-act-debate-was-about-library-records.

203 **Eventually they decided to argue:** Mike Masnick (17 Sep 2013), "Court reveals 'secret interpretation' of the Patriot Act, allowing NSA to collect all phone call data," *Tech Dirt*, https://www.techdirt.com/articles/20130917/13395324556/court-reveals-secret-interpretation-patriot-act-allowing-nsa-to-collect-all-phone-call-data.shtml.

203 **Even Congressman Jim Sensenbrenner:** Andrea Peterson (11 Oct 2013), "Patriot Act author: 'There has been a failure of oversight,'" *Washington Post*, http://www.washingtonpost.com/blogs/the-switch/wp/2013/10/11/patriot-act-author-there-has-been-a-failure-of-oversight.

203 **"It's like scooping up":** Jennifer Valentino-DeVries and Siobhan Gorman (8 Jul 2013), "Secret court's redefinition of 'relevant' empowered vast NSA data-gathering," *Wall Street Journal*, http://online.wsj.com/news/articles/SB10001424127887323873904578571893758853344.

205 **We saw this in the 1970s:** US Senate (23 Apr 1976), "Final report of the Select Committee to Study Governmental Operations with Respect to Intelligence Activities: National Security Agency Surveillance affecting Americans," US Government Printing Office, http://www.aarclibrary.org/publib/church/reports/book3/pdf/ChurchB3_10_NSA.pdf.

205 **the same thing happened in the UK:** Caspar Bowden (23 Aug 2012), "Submission to the Joint Committee on the draft Communications Data Bill," http://www.academia.edu/6002584/Submission_to_the_Joint_Committee_on_the_draft_Communications_Data_Bill.

205 **It was intentionally drafted:** During one recent litigation, one judge called it a "difficult if not impenetrable statute," and the government's own attorney called it "convoluted legislation." Owen Bowcott (18 Jul 2014), "Intelligence services 'creating vast databases' of intercepted emails," *Guardian*, http://www.theguardian.com/uk-news/2014/jul/18/intelligence-services-email-database-internet-tribunal.

205 **didn't actually legalize mass surveillance:** EU law also applies to the UK, and mass surveillance under RIPA violates the European Convention on Human Rights. Nick Hopkins (28 Jan 2014), "Huge swath of GCHQ mass surveillance is illegal, says top lawyer," *Guardian*, http://www.theguardian.com/uk-news/2014/jan/28/gchq-mass-surveillance-spying-law-lawyer.

205 **President Obama tried to reassure:** President Obama said that the NSA programs were "under very strict supervision by all three branches of government." Barack Obama (7 Jun 2013), "Transcript: Obama's remarks on NSA controversy," *Wall Street Journal*, http://blogs.wsj.com/washwire/2013/06/07/transcript-what-obama-said-on-nsa-controversy.

205 **His statement was deeply misleading:** Electronic Privacy Information Center (2014), "Foreign Intelligence Surveillance Act court orders 1979–2014," https://epic.org/privacy/wiretap/stats/fisa_stats.html.

205 **telephone metadata collection program:** The ACLU discusses why this needs to

be reformed. American Civil Liberties Union (2014), "Reform the Patriot Act Section 215," https://www.aclu.org/free-speech-national-security-technology-and-liberty/reform-patriot-act-section-215.

205 **bulk records collection:** The ACLU also discusses why this needs to be reformed. Jameel Jaffer (19 Mar 2014), "Submission of Jameel Jaffer, Deputy Legal Director, American Civil Liberties Union," Privacy and Civil Liberties Oversight Board Public Hearing on Section 702 of the FISA Amendments Act, http://www.pclob.gov/Library/Meetings-Events/2014-March-19-Public-Hearing/Testimony_Jaffer.pdf.

206 **There's just too much secrecy:** There was a telling exchange at a US Senate Intelligence Committee hearing between Senator Ron Wyden of Oregon and then NSA director Keith Alexander. Wyden asked Alexander whether the NSA collected Americans' cell phone location data in bulk. Alexander replied that the NSA did not collect it under the authority delineated in Section 215 of the PATRIOT Act. Wyden then asked Alexander whether the NSA collected it under any other authority. Alexander refused to answer. Robyn Greene (27 Sep 2013), "It's official: NSA wants to suck up all American's phone records," *Washington Markup*, https://www.aclu.org/blog/national-security/its-official-nsa-wants-suck-all-americans-phone-records.

206 **When companies refuse:** Marcy Wheeler (14 Aug 2014), "The majority of 215 orders come from Internet companies that refuse NSLs," *Empty Wheel*, http://www.emptywheel.net/2014/08/14/the-bulk-of-215-orders-come-from-internet-compa nies-that-refuse-nsls.

206 **the NSA has repeatedly threatened:** Marcy Wheeler (23 Jun 2014), "The single branch theory of oversight," *Cato Unbound*, http://www.cato-unbound.org/2014/06/23/marcy-wheeler/single-branch-theory-oversight.

206 **They produced:** Richard A. Clarke et al. (12 Dec 2013), "Liberty and security in a changing world: Report and recommendations of the President's Review Group on Intelligence and Communications Technologies," US Executive Office of the President, http://www.whitehouse.gov/sites/default/files/docs/2013-12-12_rg_final_report.pdf.

206 **President Obama agreed:** Barack Obama (17 Jan 2014), "Remarks by the President on review of signals intelligence," US Executive Office of the President, http://www.whitehouse.gov/the-press-office/2014/01/17/remarks-president-review-signals-intelligence.

206 **In 2004, Congress created:** Garrett Hatch (27 Aug 2012), "Privacy and Civil Liberties Oversight Board: New independent agency status," Congressional Research Service, http://www.fas.org/sgp/crs/misc/RL34385.pdf.

206 **The group's 2014 report:** Privacy and Civil Liberties Oversight Board (2 Jul 2014), "Report on the surveillance program operated pursuant to Section 702 of the Foreign Intelligence Surveillance Act," http://www.pclob.gov/All%20Documents/Report%20on%20the%20Section%20702%20Program/PCLOB-Section-702-Report.pdf.

206 **It was widely panned:** American Civil Liberties Union (2 Jul 2014), "Government privacy watchdog signs off on much of NSA warrantless wiretapping program," https://www.aclu.org/national-security/government-privacy-watchdog-signs-much-nsa-warrantless-wiretapping-program. Jennifer Granick (2 Jul 2014), "Did PCLOB answer my eight questions about Section 702?" *Just Security*, http://justsecurity.org/12516/pclob-answer-questions-section-702.

206 **We need meaningful rules:** Frederick A. O. Schwarz Jr. (12 Mar 2014), "Why we

need a new Church Committee to fix our broken intelligence system," *Nation*, http://www.thenation.com/article/178813/why-we-need-new-church-committee-fix-our-broken-intelligence-system.

207 **Contrary to what many:** This is one example. Gregory Conti, Lisa Shay, and Woodrow Hartzog (Summer 2014), "Deconstructing the relationship between privacy and security," *IEEE Technology and Society Magazine* 33, http://ieeexplore.ieee.org/xpl/articleDetails.jsp?arnumber=6824305.

207 **Secret warrants don't work:** Jameel Jaffer (19 Mar 2014), "Submission of Jameel Jaffer, Deputy Legal Director, American Civil Liberties Union," Privacy and Civil Liberties Oversight Board Public Hearing on Section 702 of the FISA Amendments Act, http://www.pclob.gov/Library/Meetings-Events/2014-March-19-Public-Hearing/Testimony_Jaffer.pdf.

207 **Some surveillance orders bypass:** Privacy SOS (10 Dec 2013), "No evidence, no worries: on the use of secret subpoenas," http://www.privacysos.org/node/1263.

207 **Start with the FISA Court:** Andrew Nolan, Richard M. Thompson II, and Vivian S. Chu (25 Oct 2013), "Introducing a public advocate into the Foreign Intelligence Surveillance Act's courts: Select legal issues," Congressional Research Service, http://fas.org/sgp/crs/intel/advocate.pdf. Stephen I. Vladeck et al. (29 May 2013), "The case for a FISA 'Special Advocate,'" Constitution Project, http://www.constitutionproject.org/wp-content/uploads/2014/05/The-Case-for-a-FISA-Special-Advocate_FINAL.pdf. Covington & Burling (May 2014), "The constitutionality of a public advocate for privacy," http://www.insideprivacy.com/files/2014/07/The-Constitutionality-of-a-Public-Advocate-for-Pri.pdf.

207 **more steps are needed:** Joel Reidenberg (2 Nov 2013), "The data surveillance state in the US and Europe," *Wake Forest Law Review* (forthcoming), http://papers.ssrn.com/sol3/papers.cfm?abstract_id=2349269.

208 **Snowden was rebuffed repeatedly:** Edward Snowden (7 Mar 2014), "Statement to European Parliament," http://www.europarl.europa.eu/document/activities/cont/201403/20140307ATT80674/20140307ATT80674EN.pdf.

208 **Other law enforcement agencies:** Merrick Bobb (16 Nov 2005), "Internal and external police oversight in the United States," Police Assessment Resource Center, http://www.parc.info/client_files/altus/10-19%20altus%20conf%20paper.pdf.

208 **more transparency, the better:** Michael P. Weinbeck (3 Jun 2010), "Watching the watchmen: Lessons for federal law enforcement from America's cities," *William Mitchell Law Review* 36, http://www.wmitchell.edu/lawreview/documents/12.weinbeck.pdf. Eduardo L. Calderon and Maria Hernandez-Figueroa (Jan 2013), "Citizen oversight committees in law enforcement," California State University Fullerton Center for Public Policy, http://cpp.fullerton.edu/cpp_policeoversight_report.pdf.

208 **democracies need to be leaky:** David Pozen (20 Dec 2013), "The leaky leviathan: Why the government condemns and condones unlawful disclosures of information," *Harvard Law Review* 127, http://harvardlawreview.org/2013/12/the-leaky-leviathan-why-the-government-condemns-and-condones-unlawful-disclosures-of-information. Rahul Sagar (20 Dec 2013), "Creaky leviathan: A comment on David Pozen's *Leaky Leviathan*," *Harvard Law Review Forum* 127, http://cdn.harvardlawreview.org/wp-content/uploads/pdfs/forvol127_sagar.pdf.

208 **whistleblowing the civil disobedience:** These two essays make this point. danah

boyd (19 Jul 2013), "Whistleblowing is the new civil disobedience: Why Edward Snowden matters," *apophenia*, http://www.zephoria.org/thoughts/archives/2013/07/19/edward-snowden-whistleblower.html. William E. Scheuerman (Sep 2014), "Whistleblowing as civil disobedience: The case of Edward Snowden," *Philosophy and Social Criticism* 40, http://psc.sagepub.com/content/40/7/609.abstract.

208 **The NGO Human Rights Watch:** G. Alex Sinha (28 Jul 2014), "With liberty to monitor all," Human Rights Watch, http://www.hrw.org/reports/2014/07/28/liberty-monitor-all-0.

208 **whistleblowers provide another oversight:** Rahul Sagar (2013), *Secrets and Leaks: The Dilemma of State Secrecy*, Princeton University Press, http://press.princeton.edu/titles/10151.html.

208 **Just as we have laws:** Mary-Rose Papandrea (Mar 2014), "Leaker traitor whistleblower spy: National security leaks and the First Amendment," *Boston University Law Review* 94, http://www.bu.edu/bulawreview/files/2014/05/PAPANDREA.pdf.

208 **Once they are in place:** Bruce Schneier (6 Jun 2013), "What we don't know about spying on citizens: Scarier than what we know," *Atlantic*, http://www.theatlantic.com/politics/archive/2013/06/what-we-dont-know-about-spying-on-citizens-scarier-than-what-we-know/276607.

209 **The clever thing about this:** Yochai Benkler delineated criteria that the courts can use to decide this. Yochai Benkler (Jul 2014), "A public accountability defense for national security leakers and whistleblowers," *Harvard Review of Law and Policy* 8, http://benkler.org/Benkler_Whistleblowerdefense_Prepub.pdf.

209 **Someone like Snowden:** Yochai Benkler makes the case that the smartest thing the US could do is to give Edward Snowden immunity and let him return to the US. Yochai Benkler (8 Sep 2014), "Want to reform the NSA? Give Edward Snowden immunity," *Atlantic*, http://www.theatlantic.com/politics/archive/2014/09/want-to-reform-the-nsa-give-edward-snowden-immunity/379612/2.

209 **We encourage individuals:** US Department of Labor (2014), "The Whistleblower Protection Programs," http://www.whistleblowers.gov.

209 **we need to protect whistleblowing:** Glenn Reynolds has some ideas on how to maximize the benefits of whistleblowing while minimizing the harm. Glenn Reynolds (15 Sep 2014), "Don't fear the leaker: Thoughts on bureaucracy and ethical whistleblowing," Social Sciences Research Network, http://papers.ssrn.com/sol3/papers.cfm?abstract_id=2496400.

210 **Axel Arnbak said about:** Axel Arnbak (30 Sep 2013), "The question lawyers don't ask: Can law address total transnational surveillance?" Congress on Privacy and Surveillance, Lausanne, Switzerland, http://ic.epfl.ch/privacy-surveillance.

210 **2014 UN report concluded:** Ben Emmerson (23 Sep 2014), "Report of the Special Rapporteur on the promotion and protection of human rights and fundamental freedoms while countering terrorism," United Nations General Assembly, Sixty-ninth session, Agenda item 68(a), https://docs.google.com/document/d/18U1aHmKx9jfDQjCZeAUYZdRjl6iF4QjuS_aJO2Uy7NY/edit?pli=1.

210 **a baby step in this direction:** Kim Zetter (22 Oct 2013), "Court rules probable-cause warrant required for GPS trackers," *Wired*, http://www.wired.com/2013/10/warrant-required-gps-trackers.

210 **another in 2014:** Robert Barnes (25 Jun 2014), "Supreme Court says police must get

warrants for most cellphone searches," *Washington Post*, http://www.washington post.com/national/supreme-court-police-must-get-warrants-for-most-cellphone-searches/2014/06/25/e2ff1326-fc6b-11e3-8176-f2c941cf35f1_story.html.

210 **we need to overturn:** Orin Kerr and Greg Nojeim (1 Aug 2012), "The data question: Should the third-party records doctrine be revisited?" *ABA Journal*, http://www .abajournal.com/magazine/article/the_data_question_should_the_third-party_ records_doctrine_be_revisited. Colleen Maher Ernst (Jan 2014), "A proposed revision of the third-party doctrine," *Harvard Journal of Law and Public Policy* 37, http:// www.harvard-jlpp.com/wp-content/uploads/2014/01/37_1_329_Maher.pdf. Richard M. Thompson II (5 Jun 2014), "The Fourth Amendment third-party doctrine," Congressional Research Service, http://fas.org/sgp/crs/misc/R43586.pdf.

210 **The police should need a warrant:** Currently, Justice Sotomayor is the only Supreme Court justice who has written in favor of making these changes. Richard M. Thompson II (5 Jun 2014), "The Fourth Amendment third-party doctrine," Congressional Research Service, http://fas.org/sgp/crs/misc/R43586.pdf.

211 **also hoarding vulnerabilities:** In 2014, the Russians used a zero-day vulnerability in Windows to spy on both NATO and the Ukrainian government. Ellen Nakashima (13 Oct 2014), "Russian hackers use 'zero-day' to hack NATO, Ukraine in cyber-spy campaign," *Washington Post*, http://www.washingtonpost.com/world/ national-security/russian-hackers-use-zero-day-to-hack-nato-ukraine-in-cyber-spy-campaign/2014/10/13/f2452976-52f9-11e4-892e-602188e70e9c_story.html.

211 **Some people believe the NSA:** Cory Doctorow (11 Mar 2014), "If GCHQ wants to improve national security it must fix our technology," *Guardian*, http://www .theguardian.com/technology/2014/mar/11/gchq-national-security-technology. Dan Geer (2013), "Three policies," http://geer.tinho.net/three.policies.2013Apr 03Wed.PDF.

211 **Others claim that this would:** David E. Sanger (29 Apr 2014), "White House details thinking on cybersecurity flaws," *New York Times*, http://www.nytimes.com/ 2014/04/29/us/white-house-details-thinking-on-cybersecurity-gaps.html.

211 **President Obama's NSA review group:** It's recommendation 30. Richard A. Clarke et al. (12 Dec 2013), "Liberty and security in a changing world: Report and recommendations of The President's Review Group on Intelligence and Communications Technologies," US Executive Office of the President, http://www.white house.gov/sites/default/files/docs/2013-12-12_rg_final_report.pdf.

211 **I have made this point myself:** Bruce Schneier (19 May 2014), "Should U.S. hackers fix cybersecurity holes or exploit them?" *Atlantic*, http://www.theatlantic.com/ technology/archive/2014/05/should-hackers-fix-cybersecurity-holes-or-exploit-them/371197.

212 **This is what the NSA:** Michael Daniel (28 Apr 2014), "Heartbleed: Understanding when we disclose cyber vulnerabilities," *White House Blog*, http://www.whitehouse .gov/blog/2014/04/28/heartbleed-understanding-when-we-disclose-cyber-vulnera bilities. David E. Sanger (28 Apr 2014), "White House details thinking on cybersecurity flaws," *New York Times*, http://www.nytimes.com/2014/04/29/us/white-house-de tails-thinking-on-cybersecurity-gaps.html. Christopher Joye (8 May 2014), "Interview transcript: Former head of the NSA and commander of the US cyber command, General Keith Alexander," *Australian Financial Review*, http://www.afr.com/Page/Uuid/ b67d7b3e-d570-11e3-90e8-355a30324c5f.

213 **why the technical community:** Bruce Schneier (5 Sep 2013), "The US government has betrayed the internet. We need to take it back," *Guardian*, http://www.theguard ian.com/commentisfree/2013/sep/05/government-betrayed-internet-nsa-spying. Stephen Farrell (2013), "Pervasive monitoring is an attack," Internet Engineering Task Force Trust, Network Working Group, http://tools.ietf.org/pdf/draft-farrell-perpass-attack-00.pdf.

213 **the FBI is continually trying:** Charlie Savage (27 Sep 2010), "U.S. tries to make it easier to wiretap the Internet," *New York Times*, http://www.nytimes.com/2010/09/27/us/27wiretap.html. Ryan Singel (17 Feb 2011), "FBI pushes for surveillance backdoors in Web 2.0 tools," *Wired*, http://www.wired.com/2011/02/fbi-backdoors. Valerie Caproni (17 Feb 2011), "Statement before the House Judiciary Committee, Subcommittee on Crime, Terrorism, and Homeland Security, Washington, D.C.," US Federal Bureau of Investigation, http://www.fbi.gov/news/testimony/going-dark-lawful-elec tronic-surveillance-in-the-face-of-new-technologies.

213 **and to each other's:** This isn't new. In the 1980s and 1990s, the NSA inserted backdoors into the hardware encryption products sold by the Swiss company Crypto AG. Scott Shane and Tom Bowman (4 Dec 1995), "Rigging the game," *Baltimore Sun*, http://cryptome.org/jya/nsa-sun.htm. Wayne Madsen (Winter 1998), "Crypto AG: The NSA's Trojan whore?" *Covert Action Quarterly* 63, http://mediafilter.org/caq/cryptogate.

213 **observers have concluded:** Christopher Ketcham (27 Sep 2008), "An Israeli Trojan horse," *Counterpunch*, http://www.counterpunch.org/2008/09/27/an-israeli-trojan-horse. James Bamford (3 Apr 2012), "Shady companies with ties to Israel wiretap the U.S. for the NSA," *Wired*, http://www.wired.com/2012/04/shady-companies-nsa/all. Richard Sanders (Spring 2012), "Israeli spy companies: Verint and Narus," *Press for Conversion!* 66, http://coat.ncf.ca/P4C/66/spy.pdf.

213 **Security has to come first:** Back in the 1990s, the National Academies made the same recommendation: "Recommendation 1—No law should bar the manufacture, sale, or use of any form of encryption within the United States. Specifically, a legislative ban on the use of unescrowed encryption would raise both technical and legal or constitutional issues. Technically, many methods are available to circumvent such a ban; legally, constitutional issues, especially those related to free speech, would be almost certain to arise, issues that are not trivial to resolve. Recommendation 1 is made to reinforce this particular aspect of the Administration's cryptography policy." Kenneth W. Damm and Herbert S. Lin, eds. (1995), *Cryptography's Role in Securing the Information Society*, National Academies Press, http://www.nap.edu/catalog.php?record_id=5131.

214 **law enforcement officials:** Bruce Schneier (4 Oct 2014), "Stop the hysteria over Apple encryption," CNN, http://edition.cnn.com/2014/10/03/opinion/schneier-ap ple-encryption-hysteria/index.html.

214 **exactly one involved kidnapping:** Administrative Office of the US Courts (11 Jun 2014), "Table 3: Major offenses for which court-authorized intercepts were granted pursuant to 18 U.S.C. 2519 January 1 through December 31, 2013," from *Wiretap Report* 2013, http://www.uscourts.gov/Statistics/WiretapReports/wiretap-report-2013.aspx.

214 **there's no evidence that encryption:** Andy Greenberg (2 Jul 2014), "Rising use of encryption foiled cops a record 9 times in 2013," *Wired*, http://www.wired .com/2014/07/rising-use-of-encryption-foiled-the-cops-a-record-9-times-in-2013.

214 **They have the right and ability:** Steven Bellovin et al. (6–7 Jun 2013), "Lawful hacking: Using existing vulnerabilities for wiretapping on the Internet," Privacy Legal Scholars Conference, Berkeley, California, http://papers.ssrn.com/sol3/papers.cfm?abstract_id=2312107.

215 **the NSA eavesdropped on:** Jacob Appelbaum et al. (23 Oct 2013), "Berlin complains: Did US tap Chancellor Merkel's mobile phone?" *Der Spiegel*, http://www.spiegel.de/international/world/merkel-calls-obama-over-suspicions-us-tapped-her-mobile-phone-a-929642.html. Ian Traynor, Philip Oltermann, and Paul Lewis (23 Oct 2013), "Angela Merkel's call to Obama: Are you bugging my mobile phone?" *Guardian*, http://www.theguardian.com/world/2013/oct/23/us-monitored-angela-merkel-german.

215 **the NSA spied on embassies:** Ewan MacAskill and Julian Borger (30 Jun 2013), "New NSA leaks show how US is bugging its European allies," *Guardian*, http://www.theguardian.com/world/2013/jun/30/nsa-leaks-us-bugging-european-allies. Glenn Greenwald (2014), *No Place to Hide: Edward Snowden, the NSA and the US Surveillance State*, Macmillan, http://glenngreenwald.net.

215 **the NSA spied on the UN:** Laura Poitras, Marcel Rosenbach, and Holger Stark (26 Aug 2013), "Codename 'Apalachee': How America spies on Europe and the UN," *Der Spiegel*, http://www.spiegel.de/international/world/secret-nsa-documents-show-how-the-us-spies-on-europe-and-the-un-a-918625.html.

215 **It's actually stabilizing:** Uncertainties between exploit and attack can lead to unwanted escalations. Herbert Lin (Fall 2012), "Escalation dynamics and conflict termination in cyberspace," *Strategic Studies Quarterly* 6, http://www.au.af.mil/au/ssq/2012/fall/lin.pdf.

216 **The increasing militarization:** Peter B. Kraska (Jan 2007), "Militarization and policing: Its relevance to 21st century police," *Policing* 1, http://cjmasters.eku.edu/sites/cjmasters.eku.edu/files/21stmilitarization.pdf. John Paul and Michael L. Birzer (Mar 2008), "The militarization of the American police force: A critical assessment," *Critical Issues in Justice and Politics* 1, http://www.suu.edu/hss/polscj/journal/V1N1.pdf#page=25. Abigail R. Hall and Christopher J. Coyne (Spring 2013), "The militarization of U.S. domestic policing," *Independent Review* 17, http://www.independent.org/pdf/tir/tir_17_04_01_hall.pdf. Matthew Witt (Mar 2013), "Morewell than Orwell: Paramilitarization in the United States post-9/11," *Journal of 9/11 Studies* 36, http://www.journalof911studies.com/resources/2013WittVol36Mar.pdf.

216 **that's a topic for another book:** This is a good one to start with. Radley Balko (2013), *Rise of the Warrior Cop: The Militarization of America's Police Forces*, Public Affairs Press, http://books.google.com/books?id=M3KSMQEACAAJ.

216 **he would extend some:** Barack Obama (17 Jan 2014), "Transcript of President Obama's Jan. 17 speech on NSA reforms," *Washington Post*, http://www.washingtonpost.com/politics/full-text-of-president-obamas-jan-17-speech-on-nsa-reforms/2014/01/17/fa33590a-7f8c-11e3-9556-4a4bf7bcbd84_story.html.

217 **when you're being attacked in cyberspace:** Scott Charney (30 Apr 2010), "Rethinking the cyber threat: A framework and path forward," Microsoft Corporation, http://www.microsoft.com/en-us/download/details.aspx?id=747.

217 **the Internet doesn't have borders:** On the blurring between crimes and acts of war. Benjamin J. Priester (24 Aug 2007), "Who is a 'terrorist'? Drawing the line between criminal defendants and military enemies," Florida State University Col-

lege of Law, Public Law Research Paper No. 264, http://papers.ssrn.com/sol3/papers
.cfm?abstract_id=1009845.

217 **A "cybersiege" mentality is becoming:** Far too many people use this emotionally
charged term. Richard Behar (13 Oct 2008), "World Bank under cybersiege in
'unprecedented crisis,'" *FOX News*, http://www.foxnews.com/story/2008/10/13/
world-bank-under-cyber-siege-in-unprecedented-crisis. Scott Harkey (3 Jul 2012),
"Our view: Arizona must rise to challenge of cybersiege," *East Valley Tribune*, http://
www.eastvalleytribune.com/opinion/article_fcfd880c-a421-11e0-a8e5-001cc4c002e0
.html. Kaspersky Lab (2014), "Under cybersiege: What should America do?" *Kaspersky Government Cybersecurity Forum*, http://kasperskygovforum.com.

218 **These tend to be totalitarian:** Here's a proposal to institute a sort of "cyber draft" to
conscript networks in the event of a cyberwar. Susan W. Brenner and Leo L. Clarke
(Oct 2010), "Civilians in cyberwarfare: Conscripts," *Vanderbilt Journal of Transnational Law* 43, http://www.vanderbilt.edu/jotl/manage/wp-content/uploads/Brenner-_Final_1.pdf.

218 **The 1878 Posse Comitatus Act:** RAND Corporation (20 Mar 2001), "Overview of
the Posse Comitatus Act," in *Preparing the U.S. Army for Homeland Security*, http://
www.rand.org/content/dam/rand/pubs/monograph_reports/MR1251/MR1251
.AppD.pdf. Charles Doyle and Jennifer K. Elsea (16 Aug 2012), "The Posse Comitatus
Act and related matters: The use of the military to execute civilian law," Congressional Research Service, http://www.fas.org/sgp/crs/natsec/R42659.pdf.

218 **In the US, that's Cyber Command:** Rhett A. Hernandez (Oct 2012), "U.S. Army
Cyber Command: Cyberspace for America's force of decisive action," *Army*, http://
connection.ebscohost.com/c/articles/82115370/u-s-army-cyber-command-
cyberspace-americas-force-decisive-action.

219 **NSA's defensive capabilities:** In recent decades, the NSA has been doing more to
provide data and communications security to US private companies. The companies need government help, but it needs to be much more public. Susan Landau (29
Sep 2014), "Under the radar: NSAs efforts to secure private-sector telecommunications infrastructure," *Journal of National Security Law and Policy*, http://jnslp
.com/2014/09/29/under-the-radar-nsas-efforts-to-secure-private-sector-telecom
munications-infrastructure.

219 **The Computer Security Act of 1987:** Robert A. Roe et al. (11 Jun 1987), "Computer
Security Act of 1987: Report," Committee on Science, Space, and Technology, US
House of Representatives, https://beta.congress.gov/congressional-report/107th-con
gress/senate-report/239/1. Electronic Privacy Information Center (2014), "Computer
Security Act of 1987," http://epic.org/crypto/csa.

220 **They want an Internet that recognizes:** Milton Mueller (21 Jun 2012), "Threat analysis of the WCIT part 4: The ITU and cybersecurity," Internet Governance Project,
http://www.internetgovernance.org/2012/06/21/threat-analysis-of-the-wcit-4-cy
bersecurity.

220 **Countries like Brazil:** Brazil's government even proposed a law mandating this, but
then backed down. Esteban Israel and Anthony Boadle (28 Oct 2013), "Brazil to insist on
local Internet data storage after U.S. spying," Reuters, http://www.reuters.com/arti
cle/2013/10/28/net-us-brazil-internet-idUSBRE99R10Q20131028. Anthony Boadle (18
Mar 2014), "Brazil to drop local data storage rule in Internet bill," Reuters, http://www
.reuters.com/article/2014/03/19/us-brazil-internet-idUSBREA2I03O20140319.

220 **and Germany:** Michael Birnbaum (1 Nov 2013), "Germany looks at keeping its Internet, e-mail traffic inside its borders," *Washington Post*, http://www.washing tonpost.com/world/europe/germany-looks-at-keeping-its-internet-e-mail-traffic-inside-its-borders/2013/10/31/981104fe-424f-11e3-a751-f032898f2dbc_story.html.

220 **Russia passed a law in 2014:** Charles Maynes (11 Jul 2014), "Russia tightens Internet screws with 'server law,'" Deutsche Welle, http://www.dw.de/russia-tightens-internet-screws-with-server-law/a-17779072. Adrien Henni (12 Jul 2014), "New personal data storage rules to affect both foreign and domestic players—but still no "Chinese wall" surrounding Russia," *East-West Digital News*, http://www.ewdn .com/2014/07/12/new-personal-data-storage-rules-to-affect-both-foreign-and-do mestic-players-but-no-chinese-wall-surrounding-russia.

221 **We don't perceive:** Jacquelyn Burkell et al. (2 Jan 2014), "Facebook: Public space, or private space?" *Information, Communication and Society*, http://www.tandfonline .com/doi/abs/10.1080/1369118X.2013.870591.

221 **But because we didn't bother:** Even if we had, we would have found that the agreement was vague, and gave the company the right to do whatever it wanted . . . and to change the agreement at will without notice or consent.

222 **These laws don't apply:** Scott Lybarger (1999), "Conduit or forum? Regulatory metaphors for the Internet," *Free Speech Yearbook* 37, http://www.tandfonline.com/doi/ abs/10.1080/08997225.1999.10556239.

222 **things we say on Facebook:** Noah D. Zatz (Fall 1998), "Sidewalks in cyberspace: Making space for public forums in the electronic environment," *Harvard Journal of Law & Technology* 12, http://jolt.law.harvard.edu/articles/pdf/v12/12HarvJLTech149 .pdf. Laura Stein (Jan 2008), "Speech without rights: The status of public space on the Internet," *Communication Review* 11, http://www.tandfonline.com/doi/abs/10.1080/ 10714420801888385. Lyrissa Lidsky (Dec 2011), "Public forum 2.0," *Boston University Law Review* 91, http://www.bu.edu/law/central/jd/organizations/journals/bulr/volume91 n6/documents/LIDSKY.pdf.

14: SOLUTIONS FOR CORPORATIONS

224 **what sorts of inventions:** It is much more likely that we will invent our way out of the ecological disaster that is climate change than conserve our way out of it. Bjørn Lomborg (2001), *The Skeptical Environmentalist: Measuring the Real State of the World*, Cambridge University Press, https://encrypted.google.com/books?id=JuLk o8USApwC.

224 **1980 OECD Privacy Framework:** Organization for Economic Cooperation and Development (2013), "The OECD privacy framework," http://www.oecd.org/sti/ ieconomy/oecd_privacy_framework.pdf.

224 **EU Data Protection Directive:** European Parliament and Council of Europe (24 Oct 1995), "Directive 95/46/EC of the European Parliament and of the Council of 24 October 1995 on the protection of individuals with regard to the processing of personal data and on the free movement of such data," http://eur-lex.europa.eu/Lex UriServ/LexUriServ.do?uri=CELEX:31995L0046:en:HTML. Neil Robinson et al. (2009), "Review of the European Data Protection Directive," Report TR-710-ICO, Information Commissioner's Office, RAND Corporation, http://ico.org.uk/~/media/

documents/library/data_protection/detailed_specialist_guides/review_of_eu_
dp_directive.ashx.

224 **American corporations:** Karlin Lillington (14 May 2014), "Analysis: Google takes
another hit with EU privacy rulings," *Irish Times*, http://www.irishtimes.com/busi
ness/sectors/technology/analysis-google-takes-another-hit-with-eu-privacy-rul
ings-1.1793749. Price Waterhouse Coopers (Jul 2014), "EU data protection reforms:
Challenges for businesses," http://www.pwc.com/en_US/us/risk-assurance-ser
vices/publications/assets/pwc-eu-data-protection-reform.pdf.

224 **bringing that law up to date:** European Commission (25 Jan 2012), "Commission
proposes a comprehensive reform of the data protection rules," http://ec.europa.eu/
justice/newsroom/data-protection/news/120125_en.htm. European Commission (25
Jan 2012), "Why do we need an EU data protection reform?" http://ec.europa.eu/jus
tice/data-protection/document/review2012/factsheets/1_en.pdf. European Commission (12 Mar 2014),"Progress on EU data protection now irreversible following
European Parliament vote," http://europa.eu/rapid/press-release_MEMO-14-186_
en.htm.

225 **By raising the cost of privacy breaches:** This is a good introduction to the economics of data privacy. Tyler Moore (2011), "Introducing the economics of cybersecurity: Principles and policy options," in *Proceedings of a Workshop on Deterring
CyberAttacks: Informing Strategies and Developing Options for U.S. Policy*, National
Academies Press, http://cs.brown.edu/courses/csci1800/sources/lec27/Moore.pdf.

226 **OECD Privacy Framework (1980):** Organization for Economic Cooperation and
Development (2013), "The OECD privacy framework," http://www.oecd.org/sti/
ieconomy/oecd_privacy_framework.pdf.

227 **doing this in the US with healthcare data:** Healthcare data breach violations,
and accompanying fines, are common. Patrick J. O'Toole, Corey M. Dennis, and
Douglas Levy (28 Mar 2014), "Best practices for avoiding data breach liability," *Michigan Lawyers Weekly*, http://milawyersweekly.com/news/2014/03/28/commentary-
best-practices-for-avoiding-data-breach-liability.

227 **it's starting to happen here:** Sasha Romanosky, David Hoffman, and Alessandro
Acquisti (25–26 Jun 2012), "Empirical analysis of data breach litigation," 11th Annual
Workshop on the Economics of Information Security, Berlin, Germany, http://
weis2012.econinfosec.org/papers/Romanosky_WEIS2012.pdf.

227 **Target is facing several lawsuits:** Target Corporation is a defendant in multiple
lawsuits stemming from its 2013 data breach. Alex Williams (23 Dec 2013), "Target
may be liable for up to $3.6 billion for card data breach," *Tech Crunch*, http://tech
crunch.com/2013/12/23/target-may-be-liable-for-up-to-3-6-billion-from-credit-
card-data-breach. Lance Duroni (3 Apr 2014), "JPML centralizes Target data breach
suits in Minn.," *Law360*, http://www.law360.com/articles/524968/jpml-centralizes-
target-data-breach-suits-in-minn.

227 **banks are being sued:** Brian Krebs (8 Jan 2014), "Firm bankrupted by cyberheist
sues bank," *Krebs on Security*, http://krebsonsecurity.com/2014/01/firm-bankrupt
ed-by-cyberheist-sues-bank. Brian Krebs (20 Jun 2014), "Oil Co. wins $350,000
cyberheist settlement," *Krebs on Security*, http://krebsonsecurity.com/2014/06/
oil-co-wins-350000-cyberheist-settlement. Brian Krebs (13 Aug 2014), "Tenn. firm
sues bank over $327K cyberheist," *Krebs on Security*, http://krebsonsecurity
.com/2014/08/tenn-utility-sues-bank-over-327k-cyberheist.

227 **These cases can be complicated:** Here's one proposal. Maurizio Naldi, Marta Flamini, and Giuseppe D'Acquisto (2013), "Liability for data breaches: A proposal for a revenue-based sanctioning approach," in *Network and System Security* (Lecture Notes in Computer Science Volume 7873), Springer, http://link.springer.com/chapter/10.1007%2F978-3-642-38631-2_20.

228 **There's a parallel with how:** Much has been written about what privacy regulation can learn from environmental regulation. Dennis D. Hirsch (Fall 2006), "Protecting the inner environment: What privacy regulation can learn from environmental law," *Georgia Law Review* 41, http://papers.ssrn.com/sol3/papers.cfm?abstract_id=1021623. Ira S. Rubinstein (2011), "Privacy and regulatory innovation: Moving beyond voluntary codes," *I/S, A Journal of Law and Policy for the Information Society* 6, http://www.ftc.gov/sites/default/files/documents/public_comments/privacy-roundtables-comment-project-no.p095416-544506-00022/544506-00022.pdf.

228 **The US Code of Fair Information Practices:** Willis H. Ware et al. (Jul 1973), "Records, computers and the rights of citizens: Report of the Secretary's Advisory Committee on Automated Personal Data Systems," DHEW Publication (OS) 73-94, US Department of Health, Education and Welfare, http://www.justice.gov/sites/default/files/opcl/docs/rec-com-rights.pdf.

229 **Making companies liable for breaches:** There would need to be some exception for free and open-source software, and other instances where the user does not have any contractual relationship with the software vendor.

229 **The relevant term from economics:** Giuseppe Dari-Matiacci and Nuno Garoupa (May 2009), "Least cost avoidance: The tragedy of common safety," *Journal of Law, Economics, and Organization* 25, http://papers.ssrn.com/sol3/papers.cfm?abstract_id=560062. Paul Rosenzweig (5 Nov 2013), "Cybersecurity and the least cost avoider," *Lawfare*, http://www.lawfareblog.com/2013/11/cybersecurity-and-the-least-cost-avoider.

229 **personal information about you:** The notion of ownership is actually very complicated. Ali M. Al-Khouri (Nov 2012), "Data ownership: Who owns 'my data'?" *International Journal of Management and Information Technology* 2, http://www.id.gov.ae/assets/FNukwmhbQ4k.pdf.aspx. Jacob M. Victor (Nov 2013), "The EU General Data Protection Regulation: Toward a property regime for protecting data privacy," *Yale Law Journal* 123, http://www.yalelawjournal.org/comment/the-eu-general-data-protection-regulation-toward-a-property-regime-for-protecting-data-privacy.

229 **They pay for this information:** Jennifer Valentino-DeVries and Jeremy Singer-Vine (7 Dec 2012), "They know what you're shopping for," *Wall Street Journal*, http://online.wsj.com/news/articles/SB10001424127887324784404578143144132736214. Jeremy Singer-Vine (7 Dec 2012), "How Dataium watches you," *Wall Street Journal*, http://blogs.wsj.com/digits/2012/12/07/how-dataium-watches-you.

230 **transparency trumps proprietary claims:** Frank Pasquale (21 Apr 2009), "The troubling trend toward trade secret-protected ranking systems," Chicago Intellectual Property Colloquium, Chicago, Illinois, http://www.chicagoip.com/pasquale.pdf.

230 **more algorithms can be made public:** Ethan Zuckerman (5 Sep 2012), "TSA pre-check, fairness and opaque algorithms," *My Heart's in Accra*, http://www.ethanzuckerman.com/blog/2012/09/05/tsa-pre-check-fairness-and-opaque-algorithms.

230 **there are ways of auditing algorithms:** Daniel Weitzner (29–30 Jan 2014), "The

jurisprudence of accountability," 2nd International Workshop on Accountability: Science, Technology and Policy, Cambridge, Massachusetts, http://dig.csail.mit.edu/2014/AccountableSystems2014/abs/weitzner-account-jurisprudence-abs.pdf. Ed Felten (19 Mar 2014), "Algorithms can be more accountable than people," *Freedom to Tinker*, https://freedom-to-tinker.com/blog/felten/algorithms-can-be-more-accountable-than-people. Ed Felten (12 Sep 2012), "Accountable algorithms," *Freedom to Tinker*, https://freedom-to-tinker.com/blog/felten/accountable-algorithms.

231 **There's been a concerted:** Examples include Microsoft Corporation and the World Economic Forum. Craig Mundie (Mar/Apr 2014), "Privacy pragmatism: Focus on data use, not data collection," *Foreign Affairs* 93, http://www.foreignaffairs.com/articles/140741/craig-mundie/privacy-pragmatism. William Hoffman et al. (May 2014), "Rethinking personal data: A new lens for strengthening trust," World Economic Forum, http://reports.weforum.org/rethinking-personal-data. William Hoffman et al. (May 2014), "Rethinking personal data: Trust and context in user-centred data ecosystems," World Economic Forum, http://www3.weforum.org/docs/WEF_RethinkingPersonalData_TrustandContext_Report_2014.pdf. William H. Dutton et al. (May 2014), "The Internet trust bubble: Global values, beliefs and practices," World Economic Forum, http://www3.weforum.org/docs/WEF_InternetTrustBubble_Report2_2014.pdf. Fred H. Cate, Peter Cullen, and Viktor Mayer-Schonberger (Mar 2014), "Data protection principles for the 21st century: Revising the 1980 OECD Guidelines," Oxford Internet Institute, University of Oxford, http://www.oii.ox.ac.uk/publications/Data_Protection_Principles_for_the_21st_Century.pdf. President's Council of Advisors on Science and Technology (May 2014), "Big data and privacy: A technology perspective," http://www.whitehouse.gov/sites/default/files/microsites/ostp/PCAST/pcast_big_data_and_privacy_-_may_2014.pdf.

231 **the privacy harms come from:** Chris Jay Hoofnagle (2 Sep 2014), "The Potemkinism of privacy pragmatism," *Slate*, http://www.slate.com/articles/technology/future_tense/2014/09/data_use_regulation_the_libertarian_push_behind_a_new_take_on_privacy.single.html.

232 **One intriguing idea has been:** A. Michael Froomkin (23 Feb 2014), "Regulating mass surveillance as privacy pollution: Learning from environmental impact statements," University of Miami, http://papers.ssrn.com/sol3/papers.cfm?abstract_id=2400736.

233 **The regulatory agencies:** Julie Brill (2 Jun 2014), "Weaving a tapestry to protect privacy and competition in the age of Big Data," European Data Protection Supervisor's Workshop on Privacy, Consumer Protection and Competition in the Digital Age, Brussels, Belgium, http://www.ftc.gov/system/files/documents/public_statements/313311/140602edpsbrill2.pdf. Jules Polonetsky and Omer Tene (6 Dec 2012), "It's not how much data you have, but how you use it: Assessing privacy in the context of consumer data integration," Future of Privacy Forum, http://www.futureofprivacy.org/wp-content/uploads/FPF-White-Paper-Its-Not-How-Much-Data-You-Have-But-How-You-Use-It_FINAL.pdf.

233 **what the United States needs:** European Union (9 Dec 2013), "National data protection authorities," http://ec.europa.eu/justice/data-protection/bodies/authorities/index_en.htm.

234 **Other applications prefer having:** Alon Halevy, Peter Norvig, and Fernando

Pereira (Mar/Apr 2009), "The unreasonable effectiveness of data," *IEEE Intelligent Systems* 24, https://static.googleusercontent.com/media/research.google.com/en/us/pubs/archive/35179.pdf.

234 **Twitter . . . is giving its data:** Doug Gross (7 Jan 2013), "Library of Congress digs into 170 billion tweets," CNN, http://www.cnn.com/2013/01/07/tech/social-media/library-congress-twitter.

234 **the German language:** Martin Fowler (12 Dec 2013), "Datensparsamkeit," http://martinfowler.com/bliki/Datensparsamkeit.html.

235 **The US is the only Western country:** Of course, legal protections do not necessarily translate to actual protection. In 2011, the German government was found to be using a Trojan to spy on German citizens, in violation of its very strong data protection laws. As we've learned again and again, no law can secure us from a government that refuses to abide by it. Chaos Computer Club (8 Oct 2011), "Chaos Computer Club analyzes government malware," http://ccc.de/en/updates/2011/staatstrojaner.

235 **We do have protections for certain:** DLA Piper (7 Mar 2013), "Data protection laws of the world," http://files.dlapiper.com/files/Uploads/Documents/Data_Protection_Laws_of_the_World_2013.pdf. Theodore J. Kobus III and Gonzalo S. Zeballos (19 Feb 2014), "2014 international compendium of data privacy laws," Baker Hostetler, http://www.bakerlaw.com/files/Uploads/Documents/Data%20Breach%20documents/International-Compendium-of-Data-Privacy-Laws.pdf.

235 **Google has my lifelong search history:** I can get at some of it if I have search history enabled. Dave Greenbaum (12 Jul 2014), "Google's new account history page helps further control your privacy," *Life Hacker*, http://lifehacker.com/googles-new-account-history-page-helps-further-control-1603125500.

235 **Medtronic maintains that data:** Hugh Campos (19 Nov 2011), "Hugo Campos fights for the right to open his heart's data," TEDxCambridge, Cambridge, Massachusetts, http://tedxtalks.ted.com/video/TEDxCambridge-Hugo-Campos-fight.

235 **different types of data:** Bruce Schneier (Jul/Aug 2010), "A taxonomy of social networking data," *IEEE Security & Privacy* 8 (4), http://ieeexplore.ieee.org/xpls/abs_all.jsp?arnumber=5523874.

236 **you could either make your Facebook:** Blake Ross (13 Sep 2011), "Improved friend lists," *Facebook*, https://www.facebook.com/notes/facebook/improved-friend-lists/10150278932602131.

236 **Tweets are either direct messages:** Tony Bradley (13 Oct 2010), "Think your tweet is private? Think again," *PC World*, http://www.pcworld.com/article/207710/think_your_twitter_dm_is_private_think_again.html.

236 **Instagram posts can be either:** Leslie Meredith (15 Jan 2013), "Why you should make Instagram private before Saturday," *NBC News*, http://www.nbcnews.com/tech/internet/why-you-should-make-instagram-private-saturday-f1B7987618.

236 **Pinterest pages have public:** Serge Malenkovich (25 Jan 2013), "How to protect your privacy on Pinterest," *Kaspersky Lab Daily*, http://blog.kaspersky.com/protect-your-privacy-on-pinterest.

236 **In 2014, a presidential review group:** US Executive Office of the President (1 May 2014), "Big data: Seizing opportunities, preserving values," http://www.whitehouse.gov/sites/default/files/docs/big_data_privacy_report_may_1_2014.pdf.

236 **Jaron Lanier proposes a scheme:** Jaron Lanier (2013), *Who Owns the Future?* Simon and Schuster, http://books.google.com/books?id=w_LobtmRYmQC.

237 **US Consumer Privacy Bill of Rights:** US Executive Office of the President (Feb 2012), "Consumer data privacy in a networked world: A framework for protecting privacy and promoting innovation in the global digital economy," http://www.whitehouse.gov/sites/default/files/privacy-final.pdf.

238 **the EU is currently grappling with:** European Commission (8 Jul 2014), "Factsheet on the 'Right to be Forgotten' ruling (C-131/12)," http://ec.europa.eu/justice/data-protection/files/factsheets/factsheet_data_protection_en.pdf.

238 **European Court of Justice ruled:** Rory Cellan-Jones (13 May 2014), "EU court backs 'right to be forgotten' in Google case," *BBC News*, http://www.bbc.com/news/world-europe-27388289. Court of Justice of the European Union (13 May 2014), "Judgment in Case C-131/12: *Google Spain SL, Google Inc. v Agencia Española de Protección de Datos, Mario Costeja González*," http://curia.europa.eu/jcms/upload/docs/application/pdf/2014-05/cp140070en.pdf.

238 **This caused a torrent of people:** Jane Wakefield (15 May 2014), "Politician and pedophile ask Google to 'be forgotten,'" *BBC News*, http://www.bbc.com/news/technology-27423527.

238 **this is an important right:** Alessandro Mantelero (Jun 2013), "The EU Proposal for a General Data Protection Regulation and the roots of the 'right to be forgotten,'" *Computer Law and Security Review* 29, http://www.sciencedirect.com/science/article/pii/S0267364913000654.

239 **What they're consenting to:** There have been lots of experiments to demonstrate this. Patricia A. Norberg, Daniel R. Horne, and David A. Horne (Summer 2007), "The privacy paradox: Personal information disclosure intentions versus behaviors," *Journal of Consumer Affairs* 41, http://onlinelibrary.wiley.com/doi/10.1111/j.1745-6606.2006.00070.x/abstract. Leslie K. John, Alessandro Acquisti, and George Loewenstein (6 Jul 2009), "The best of strangers: Context-dependent willingness to divulge personal information," Social Sciences Research Network, http://papers.ssrn.com/sol3/papers.cfm?abstract_id=1430482. Susan Waters and James Ackerman (Oct 2011), "Exploring privacy management on Facebook: Motivations and perceived consequences of voluntary disclosure," *Journal of Computer-Mediated Communication* 17, http://onlinelibrary.wiley.com/doi/10.1111/j.1083-6101.2011.01559.x/full. Fred Stutzman, Ralph Gross, and Alessandro Acquisti (Apr 2013), "Silent listeners: The evolution of privacy and disclosure on Facebook," *Journal of Privacy and Confidentiality* 4, https://www.cylab.cmu.edu/news_events/news/2013/acquisti-7-year-study-facebook-privacy.html.

239 **systems we use are deliberately:** It turns out that it's surprisingly easy to manipulate people into ignoring their privacy concerns. Idris Adjerid et al. (22 Mar 2013), "Sleights of privacy: Framing, disclosures, and the limits of transparency," *SOUPS '13: Proceedings of the Ninth Symposium on Usable Privacy and Security*, http://www.heinz.cmu.edu/~acquisti/papers/acquisti-sleights-privacy.pdf.

239 **Companies will be less inclined:** Sara M. Watson (29 Apr 2014), "If customers knew how you use their data, would they call it creepy?" *HBR Blog Network*, http://blogs.hbr.org/2014/04/if-customers-knew-how-you-use-their-data-would-they-call-it-creepy.

240 **And users will be less likely:** Chris Jay Hoofnagle and Jan Whittington (28 Feb 2014), "Free: Accounting for the costs of the Internet's most popular price," *UCLA Law Review* 61, http://papers.ssrn.com/sol3/papers.cfm?abstract_id=2235962.

240 **Notice, choice, and consent:** Kirsten Martin (2 Dec 2013), "Transaction costs, pri-

vacy, and trust: The laudable goals and ultimate failure of notice and choice to respect privacy online," *First Monday* 18, http://firstmonday.org/ojs/index.php/fm/article/view/4838/3802.

241 **We need information fiduciaries:** Near as I can tell, this idea has been independently proposed by two law professors. Jerry Kang et al. (Mar 2012), "Self-surveillance privacy," *Iowa Law Review* 97, http://papers.ssrn.com/sol3/papers.cfm?abstract_id=1729332. Jack M. Balkin (5 Mar 2014), "Information fiduciaries in the digital age," *Balkinization*, http://balkin.blogspot.co.uk/2014/03/information-fiduciaries-in-digital-age.html.

241 **comparable to investment advisors:** Jonathan Zittrain (1 Jun 2014), "Facebook could decide an election without anyone ever finding out," *New Republic*, http://www.newrepublic.com/article/117878/information-fiduciary-solution-facebook-digital-gerrymandering.

241 **Dan Geer proposed that Internet:** Dan Geer (9 Oct 2013), "Tradeoffs in cyber security," http://geer.tinho.net/geer.uncc.9x13.txt.

242 **Surveillance became the business model:** The inventor of the pop-up ad has apologized. Ethan Zuckerman (14 Aug 2014), "The Internet's own original sin," *Atlantic*, http://www.theatlantic.com/technology/archive/2014/08/advertising-is-the-internets-original-sin/376041.

242 **a lot of research on building privacy:** Ann Cavoukian (Jan 2011), "Privacy by Design: The 7 foundational principles," *Privacy by Design*, http://www.privacybydesign.ca/content/uploads/2009/08/7foundationalprinciples.pdf. US Federal Trade Commission (Mar 2012), "Protecting consumer privacy in an era of rapid change: Recommendations for businesses and policymakers," http://www.ftc.gov/sites/default/files/documents/reports/federal-trade-commission-report-protecting-consumer-privacy-era-rapid-change-recommendations/120326privacyreport.pdf.

242 **Companies like Google and Facebook:** Ingrid Lunden (30 Sep 2013), "Digital ads will be 22% of all U.S. ad spend in 2013, mobile ads 3.7%; total global ad spend in 2013 $503B," *Tech Crunch*, http://techcrunch.com/2013/09/30/digital-ads-will-be-22-of-all-u-s-ad-spend-in-2013-mobile-ads-3-7-total-gobal-ad-spend-in-2013-503b-says-zenithoptimedia. Marketing Charts (23 Dec 2013), "Data dive: US TV ad spend and influence (Updated—Q3 2013 data)," http://www.marketingcharts.com/wp/television/data-dive-us-tv-ad-spend-and-influence-22524.

242 **Journalist James Kunstler calls this:** James Kunstler (21 Oct 2005), "The psychology of previous investment," *Raise the Hammer*, http://www.raisethehammer.org/article/181.

243 **Some fought in court:** Charlie Savage (14 May 2014), "Phone company pushed back against NSA's data collection, court papers show," *New York Times*, http://www.nytimes.com/2014/05/15/us/politics/phone-company-pushed-back-against-nsas-data-collection-court-papers-show.html. Claire Cain Miller (13 Jun 2013), "Secret court ruling put tech companies in data bind," *New York Times*, http://www.nytimes.com/2013/06/14/technology/secret-court-ruling-put-tech-companies-in-data-bind.html.

243 **Many computer companies:** Ewen MacAskill (9 Sep 2013), "Yahoo files lawsuit against NSA over user data requests," *Guardian*, http://www.theguardian.com/world/2013/sep/09/yahoo-lawsuit-nsa-surveillance-requests. Mike Masnick (27 Jan 2014), "Feds reach settlement with Internet companies allowing them to report not

nearly enough details on surveillance efforts," *Tech Dirt*, https://www.techdirt.com/articles/20140127/17253826014/feds-reach-settlement-with-internet-companies-allowing-them-to-report-not-nearly-enough-details-surveillance-efforts.shtml. Spencer Ackerman (3 Feb 2014), "Microsoft, Facebook, Google and Yahoo release US surveillance requests," *Guardian*, http://www.theguardian.com/world/2014/feb/03/microsoft-facebook-google-yahoo-fisa-surveillance-requests.

243 **Google says it turned over:** Google (2014), "Transparency report," https://www.google.com/transparencyreport/userdatarequests/US.

244 **starting with CREDO Mobile:** Brian Fung (9 Jan 2014), "The first phone company to publish a transparency report isn't AT&T or Verizon," *Washington Post*, http://www.washingtonpost.com/blogs/the-switch/wp/2014/01/09/the-first-phone-company-to-publish-a-transparency-report-isnt-att-or-verizon.

244 **Verizon, for example, reports:** Verizon (22 Jan 2014), "Verizon transparency report," http://transparency.verizon.com/us-data.

244 **every three months Verizon:** Glenn Greenwald (5 Jun 2013), "NSA collecting phone records of millions of Verizon customers daily," *Guardian*, http://www.theguardian.com/world/2013/jun/06/nsa-phone-records-verizon-court-order.

244 **Apple announced that it would inform:** Craig Timberg (1 May 2014), "Apple, Facebook, others defy authorities, notify users of secret data demands," *Washington Post*, http://www.washingtonpost.com/business/technology/apple-facebook-others-defy-authorities-increasingly-notify-users-of-secret-data-demands-after-snowden-revelations/2014/05/01/b41539c6-cfd1-11e3-b812-0c92213941f4_story.html.

244 **Microsoft and Google have teamed:** Jacob Siegal (30 Aug 2013), "Microsoft, Google team up to sue federal government over NSA spying," *BGR*, http://bgr.com/2013/08/30/microsoft-google-nsa-lawsuit.

244 **Yahoo is doing the same:** Ewan MacAskill (9 Sep 2013), "Yahoo files lawsuit against NSA over user data requests," *Guardian*, http://www.theguardian.com/world/2013/sep/09/yahoo-lawsuit-nsa-surveillance-requests. Kevin Collier (15 Jul 2013), "Yahoo wins court order to release records of its fight against PRISM," *Daily Dot*, http://www.dailydot.com/news/yahoo-prism-court-win-fisa-declassified. Craig Timberg (11 Sep 2014), "U.S. threatened massive fine to force Yahoo to release data," *Washington Post*, http://www.washingtonpost.com/business/technology/us-threatened-massive-fine-to-force-yahoo-to-release-data/2014/09/11/38a7f69e-39e8-11e4-9c9f-ebb47272e40e_story.html.

244 **companies are employing "warrant canaries":** Cyrus Farivar (5 Nov 2013), "Apple takes strong privacy stance in new report, publishes rare 'warrant canary,'" *Ars Technica*, http://arstechnica.com/tech-policy/2013/11/apple-takes-strong-privacy-stance-in-new-report-publishes-rare-warrant-canary.

244 **valiant and clever effort:** In fact, Apple's canary disappeared in the report following the one where it debuted. No one is sure what it means. Jeff John Roberts (18 Sep 2014), "Apple's 'warrant canary' disappears, suggesting new Patriot Act demands," *Gigaom*, https://gigaom.com/2014/09/18/apples-warrant-canary-disappears-suggesting-new-patriot-act-demands.

244 **many companies are stepping up:** The Electronic Frontier Foundation is keeping a scorecard. Nate Cardozo, Parker Higgins, and Kurt Opsahl (13 Mar 2014), "Update: Encrypt the Web report: Who's doing what," Electronic Frontier Foundation, https://www.eff.org/deeplinks/2013/11/encrypt-web-report-whos-doing-what.

244 **After Google learned that the NSA:** Sean Gallagher (6 Nov 2013), "Googlers say 'F*** you' to NSA, company encrypts internal network," *Ars Technica*, http://arstechnica.com/information-technology/2013/11/googlers-say-f-you-to-nsa-company-encrypts-internal-network.

244 **After Yahoo learned that the NSA:** Barton Gellman and Ashkan Soltani (14 Oct 2013), "NSA collects millions of e-mail address books globally," *Washington Post*, http://www.washingtonpost.com/world/national-security/nsa-collects-millions-of-e-mail-address-books-globally/2013/10/14/8e58b5be-34f9-11e3-80c6-7e6dd8d22d8f_story.html.

245 **both Yahoo:** Andrea Peterson, Barton Gellman, and Ashkan Soltani (14 Oct 2013), "Yahoo to make SSL encryption the default for Webmail users. Finally," *Washington Post*, http://www.washingtonpost.com/blogs/the-switch/wp/2013/10/14/yahoo-to-make-ssl-encryption-the-default-for-webmail-users-finally.

245 **and Microsoft:** Craig Timberg, Barton Gellman, and Ashkan Soltani (26 Nov 2013), "Microsoft, suspecting NSA spying, to ramp up efforts to encrypt its Internet traffic," *Washington Post*, http://www.washingtonpost.com/business/technology/microsoft-suspecting-nsa-spying-to-ramp-up-efforts-to-encrypt-its-internet-traffic/2013/11/26/44236b48-56a9-11e3-8304-caf30787c0a9_story.html.

245 **Several large e-mail providers:** Some examples. Danny Yadron (3 Jun 2014), "Comcast to encrypt email for security," *Wall Street Journal*, http://online.wsj.com/articles/comcast-to-encrypt-email-for-security-1401841512. Mikey Campbell (13 Jun 2014), "Apple will soon encrypt iCloud emails in transit between service providers," *Apple Insider*, http://appleinsider.com/articles/14/06/13/apple-will-soon-encrypt-icloud-emails-in-transit-between-service-providers-.

245 **Other companies are doing more:** Nate Cardozo, Parker Higgins, and Kurt Opsahl (13 Mar 2014), "Update: Encrypt the web report: Who's doing what," Electronic Frontier Foundation, https://www.eff.org/deeplinks/2013/11/encrypt-web-report-whos-doing-what. Claire Cain Miller (13 Jun 2013), "Secret court ruling put tech companies in data bind," *New York Times*, http://www.nytimes.com/2013/06/14/technology/secret-court-ruling-put-tech-companies-in-data-bind.html.

245 **Both iPhones and Android phones:** In late 2014, Apple modified its system so everything is encrypted. Android phones had encryption capability since 2011, but Google made it the default in 2014 to match Apple. David E. Sanger and Brian X. Chen (26 Sep 2014), "Signaling post-Snowden era, new iPhone locks out NSA," *New York Times*, http://www.nytimes.com/2014/09/27/technology/iphone-locks-out-the-nsa-signaling-a-post-snowden-era-.html. Craig Timberg (18 Sep 2014), "Newest Androids will join iPhones in offering default encryption, blocking police," *Washington Post*, http://www.washingtonpost.com/blogs/the-switch/wp/2014/09/18/newest-androids-will-join-iphones-in-offering-default-encryption-blocking-police.

245 **Google is now offering:** Google (3 Jun 2014), "Transparency report: Protecting emails as they travel across the web," *Google Official Blog*, http://googleblog.blogspot.com/2014/06/transparency-report-protecting-emails.html.

245 **Yahoo secretly fought the NSA:** Claire Cain Miller (13 Jun 2013), "Secret court ruling put tech companies in data bind," *New York Times*, http://www.nytimes.com/2013/06/14/technology/secret-court-ruling-put-tech-companies-in-data-bind.html. Craig Timberg (11 Sep 2014), "U.S. threatened massive fine to force Yahoo to release data," *Washington Post*, http://www.washingtonpost.com/business/technology/us-threatened-

massive-fine-to-force-yahoo-to-release-data/2014/09/11/38a7f69e-39e8-11e4-9c9f-ebb47272e40e_story.html.

245 **Twitter unsuccessfully fought:** Kim Zetter (28 Aug 2012), "Twitter fights back to protect 'Occupy Wall Street' protester," *Wired,* http://www.wired.com/2012/08/twitter-appeals-occupy-order. Tiffany Kary (14 Sep 2012), "Twitter turns over Wall Street protester posts under seal," *Bloomberg News,* http://www.bloomberg.com/news/2012-09-14/twitter-turns-over-wall-street-protester-posts-under-seal.html.

245 **Facebook is fighting a court order:** Vindu Goel and James C. McKinley Jr. (26 Jun 2014), "Forced to hand over data, Facebook files appeal," *New York Times,* http://www.nytimes.com/2014/06/27/technology/facebook-battles-manhattan-da-over-warrants-for-user-data.html.

245 **none of the big e-mail providers:** Amicus curiae briefs were filed by three non-profit organizations: EFF, ACLU, and Empeopled LLC. Electronic Frontier Foundation (24 Oct 2013), "Brief of amicus curiae," *United States of America v. Under Seal 1; Under Seal 2* [Lavabit], Case Nos. 13-4625, 13-4626, United States Court of Appeals for the Fourth Circuit, https://www.eff.org/document/lavabit-amicus. American Civil Liberties Union (25 Oct 2013), "Brief of amicus curiae," *United States of America v. Under Seal 1; Under Seal 2* [Lavabit], Case Nos. 13-4625, 13-4626, United States Court of Appeals for the Fourth Circuit, https://www.aclu.org/sites/default/files/assets/stamped_lavabit_amicus.pdf. Empeopled LLC (24 Oct 2013), "Brief of amicus curiae," *United States of America v. Under Seal 1; Under Seal 2* [Lavabit], Case Nos. 13-4625, 13-4626, United States Court of Appeals for the Fourth Circuit, http://justsecurity.org/wp-content/uploads/2013/10/empeopled-lavabit-amicus.pdf.

245 **On four occasions in the early 2000s:** Rebecca MacKinnon (2006), "'Race to the bottom': Corporate complicity in Chinese Internet censorship," Human Rights Watch, http://www.hrw.org/reports/2006/china0806/5.htm.

246 **lobbying for legislative restrictions:** Thomas Lee (25 May 2014), "Mind your business: Slow flex of tech's lobbying muscle," *San Francisco Chronicle,* http://www.sfgate.com/technology/article/Mind-Your-Business-Slow-flex-of-tech-s-lobbying-5504172.php. Joseph Menn (5 Jun 2014), "U.S. technology companies beef up security to thwart mass spying," Reuters, http://www.reuters.com/article/2014/06/05/us-cybersecurity-tech-idUSKBN0EG2BN20140605. Reform Government Surveillance (2014), https://www.reformgovernmentsurveillance.com.

246 **The EU has been trying to pass:** Zack Whittaker (4 Feb 2013), "Privacy groups call on US government to stop lobbying against EU data law changes," *ZDNet,* http://www.zdnet.com/privacy-groups-call-on-us-government-to-stop-lobbying-against-eu-data-law-changes-7000010721. James Fontanella-Khan (26 Jun 2013), "Brussels: Astroturfing takes root," *Financial Times,* http://www.ft.com/cms/s/0/74271926-dd9f-11e2-a756-00144feab7de.html. David Meyer (12 Mar 2014), "Web firms face a strict new set of privacy rules in Europe: Here's what to expect," *Gigaom,* http://gigaom.com/2014/03/12/web-firms-face-a-strict-new-set-of-privacy-rules-in-europe-heres-what-to-expect.

246 **a new Magna Carta:** Tim Berners-Lee (Dec 2010), "Long live the Web," *Scientific American,* http://www.cs.virginia.edu/~robins/Long_Live_the_Web.pdf.

246 **that imposes responsibilities:** Jemima Kiss (11 Mar 2014), "An online Magna Carta: Berners-Lee calls for bill of rights for web," *Guardian,* http://www.theguardian.com/technology/2014/mar/12/online-magna-carta-berners-lee-web.

247 **the prevailing political philosophy:** Thomas Hobbes (1651), *Leviathan*, Printed for Andrew Crooke, http://www.gutenberg.org/files/3207/3207-h/3207-h.htm.

247 **John Locke argued:** John Locke (1690), *Two Treatises of Government*, Printed for Awnsham Churchill, http://books.google.com/books/?id=LqA4nQEACAAJ.

247 **Rebecca MacKinnon makes this point:** Rebecca MacKinnon (2012), *Consent of the Networked: The Worldwide Struggle for Internet Freedom*, Basic Books, http://www.owlasylum.net/owl_underground/social/ConsentoftheNetworked.pdf.

247 **Madrid Privacy Declaration (2009):** The Public Voice (3 Nov 2009), "The Madrid Privacy Declaration," International Conference of Data Protection and Privacy Commissioners, Madrid, Spain, http://privacyconference2011.org/htmls/adopted Resolutions/2009_Madrid/2009_M1.2.pdf.

15: SOLUTIONS FOR THE REST OF US

251 **Law professor Eben Moglen wrote:** Eben Moglen (27 May 2014), "Privacy under attack: The NSA files revealed new threats to democracy," *Guardian*, http://www.theguardian.com/technology/2014/may/27/-sp-privacy-under-attack-nsa-files-revealed-new-threats-democracy.

251 **I'm going to break them down:** Sociologist Gary Marx cataloged 11 different ways people resist surveillance; I'm going to be drawing on his taxonomy in this section. Gary T. Marx (May 2003), "A tack in the shoe: Neutralizing and resisting the new surveillance," *Journal of Social Issues* 59, http://web.mit.edu/gtmarx/www/tack.html.

252 **Privacy enhancing technologies:** R. Jason Cronk (25 Nov 2013), "Thoughts on the term 'privacy enhancing technologies,'" *Privacy Maverick*, http://privacymaverick.com/2013/11/25/thoughts-on-the-term-privacy-enhancing-technologies.

252 **Privacy Badger:** Jon Brodkin (2 May 2014), "EFF 'Privacy Badger' plugin aimed at forcing websites to stop tracking users," *Ars Technica*, http://arstechnica.com/information-technology/2014/05/eff-privacy-badger-plugin-aimed-at-forcing-websites-to-stop-tracking-users.

252 **and others:** Electronic Privacy Information Center (2014), "EPIC online guide to practical privacy tools," http://epic.org/privacy/tools.html.

252 **Remember that the private browsing:** Sara M. Watson (24 Sep 2014), "Ask the Decoder: How private is private browsing, really?" Al Jazeera, http://america.aljazeera.com/articles/2014/9/24/private-browsing.html.

252 **Microsoft's BitLocker:** Microsoft Corporation (21 Aug 2013), "BitLocker overview," http://technet.microsoft.com/en-us/library/hh831713.aspx.

252 **Apple's FileVault:** Apple Corporation (Aug 2012), "Best practices for deploying FileVault 2," http://training.apple.com/pdf/WP_FileVault2.pdf.

252 **I recommended TrueCrypt:** James Lyne (29 May 2014), "Open source crypto TrueCrypt disappears with suspicious cloud of mystery," *Forbes*, http://www.forbes.com/sites/jameslyne/2014/05/29/open-source-crypto-truecrypt-disappears-with-suspicious-cloud-of-mystery.

252 **a chat encryption program:** Nikita Borisov, Ian Goldberg, and Eric Brewer (28 Oct 2004), "Off-the-record communication, or, Why not to use PGP," ACM Workshop on Privacy in the Electronic Society (WPES'04), Washington, D.C., https://otr.cypherpunks.ca/otr-wpes.pdf.

253 **Google is now offering encrypted e-mail:** Stephan Somogyi (3 Jun 2014), "Making end-to-end encryption easier to use," *Google Online Security Blog*, http://googleonli nesecurity.blogspot.com/2014/06/making-end-to-end-encryption-easier-to.html.

253 **TLS—formerly SSL—is a protocol:** Tim Dierks and Eric Rescorla (17 Apr 2014), "The Transport Layer Security (TLS) Protocol Version 1.3," Internet Engineering Task Force Trust, Network Working Group, http://tools.ietf.org/html/draft-ietf-tls-rfc5246-bis-00.

253 **You can make sure it's always on:** Electronic Frontier Foundation (2014), "HTTPS Everywhere," https://www.eff.org/Https-everywhere.

253 **go on the Internet to find out:** Here's a good guide. Electronic Privacy Information Center (2014), "EPIC online guide to practical privacy tools," http://epic.org/privacy/tools.html.

253 **very annoying to use:** Peter Bright and Dan Goodin (14 Jun 2013), "Encrypted e-mail: How much annoyance will you tolerate to keep the NSA away?" *Ars Technica*, http://arstechnica.com/security/2013/06/encrypted-e-mail-how-much-annoy ance-will-you-tolerate-to-keep-the-nsa-away.

253 **The standards bodies that run the Internet:** Here's the Internet Engineering Task Force's statement on security and pervasive monitoring. Jari Arkko and Stephen Farrell (7 Sep 2014), "Security and pervasive monitoring," Internet Engineering Task Force, https://www.ietf.org/blog/2013/09/security-and-pervasive-monitoring.

254 **various proxies can be used:** Mirimir (2014), "Advanced privacy and anonymity using VMs, VPN's, Tor, etc," *IVPN*, https://www.ivpn.net/privacy-guides/advanced-pri vacy-and-anonymity-part-1.

254 **The program Onionshare:** Andy Greenberg (21 May 2014), "Free app lets the next Snowden send big files securely and anonymously," *Wired*, http://www.wired .com/2014/05/onionshare.

254 **cell phones in a refrigerator:** Most modern refrigerators are not metal boxes, and don't make good Faraday cages. Check the details of your model before trying this yourself.

255 **hire someone to walk behind your car:** John Farrier (16 Apr 2014), "What is a job that exists only in your country?" *Neatorama*, http://www.neatorama.com/2014/04/16/ What-Is-a-Job-That-Exists-Only-in-Your-Country.

255 **face paint to fool facial recognition:** Robinson Meyer (24 Jul 2014), "Anti-surveil-lance camouflage for your face," *Atlantic*, http://www.theatlantic.com/features/ archive/2014/07/makeup/374929. Joseph Cox (14 Sep 2014), "The rise of the anti-facial recognition movement," *Kernel*, http://kernelmag.dailydot.com/issue-sec tions/features-issue-sections/10247/anti-facial-recognition-movement.

255 **special clothing to confuse drones:** Adam Harvey (2013), "Stealth wear," *AH Proj-ects*, http://ahprojects.com/projects/stealth-wear.

255 **there are lots of tricks:** A good list of techniques is here. Finn Brunton and Helen Nissenbaum (2 May 2011), "Vernacular resistance to data collection and analysis: A political theory of obfuscation," *First Monday* 15, http://firstmonday.org/article/ view/3493/2955.

255 **puts rocks in his shoes:** That trick also appears in Robert A. Heinlein's *Double Star*. Robert A. Heinlein (1956), *Double Star*, Doubleday, http://books.google.com/ books?id=bnoGAQAAIAAJ.

256 **your kids do it all the time:** danah boyd et al. (7 Nov 2011), "Why parents help their

children lie to Facebook about age: Unintended consequences of the 'Children's Online Privacy Protection Act,'" *First Monday* 16, http://firstmonday.org/ojs/index .php/fm/article/view/3850/3075.

256 **that was socially awkward:** Overcoming this awkwardness is important. There's a story where a customer refused to give Comcast a reason why he was disconnecting. At first, it seems rude. But when you think about it, Comcast is not entitled to this information. Xeni Jardin (14 Jul 2014), "Listen to Comcast torture Ryan Block and Veronica Belmont as they try to cancel service," *Boing Boing*, http://boingboing .net/2014/07/14/listen-to-comcast-torture-ryan.html.

257 **You'll find your own sweet spot:** Julia Angwin wrote an excellent account of her year-long quest to evade surveillance in the Internet age. Julia Angwin (2014), *Dragnet Nation: A Quest for Privacy, Security, and Freedom in a World of Relentless Surveillance*, Times Books, http://books.google.com/books?id=bbS6AQAAQBAJ.

257 **Geopolitical conflicts aren't going away:** Stewart Baker makes this point. Stewart A. Baker (29 Oct 2013), "Potential amendments to the Foreign Intelligence Surveillance Act," Testimony before the Permanent Select Committee on Intelligence of the United States House of Representatives, http://intelligence.house.gov/sites/ intelligence.house.gov/files/documents/Baker10292013.pdf.

258 **NSA director General Keith Alexander said:** David E. Sanger (13 Aug 2013), "NSA leaks make plan for cyberdefense unlikely," *New York Times*, http://www.nytimes .com/2013/08/13/us/nsa-leaks-make-plan-for-cyberdefense-unlikely.html.

259 **You're going to be affected:** DLA Piper (7 Mar 2013), "Data protection laws of the world," DLA Piper, http://files.dlapiper.com/files/Uploads/Documents/Data_Pro tection_Laws_of_the_World_2013.pdf.

259 **because Microsoft is a US company:** In 2014, Microsoft unsuccessfully challenged a US demand for data stored solely in Ireland. The court demanded that the company turn it over to the US government. The decision is currently stayed while it is being appealed. Joseph Ax (31 Jul 2014), "U.S. judge orders Microsoft to submit customer's emails from abroad," Reuters, http://www.reuters.com/article/2014/07/31/usa-tech-warrants-idUSL2N0Q61WN20140731.

259 **The UK wants similar access:** Guardian (19 Sep 2014), "Former UK ambassador to the United States given data-access role," *Guardian*, http://www.theguardian.com/ technology/2014/sep/19/sir-nigel-shienwald-data-access-role-david-cameron.

260 **Apple's business model protects:** Rich Mogull (25 Jun 2014), "Why Apple really cares about your privacy," *Macworld*, http://www.macworld.com/article/2366921/ why-apple-really-cares-about-your-privacy.html. Charles Arthur (18 Sep 2014), "Apple's Tim Cook attacks Google and Facebook over privacy flaws," *Guardian*, http://www.theguardian.com/technology/2014/sep/18/apple-tim-cook-google-facebook-privacy-surveillance.

260 **Do you trust a company:** European countries allow for far more permissive government access than the US does. Cyrus Farivar (13 Oct 2013), "Europe won't save you: Why e-mail is probably safer in the US," *Ars Technica*, http://arstechnica.com/ tech-policy/2013/10/europe-wont-save-you-why-e-mail-is-probably-safer-in-the-us.

260 **European Court of Justice struck down:** James Kanter (8 Apr 2014), "European court rejects data retention rules, citing privacy," *New York Times*, http://www .nytimes.com/2014/04/09/business/international/european-court-rejects-data-re tention-rules-citing-privacy.html.

261 **the UK government rushed through:** David Meyer (17 Jul 2014), "The UK's 'emergency' DRIP surveillance law is now a done deal," *Gigaom*, http://gigaom.com/2014/07/17/the-uks-emergency-drip-surveillance-law-is-now-a-done-deal.

261 **It was an ugly political railroad job:** Ray Corrigan (11 Jul 2014), "Mass surveillance and scared politicians," *B2fxxx*, http://b2fxxx.blogspot.com/2014/07/mass-surveillance-and-scared-politicians.html.

262 **sites that identify surveillance cameras:** No CCTV, http://www.no-cctv.org.uk/camera_locations/default.asp. The CCTV Treasure Hunt, http://cctvtreasurehunt.wordpress.com. NYC Surveillance Camera Project, http://www.mediaeater.com/cameras.

263 **South Korean teachers objecting:** Christian (24 Jun 2004), "After the Saturday large demonstration against NEIS South Korean government shows how it understand the democracy," *Jinbo*, http://act.jinbo.net/drupal/node/5819. Seoyong Kim and Sunhee Kim (Oct 2004), "The conflict over the use of information technology in South Korean schools," *Innovation* 17, http://ajou.ac.kr/~seoyong/paper/Seoyong%20Kim-2004-The%20Conflict%20Over%20the%20Use%20of%20Information%20Technology.pdf.

263 **German consumers opposing:** IBM Corporation (16 Dec 2004), "METRO Group's Future Store takes German public by storm—thanks to wireless technology," ftp://ftp.software.ibm.com/software/solutions/pdfs/10704035_Metro_cs_1b.pdf. Kim Zetter (28 Feb 2004), "Germans protest radio-ID plans," *Wired*, http://archive.wired.com/techbiz/media/news/2004/02/62472. Jan Libbenga (1 Mar 2004), "German revolt against RFID," *Register*, http://www.theregister.co.uk/2004/03/01/german_revolt_against_rfid.

263 **Facebook users objecting:** K. C. Jones (17 Feb 2009), "Facebook's terms of use draw protest," *Information Week*, http://www.informationweek.com/software/social/facebooks-terms-of-use-draw-protest/d/d-id/1076697. Bobbie Johnson and Afua Hirsch (18 Feb 2009), "Facebook backtracks after online privacy protest," *Guardian*, http://www.theguardian.com/technology/2009/feb/19/facebook-personal-data.

263 **US airline travelers objecting to:** Ashley Halsey III and Derek Kravitz (25 Nov 2010), "Protests of TSA airport pat-downs, body scanners don't delay Thanksgiving travel," *Washington Post*, http://www.washingtonpost.com/wp-dyn/content/article/2010/11/24/AR2010112406989.html. Jason Keyser (25 Oct 2012), "TSA quietly removing some full body scanners," Associated Press, http://bigstory.ap.org/article/government-replaces-body-scanners-some-airports-0.

263 **It's how worldwide change happens:** It's the idea of incremental change, or muddling through. Charles E. Lindblom (Spring 1959), "The science of 'muddling through,'" *Public Administration Review* 19, http://www.jstor.org/stable/973677.

16: SOCIAL NORMS AND THE BIG DATA TRADE-OFF

267 **No one in Congress read it:** Paul Blumenthal (2 Mar 2009), "Congress had no time to read the USA PATRIOT Act," Sunlight Foundation, http://sunlightfoundation.com/blog/2009/03/02/congress-had-no-time-to-read-the-usa-patriot-act.

267 **almost everyone in the country:** Leonie Huddy and Stanley Feldman (Sep 2011), "Americans respond politically to 9/11: Understanding the impact of the terrorist

attacks and their aftermath," *American Psychologist* 66, http://www.ncbi.nlm.nih
.gov/pubmed/21823777.

267 **tried to improve the messaging:** Tim Dawson (9 Jun 2014), "More like the Stasi
than James Bond," National Union of Journalists, http://www.nuj.org.uk/news/
more-like-the-stasi-than-james-bond.

267 **if listeners are scared of terrorists:** Joseph H. Campos III (7 Sep 2013), "Memory
and remembrance: The diffusion of fear, horror and terror into control and legitimacy," At the Interface, Mansfield College, Oxford, UK, http://www.inter-disci
plinary.net/at-the-interface/wp-content/uploads/2013/07/camposfhtpaper.pdf.

267 **more congressional oversight:** Jack Goldsmith (9 Aug 2013), "Reflections on NSA
oversight, and a prediction that NSA authorities (and oversight, and transparency)
will expand," *Lawfare*, http://www.lawfareblog.com/2013/08/reflections-on-nsa-
oversight-and-a-prediction-that-nsa-authorities-and-oversight-and-transparency-
will-expand.

267 **Fear trumps privacy:** Donna G. Bair-Mundy (Aug 2009), "Of terrorists, tyrants, and
social turmoil: A competing-fears theoretical model for the evolution of law relating
to telecommunication privacy vis-a-vis law enforcement surveillance in America,"
University of Hawai'i at Manoa, http://books.google.com/books?id=8LveYgEACAAJ.
Samuel Best et al. (Dec 2012), "Al Qaeda versus Big Brother: Anxiety about government
monitoring and support for domestic counterterrorism policies," *Political Behavior* 34,
http://link.springer.com/article/10.1007%2Fs11109-011-9177-6. Keven G. Ruby (2012),
*Society, State, and Fear: Managing National Security at the Boundary between Compla-
cency and Panic*, University of Chicago Press, http://books.google.com/books?id=
UPILnwEACAAJ.

267 **If strong enough, it trumps all:** Dawn Rothe and Stephen L. Muzzatti (Nov 2004),
"Enemies everywhere: Terrorism, moral panic, and U.S. civil society," *Critical Crim-
inology* 12, http://www.researchgate.net/publication/227209259_Enemies_Every
where_Terrorism_Moral_Panic_and_US_Civil_Society/file/32bfe50d3c7fe0d03b
.pdf. David Rothkopf (6 Aug 2013), "The real risks," *Foreign Policy*, http://www.for
eignpolicy.com/articles/2013/08/06/the_real_risks_war_on_terror.

267 **they believe they have to do:** It's CYA security. Bruce Schneier (22 Feb 2007), "Why
smart cops do dumb things," *Wired*, http://archive.wired.com/politics/security/
commentary/securitymatters/2007/02/72774.

267 **Keeping the fear stoked:** Leaked NSA talking points specifically reference 9/11: "I
much prefer to be here today explaining these programs, than explaining another
9/11 event that we were not able to prevent." Jason Leopold (30 Oct 2013), "Revealed:
NSA pushed 9/11 as key 'sound bite' to justify surveillance," Al Jazeera, http://amer
ica.aljazeera.com/articles/2013/10/30/revealed-nsa-pushed911askeysoundbiteto
justifysurveillance.html.

268 **Clay Shirky has noted:** Clay Shirky (14 Mar 2010), Remarks at South by Southwest
(SXSW), Austin, TX, quoted in Kevin Kelly (2 Apr 2010), "The Shirky principle," *Kevin
Kelly*, http://kk.org/thetechnium/2010/04/the-shirky-prin.

268 **And then the laws will change:** Stewart Baker (24 Feb 2014), Remarks at 2014
Executive Security Action Forum Annual Meeting, RSA Conference, San Francisco,
California.

268 **Jack Goldsmith again:** Jack Goldsmith (9 Aug 2013), "Reflections on NSA over
sight, and a prediction that NSA authorities (and oversight, and transparency) will

expand," *Lawfare*, http://www.lawfareblog.com/2013/08/reflections-on-nsa-over
sight-and-a-prediction-that-nsa-authorities-and-oversight-and-transparency-
will-expand.

268 **we need to take risks:** I think the people of North Korea and Cuba are safe from
terrorist attacks, but at what price?

268 **It's not just politicians:** Bruce Schneier (17 May 2007), "Virginia Tech lesson: Rare
risks breed irrational responses," *Wired*, http://archive.wired.com/politics/secu
rity/commentary/securitymatters/2007/05/securitymatters_0517.

268 **We also need to counter the notion:** The phrase is much older, from a Supreme
Court decision. "The choice is not between order and liberty. It is between liberty with
order and anarchy without either. There is danger that, if the Court does not temper
its doctrinaire logic with a little practical wisdom, it will convert the constitutional
Bill of Rights into a suicide pact." US Supreme Court (16 May 1949), Opinion, *Termini-
ello v. Chicago*, http://caselaw.lp.findlaw.com/scripts/getcase.pl?court=us&vol=337&
invol=1.

268 **a sentiment based in fear:** Linda Greenhouse (22 Sep 2002), "Suicide pact," *New
York Times*, http://www.nytimes.com/2002/09/22/weekinreview/the-nation-sui
cide-pact.html.

269 **What it says is something like this:** There's even a book with the title. Richard A.
Posner (2006), *Not a Suicide Pact: The Constitution in a Time of National Emergency*,
Oxford University Press, http://books.google.com/books?id=hP6PAAAAMAAJ.

269 **massacre in Norway:** Richard Orange (14 Apr 2012), "'Answer hatred with love':
How Norway tried to cope with the horror of Anders Breivik," *Guardian*, http://
www.theguardian.com/world/2012/apr/15/anders-breivik-norway-copes-horror.
Balazs Koranyi and Victoria Klesty (26 Apr 2012), "Tens of thousands protest at Norway Breivik trial," Reuters, http://in.reuters.com/article/2012/04/26/norway-brei
vik-protest-idINDEE83P0B720120426. Tim Cushing (26 Jul 2012), "One year after
the Breivik massacre, Norway continues to fight terrorism with democracy, openness and love," *Tech Dirt*, https://www.techdirt.com/articles/20120724/203635
19819/one-year-after-breivik-massacre-norway-continues-to-fight-terrorism-
with-democracy-openness-love.shtml.

269 **Indomitability is the correct response:** Bruce Schneier (7 Jan 2012), "Our reaction is the real security failure," *AOL News*, https://www.schneier.com/essays/
archives/2010/01/our_reaction_is_the.html.

269 **There's hope for the US:** John Mueller and Mark G. Stewart (2011), *Terror, Security, and
Money: Balancing the Risks, Benefits, and Costs of Homeland Security*, Oxford University
Press, chap. 9, http://books.google.com/books?id=l1IrmjCdguYC&pg=PA172.

270 **it's well past time to move beyond fear:** I even wrote a book with that title. Bruce
Schneier (2003), *Beyond Fear: Thinking Sensibly about Security in an Uncertain World*,
Wiley, http://books.google.com/books/about/?id=wuNImmQufGsC.

270 **shift in Americans' perceptions:** Nate Silver (10 Jul 2013), "Public opinion shifts
on security-liberty balance," *Fivethirtyeight*, *New York Times*, http://fivethirty
eight.blogs.nytimes.com/2013/07/10/public-opinion-shifts-on-security-liberty-
balance.

270 **Our personal definitions of privacy:** New York University law professor Helen
Nissenbaum argues that privacy can only be properly understood in terms of context and expectations. Helen Nissenbaum (Fall 2011), "A contextual approach to

privacy online," *Daedalus* 11, http://www.amacad.org/publications/daedalus/11_fall_nissenbaum.pdf. Alexis C. Madrigal (29 Mar 2012), "The philosopher whose fingerprints are all over the FTC's new approach to privacy," *Atlantic*, http://www.theatlantic.com/technology/print/2012/03/the-philosopher-whose-fingerprints-are-all-over-the-ftcs-new-approach-to-privacy/254365.

270 **They're different in the US:** This means there will always be some regional differences in the Internet, although its international nature necessitates more homogeneity.

270 **Lawyers look up potential jurors:** Sarah Grider Cronan and Neal F. Bailen (5 Apr 2007), "'Should I Google the jury?' and other ethical considerations," Section of Litigation, American Bar Association, http://apps.americanbar.org/litigation/committees/products/articles/0407_cronan.html.

270 **people look up each other:** Samantha Henig (Mar 2013), "Why you should stop Googling your dates," *Glamour*, http://www.glamour.com/sex-love-life/2013/03/why-you-should-stop-googling-your-dates. This video shows how creepy this sort of thing can get. Mario Contreras (29 May 2014), "Meet in a public place," *Vimeo*, http://vimeo.com/96870066.

270 **Google stalking:** Andrea Bartz and Brenna Ehrlich (7 Dec 2011), "The dos and don'ts of Googling people," CNN, http://www.cnn.com/2011/12/07/tech/social-media/netiquette-google-stalking.

271 **Julian Assange's old OKCupid:** Joe Coscarelli (12 Dec 2010), "Does Julian Assange have a profile on OKCupid?" *Village Voice*, http://blogs.villagevoice.com/runnin scared/2010/12/does_julian_ass.php.

271 **Revenge porn . . . is an extreme example:** Economist (5 Jun 2014), "Misery merchants," *Economist*, http://www.economist.com/news/international/21606307-how-should-online-publication-explicit-images-without-their-subjects-consent-be.

271 **Mug shot extortion sites:** David Kravets (15 Jul 2013), "Mugshot-removal sites accused of extortion," *Wired*, http://www.wired.com/2013/07/mugshot-removal-extortion. David Segal (6 Oct 2013), "Mugged by a mug shot online," *New York Times*, http://www.nytimes.com/2013/10/06/business/mugged-by-a-mug-shot-online.html.

271 **This is essentially the point of:** David Brin (1998), *The Transparent Society: Will Technology Force Us to Choose between Privacy and Freedom?* Basic Books, http://www.davidbrin.com/transparentsociety1.html.

271 **Clay Shirky pointed out:** Emily Nussbaum (12 Feb 2007), "Say everything," *New York Magazine*, http://nymag.com/news/features/27341.

272 **grow up with more surveillance:** Jessy Irwin (7 Oct 2014), "Grooming students for a lifetime of surveillance," *Model View Culture*, http://modelviewculture.com/pieces/grooming-students-for-a-lifetime-of-surveillance.

272 **schools with ID checks:** Some schools are requiring students to wear electronic badges: the same technology that farmers use with livestock. Associated Press (11 Oct 2010), "Houston-area schools tracking students with radio frequency badges," *Dallas Morning News*, http://www.dallasnews.com/news/education/headlines/20101011-Houston-area-schools-tracking-students-with-6953.ece.

272 **Charter of Fundamental Rights:** The charter was declared in 2000, but didn't have full force of law until it was ratified as part of the Treaty of Lisbon in 2009.

European Union (18 Dec 2000), "Charter of Fundamental Rights of the European Union," http://ec.europa.eu/justice/fundamental-rights/charter/index_en.htm.

273 **Privacy is recognized as a fundamental right:** United Nations (10 Dec 1948), "The Universal Declaration of Human Rights," http://www.un.org/en/documents/udhr.

273 **European Convention on Human Rights:** The convention was revised in 2010. European Court of Human Rights (1 Jun 2010), "European Convention of Human Rights," Council of Europe, http://www.echr.coe.int/documents/convention_eng.pdf.

273 **It's in the US Constitution:** Doug Linder (2014), "Exploring constitutional conflicts: The right of privacy," University of Missouri, Kansas City, http://law2.umkc.edu/faculty/projects/ftrials/conlaw/rightofprivacy.html.

273 **It's part of the 2000 Charter:** European Union (18 Dec 2000), "Charter of Fundamental Rights of the European Union," http://ec.europa.eu/justice/fundamental-rights/charter/index_en.htm.

273 **the UN General Assembly approved:** The document reaffirms "the human right to privacy, according to which no one shall be subjected to arbitrary or unlawful interference with his or her privacy, family, home or correspondence, and the right to the protection of the law against such interference, and recognizing that the exercise of the right to privacy is important for the realization of the right to freedom of expression and to hold opinions without interference, and is one of the foundations of a democratic society." United Nations General Assembly (21 Jan 2014), "Resolution adopted by the General Assembly on 18 December 2013, 68/167, The right to privacy in the digital age," http://www.un.org/ga/search/view_doc.asp?symbol=A/RES/68/167.

273 **privacy is not something to be traded:** Benjamin Franklin said, "Those who would give up essential Liberty, to purchase a little temporary Safety, deserve neither Liberty nor Safety."

274 **There's an opportunity for real change:** Marcia Stepanek (8 Aug 2013), "The Snowden effect: An opportunity?" *Stanford Social Innovation Review,* http://www.ssireview.org/blog/entry/the_snowden_effect_an_opportunity.

274 **Rahm Emanuel said:** Gerald F. Seib (21 Nov 2008), "In crisis, opportunity for Obama," *Wall Street Journal,* http://online.wsj.com/news/articles/SB122721278056345271.

276 **group interest against self-interest:** Bruce Schneier (2012), *Liars and Outliers: Enabling the Trust That Society Needs to Thrive,* Wiley, http://www.wiley.com/WileyCDA/WileyTitle/productCd-1118143302.html.

277 **humanity will benefit:** Charles Safran et al. (Jan/Feb 2007), "Toward a national framework for the secondary use of health data: An American Medical Informatics Association white paper," *Journal of the American Medical Informatics Association* 14, https://www.sciencedirect.com/science/article/pii/S106750270600212X. Peter B. Jensen, Lars J. Jensen, and Søren Brunak (Jun 2012), "Mining electronic health records: Towards better research applications and clinical care," *Nature Reviews: Genetics* 13, http://www.dartmouth.edu/~cbbc/courses/bio270/PDFs-13S/Tim_Byounggug.pdf.

277 **analyzes the study habits:** Reynol Junco (2014), *Engaging Students through Social Media: Evidence Based Practices for Use in Student Affairs,* Wiley/Jossey-Bass, http://www.wiley.com/WileyCDA/WileyTitle/productCd-1118647459.html.

277 **OKCupid has been experimenting:** Christian Rudder (28 Jul 2014), "We experiment on human beings!" *OK Trends,* http://blog.okcupid.com/index.php/we-exper

iment-on-human-beings. Christian Rudder (4 Sep 2014), "When websites peek into private lives," *Wall Street Journal*, http://online.wsj.com/articles/when-websites-peek-into-private-lives-1409851575.

277 **it's hard to justify:** Mark Weinstein (2 Sep 2014), "OKCupid, that's OKStupid," *Huffington Post*, http://www.huffingtonpost.com/mark-weinstein/okcupid-thats-okstupid_b_5739812.html.

278 **value in our collective data:** US Executive Office of the President (2013), "Digital government: Building a 21st century platform to better serve the American people," http://www.whitehouse.gov/sites/default/files/omb/egov/digital-government/digital-government.html. Microsoft Corporation (27 Mar 2013), "State and local governments adopt Microsoft Dynamics CRM to improve citizen service delivery," *Microsoft News Center*, http://www.microsoft.com/en-us/news/press/2013/mar13/03-27dynamicscrmpr.aspx.

278 **we need to get involved:** The UK's GCHQ explicitly fears this debate. One of the Snowden documents repeatedly talks about avoiding a "damaging public debate" about the extent of surveillance. James Ball (25 Oct 2013), "Leaked memos reveal GCHQ efforts to keep mass surveillance secret," *Guardian*, http://www.theguardian.com/uk-news/2013/oct/25/leaked-memos-gchq-mass-surveillance-secret-snowden.

279 **I often turn to a statement:** It is actually his paraphrase of an older statement by the abolitionist Theodore Parker, from 1853: "I do not pretend to understand the moral universe, the arc is a long one, my eye reaches but little ways. I cannot calculate the curve and complete the figure by experience of sight; I can divine it by conscience. But from what I see I am sure it bends towards justice." garson (15 Nov 2012), "The arc of the moral universe is long but it bends toward justice," *Quote Investigator*, http://quoteinvestigator.com/2012/11/15/arc-of-universe.

Index

Page numbers beginning with 285 refer to notes.

About the Author

Bruce Schneier is an internationally renowned security technologist, called a "security guru" by *The Economist*. He is the author of twelve books—including *Liars and Outliers: Enabling the Trust Society Needs to Survive*—as well as hundreds of articles, essays, and academic papers. His influential newsletter "Crypto-Gram" and blog "Schneier on Security" are read by over 250,000 people. Schneier is a fellow at the Berkman Center for Internet and Society at Harvard Law School, a program fellow at the New America Foundation's Open Technology Institute, a board member of the Electronic Frontier Foundation, and an Advisory Board member of the Electronic Privacy Information Center. He is also the Chief Technology Officer of Resilient Systems, Inc.

You can read his blog, essays, and academic papers at www.schneier .com. He tweets at @schneierblog.